Veiled in *Flesh*
THE GODHEAD SEE

Advent Sermons

David W. Hall

Covenant Foundation
© 2019

Hall, David W.
Veiled in Flesh, the Godhead See

1. Christmas Sermons; 2. Advent;
3. Pastoral Aids; 4. Christology;

First Edition 2019

TABLE OF CONTENTS

PART 2: MEDITATIONS AND DEVOTIONALS

Preface

I have served as a Pastor for 4 decades, mainly in one church in Tennessee (20 years) and one in Georgia (17 years). After that span of time, one accumulates a number of seasonal sermons. All of these, thus, have been preached to average congregations in the context of normal pastoral ministry. These are far from celebrity sermons—hopefully, emitting a humble tone in keeping with Advent. Having also felt the stress of desperation in finding another Advent sermon occasionally, without becoming overly fictional, I offer this collection to the many stressed, busy, and faithful pastors and people, who also look for biblical reflections on these amazing passages. If any of these help you and your church, I am blessed. Each normally takes a simple portion of the ancient text and draws a few points, explanations, and applications from it.

In the spirit of "Freely have you received, so freely give," I am happy for others to borrow from any of these. Things like citations, attributions, and acclaim, probably should have little place in normal ministry. Below and throughout, I've borrowed freely from the likes of Spurgeon, Ryle, MacLaren, Calvin, Luther, and many others. This primer should not be viewed as an attempt at pure originality or rigorous scholarship; instead, it is an attempt at fellowship and rhetoric. I also have used, as with most working pastors, so many of these sources, so often, that the best I could do is refer to the author when the language is so clearly not my own. No intent to plagiarize nor aggrandize is herein intended; so let the reader be merciful and enjoy. Accordingly, pastors may borrow (as I certainly have), as long as they understand that my borrowings are from betters. Somehow, I think Ryle, Luther, Spurgeon, *et al*, would be fine with their voices still speaking succinctly, even though they have joined the heavenly chorus above. Where convenient, I have even at times simply placed the names of these worthies in parentheses. But I'd not want anyone to fail to recognize how greatly indebted I am to my predecessors. A few of these, as noted, are almost verbatim, so skilled were the original expositors.

It is my prayer that the flesh-veiled Godhead of Jesus will be seen clearly through these sermons.

Faith Just Prior to Jesus' Advent

Luke 1:5-25

There are more details provided by Luke about the family, the cousins of our Master, and other mundane matters than any other gospel. Surely, this context and details are important.

Geoff Thomas notes: "The purpose of the book is fourfold. First, it is full of teaching to tell Christians what they are to believe. Second, it is full of ethics to tell Christians how they should live. Third, it is full of comfort to tell Christians why they should rejoice (Luke's gospel begins with five songs, while the final two words of this gospel are "praising God"). Fourth, it is full of prophecy to tell Christians what they are to expect. In this world of ignorance, wickedness, despair and confusion, how important is the gospel of Luke."

"Important as every book of the Bible is in its own way," says Rob Rayburn, "the Gospels are unique in their fundamental importance, providing as they do the raw material from which our entire Christian faith is constructed. One early church father put it this way: 'The Gospels supply the wool . . . the epistles weave the dress.'"

Today, we've inherited all kinds of religious environments. We take a lot for granted. But what was the life of faith like just before Jesus burst on the scene?

Several of these leading characters are described as: upright, observing commandments (v. 6) (Can we be blameless? In what sense?)

Luke provides a prologue in 1:1-4. After that we are introduced to Zechariah and Elizabeth. In his prologue, Luke has stated:

- This is a historic account.
- It is well investigated by Luke, using eyewitnesses.
- It was presented to a Roman official.
- Its purpose was: to know the life of Christ with certainty.

Now turn your attention to Zechariah and the birth of John the Baptist. From these verses we can learn about salvation just before the First Advent:

1. The first question to ask is this: Can a person be righteous because of family lineage?

Have you ever known a person who acted as though he/she was "in" with God because of his/her parents' spiritual activity? Regardless of attempts to make that happen, true spirituality is not passed on biologically. As we approach holidays and at the onset of what we pray will be a blessed Advent, with many rich family celebrations, make sure that you understand that your family cannot secure your spiritual life for you. Oh, how we might wish!!

Some Pharisees at the time of Jesus seemed to think so, but that is not true. As Zechariah is introduced, his lineage is given. He was a priest; thus he had to be a descendant of Levi. More particularly, he was from the division of Abijah, and his wife traced her lineage all the way back to Aaron.

As a priest, Zechariah would serve at the temple for two one-week periods each year, as part from the three great Jewish festivals (Howard Marshall, *Commentary on Luke* [Eerdmans], p. 52). Because of the great number of priests, estimated at 18,000-20,000, they cast lots to determine which priests got to offer the incense on the altar in the holy place. This was a once in a lifetime privilege (*Mishnah*, Tamid 5.2), and so it would have been the high point of Zechariah's priestly service.

So they met the lineage requirements. Then v. 6 says, "Both of them were upright in the sight of God, observing all the Lord's commandments and regulations blamelessly." Still "God was breaking into the ancient routine of Jewish ritual with the word of his decisive saving act" (W. Liefeld, *Expositor's Bible Commentary* [Zondervan], 8:826).

Here's where Luke differs with those who chop-up Scripture and divide it, confusing cause with effect. I side with Paul's teaching in

Galatians 3 that I'll come back to below. When v. 6 affirms that Zechariah was upright and observed the Lord's commands, neither lineage nor effort is what put him in right relationship with God. Instead, that was a by-product of already being in right relationship with God.

God never saves a person who is already morally perfect. If already perfect, that person would not need saving. The apostle Paul makes it clear in Gal. 3:11 that "No one is justified before God by the law." It is not by keeping the law that we come into good standing with God. Instead, it is by God's grace that we are changed, then made righteous, and then obey. That is true for your life and that was true for Abraham and for Zechariah.

Earlier, the OT agreed and made it plain: "Not by might, nor by power, but by my power, saith the Lord."

Romans 9 teaches similarly: It is not by a human being's running nor by his effort that one is saved. It is all of grace—regardless of what period of history you live.

From cover to cover, the Bible is a book that proclaims a unified message: No person is saved by keeping the law, nor by being good, nor by religious activity. No priest before the time of Jesus could meet God's standard of holiness by his own human behavior.

Geoff Thomas: puts it this way:

> Mary and Joseph, Simeon and Anna, Luke and Theophilus were all true Israelites though Jews or Gentiles. They were true Israelites not because they were the natural descendants of Abraham through Jacob, because both Luke and Theophilus were not, but they all trusted in that same Lord in whom Abraham had put his trust. Paul says to the Galatian Christians who were mostly Gentile believers – "If you are Christ's, then are you Abraham's seed, and heirs according to the promise" (3:29). So Luke and Theophilus would not feel that they were Johnny-come-latelys or second class Christians. God had started with the Jews; they alone he had known of all the nations of the earth. So the New Testament must start with the Jews, but then God invited the Gentiles also into his banqueting house and his banner over them was the very same love.

Zechariah, as I think the rest of this chapter shows, was saved by God's Spirit, and had sincere desires to live according to God's ways. He did make efforts to keep God's law, but it was because his heart had been reborn. That could happen to Jewish people, after all. Isn't that the way you become once you are converted, too? Once your heart is won to the Lord, you want to live obediently to please him.

There is nothing in the Bible that teaches that a person in the OT could not have a change of heart by the work of the Holy Spirit. Zechariah lived an upright life because he knew the error of not doing so, and he loved God. He tried to serve God with the limited knowledge he had.

But he was not so foolish as to be a chopper of Scripture. He knew the human heart was sinful. He knew within himself what you have come to know: that no one can save himself. No person can take a self-improvement class and make himself holy. Only God can heal the human heart. Since the Fall of Adam, no person has the spiritual ability to save himself.

Verse 6 describes the EFFECT of salvation, certainly not the CAUSE of it.

OT saints, before the coming of Jesus, knew that humans were not righteous because of lineage, nor were they righteous because of keeping the law. The Law, according to Gal. 3:21, does not have the power to make us righteous. "For if the law . . . could impart life, then righteousness would certainly have come by the law."

Luke "does not mean that they were sinlessly perfect, which no one is. Rather, they walked consistently in the fear of the Lord, seeking to obey Him in all their ways. Mary and Joseph were another godly couple in Israel. It was through such obscure people, quietly living in godliness, going about their normal duties, that the Lord brought about this" Marvelous Advent.

The combined picture is this: We do not make ourselves upright or blameless with God—who cannot easily be fooled—by straining, keeping the law, or by anything external. Yet, once saved, our nature is changed and we keep God's commands. We are upright, in contrast to a life of overt sinfulness. While we don't MAKE ourselves upright or blameless, we are called to live uprightly. By God's spirit, which is necessary.

2. Note, next, other dynamics of spirituality—for those who are saved—that were the same for Zechariah as for us.

Verse 9 speaks of Zechariah chosen by lot to go into the temple for special service at a definite point of time. Now this may seem mechanical, but it actually takes a good bit of faith to do things by lot. In Zechariah's case, he was chosen by lot, and he trusted God to make his sovereign will known by that method. That requires faith.

Then right after that, as you continue to scan this passage, you note in v. 10 that people were gathered together worshipping and praying. That shows they trusted the Lord.

Note these other tokens of genuine faith.

Prayer (incense in 9-10 symbolized): "your prayer has been heard" (13a) Zechariah and true believers at the birth of Jesus knew and believed in prayer. They knew the God of prayer and were connected to him.

Ligon Duncan points out that your prayers are not rejected just because God's answers are delayed. How long had it been since Zechariah and Elizabeth had prayed that prayer? My guess is they started praying that prayer early on in their marriage, and now he says, "I'm old." And, he says very tactfully, "And my wife is . . . advanced in years." He's old, but she's just "advanced in years." They'd started praying that prayer, my guess is, a long time ago. And maybe they'd even forgotten about it. A motto for Advent about God: "He may not come when you want Him, but He's always on time."

The presence and activity of Angels (11-13, 19-21).

An angel appeared to Zechariah in v. 11. I have never seen an Angel. Have you? I have never had an angel appear to me while I was standing in a sanctuary. I have to admit, thus, that the spirituality of Zechariah is above my own. This spirituality at the hinge of the OT era is certainly not impoverished.

An angel appears to Zechariah, and his reaction is another confirmation of true spirituality. When Zechariah sees the angel, he does not say, "Oh yeah, you again," or "Hey Big Guy, what's up?" Zechariah is startled and gripped with fear. He knows the proper reaction is fear. That is how Moses and all the great OT saints reacted when they were ushered into the presence of God.

The Angel speaks to Zechariah and reassures him. He tells him that his prayer has been answered and that Elizabeth will conceive and bear him a son. That is news he has wanted to hear for a long time. Zechariah quickly realizes that he cannot have a child unless

God miraculously intervenes. This OT saint realized that we don't live in a universe that is only bound by natural process.

As you approach Advent, will you recall that we live in a universe that is more saturated with the miraculous than we often think? Or will you live out a spirituality that is lesser than that of Zechariah? One spirituality is filled with God's presence.

Later in v. 19 the Angel says that he stands "in the presence of God."

The next verses tell us about prayer and joy. Zechariah's prayer life was evidently pretty strong. He did not merely try to keep the law. He prayed for help, and did so regularly. The Angel told him that God heard prayers. The birth of a son, John, would also bring joy and delight to Zechariah (v. 14).

J. C. Ryle writes: "The ministry of angels is undoubtedly a deep subject. Nowhere in the Bible do we find such frequent mention of them, as in the period of our Lord's earthly ministry. At no time do we read of so many appearances of angels, as near the time of our Lord's incarnation and entrance into the world. The meaning of this circumstance is sufficiently clear. It was meant to teach the church that Messiah was no angel, but the Lord of angels, as well as of men. Angels announced his coming. Angels proclaimed his birth. Angels rejoiced at his appearing. And by so doing they made it plain that He who came to die for sinners, was not one of themselves, but one far above them, the King of kings and Lord of lords."

One thing, at all events, about angels, we must never forget. They take a deep interest in the work of Christ, and the salvation that Christ has provided. They sang high praise when the Son of God came down to make peace by his own blood between God and man. They rejoice when sinners repent, and sons are born again to our Father in heaven. They delight to minister to those who shall be heirs of salvation. Let us strive, while we are upon earth—to be of their mind, and to share their joys. This is the way to be in tune for heaven. It is written of those who enter in there, that they shall be "as the angels." (Mk 12:25)

The role and spirituality of John the Baptizer. Verses 14-17), especially tied to Malachi (below) are strong in their emphasis on repentance. Repentance and turning back are required (16-17).

Later, v. 16 indicates that Zechariah understood something about true conversion. His son, according to that verse, would be used to "turn back" many to the Lord. Zechariah knew the people were straying from God's ways, just like the OT prophets taught. They needed heart change, and God promises to provide that through the ministry of Zechariah's son, John the Baptist.

Moreover, John the Baptist would minister in the power of the Spirit (see v. 17), that same spirit that animated Elijah.

The OT concludes with the prophet Malachi predicting that when the forerunner came, the one who would level things out for the Coming King-Messiah, that he would turn the hearts of the fathers back to their children. And Messiah would come to purify. Verse 25, then, identifies this with the 'favor of the Lord.'

Let's briefly review and summarize these, by asking: does the rest of the NT teach these?

Does the faith change or is it similar?

In order for people to be prepared for the Messiah, a great spiritual work had to be done—then and now! This required massive changes of heart. Conversion was a change of heart, and people needed the Holy Spirit to work first, and prepare them. OT saints knew this, despite the claims of some dispensationalists.

Focus also for a minute on *what Zechariah knew about the Holy Spirit.* Dispensationalists have a faulty view of the work of the Spirit. They think that he did not work in the lives of regular believers in the OT period. Their roadblock from seeing this—erected by their own theory, I might add—is their assumption that OT people are saved differently from those in the NT, and only by keeping the law.

A crucial argument against this is the teaching here on the work of the Holy Spirit before the arrival of Jesus. Already, Zechariah knew several things about the Holy Spirit.

Start in v. 15. When the angel first promised Zechariah that he would have a son, he also told him that John the Baptist would be filled with the Holy Spirit from birth. Now that challenges several ideas. First it discounts the notion that children have to attain a certain age before they can walk with the Lord. Young John the Baptist would not only walk with the Lord, he would be filled with the Spirit at the soonest moment possible. True, not all our children are the forerunners of the Messiah, but this indicates that human nature does not require great age or maturity prior to the Spirit's indwelling.

Secondly, it shows that the Spirit indwelt believers prior to the Resurrection of Christ and the Day of Pentecost. This passage reminds us that the Holy Spirit was not first given on the Day of Pentecost. That was not a new beginning of the work of the Spirit.

In the OT, the Holy Spirit filled believers just as today. Think of it this way: If we begin with the teaching of Genesis, and see that all people are sinners, then we understand that no person has the intellect, will, or strength to turn to God on his own. All have sinned and fallen short of the glory of God. We are innately incapable of salvation, unless something is radically changed within us. And we do not have the power to change or alter our own nature. Only a power greater than us can do that. That Power is the Holy Spirit, and any person who is ever saved, had to have the Holy Spirit change his nature. Else he would never call out to or believe in God. So, if any OT saints were saved, they were necessarily saved by the operations of the HS, who worked long before the incarnation of Christ and Pentecost. The numerous references in the OT to the spirit's work indicate that the same Spirit has always been working among God's covenant people.

God promised Zechariah that the Holy Spirit would be given to his child from birth.

Six months later, in v. 41. the Angel Gabriel visits Mary. Shortly, thereafter, she goes to visit her cousin, Elizabeth. When Mary walks in, we see more of the work of the Holy Spirit. When she greeted her cousin, little John the Baptist jumped in her womb, and Elisabeth was "filled with the HS." She realized that this experience was unusual. She knew that the Holy Spirit's presence was real.

This also may indicate a strong outpouring of the Holy Spirit, not so much the first time, Elizabeth ever had the Holy Spirit. There were already present the signs of rebirth; it may be that they were just strengthened at this experience.

At Advent, shouldn't we have a proper hunger for and seek a renewal by God's Holy Spirit? Make that one of your prayers this season. Will we seek the Spirit of Holiness, his power and glory, less than these OT saints? Or more?

Elizabeth seems to know a great deal (42-43) about Mary and God's plan. When Elizabeth becomes pregnant she praises God for "showing favor." (v. 25) When she feels the infant John leap in her womb, she is filled with the Holy Spirit—again, this did not await some future age. He praised God in a loud voice to recognize the blessing that Mary would be. Mary's child would be blessed. And

Elizabeth reflected an appropriate humility, too, in v. 43. She knew that blessing was related to believing the Lord.

Zechariah had been miraculously struck deaf. God was working in much more of his life than externals only. The angel rebuked him for his skepticism.

UnBELIEF is everywhere a great sin, and a grievous mistake. Unbelief has proved the ruin of those countless multitudes who, having heard the gospel, rejected it, died in their sins, have been consigned to the place of torment, and await the fiercer judgment of the last day. I might ask the question concerning this innumerable host, "Who slew all these?" The answer would be, "Unbelief." And when unbelief comes into the Christian's heart, as it does at times — for the truest believer has his times of doubt; even Abraham, the father of the faithful, sometimes had his misgivings—that unbelief does not assail his thoughts without withering his joys, and impairing his energies.

Unless otherwise shown, all other characters in the Advent narratives should be understood as knowing roughly the same things about spirituality. And it was a vital spirituality at the time for some. Just as it is FOR SOME today. The reason for this is rooted in the nature of God: He is unchangeable!!

Now, as your families gather for Advent, read the OT with new eyes, knowing that they too are God's people. I think one of the best things you and your family can do for the coming weeks is to focus on the OT, read those prophecies, learn the anticipation as God's people awaited the Messiah. And know something of the hunger, which waited for the Redeemer.

From this passage, we learn about:
1. The Plan of God.
2. The working of the Spirit in all ages.
3. The proper fear of God and prayer.
4. Repentance and Advent. As Ligon Duncan put it: repentance is an indication of the work of God's Spirit in us to show us what we really are, to show us how we need God's grace; and until we see our sin, we're not ready to see the marvelous grace of our Savior. Zechariah had a sin that needed to be forgiven. What was it? Unbelief. He didn't believe God's word. The Lord had sent him Gabriel himself to announce His promises, and Zechariah's response is, 'How do I believe

this?' When the Lord gives you a promise, your answer is, "Yes, sir. I believe."

What do you need to repent of this day? What sin of yours do you need to reckon with so that you can see the marvelous grace of our loving Lord forgiving you where you don't deserve forgiveness?

So, how could people before the birth of Christ be saved or have true faith? The same way you and I do today? It is by grace that you are saved through faith, not of yourself. It is the gift of God. And God has been giving gifts for thousands of years. All who have received this gift, praise the Lord.

What do you need to embrace or avoid from this?

EMBRACE these:

1. Angel appeared while Zechariah was in the temple. Expect God to bless at worship.
2. Look to God to provide children. God can bless, even while we are experiencing consequences for disobeying

AVOID these:

1. Doubting God, even if it seems impossible.
2. Putting off obedience.
3. Trusting in self and inherited ways.

What to Think of Mary's Faith as God Predicts Jesus' Birth

Luke 1:26-56

Dr. Rob Rayburn noted in a sermon on this passage that Dorothy Sayers said of the history of the incarnation, "this is the only thing that ever happened." She meant that in comparison to this event, its significance, its wonder, there are no other happenings worthy to be called happenings. That is why G. K. Chesterton called Advent "that incredible interruption, as a blow that broke the very backbone of history."

Mary has had a prominent role in religious art and theory; of course, she is fairly prominent in this opening chapter of Luke, too. What do we make of that? Ryle observes that she is formally declared by the Roman Catholic Church to have been "conceived without sin." She is held up to Roman Catholics as an object of veneration, and prayed to as a mediator between God and man, no less powerful than Christ Himself. For all this, recall, there is not the slightest evidence in Scripture. There is no warrant in the verses before us now. There is no warrant in any other part of God's Word.

Should we—like Medieval Roman Catholics—elevate her to a plane above all other women? Or should we see her in some other light. Some folks believe that Mary provides a "kinder and gentler" side of God that comforts believers. However, that reflects a serious misunderstanding of who God is. For he himself is abundantly gentle and kind, and doesn't lack for a kinder side. He is compassionate and gracious and slow to anger—just not approving of all behaviors. As

Zechariah praised in this very chapter, God is known for his forgiveness and "tender mercy" even before the birth of Jesus. It is only a mis-shapened, twisted God that needs Mary as an assistant to be venerated.

And the Lord Jesus Christ, who is God in the flesh and who shows us the Father, is a perfect image to embrace, whereas Mary was imperfect and in fact a sinner like us. Still, since she is prominent in this opening chapter, we should see what God wants us to learn from her. I'll focus on 2 sections that are called the Annunciation or grand announcement (1:26-38) and the *Magnificat*, her response in her song (1: 46-56). Both of these poetic, or hymn-like writings, teach us much.

Mary was a young woman about the age of some of our teenage girls [Leah, Jodi, Gabby, or Susie]. In her mid-teens, she was about to marry, and she met the crisis of her life. The angel Gabriel appeared to her. That setting is given in 1:26-28.

This angel had appeared to Zechariah and predicted the birth of his son, John. He was walking with the Lord already, but struggled with unbelief. After Zechariah completed his priestly turn, he returned home and Elizabeth became pregnant. Taking the safe route, she stayed as secluded as possible for the first 5 months of her pregnancy. A month later, in the sixth month, Gabriel was dispatched with the highest of assignments. He went to Nazareth and appeared to the Virgin Mary, who was engaged to Joseph, a descendant of David. Gabriel began his communication to her by greeting her as one who was highly favored; and he told her that the Lord was with her. That covenant promise, that God is with us, had a long history of meaning, dating back to the OT patriarchs. It was an assuring message.

However, Gabriel's announcement about her future was met with equal parts of excitement and confusion. According to Luke's account, she wondered just what kind of greeting this might be. Was it a trick? Was she really seeing an angel? Did this appearance mean that she was in big trouble with the Lord? All of those questions would cause her confusion. As this episode continues, however, it unfolds for us how God works with his people in all ages. At the heart of this passage is the call for the believer to submit to God's will and be a servant, just like Christ.

The angel tells her not to fear but that she'll give birth to a blessed child.

For a brief moment, consider things from Mary's perspective. She is young; she knows she is a virgin. She knew that she had not been immoral. Have you ever been wrongfully accused of something, you really did not do? Mary knew what kind of accusations would surely come her way. In fact, her son would later be falsely accused as well, and perhaps this early lesson would prepare her to care for him when that happened.

Think of how much criticism a young woman would attract if she claimed to have a virgin-born child? She'd be the laughing stock of the town. And imagine what all the other women would say!

The Angel speaks blessings similar to those for Zechariah to her. She is "highly favored" and he comforts her, telling her not to be afraid. After the Angel tells her what will transpire, she has a few basic questions. And I hope that you'll notice as we proceed that there are different kinds of questions: some reflect doubt (as Zechariah's 'How can I be sure of this?' in v. 18), and others are honest queries. To begin, though, see:

I.   Mary Perplexed

First consider Mary—please understand from the outset that Mary was a great saint, but she was not deified in any way; she was exactly like we are. We should respect her, even admire her spiritual courage, but never worship her or any other human being. First Mary, wonders, "Why me?"

Do you ever mutter that? Usually it is not because things are so great, but because we don't like the hand we're dealt that we ask that question. I'm sure Mary had to think this. She was just going about her business—didn't ask to be the special virgin; never had asked for that in all her 16 years. And, come to think of it: she was too young and unprepared for all that responsibility. That's part of why the Scripture records in v. 29, "she was greatly troubled."

She wondered what kind of message this was. You have to note that she was spiritual enough to consider this but not so spiritual as to embrace this notion immediately. Mary had to mull this over a little. That emphasizes two things: (1) this is real history, *not made-up*, high-gloss fantasy portrait—yes, she wrestled with this announcement; and (2) she struggled with parts of God's plan just like everyone else.

Noting this doubt, the angel tries to calm her. First, he comforts her with "be not afraid." And he tells her that she has found favor with God. Perched on the edge of the OT, this term, "found favor with God," frequently signified the presence of God's grace.

The Angel continues to tell her . . . that the child's name would be Jesus. Matthew explains that that name means, "he shall save his people." He would fulfill the expectations for the Messiah, he would be the Son of the Most High. Mary's child would also receive the throne long promised to David, and his kingdom will never end. (31-33) The heir to David's throne had been expected for a thousand years, and now it was about to come true.

That's not your average baby. Mary had asked, and the Angel had answered. In her most challenging and difficult moment, she was given assurance and promise. Even if you are not given those exact promises, God still gives other promises. And he gives exactly what we need when challenges come our way. His gifts match our true needs.

Most of us would react to similar information in one of three ways:

Incredulity: We simply would not believe. We'd raise our eyebrows and not give it much more thought. Or dismiss it as ludicrous.

Ecstasy: We would be thrilled and begin to plan ways to have some star commend our book about the experience on the way to wealth and fame.

Honest Doubt: We would want to believe the Angel—really trust God, but occasionally known-reality would creep through, and we would wonder. In the end, we would have to be quite skeptical about this.

This last reaction, honest doubt, closest describes Mary's reaction. Verse 34 records her thinking: How shall this be, since I am a Virgin? She questioned this, since it had never happened before. "How can this happen? I want to believe, Lord, but this defies all I know." How?

Good question. Let me simply mention in passing, that the teaching that Jesus was born of a virgin is absolutely clear, it was prophesied in the OT, it is miraculous, and the wording need not be twisted to mean anything else. The only reason some people do not believe in it is that they willfully reject the miracle as it is reported here. [see the sermon on that subject below.]

In the 1950s, one version of the Bible, sought to tone down the
miraculous so that moderns would find it more in keeping with their
thinking. To do so, the RSV translated this as "young maiden" instead
of virgin, and there is no reason to do so.

Luke makes it abundantly clear that Mary—who should know
best—saw herself as a virgin. She should, after all, know. Yes, this
goes against any medical or scientific knowledge of her day and our
day, but God can work a miracle whenever he wishes. *Our job is not
to work miracles but to believe them.*

She begins perplexed and moves gradually toward God (Tim
Keller develops her cognition below). She starts with:

1. Pondering (an auditing term; carefully examined) and
   measured incredulity.
2. Then, she moves to simple resignation ('As the Lord says').
3. Next, to faith in action and praise. Is this your path?

It's not a process of which you are in control. Most of us are deeply
prejudiced against the idea that we are not in charge of our own lives.
We are incapable, on our own, of simply believing in Jesus. People
don't come to Christ by simply deciding to develop faith and then
carrying out their plan. No, God has to open our hearts and help us
break through our prejudices and denials. One of the marks of real
Christian faith, then, is a sense that there is some kind of power
outside of you putting its finger on you, coming to you, and dealing
with you. It shows you things you find incredible, helps you see that it
is true, and then enables you to rejoice and give yourself. The One
who made you at the beginning is making you again (Titus 3: 4–7).
Unless he comes and reveals himself to us, as he did to Mary, we
would never be able to find him.

4. She responds, then, in wonder [Keller, Timothy (2016-10-25).
Hidden Christmas: The Surprising Truth Behind the Birth of Christ
(p. 87). Kindle Ed.] Mary is not saying, "I think this could add value
to my life" or "This is just what I need to reach my goals in life."
[Keller, Timothy (2016-10-25)].

5. Finally, she grows into amazement. She stands amazed,
dazzled: "I would argue that despite the unique features of Mary's
situation, we should all be amazed that we are Christians, that the
great God is working in us. In "O Little Town of Bethlehem" we sing,
"O holy child of Bethlehem, descend to us, we pray; cast out our sin,
and enter in, be born in us today." It's a bold image, but quite right.

Every Christian is like Mary. Everyone who puts faith in Christ receives, by the Holy Spirit, "Christ in you, the hope of glory" (Col 1: 27, emphasis mine). We should be just as shocked that God would give us—with all our smallness and flaws—such a mighty gift. And so no Christian should ever be far from this astonishment that "I, I of all people, should be loved and embraced by his grace!" [Keller, Timothy (2016-10-25). *Hidden Christmas: The Surprising Truth Behind the Birth of Christ* (pp. 88-89). Penguin Publishing Group. Kindle Edition.] If [salvation] is something done for you, and to you, and in you, then there is a constant note of surprise and wonder.

Mary models this: "Becoming a Christian is not like signing up for a gym; it is not a 'living well' program that will help you flourish and realize your potential. Christianity is not another vendor supplying spiritual services you engage as long as it meets your needs at a reasonable cost. [Keller, Timothy (2016-10-25). *Hidden Christmas: The Surprising Truth Behind the Birth of Christ* (p. 93).]

But she still queried. Belief does not mean that we never question. In fact, when we have child-like faith, that does not mean that we do not seek more under-standing. Children, do, after all, ask quite a few questions, but they are wanting to learn. That kind of questioning is fine; it is only the skeptical kind that is not in line. *Faith means that after we question, we accept God's answer.*

Mary knew the difference, and it was a big one. Do you ever ask God about certain things, and after he gives the answer, you just continue to raise even more questions? Some characters in the Bible did that, and it exemplifies doubt and sin, not belief and trust. Belief may question, but if honest, it must also accept divine answers and not merely throw up objections dressed as questions. You can tell the difference. And Mary moves from initially being perplexed to:

II. Focusing on the POWER of God (in the Person of the Holy Spirit).

Since Mary asked an honest query, the Angel gave her this answer: It relies once again on the Holy Spirit. Gabriel responds: "The Holy Spirit will come upon you, and the power of the Most High will overshadow you."

Note that the Holy Spirit is a person, distinguishable from his power. Some theologians, having watched too many Star Wars movies, confuse the Holy Spirit with the Force. This chapter makes a distinction. The "force" is not with Mary. The "power of the Most High" is a person, not a blind power.

The Holy Spirit was at work in Mary. She knew this world was more than nuts and bolts. It was filled with the presence of God who was mightily at work. Whenever you think about Jesus' birth this season, you should re-pledge yourself to that work of the Spirit in this universe. We are more surrounded by God's invisible workings than we many times can guess. We live, as the Advent narratives teach, in a world that is tinged with the miraculous.

To demonstrate this to Mary, the Angel gives her a concrete sign. He says: to confirm this, you can visit your cousin and find her pregnant. Elizabeth was much older and considered barren. Everyone thought that it was impossible for her to bear a son. Similarly, everyone thought a 16 year-old virgin could not be with child. But God works through the impossibilities.

Sure, the Lord does not always conquer death, illness, and pain, nor give us everything we wish for. That would render us spoiled spiritual brats. The college student, for example, who takes this verse and applies it to upcoming exams may be surprised to find that his/her application of Scripture is wrong. Sure, God could cause you to make an 'A' on your exam, when you haven't studied at all, but I'll bet against it.

What is affirmed here is not so much that God gives us exactly what we want as this: God must always be approached by believers with them knowing that he is fully able to do anything. No material conditions or physical forces block him from doing exactly what his will is. His will, will come about.

You can depend on him for that, just as much as Mary did. Let me repeat that, because we are tempted to forget it or minimize it: No material conditions or physical forces block him from doing exactly what his will is. His will, will come about.

Note that Mary's Primary Response to the Power of God is: *Your will be done!!*

And, notice, when the Angel finishes this message, Mary's faith shows through. She accepts the answer and responds with humility: "I am the Lord's servant. May it be as you have said." *Can you say that this morning, about some big matter that the Lord has laid before you?* We all have burdens or callings that we at times think we cannot bear. We all have things that happen that we cannot imagine or that we do not like at all—likely something this morning has already occurred to you. Can you take that area of difficulty and ask the Lord one time, "How shall this be?" and then leave it with the Lord—as Mary did—saying, "I am the Lord's servant. You have answered, and I will walk in it." Does your calling to servanthood extend that far? Or are you only a partial servant?

That's tough. But Mary did that. She took the largest burden possible, even something that was potentially embarrassing, and entrusted that to the Lord. She knew he could be trusted.

She also went to visit Elizabeth, as v. 56 notes. You may even wish to view this as her seeking confirmation of the Angel's message. That is fine, as long as you accept the answer when it is given.

Mary visited her older cousin, and found sure enough, she was pregnant. The details that Luke gives indicate that this was no dream. Mary went to the hill country of Judah (particular region), she visited a definite house, John the Baptist responded in her womb, and Elizabeth praised God for the miraculous blessings he was given. All of this is history.

III. Finally, see how the Lord moves Mary to praise.

Still there is another major part of Mary's story. It is a song that is recorded in vss. 46-55. Mary, an OT saint at this point, composed a Psalm of praise. It may have been written down, or else Mary herself may have told it to Luke later. Either way, God made sure this was preserved in holy writ. Review Mary's sincere faith and spiritual outlook, as it is contained in this Psalm. Like Zechariah's, it can still serve as a guide for our thoughts and actions today.

A. First, you should note her *view of God.*

God, for Mary, was her Savior (47). She knew humans were lost and needed finding. Do you know that about all human beings as well as about yourself?

She also knew God as the "mindful" God. He was the all-seeing, all-knowing God. Nothing could escape his knowledge or attention. Mary knew God was neither a local deity, nor was he the limited God. There are actually some evangelicals today, who are taking their theology to its logical but perverted conclusion who are arguing: If humans have free choice, then God cannot know everything. That, of course, is unbiblical and denies, at heart, that he is the mindful God.

But this humble Galilean girl knew God was the mindful God—she was more on target than some modern theologians. And she loved him for that. He is mindful or your thoughts and condition today.

She also knew him as The "Mighty One." (49) He was all-powerful. He performed "mighty deeds with his arm." (51). David and other OT Psalms had affirmed the same thing. God did not perform merely small miracles but he did mighty deeds.

And God was the stupefying God. He surprised many with the way he consistently turned expectations on their heads. He would scatter the proud (51). Those who thought they were either most secure, or strongest, or most able to hide from God—he would reduce them to rubble and scatter the proud.

He would also bring down rulers. Those with the most powerful thrones, those who thought themselves immune from human movements, God would find more easily than Google finds a name on the internet or than a search utility finds a file with on a computer hard drive, and then he would bring them down, while also lifting up the humble (52).

God, the surprising God, would also fill the hungry and starve the rich. Mary knew how God worked. She knew his ways, his tell-tale marks and finger-prints. She knew God was immutable, merciful, and good.

God was faithful to his servant Abraham. These are things all believers should know about God today. And in consistency with the message last week, these were things that believers knew in the OT era as well.

B. Second, observe her *response to God.*

Mary does the best thing: She praises God, and her spirit rejoices in her savior.

This experience, rather than puffing up her self-esteem, makes her humble. She knows her position. She knows she is undeserving. She realizes that she is called to be a "servant." *So was her son.* That's why we say we are all called to servanthood. We are called to give ourselves away, to exhaust ourselves in service to our Savior. That is what he did. And that is what God called Mary to do. For that, she deserves high respect.

Mary had faith, and yet, at the same time she must have been awe-stricken by the revelation. That she should give birth to the Son of the

Highest must have utterly abashed and overwhelmed her. Now both these states of mind are here—faith and awe. Faith says, "I know that the angel's message is true, and therefore my soul doth magnify the Lord." Awe says, "What a solemn thing it is that God should come to dwell in me! My soul doth magnify the Lord." Thus in these words confidence and reverence have met together, assurance and adoration have kissed each other. Here is faith with its familiarity, and devotion with its godly fear.

Mary sang reverently, with devotion and true spirituality, intelligently, enthusiastically, evangelically, and with full assurance. Think of his greatness; it will be really praising him if we thus think of him. You need not speak, but just ponder, weigh, consider, con-template, meditate, ruminate upon the attributes of the Most High. Begin with his mercy if you cannot begin with his holiness; but take the attributes one by one, and think about them. I don't know any attribute of God that is not wonderfully quickening and powerful to a true Christian. As you think of any one of them, it will ravish you, and carry you away. You will be lost in wonder, love, and praise as you consider it; you will be astonished and amazed as you plunge into its wondrous depths, and everything else will vanish from your vision. That is one way of making God great,—by often thinking about him.

Mary gave birth to the greatest person in world history. But he did not ask for or seek the trappings of royalty in his birth or his life. He did not request an entourage as any other king would. He was lowly born, and lived his entire life as a slave. His will was severely diminished in this respect: Harnessed to his saving task, he was not free to serve himself, center on himself, nor have the world revolve around his comfort, pleasure, or agenda. Christ was taking on the shroud of a servant in Mary's womb.

He would not live for himself. Will you this Advent? No, he realized that others were to be served, and that is what he did. He gave himself away, *first melting into the cradle and later dissolving into the wood of the cross.*

The cradle cannot be separated from the cross. And that cross is held before us today. It was Mary's sinless baby whose body would be broken and whose blood was shed.

The Advent birth reminds us that Greatness does not lead to privilege; greatness leads to service. We are quite misguided if we think that God's call to us means that we are called to the stage.

Instead, many are called to work in the kitchen or take out the garbage.

Jesus himself shows this. Just like Mary and Jesus we find our contentment in that which the world so misunderstands. We find that serving God is greater than all the honors the world could bring. At Advent we join Mary as a servant.

It's better, as Psalm 84:10 expresses it: "I'd rather be a doorkeeper in the palace of the Almighty than dwell anywhere else. Better is one day in your courts than a thousand elsewhere." Do you love to worship God and serve him in his house? Mary did.

Most of us still have to make that choice in one way or another. She had learned, as some of you are, to reject the most instinctive human prayer, "Thy Will be changed," and began to pray as her son would: "Thy Will be Done."

Application:

Can you join with Mary and sing, 'my soul magnifies the Lord'? Or would that be a hypocritical statement today? 'If you cannot magny God, it probably is because you are magnifying yourself. When you sink in your own estimation, then will God rise in your esteem." This is a calling for all people who know the Lord as Mary did. Do this as you are driving in traffic this week, as you gather for worship, as you reflect in your homes. It is always appropriate. 'To magnify the Lord is the grandest thing we mortals do, for, it is the occupation of heaven. The word signifies to "greaten God." We cannot make him really greater, but we can show forth his greatness. We can focus more on his greatness and point others to greater thoughts of him, and that we do when we are praising him.

This is also A SURE REMEDY FOR Self-Congratulation. The more God gives you, the more you should magnify him, and not yourself. Let this be your rule—"He must increase, but I must decrease." Be less and less. Be the Lord's humble handmaid, yet bold and confident in thy praise of him who hath done for thee great things.

There are countless holy influences that flow from the habitual focusing of thoughts on God's greatness, as there are incalculable mischiefs which flow from our small thoughts of him. The root of false theology is belittling God; and the essence of true divinity is greatening God, magnifying him, and enlarging our conceptions of his majesty and his glory.

"Greaten God, my friends; greaten God," preached Charles Spurgeon. That's what Mary's faith did!" Believe great things of him. Believe that China can be made into a province of the celestial kingdom. Believe that India, [Iraq, the Ukraine, and Afghanistan] will cast their riches at Jesus' feet. Believe that the round world will yet be a pearl on Christ's finger-ring." God is able!

Note well: The great joy that is in the Lord. "My soul doth magnify the Lord, and my spirit hath rejoiced in God my Savior." Let us bless God that our religion is not one of gloom. I do not know of any command anywhere in Scripture that says, "Groan in the Lord always; and again I say, Groan." Sing joyfully that God is your Savior, and that he has looked on those who are downtrodden, and of the combination of Grace and Holiness.

So, what to make of Mary's Faith? Should she sing all alone?

We should not overlook the fact that the choice poem before us is a hymn of faith. "As yet there was no Savior born, nor, as far we can judge had the virgin any evidence such as carnal sense required to make her believe that a Savior would be born of her. 'How can this thing be?' was a question which might very naturally have suspended her song until it received an answer convincing to flesh and blood; but no such answer had been given. She knew that with God all things are possible, she had his promise delivered by an angel, and this was enough for her: on the strength of the Word which came forth from God, her heart leaped with pleasure and her tongue glorified his name. . . . Today there are far too many among us who have little or no conscious enjoyment of the Savior's presence; they walk in darkness and see no light; they are defeated by sin." (Spurgeon)

This is not a "Song for Self"; that straight, stiffbacked letter "I" makes a very poor song. The less we sing about it, the better. There is no such note in the whole gamut, so let us never attempt to sing it; but when we sing, let us sing unto the Lord, and let our song be concerning what he has done.

Mary knew her parents' faith; she was not a stranger to God's ways in the OT. The true Christian should always give close attention to Bible history, and the lives of saints. Let us often examine the previous ways that God deals with His people. He is of one mind. What He does for them, and to them, in time past, He is likely to do in time to come. Such study will teach us what to expect, check unwarrantable expectations, and encourage us when cast down. Happy is that man whose mind is well stored with such knowledge. It will make him patient and hopeful. (Ryle)

A Baptist Birth and Zechariah's Psalm

Luke 1:57-80

Dr. W. Robert Godfrey recently shared this comment with me on Luke. "This concern to show Christ as the fulfillment of Israel explains why Luke presents so much of Israel and its institutions in a positive way. Especially early in the Gospel Luke shows the people and institutions of Israel as good and faithful. Zechariah, Elizabeth, Mary, Simeon, and Anna are all presented as devout covenant people, and the Temple is a center of faithful worship and piety. Luke's point is that Christianity is not the rejection of Israel, but the fulfillment of it."

We will see in these verses: (1) Notes of God's work in a birth; (2) a NT Psalm; and (3) Scripture confirmed.

Charles Spurgeon preached on this passage; "There is nothing in the world that costs a saint so dear as doubt. If he disbelieves his God, he most assuredly robs himself of comfort, deprives himself of strength, and does himself a real injury. The case of Zechariah may be a lesson to the Lord's people. Don't be like Zechariah—a believer— and respond: "\'How shall I know that these things shall be?' The higher a man's position, the greater his responsibility; and in the event of any delinquency, the graver his offense." (Lu 1:20 Judgment Upon Zacharias, s3495)

That reminds me of what it says elsewhere in Scripture: That God rebukes those he loves. He surely loved and rebuked OT characters in similar fashion as he does today.

I. First, note how the Lord works in this birth with notes of miracles (57-66).

All of what is stated in these verses fulfills the previous predictions. Elizabeth gave birth to a lad. On the 8th day (59), when the family brought him for circumcision, with Zechariah still mute, Elizabeth halted things and stated that the baby boy was to be named 'John.' Some folks protested (v. 61) that there was no one in his family with that name.

They brought Zechariah into the conversation and wanted his input, even if only by nodding and signing. So he wrote on a tablet (v. 63) that John was to be his name. And immediately, his speech returned, and the first thing he does is to speak praise for God.

That sets the neighbors talking—big time, far and near. It was becoming obvious that the Lord's hand was on this family. That's the kind of witness they had. Thus, the birth of the first Baptist in the Bible.

It leads to a Psalm that also confirms that a remnant of faith was living still.

What can we learn from this birth, so filled with the miraculous?
    a. God is faithful; when he speaks something will happen.
    b. We can trust God to give us children; this is far from naturalistic.
    c. God wants the attention of fathers (and mothers, too, of course), but none of us can take these things for granted.
    d. The Holy Spirit was certainly prominent and at work before Pentecost.

II. Second, note Zechariah's sincere and deep faith in this NT Psalm, contained in vss 67-79.

This, note, was a product of being filled with the Spirit and exercising the gift of prophesy prior to Pentecost. I am amazed as I review these two chapters how many times the Holy Spirit is shown to be quite active in the lives of these believers long before Pentecost. When Zechariah is filled with the Holy Spirit, he declares God. This could almost be lifted from the Psalter, Israel's ancient hymnbook.

Zechariah praises God because he has redeemed his people. He understands, thus, at an early point, that we are sinners and in need of redemption.

He also sees how God rises up a leader for salvation (69) for us.

This passage can well be outlined and explained like the Psalm it is.

a. Like with worship and a good psalm, this begins with praise and the reasons for praise. Shouldn't songs used in worship have those two notes?

"Praise" is similar to the OT term, "Bless" the Lord (*barukah*). Praise is not for man, nor for people or race. It is praise for the Lord, the God of Israel.

This God is identified. He is the God who worked long ago in Israel and who worked consistently. He is the KNOWN God, not the unknown one as in Athens. The God of Israel was known for his amazing work in or with:

- Creation—it begins there, and God provides curious souls with information!
- The Patriarchs: Abraham, Isaac, and Jacob.
- The Exodus and deliverance.
- The Giving of the Law.
- The possession of the Land; building the Temple.
- Great Dynasty of Kings.
- The prophets.
- Coming Messiah.

God had a clear resume, in other words, as the Known God.

a. First, Praise is for God as he wishes to be known. As this year winds down, and as we look to Advent, this is a fitting reminder not to praise our own works but to reserve praise and worship for God alone.

b. Second, see the *reasons* for praise in this psalm: the attributes of God are noted, over and over again in Psalms. Like a typical psalm-hymn of its day, there are several primary attributes of God that are mentioned (68b-70).

1. He is the Arriving God, "Because he has come." God does not sit, entirely removed in heaven. He comes to his people. He initiates. He arrives. Far more than us, He is the One on the Journey! That is at the heart of Advent in fact. Had God

remained comfortably in heaven, Jesus would never have come.

Older translations speak of God 'visiting' us (cf. Gen 50:24-25 and Ex. 4:31).

2. He is the God who comes, though, with a targeted purpose; "he has come and redeemed his people." Redemption is a great concept—and it is more of a NT term than OT.

Isaiah seems to be a primary user of this term: "Fear not, for I have redeemed you." (43:1) It also occurs in the Psalter: 130:7, "with God is full redemption." Prior to that, it is used symbolically of the Exodus (6:6), but it's more of a NT term.

As God's people become more familiar with slavery, this term takes on a richness. And there were two 400-year periods of slavery that Zechariah's people had known: (a) in Egypt, prior to Moses; and (b) in the 400 years prior to Zechariah between the testaments, when the Temple had been destroyed, a smaller one rebuilt, but most of Israel was scattered.

Now, they were under the control of the Roman army. Israel was a police state. They were slaves of sorts. Of course, the NT will expand this concept to show that we are all slaves to sin.

For what does a slave pray? If not a merciful master, then emancipation is his dream. Redemption is when a slave is bought at the market by someone who loves him and will care for him.

Imagine being born into slavery, not in any way due to your own actions. And then spend your life constrained, chained, laboring for someone else and never for yourself. And when you try to break free of those chains, it only gets worse. Then one day . . . you are freed! A merciful Master comes and crushes those chains. You can now run, work, and enjoy. That's what Mary and Zechariah knew early on, on the final page of the OT.

Redemption is a prime ground for comparison to God. He is the one who goes shopping for his people. And he has the deepest of pockets to buy us back. He purchases us, that is redemption. And he is known as our Redeemer—a great portrait of God. Do you know this redemption today? Do you realize that you've been the slave—to sin—and your Master has the power AND LOVE to free you?! He has bought you at the market and brought you into his home. Zechariah knew this.

Thus far, God is the Arriving God, the Redeeming God; he is also:

3. The Strong Saving God. The "horn" symbolizes that things are secure and cannot be torn away. A bull's horns would stay attached to his head as long as anything stays intact. And such a horn would be powerful. The "horn" of our salvation, then, became a term that referred to the security that our Savior would bring (cf. it is used in Ps. 18:2-3 and 132:17). Once he saves us, we are not separated. He is a horn that we can anchor to!

4. Finally, he is the Holy God who raised up prophets (70a).

So, God is Holy, he is praised as our Savior and Redeemer, who is on a mission to purchase his people. Zechariah and true saints of the OT knew this much about God—far more than some of our contemporaries. What a portrait!

These are reasons related to the character of God that set our hearts to song. Next, this NT Psalm moves to praise God for:

c. The benefits to the redeemed (in 71-75); among the benefits to the redeemed are:

- He will bring salvation from our enemies. Most Jews thought this meant deliverance from the Romans. But as the scriptures make clear, it is salvation from Sin—that is far stronger than any nation. God brings salvation from that enemy by his power.

- v. 72: He will show mercy to our fathers. God is a promise-keeping God. He does not forget. And when he keeps his promise, that is a token of mercy. One Pastor illustrated mercy this way: We are like poor children peeking through the window of a mansion, watching the family children open their gifts on Christmas morning. Suddenly we turn around and find the father standing behind us. But instead of him running us off, he ushers us into the house and presents us with wonderful gifts as well. The mercy of God opens the door for us.

- Specifically, he will "remember his Holy covenant." Yes, God is praised for keeping his oath, going all the way back to Abraham. Already in the NT, we see how we are grafted into Abraham and that God was always looking for a holy people—not so much from one nation or stock.

- He rescues us (v. 74a) from our enemies.
- This next one in 74b is big: "He enables us to serve him without fear." That is huge. We come to the Lord, knowing that he loves us—not that he is looking to cast us away. That makes a tremendous difference in your worship and walk. Can you apply this? To stand before him in holiness and righteousness all our days?

d. Fourth, this Psalm itemizes praise and predictions for Zechariah's child

The News about what the Messiah and his Forerunner do (76-79).

1. John would be called the prophet of the Most High. He would fulfill Malachi's prophecy and go before the Lord to prepare the way for him. John's role was a bulldozer of sorts . . . in fulfillment of several OT prophecies, an Elijah-figure would arise just before the Messiah. And this Elijah would prepare the highway. As Is. 40 puts it "Every valley shall be exalted, the crooked roads made straight—for quick travel—and the rough places plain. John, Zechariah's son, was designed for that.

2. He would also point to Christ who would "give his people the knowledge of Salvation. (77a) That is not something that we inherently have. We are not born with this encoded information. It comes from outside of our insight, and the Lord has to reveal salvation to us. Else, we'd never have it. This is what Jesus uniquely brings.

3. Messiah also would bring forgiveness of sins (77b). Our sin problem is actually handled. We don't sweep it under the rug; nor do we remove sins ourselves. We do not have that power; this must be done for us. And one of the beauties of Christianity is that Christ disposes of our sins against him.

Rob Rayburn notes that Zechariah's NT song is perfectly in keeping with the OT psalms where we read repeatedly of forgiveness sought and received. Time after time we are given beautiful and powerful images of divine forgiveness—and Zechariah knew these:

a. God has separated our sins from us as far as the east is from the west;
b. He has trampled our sins under his feet;
c. He remembers them no more;
d. Though our sins are as scarlet, they shall be made as white as snow;
e. He buries our sins in the deepest sea;
f. He does not count our sins against us;
g. He casts them behind his back; and so on.

4. Messiah would bring home the tender mercy of God (78a). The tender mercy is derived from a term from anatomy that refers to the deep sympathetic feeling for another's pain. It is taken from the word "bowels, or guts." Mercy feels the pain of sin deep within. God has shown this to Zechariah, and he sings it to others. These characters on the verge of the OT, know mercy so well that: this becomes a central theme of this second half of chapter one. The word "mercy" occurs 5 times, twice in each of the songs and here in v. 58 between them. (Rayburn)

The reference to the sun rising comes from Malachi 4:2. It means the sun rise or "dayspring" as some hymns have it. And it depicts the beginning dawn of God's mercy, with much more to come. It's not the sunset of mercy but the Rise.

5. Messiah would shine ethical light and give guidance to all (79). Again, human nature is blind and needs help. We do not see the light on our own. We live in darkness—certainly that is the depiction of life just before the coming of the Messiah, as much of this is taken from Is. 9:1-2 ("no gloom," distress relieved," Light shining "amidst darkness") and Is. 55:12. Now, is a good time to consult those and factor them into your thinking.

This is the kind of God Zechariah knew and expected.

And he believes that God's prophets from long ago are truthful. The Lord planned to show mercy (72) to our fathers and remember his holy covenant. That's the kind of God Zechariah knew, not a God who was looking for legal perfection. Yes, he showed mercy in the OT and rescued his people (74) from their enemies. In fact, look at how v. 74-75 illustrates the beauty of OT relationships with the Lord. These saints before the birth of Christ understood that God enabled them—he gave them grace—to serve him without fear in holiness and righteousness. No fear!! That could only come from a standing that knew forgiveness. It also meant that righteousness would come from Another.

Furthermore, Zechariah knew something about God's plan to prepare for a Messiah. He knew that the Messiah would come and "give his people the knowledge of salvation through the forgiveness of sins." (77) Now that's pretty powerful gospel theology prior to the birth of Christ, isn't it!! Zechariah knew the forgiveness of his sins.

And he also knew the basis of it, as v. 78 says, "Because of the *tender mercy* of our God." The tender mercy of our God . . . if that was known, these OT era saints were not trying to earn God's favor by keeping the law. What grace!!

They also had a future hope (78b-79).

It's fairly amazing to see how close some of these OT saints were to God and how much genuine spirituality they had. Can we really think we are above them?

Zechariah, in this his joyful song, extolled the remission of sins, as one of the most extraordinary proofs of the tender mercy of our God. He had been dumb for a season, as a chastisement for his unbelief; and therefore he used his recovered speech to sing of pardoning mercy. No salvation is possible without forgiveness, and so Zechariah says, "To give knowledge of salvation unto his people by the remission of their sins." The Lord could not forgive them on the ground of justice, and therefore he did so because of his tender mercy—the tender mercy of our God, who has made himself "our God" by the covenant of grace. He passes by the transgression of his people because he delights in mercy.

"Mercy" is music, said one pastor, and "tender mercy" is the most exquisite melody, especially to a broken heart. To one who is despondent and despairing, this word is life from the dead. A great sinner, much bruised by the lashes of conscience, will bend his ear this way, and cry, "Let me hear again the dulcet sound of these words, tender mercy." If you think of this tenderness in connection with God, it will strike you with wonder, for an instant, that one so great should be so tender; for we are apt to impute to Omnipotence a crushing energy, which can scarcely take account of little, and feeble, and suffering things.

It was a proof of great tenderness, on God's part, to think of his sinful creature, man, at all. When the created one had willfully set himself in opposition to his Creator, that Creator might at once have destroyed him, or have left him to himself, to work out his own destruction. It was divine tenderness that looked on such an insignificant creature, impudently engaging in so gross a revolt. It was also infinite tenderness which had, long before that, considered man so carefully as, practically, to frame a plan by which the fallen might be restored. It was a wonder of mercy that infallible wisdom should unite with almighty power to prepare a method by which rebellious man might be reconciled to his Maker. It was the highest possible degree of tenderness that God should give up his own Son, his only-begotten Son, that he might bleed and die in order to accomplish the great work of our redemption. It is also indescribable tenderness that God should, in addition to the gift of his Son, take such pity upon our weakness and our wickedness as to send the Holy Spirit to lead us to accept of that unspeakable gift. It is divine tenderness which bears with our obstinacy in rejecting Christ, divine tenderness that plies us with incessant expostulation and invitation, all to induce us to be merciful to ourselves by accepting the immeasurable boon which God's tender mercy so freely gives to us.

Application: This is a good reason to sing Psalms. That's why I am thankful that we have begun to integrate these great songs of faith in our worship. They are timeless and fresh, holding forth deep, timeless, and true spirituality.

A summary of these teachings, shows that Zechariah, contrary to being spiritually challenged, was ahead of most understanding: In Sum (From Ryle):

1. We should notice, firstly, the deep thankfulness of a Jewish believer's heart in the prospect of Messiah's appearing. Praise is the first word that falls from the mouth of Zechariah as soon as his speechlessness is removed, and his tongue restored.
2. We should notice, secondly, in this hymn of praise, how much emphasis Zechariah lays on God's fulfillment of His promises. Let us learn to rest on promises and embrace them as Zechariah did. Let us not doubt that every word of God about his people concerning things future, shall as surely be

fulfilled as every word about them has been fulfilled concerning things past. Their safety is secured by promise.

3. We should notice, thirdly, in this hymn, what clear views of Christ's kingdom Zechariah possessed. He speaks of being "saved and delivered from the hands of enemies," as if he had in view a temporal kingdom and a temporal deliverer from Gentile power.

4. We should notice, finally, what clear views of doctrine Zechariah enjoyed. He ends his hymn of praise by addressing his infant son John the Baptist. He foretells that he shall "go before the face" of Messiah, and "give knowledge of the salvation" that He is about to bring in--a salvation which is all of grace and mercy--a salvation of which the leading privileges are "remission of sins," "light," and "peace."

Let's sing like this at Advent; first, believing and then trusting like this!

Let us end the chapter by examining what we know of these glorious privileges. Do we know anything of pardon? Have we turned from darkness to light? Have we tasted peace with God? These, after all, are the realities of Christianity. Let us never rest until we are experimentally acquainted with them. Mercy and grace have provided them. Mercy and grace will give them to all who call on Christ's name. Let us never rest until the Spirit witnesses with our spirit that our sins are forgiven us, that we have passed from darkness to light, and that we are actually walking in the narrow way, the way of peace.

God Sovereign Over All the Details

Luke 2:1-10

I enjoy the Christmas celebration as much as anyone. Well, that is not exactly true; there are other people in my home, primarily female, who, over the years have assumed more joy than usual during Advent. Shortly after Thanksgiving the house becomes filled with light and holiday fragrances. Ann makes our home very festive when the tree arrives (often it even stays up), and she has a nearly evangelistic compulsion to light the exterior of the house, which I still resist.

During Advent, the Halls probably consume more calories per capita than some cities, and a greater volume of cheese balls than several developing nations. The whole house becomes warm, filled with memorabilia from family and different traditions. And the Mrs. Santa Claus in my house has managed to convince the next generation of Halls that this is good; for years I was outvoted 4-1 on most decorating issues. I remain an oppressed minority during the entire month of December. Over time, this phenomenon has worn me down, and lately I've surrendered to joy, no longer contending for the Evangelical Grinch of the Year award. Joy is, after all, an appropriate emotion of the season. I might advise other dads to run up the flag as well.

Over the years, we have also noted another evangelical version of Grinchism. Mine, of course, stems from seasonally affected crabbiness and fatigue as a busy year ends. There are some, however, who don't want to have any celebration of Advent at all.

The Puritans, whom I love and admire, were like that. I agree with their motive, but differ with their outworking on this issue. Their desire was to avoid anything close to a Roman Catholic holy day or any tradition that was not strictly biblical. They were right to pursue those goals, and many others are right, though, about this: One can become distracted in many different ways by our Christmas partying, but there's also something good that I've learned from my wife and from churches like this one: If Advent is a little-bit dreamy, a little bit better than daily reality, that, in itself, may not be so bad. It may be a foretaste of heaven to remind us not so much that there are undeserved gifts as to remind us of something of greater importance: Yes, there is a heaven. One day, all will be blissful. There is an entirely different level of reality that is frequently forgotten or ignored altogether. And all too often, modern materialists become convinced of their own inherited creed: they start believing that only the daily routines, the here and now, are real. A biblically-rooted Advent focus can serve to remind us of both the supernatural and also of the promise of God to make all things new.

Sometimes, Advent emphases on the miraculous may provide a partial cure for that. In a fallen world, it's not all bad to have some of heaven invade our lives. Even if only one month out of 12, it might not be so bad to reserve some emphasis on heart-preparation and supernatural. It is not wrong for children to look forward to the future and then not be disappointed. Finding oneself "beneath life's crushing load" happens enough as it is. For some, life is filled with difficulty and disappointment, but why not help our children with tangible lessons, and teach them that the Messiah does bring wonder, beauty, joy-unspeakable, and he fulfills the hope of every longing heart? It is not wrong to have some cozy moments around a fire or a lit-tree to reflect on God's providence, his blessing in our lives, and his saving work in our lives. It is not wrong for our children to look forward to good things and know that their parents will move mountains to make them happy and fulfill their dreams if at all possible. Those acts of parental love, when later remembered, may encourage a young person when he falls on his face or thinks no one loves him. Those gifts of love, may be used by the Holy Spirit in a young person's life as follows: When that person hits a brick wall in some area, he may repeat the words of the Prodigal: I can go home, my father has plenty and will love me.

So while I have become a convert away from Puritanism on this particular issue, I am still aware of another distinct danger posed by our many Christmas celebrations.

With all the festivities, and our family is not alone in this: It is possible to lose the reality of Christ's birth amidst all the preparations, parties, and lighting. This other way to lose the reality of Christ's birth is to lose it amidst the gold and glitter of smooth presentations. If everything is so perfect—or to romanticize Christmas—that may deceive us and we may forget that when Jesus was born, the surroundings were far from perfect.

At times, I wonder if we don't go a little astray by having all perfect trees and shiny garments. And with everyone on their best behavior, we are nicer than normal, and it may mislead some people into thinking that our homes are perfect, and all is harmonious. Luke seems to counter this!

Moreover, those flawless Christmas pageants are so neatly choreographed, with all the props in place, and the story always works out well.-Somehow, I doubt that the wise men sounded like Opera star Luciano Pavarotti. I'm not sure everything was quite as easy as the re-enactments make things look. The shepherds weren't a group of crack religious operatives.

At most re-enactments, you have snowflakes, controlled temps, beautiful music.

You have some of the best lighting available.

Plus, if it's really cold, you have heaters. The harsh reality is blunted.

And you see shiny outfits, fur, and glitter.

Then when churches add living Christmas trees, angelic choirs that are perfectly pitched—complete with harps—and exquisite stained-glass, it is possible, just possible, that some people can confuse the reality of Christmas with a choreographed drama. In the process, the living breathing Lord of Glory can be transformed into a God of the gaps, wrapped in tinsel and gold lamé.

The historian Luke, however, records for us a narrative with a different emphasis. He tells us the true history behind this event that has changed our lives. And the realism of this narrative should be appreciated.

In fact, glance back to the first 4 verses of Luke's gospel with me for a moment to see how clear he is that this is historical material. In his prologue, Luke states that his gospel is:

- A historic account;
- Well investigated by Luke, using eyewitnesses;
- Presented to a specific Roman official;
- Purposeful: to know the life of Christ with certainty.

Review this with me, and see if it doesn't refocus some things. Today, I wish to highlight 4 aspects that show the signs of reality from the narrative in Luke 2.

1. Christ comes into Dire Political Circumstances (1-3).

It is not into an easy environment that Christ comes.
These early verses in chapter 2 tell us a lot about the setting before Christ's birth. The ruler of the Roman Empire was Caesar Augustus. He was the latest in a series of powerful rulers, reigning from 30 BC to 14 AD. Augustus put an end to ferocious civil wars within the empire by assuming absolute powers. A landmark from Ephesus records that he also wished to be considered divine. The Roman empire itself was the most powerful government of the known world. But it had not always been that way.

Rome came to prominence by defeating the Greeks. They were the latest in a succession of aggressive powers. They were known for their military conquests—they didn't exactly live by UN Human Rights conventions; imagine how the press would have reported their brutal treatment of prisoners. They routinely trampled human rights and stole whatever properties they could confiscate.

For the past century, Rome had secured peace. During that period, the government built massive roads to expedite military travel—all at taxpayer expense. Those roads also enhanced communication and trade. The empire grew, and flourished. Roman writers like Seneca and other dramatists were the most cultured and most intelligent of the day.

The Romans were also a polytheistic people, who believed in many gods. To the Jews who had been conquered by the Romans, they were surrounded by unbelieving people.

One of the other things that the Romans did was to assess taxes. Caesar ordered a census, and the reason for the census was fairly simple: He wanted money. The other reason for the census was to supply his army, but the Jews were exempt from that service. The people were taxed, and at a pretty high rate. Each person had to stop his work, grind his life to a halt, and inconvenience his family (had to present them in person), by taking them to his own city to register. No one was exempt, except the very rich, who could buy off a census worker.

Joseph was certainly not rich, so he had to pack up his young pregnant wife, at the worst time possible, and motor down 80 miles from Nazareth to Bethlehem.

When he traveled, he did not have the safety we do. The highways were often the homes of robbers and bands of undesirables. There were not nearly enough police to protect travelers, so wherever Joseph went, he went at his own risk. Joseph and Mary traveled amidst Roman oppression.

Jewish travelers were frequently known to disappear when traveling. There were no conveniences, and few leisure stops.

Joseph and Mary were traveling amidst political instability—frequently local overlords would attack others or plunder the law-abiding citizens.

With all this, Jesus came into the world. There were no soft lights, no audio dubbing or soundtracks (except provided by the angels), no synthesizers, and little glory—except divine. Christ came into dire circumstances. The Jews were in despair; times were not good—they hadn't been for centuries. Many didn't know where the next meal would come from.

Guess what? Amidst all this backdrop, with the Fall of Adam working itself out in human society, more and more every day, the Savior was about to be born. He would come into lives that were surrounded by the most dire circumstances possible. He did not enter the universe only when it was perfect or flawless. Christ did not enter a smooth, sanded stage. He entered in rough-hewn circumstances. Lives were a mess and the whole world was far from choreographed.

He does the same still in lives today. You may feel that you are surrounded by the worst conditions possible. . .

Less than great jobs or none at all.

Disease and physical deterioration.
Emotional problems.
Scars from personal quarrels.
International tension.

Look for Christ to come when things are their worst, not when things are at their best. He comes to make his blessings flow, far as the curse is found. And all this is amidst the reality of a less-than perfect world.

2. *Christ also comes into Family Stress Circumstances (4-6).*

Not only was the society less than heavenly, there was family difficulty as well. Let me mention a few aspects in Jesus' parents. First there was the physical difficulty of transporting a pregnant lady 80 miles. There were no buses or planes. The Christmas card picture of Mary riding a donkey is likely accurate, or at least close—except for her imagined serenity. Any of you ladies who have given birth can imagine how uncomfortable it would be to ride an animal for 80 miles in that condition. The only thing worse would be to walk.

Don't think the trip went smooth. Can you recall any vacations where things were difficult? I remember my family's first real family vacation when I was 6 years old. We looked like a vagabond troupe going west. We loaded up—6 of us, three from the immediate family, grandma and grandpa, an aunt or some other person. We went out in a 1960 Chevrolet with no air conditioning to New Mexico *in the summer time.* We were sort of crammed all over each other. Know what? No one has ever made a church-play about any of our family's vacations.

The reality of difficult travel conditions on a family trip should not be forgotten. That's closer to the reality Joseph experienced than most cantatas show.

Joseph is doing the best he can. He's contending with a high level of family stress. Things are not going well, and he would never be featured on the cover of *Christianity Today.*

Like any other young couple, they had worries. They had little savings, and now with a child on the way, it's hard not to worry about providing. Remember those years when you were just getting your family going? Joseph didn't have a lot of cash lying around. He worked hard every week, and only had enough to scrape by. Do you realize that Jesus did not grow up in an upper class home, maybe not even a middle class one. Prep school was never discussed as an option for him. It's even entirely possible that this couple had less family support than most.

Could it be that Joseph's parents reacted like everyone of us would, if our son came and said, "Mom, dad, uh . . . , I'm gonna be a father, but Mary and I have not had any sexual relationship yet." Devoid of parental help, this young couple had a lot of family stress.

There were strains between Joseph and Mary as well. The economic realities seemed to crash all around them. Do you think they never snapped at each other at the First Advent?

Plus, it was all very embarrassing. All the other young couples rejoiced in their good news. All the family members were thrilled at the coming of a new grandbaby, but Joseph and Mary were out on their own. Wouldn't be a lot of baby showers for her.

It was a crowning blow, then, to have some distant Roman ruler steal some of Joseph's hard earned money. They had to load up and go to Bethlehem to pay the tax to the atheist Roman conquerors.

This was one stressed family; and frankly at times, Joseph wondered if it was all worth it. He wondered if he shouldn't leave Mary in some other town, or call it off altogether.

Does your family have any stress at this time of year? If so, Christ came to save you in the midst of that. It doesn't all disappear. Instead, he redeems it.

While Joseph and Mary were in Bethlehem, as if the trip couldn't get any worse, the time came for her to give birth. GREAT. When he left, he thought they would surely be able to get back home, but no.

3. *Christ comes into a Humble Environment (7).*

Like any parents, Joseph and Mary wanted the best for their children. Long before the day of college savings plans, Joseph and Mary still wanted to provide the best for their offspring. Mary wanted, just like all the others, to have a nice quiet nursery for her son. She couldn't quite figure out, how all this worked, but she did know how to prepare a nursery. Then when she was uprooted and the time for delivery arrived early, all those plans came crashing down. Further, after his birth, she would not be able to return home. She would be whisked off to Egypt for 2 years, away from her own family. There went the nursery.

When Christ was born, there wasn't even any room at a local inn. They had to contend with the rest of the crowds just to get space. Finally, someone felt sorry for them. An innkeeper gave them a fairly clear stall for the couple. Their distress was obvious.

Christ was enthroned in the following:

- Manger, normally reserved for crops.
- Animals sharing the birthing suite.
- Dank, cold of a cave or the musty smell of a used barn.
- First clothes were rags.

Not exactly a scripted way for the King of the universe to begin his rule. But this was God's way. Christ comes into a humble environment.

4. Finally, from these vss.: Christ comes to the least likely (8-11).

Those who first learned about Christ's birth were shepherds. These were considered unclean because they dealt with animals all the time. It was impossible for them to keep the laws of cleanliness. Shepherds were also notorious in the day for their dishonesty and for their unreliability. They were seldom rich, and they would make off with anything possible.

Interestingly, the angels did not go to CEOs, bankers, or university faculties to make this announcement. They went first to field-hands. The angel, following God's orders, knew that God did not plan to build his kingdom on the shoulders of the successful or the self-sufficient. It would have been difficult to choose more unlikely vehicles to be the first announcers of the gospel.

Angels appearing to the Shepherds in Luke 2 was a fulfillment of 1:53: God "has sent the rich away empty."

Are there any such people in the world in a spiritual sense? Yes; every now and then we come across them. They are not truly rich; they are naked, and poor, and miserable; but they are rich in their own esteem, and think they need nothing. Some think they have kept the law from their youth up; or, if they have not done that, they have done something quite as good. They are very full of grace, and sometimes they wonder that they can hold so much. They are as good as ever they can be, they hardly know how to put up with the company of some Christians, especially of those who are mourners in Zion, and are lamenting their sins and their departure from God. They have no patience with these people. They stand by themselves, as did he who was called a Pharisee, and who went up to the temple to pray; and as they hear others making confession of sin, they proudly say, "Lord, we thank thee that we are not as other men are." 'Very superior persons indeed are they—sometimes in education—sometimes in rank and station—sometimes in the weight of their money-bags but anyhow, very superior indeed—the "upper-crust" of society. They are spiritually and morally rich before God—they think.

The shepherds were out in the fields, it was night, and the Angel announced: Don't be afraid; there's great news for you and all the world. A Savior is born, and he is Christ, the Lord. (2:10-12)

Christ comes in the least likely places and times. He surprises us with that still today. He may visit in a dimly lit hospital room, or in a classroom, or when a person is little recognized by others. He may come to that nursing home where many are forgotten, or to the popular shop. But he does not need the trappings of affluence or power to dwell with us.

Play a short round of, "If you were God," with me. If you were God, and you wanted to conquer the world, would you begin:

In the outback?

In an outback that was part of a runt nation, never distinguished for much except its calamity?

An outback country that was ruled by a crushing, insurmountable power?

Born to parents who were not rich nor influential?

Born in a humble make-shift environment, fraught with family stress and universal problems?

Kinda like today.

Think about what God was planning. For him to do things this way, shows . . .

That he needs no props.

That he depends on no others.

That he is not the "fair-weather" God who can only work when things are going fairly well anyway.

That he is not captive to the plans of the Romans or any other empire.

That he does not need the powerful, nor the mighty to work his plan.

That . . . most of all, his glory and majesty is also wrapped up in his humility and weakness.

See the greatness of God!! All amidst these particulars:

He came among us as the weakest, as the most dependable. And his triumph is beyond measure.

When Jesus came, it was the "Half Dickens." It was the worst of times, and it was the worst of times.

The world and this family was surrounded by darkness, and the Lord was bringing light, and glory.

The strength and majesty of God show more clearly against this backdrop.

Advent is the magnifying glass of God. By that, I mean it focuses our attention in ways we need.

Don't get distracted by all the unreality, but do know this: the reality is even greater. God did break through in human history, he did come to earth and took on our humanity. He shattered the theological categories, and he will triumph.

This is NOT fiction!!

Dr. David Strain sums it up well: "Let's remember as we're here that Luke is telling this story to a friend. He is telling this story to a friend, Theophilus, who is probably a Roman citizen. You can sense Luke saying here in Luke chapter 2, 'Theophilus, what a time we live in. What a time we live in, it's the intersection of the ages, it's a day in time when ancient prophecies have come to pass in our lifetime, Theophilus. And Theophilus, even the greatest empire in the world has become subservient to the purposes of God in the plan of redemption.'" You can sense the excitement in Luke's words as He shares this story. Shouldn't you have the same?

The Heavenly Song and Our Reaction to It

Luke 2:10-20

Perhaps two of the most recurrent strains in our Christmas music today and in all Advent hymns are "Glory to God in the highest" and 'Peace on Earth to men." Such phraseology does make grand Christmas card poetry.

The parallel makes those two phrases easy to remember, and like most things that are memorable they can also be overlooked because of over-familiarity. With rich strains and great music like we hear at this time of year, we ought to appreciate the greatness of this theology in Luke's gospel. In some ways, these words form the theological climax; the towering crescendo of the Advent narratives is reached with these words. These words almost demand percussion and cymbals because they are so emphatic.

Briefly on the context of Luke 2:8-10, after a considerable buildup, the birth of Jesus is actually simple and to the point. Christ is born in a stable and wrapped in whatever rags they could find.

After Joseph and Mary trek to Bethlehem, she gives birth, and the shepherds are the first to hear the news. Angels have been frequent characters in this drama, but they become even more important in this announcing phase. They tell the shepherds that the good news involves the Savior, who is Christ the Lord (2:11). The term, Christ, of course, to these Bethlehemites would signify that the long-expected Messiah had arrived. This great joyful event will also lead the shepherds to find Christ in the humblest of conditions.

Following that, the first announcing angels cannot remain solo. A whole slew of angels—in the OT, a heavenly host was often associated with military conquest; now that's interesting symbolism to note—joins together in chorus to praise God. It seems that Angels know better how to respond than do humans. When they are in the presence of God, they know it, and they rejoice. That is the proper reaction, and that is why we sing so much at this time of year. "Angels who had never sinned, and needed no Savior—angels who had not fallen, and required no redeemer, and no atoning blood. The first hymn to the honor of 'God manifest in the flesh,' was sung by a multitude of the heavenly host." (Ryle)

William Hendriksen commented: "These angels, having been associated with Christ in heaven before his incarnation, knew something about his glory, riches and majesty. They had also become aware of man's fall. And they had been informed that God had provided a way of salvation for man. When Gabriel announced the salvation, they may have also included some of the following information: that in order to maintain God's perfect righteousness, the Father would devote his own son, who though he was rich, for his people's sake became poor, vicariously bearing the curse resting on those he yearned to save. We can assume at least that the very birth of Christ in a condition of poverty and deprivation must have caused these angels to stand in awe of God's indescribably marvelous love." Whether a lyrical song or not, this is an outpouring of adoration. These angels had never been so thrilled. No wonder they shout glory to God in the highest. The message of our worship does make you want to sing!

And their song is well known. I want to discuss the two strands in my meditation this Christmas morning: "glory to God in the highest" and "Peace to men." Take these in reverse order.

First, let me suggest an often overlooked meaning of the phrase, "Peace on earth to those on whom God's favor rests." After that, we'll spend a little time on the reaction in vss. 15-20.

1. The first thing many of you will hear is a significant alteration in the traditional wording that I have employed. That's what I want to explain, first.

Change is not easy, but this is "change you can believe in." I want you, at least, to understand why newer versions translate the 2nd part of this verse differently than did the court of King James in the early 1600s. Part of the problem of with King James translators was that they were searching for poetic parallels in the wrong places.

They thought they could employ marvelously prosaic language that paralleled "Glory to God in the highest" by stretching the Greek "and peace to men on earth." The contrast between God in heavens and men on earth is valid, but the message became artificially crunched when it was squeezed too drastically to fit the poetry. That is something that we preachers have to be careful to avoid: we should not artificially mold God's Word to produce poetry if that poetry harms the original meaning.

At some point, an inquiring mind will ask of this verse: Does God give peace to all men on the earth to the same degree? That may seem like a surprising question, but it is actually a very welcome one. Several scriptures come to mind. Romans 1, for example, talks about the wrath of God—not peace—being poured out on unbelievers. That wrath is not always material, so it is hard to conceive how a person could receive both the wrath of God and the peace of God at the same time, if he were an unbeliever.

Other verses describe various ways that the wrath, judgment, or disapproval of God is given to unbelievers. Consider, for example:

- The prophecy in Haggai 2 promises to shake all nations, not bring them all peace.
- God's wrath, according to 2 Peter 2, was not spared in regard to Sodom, Gomorrah, and other ungodly men in the OT.
- John 3:36 speaks of God's wrath in the present tense as remaining on unbelievers.
- Numerous psalms note how God pours out judgment on unbelievers.
- And in the final book of the Bible, the wrath of God is spoken of in Revelation:
  - 6:16—to such a degree that those who do not love God flee from him and ask the caves to cover them from the assaulting anger of God. And:
  - 19:15 depicts Christ, our Lord, as ruling with an iron scepter, treading the "winepress of the fury of the wrath of God Almighty."

So the question is: How can we understand that God gives peace to all men on earth? Does he give peace to Satan worshippers, Atheists, Muslims? If so, it is, at best, a temporary lull.

And this is one of those places where better understanding of the original languages behind our English helps us. Let me cut to the chase:

A better translation for the words that the KJV missed (and which were unfortunately perpetuated in Christmas cards by the millions) are the following. This is what the Greek NT really has and what the shepherds originally heard in 2:14b: "Glory to God in the highest. And peace on earth among/to those men with whom God is well pleased, or the objects of his favor." There is a class of men, in other words, that God is pleased with. *He is not so peaceful toward rebels!*

The word for "pleased" or "finding favor"—literally, good showing/appearing—is used elsewhere in the NT, if we but interpret Scripture by Scripture:

- In the next chapter of Luke, a dove descends on Jesus, and a voice says, "You are my Son, who I love and with you I am *well pleased."*
- Luke 12:32: "Do not fear, little flock, for your Father has been *pleased* to give you the kingdom."
- Mt. 12:18 (to fulfill Isaiah's prophecy): "Here is my servant whom I have chosen, the one I love, in whom I *delight.*"
- Rom. 15:26-27 uses this word to refer to a voluntary gift to the poor in Jerusalem made by the Macedonians, who were *pleased* to do that.
- 1 Cor. 1:21—God was *pleased*—he freely willed it—to use the foolishness of preaching to save those who believe.
- 1 Cor. 10:5: uses this term of the will of God: "Nevertheless, God was not *pleased* with most of them; their bodies were scattered over the desert."
- 2 Cor. 12:10: "I *delight* (or take good pleasure) in weaknesses."
- Gal. 1:15: "But when God, who set me apart from birth and called me by his grace, was *pleased* to reveal his Son to me . . ."
- Col. 1:19: "For God was *pleased* to have all his fullness dwell in [Christ]."

This word is used over 20 times in the NT, so we can glean a pretty clear meaning. It means: well-pleased, or delighted with; and in this case, it is of men (genitive), with whom God is well pleased. So, the NIV does us a favor of straightening that out, and we are freed from a contradiction.

Notice *three things* about that line from the original Angels' hymn:

First, it is peace on earth—it is *here and now*. Christ brings a different kind of peace, to be sure, and he brings a peace that the world cannot strip away. He also gives an eternal and heavenly peace. But this is peace on earth, and that is contrasted with glory in the heavens.

What kind of peace on earth does Christ give now? (I'm not talking about the far off, or in the end times) He gives peace of conscience to those who are his. He gives and reassures us that he has forgiven our sins and that we are reconciled to him. The soul that knows Jesus knows rest of conscience. And he reminds us that all is well and will eventually work out. That is one of God's choice gifts to believers. But unbelievers do not have that, except as they tell themselves they are innately good and deserving. So, even at this point, we should be expecting that this peace is given to some, and not others.

Secondly, it is peace from God. This peace does not come from wealth, from personal achievement, nor from international settlements. It comes from God and is given by the Holy Spirit. No amount of works or accomplishment, no diplomacy, can secure this peace. It is not the peace of man. And the *Pax Romana*, the 200 years secured by the Roman government, is a pittance compared to this. It is the only enduring peace anyone will ever know. Plus, even the Roman peace was described by the first century philosopher Epictetus as: "While the emperor my give peace from war on land and sea, he is unable to give peace from passion, grief, and envy."

Thirdly, this peace is the peculiar possession of believers. Based on what the words of Scripture actually say, I can assure believers that you have something that others don't. You have God's favor and pleasure given to you; that's what gives you peace. And, yes this peace is to those on whom his favor rests, not the parallel poetry that

King James and Christmas cards feature. Viewing our peace this way should also produce humility.

Christ brings real peace to nations and to persons, and to the degree that he is honored, there is peace on earth. (Geldenhuys) When people ignore his ways, their lives are a mess and the "earth remains in a state of disorder and strife."

The good news announced here does not confuse belief with unbelief, it keeps things clear and straight. And this way, there is no conflict with other passages. That's why the NIV had the courage to break with an ill-conceived tradition and translate it this way. *God's work is emphasized, not man's.* "His sovereign delight rests on them. . . . True and lasting peace is the portion of those, and only of those, whom God has graciously chosen. The entire work of salvation from start to finish must be ascribed to him alone." (Hendriksen)

All that you lose is the 1st stanza of "It came upon a midnight clear," that says "peace on the earth, good will to men . . ." and Christmas rhyme or two. Or sing these, knowing what they really mean.

But we'd rather follow the Bible. And sing (from 'Hark the Herald'): "Peace on earth and mercy mild, God and sinners reconciled." Whether a seemingly small point or not, the thing to grasp is this: God brings peace to his people, and it is a deep, enduring peace—not one that goes away nor one that is subject to our small minds. It surpasses all understanding, but as a grace-gift is something to cherish. And it makes us love God more.

But that is not the first, the only, nor the most important thing contained in this hymn. Take your comfort from that and know that this promise fits in with all the other scriptural teaching, but also rejoice in the other part:

Glory to God in the highest

The original and basic meaning of glory is heaviness or weight. In 2 Samuel, Absalom's hair was "heavy." It is translated, "glory." This term refers to honor that is given. The one who is glorious should be honored. Compared to the passing transience of this world, God's glory shines. It is known and revealed. The word occurs 336 times in the OT alone.

Glory begins in the OT:

1. Glory is noted at creation—splendor and majesty accompany God's creating everything out of nothing by his powerful word.

2. Glory is in the creation of man. Man, in the image of God is the crown of his handiwork. Man also is given the ability to create glory.

3. Glory is pervasive at Mt. Sinai; when Moses went atop the mountain to receive the 10 commandments, he came down with a radiant glory. It faded as he moved away from the mountaintop experience, but still it was glorious. After that, God led his people by the glory of the pillar and the cloud.

4. Glory is certainly a feature of the Temple. That is where God's presence was known. Worship is thus associated with glory.

5. Isaiah wrote: "I am the Lord . . . I will not give my glory to another or praise to idols." (Is. 42:8)

The glory may also depart (Ichabod), when a people disobey God habitually. And Israel did that with serial predictability.

Short of the 2nd Coming, God's glory seemed to peak here at the birth of Christ. The angels are thrilled over this message and believe that it suggests that God's glory is revealed in strength here.

Glory surrounds Jesus in John 1:14: "We have seen his glory, the glory of the One and Only who came from the Father, full of grace and truth."

Later, toward the end of his earthly ministry in John 17:5, he would pray, "Glorify me father in your presence, with the glory I had with you before the foundation of the world." Jesus and the Father shared a glory before the world was ever created, and it did not depend in the least on anything external.

Glory was once associated with powerful empires like Rome or Britain. Today, we normally associate glory with conquest or triumph, perhaps by a military unit against all odds or other performers. When a team has come from behind or when an individual performance is far better than we expect, if that winner is then the least bit noble or humble, he exemplifies glory. Sometimes, though, it is becoming hard to associate glory with political or entertainment leaders.

The glory that is envisioned here is the highest glory possible. It is glory to God in the highest. The angels realized that he was not confused with anything on this earth, nor was God's glory lessened by lack of human participation.

If God is glorified in all that he does, why is this one so special? Because there is more, as Charles Spurgeon said, "in that than in creation, more melody in Jesus in the manger, than there is in worlds on worlds rolling their grandeur round the throne of the Most High. Pause to consider how every attribute is here magnified. What wisdom is here! God becomes man that God may be just, and the justifier of the ungodly. What power, for where is power so great as when it concealeth power? What power, that Godhead should unrobe itself and become man! Behold, what love is thus revealed to us when Jesus becomes a man. Behold, ye what faithfulness! How many promises are this day kept? How many solemn obligations are this hour discharged? Tell me one attribute of God that is not manifest in Jesus. Ignorance would be the only reason why you have not seen it so. The whole of God is glorified in Christ; and though some part of the name of God is written in the universe, it is here best read—in Him who was the Son of Man, and, yet, the Son of God."

And if salvation glorifies God, then any focus on man as his own savior or partial redeemer reviles God.

The glory, and all that we can manufacture from our reputations, is to go to God in the highest. Finally, note:

2.   The reaction to the song in vss. 15-20.

Now the *army* of angels return to heaven—their work of announcing is done, and there's no need to remain with the shepherds. The spotlight shifts to some of the common characters in Luke's Gospel.

They begin to converse with one another. They respond in belief. Do you respond that way to the song? When you hear the above messages, does your heart thrill to it, do you pause to recognize how extraordinary this is, or do you take it for granted, ho hum?

These field hands head off to Bethlehem, speaking the language of belief that "the Lord has told us about." They do not waste time. Another token of belief is to act on the Lord's commands promptly. They didn't debate with the Lord, they didn't raise objections, nor did they list the difficulties. God was so powerful that they wanted to obey him and obey him promptly. So, off they hurry and locate Mary, Joseph, and Jesus. They find him in a manger.

Now notice how vss. 17-20 show us what our reaction to Christ's birth ought to be. It is two-fold: (1) tell the story and (2) continue to ponder what God has done.

When these shepherds find Jesus, they don't act like doubters or skeptics. Neither do they let any fears of incompetence stand in their way. What do they do? As soon as they'd seen him they spread the word about what was told and what they found. Ryle: We should "Believe implicitly, act promptly, and wait for nothing, when the" calling is clear.

You've heard the Word; now do you believe and wish to spread the word? Think what we've heard from God's Word lately:

- The miracles he works;
- How God comes to earth and takes on our flesh;
- He moves out of the way those who were thought to be powerful;
- And uses poor, common folks;
- He gives faith and saves us from sin.

The shepherds, who had no classes or expertise in public communication become the announcers of this message. Why? Only because they'd seen it and heard it so clearly. And they would not have behaved this way, had they not seen it. Could that be a clue for why many do not tell the Lord's gospel?

Best I can tell they didn't spread the word by writing but by speaking. They told those they came into contact with. These crude evangelists had wide open doors for ministry; and they took the opportunities before them. What made it happen was something stunningly simple but more effective than numerous evangelistic clinics: They saw with their own lives.

This Christmas, have you seen the Lord with your own eyes? Have you seen him work in your life? To change it, to convert you, to fill and guide you? Or have you only read about it in others?

When they told others, those who heard it were amazed at the shepherd's testimony. These weren't orators or great teachers—else they wouldn't have had the jobs they did. But God used them, and in simple language they told the truth. Verse 20 states that when they returned to their pastures, along the way, they "glorified and praised God." That means they pointed to the Lord as the one who should receive glory. They praised God for all the that they'd heard and seen. If you'll tell the story of Christ, you need not add embellishments.

The second reaction is that of Mary. She (v. 19) treasured these things up. She pondered. The original word is "thesaurus?" What a great tool on computers—to have a thesaurus at your fingertips.

She continued to meditate, on these things. At Christmas, it is a good thing to slow down and ponder some things. She may have dwelt on how Jesus would grow or fixated on her obedience.

Will one of those reactions be yours? Both would be even better.

Each of the verses sets before us a different way of sacred service. Some, it appears, published abroad the news, or told to others what they had seen and heard. Some wondered with a holy marveling and astonishment; one, at least, pondered, meditated, thought upon these things; and others, in the fourth place, glorified God and gave him praise. I don't know which of these did God the best service, but I think if we could combine all these mental emotions and outward exercises, we should be sure to praise God after a most godly and acceptable fashion.

Let me suggest to you that *holy wonder* at what God has done should be very natural to you. That God should consider his fallen creature, man, and instead of sweeping him away with destruction should devise a wonderful scheme for his redemption, and that he should himself undertake to be man's Redeemer, and to pay his ransom price, is, indeed, marvelous! Probably it is most marvelous to you in its relation to yourself, that you should be redeemed by blood; that God should forsake the thrones and royalties above to suffer ignominiously below for you. If you know yourself you can never see any adequate motive or reason in your own flesh for such a deed as this. "Why such love to me?" you will say. Had we been the most meritorious of individuals, and had unceasingly kept the Lord's commands, we could not have deserved such a priceless boon as incarnation; but sinners, offenders, who revolted and went from God, further and further, what shall we say of this incarnate God dying for us, but "Herein is love, not that we loved God but that God loved us." Let your soul lose itself in wonder, for wonder, dear friends, is in this way a very practical emotion. Holy wonder will lead you to grateful worship; being astonished at what God has done, you will pour out your soul with astonishment at the foot of the golden throne with the song, "Blessing, and honor, and glory, and majesty, and power, and dominion, and might be unto Him who sitteth on the throne and doeth these great things to me." (Spurgeon)

Filled with this wonder it will cause you a godly watchfulness; you will be afraid to sin against such love as this. You will be moved at the same time to a glorious hope. If Jesus has given himself to you, if he has done this marvelous thing on your behalf, you will feel that heaven itself is not too great for your expectation, and that the rivers of pleasure at God's right hand are not too sweet or too deep for you to drink thereof. Who can be astonished at anything when he has once been astonished at the manger and the cross? What is there wonderful left after one has seen the Savior? The nine wonders of the world! Why, you may put them all into a nutshell-machinery and modern art can excel them all; but this one wonder is not the wonder of earth only, but of heaven and earth, and even hell itself. It is not the wonder of the olden time, but the wonder of all time and the wonder of eternity. There is more of God, let us say, to be seen in the manger and the cross, than in the sparkling stars above, the rolling deep below, the towering mountain, the teeming valleys, the abodes of life, or the abyss of death.

I think it would be very difficult to draw a line between holy wonder and real worship, for when the soul is overwhelmed with the majesty of God's glory, though it may not express itself in song, or even utter its voice with bowed head in humble prayer, yet it silently adores. I am inclined to think that the astonishment which sometimes seizes upon the human intellect at the remembrance of God's greatness and goodness is, perhaps, the purest form of adoration which ever rises from mortal men to the throne of the Most High.

The angels sang this with joyful tears in their eyes; they knew it was the best of news. Let's take our clues from them, and know that this is the very best thing to discuss over the coming days. Ponder on these things for yourself, but love your neighbor and spread the word.

How will you react? These did in FAITH, in PRAISE, and CONTINUED THEIR WORK.

Learning from the Last Two OT Saints in the NT: Simeon and Anna

Luke 2:21-40

After the birth of Christ, time moves on, and one of the things I learn from studying Luke's narrative is this: Even after stupendous miracles, life goes on. A historian like Luke wants to make that point. Our faith does not fizzle or stop at the great peaks of the mighty works of the Lord.

And here, Luke's gospel shows us how life moves ahead, after Jesus' birth, with Christ even more central. Angels, kings, shepherds, and Jesus' parents may fade, but that is so Christ may *increase.*

I hope to bring several of our Advent themes forward to focus on the last OT characters in the NT. These two characters were alive at the birth of Christ, and they are privileged to see him first after the shepherds and angels. It is interesting that Mary and Joseph's obedience led to Jesus' first appearance in, of all places, a Jewish temple.

In this passage, we meet two people stranded at the edge of the testaments. As I stated in my first sermon from Luke 1 earlier in Advent, some people would think that Simeon and Anna, the two characters here, could not really know anything about Christ or walking with the Lord. That old theory of dispensationalism shows another of its faulty foundations in this passage, too. Look with me to see what Anna and Simeon knew about God and piety.

But before that, let me make one more stab at defending the piety of Joseph and Mary.

My first point is: *Faith is shown by obedience to the details of worship.*

Are you one of those who thinks that worship is so unimportant—that the real ministry is done only in small groups or via social rallies—that we either may make up worship as we think best or that it doesn't matter? As if God is so desperate to have a few followers that he'll take any pagan practices that thrill our senses and just paint over them with a bit of religious terminology?

No one in these birth narratives seemed to have that idea, leaving us with this challenge: is our religion in line with these Gospel themes or are we creating a different religion? Doesn't obedience extend even to the details that the Lord provides? Mary and Joseph presented Jesus at the Temple on the 8th day for circumcision. Now think about this for a second. If you'd just been through what Joseph and Mary had, wouldn't you think that Jesus should be treated differently than all other little Jewish boys? Wouldn't you think that the rules didn't apply? I mean, with the angelic announcements, all the miracles and attendant angels, Joseph and Mary surely knew that Jesus was unique. Yes, he cried like any other infant, and yes he was about 7-8 pounds of life, and was indistinguishable from any other baby boy. And as the 8 days progressed, it would be tempting for Joseph and Mary to think that all that earlier fuss about the birth and miracle of Jesus could be forgotten about or minimized.

But, Joseph and Mary would not have so quickly forgotten that Jesus (see his name below) was God's son. Still, they brought him to the temple on the 8th day to be circumcised. While he was not lacking and while this sign/seal would certainly not save him, yet Joseph and Mary brought him to the Lord's house in conformity to the OT rule. They were not seeking to overturn these requirements, and they did not see themselves above this. They were not looking for exemptions; they were obedient. This custom signified that the death penalty rested on the head of every sinner born. And unless God cancelled that punishment by some other sacrifice, it would belong on all children.

They were mature enough to realize that part of mature spirituality is *accepting that we all can't have our way.* To live in a society means to obey certain rules or codes. Joseph and Mary sought to obey God, who had called for children to be presented to him. We still do that in infant baptism by the way, and this was the equivalent of that in

Jesus' case. Unlike some of our Western individualistic friends, they didn't say, "Well, let's wait until he makes a decision himself; that's the only authentic decision." His parents knew that they could love God and obey his law at the same time.

They also knew the spiritual significance of his name (21b). This was the name that the angel had assigned before he was conceived. Joseph and Mary believed God and gave Jesus this name at his circumcision. According to Mt. 1:21 his name meant that "he will save his people from their sins."

This whole episode stresses how Joseph and Mary were obedient to God's word. Mary set aside the 7-day period for purification. Then they took Jesus to Jerusalem to be presented as the law required. Moreover, their poverty is noticed when you see the kind of offering they could afford: they could only afford to offer a pair of doves. This poor, young couple was unable to bring a lamb, and thankfully, God did not exclude people because they had limited resources. But Joseph and Mary did the best they could. They acted in obedience, and made an offering, dedicating Jesus on the 8th day. Have you given your children to the Lord? If not, let me urge you to give what is most precious to you to the Lord. Entrust your children to God. Even Jesus' parents did this.

In all respects, Joseph and Mary acted in faithfulness to the Lord. They knew the Lord and wanted to please him. Their obedience did not earn his favor but *was a by-product of his favor.* A person asked me over the holiday: how do I explain to a friend that we go to church because we love God—not so much as a requirement? I told her that I try to answer folks with examples sometime, and I would put it this way. What if I told my wife that I love her but never spoke to her or did anything for her? Why, you'd laugh me out of the room, and my wife would not fall for it. Similarly, we come to worship because we love God and that is one way to illustrate it.

Now, in order to glean the piety of Simeon and Anna, the last two OT characters in the NT (this is my second point), I want to look at three questions about each of these. These can be good for you to ask: (1) *How his piety described*; (2) What *each knew about God*; and (3) How each *responded to the presence of Christ*?

Alexander Maclaren says, "Here we have the Old recognising and embracing the New; the slave recognising and submitting to his

Owner (Despot); and the saint recognising and welcoming the approach of death."

SIMEON

Simeon—an aristocrat—is only mentioned here and not afterwards. Remember that God has his people, believers, even in places that are dark and hopeless. Learn from Simeon that God's true church will never be destroyed.

Ryle said: "True Christians, in every age, should remember this and take comfort. It is a truth which they are apt to forget, and in consequence to give way to despondency. 'I alone am left,' said Elijah, 'and they seek my life to take it away.' But what said the answer of God to him, 'Yet have I reserved seven thousand in Israel.' (1 Kings 19:14, 18.) Let us learn to be more hopeful. Let us believe that grace can live and flourish, even in the most unfavorable circumstances. There are more Simeons in the world than we suppose."

1. Note How his piety is described.

Righteous: This term refers to being straight in line with God; justified. He was like Zechariah: made righteous, never on own or by works. No one is made righteous by the law

And *devout*: means inwardly oriented toward the spiritual. He was reverent and not phony. This was not an external righteousness only.

More than anything, our calling card is that God has done for us what we could never do for ourselves. He has devised a way to classify us as righteous, even when we are very sinful. That is constant in all ages of history.

2. What he knew about God.

Waiting for the consolation of Israel: This is a very interesting phrase. What do you think of when you hear the word "consolation"? Some think of a second place prize. Or others think of being comforted after a death. Either way, if a person is waiting for the consolation of Israel, that follows some kind of defeat or loss or down-time. In this case, Israel needed consoling because she had forfeited her promises, and had gone so long without God's without God's blessing. The Lord had covenanted with Israel, that if she would obey him, she would receive the promises given to Abraham and have the Messiah reign in her midst. However, that promise was over 2,000 years in being fulfilled, and for the past 6-7 centuries, Israel had been in a serious downturn. The people felt as though the glory had departed, and it had.

All that was left was consolation. Even if God would not bless the entire nation, some remnant might be blessed as a consoling act of the merciful God. Simeon and some others were looking for that.

He knew that God's promises are eventually brought about. All the Lord's promises are true and never failing!

He knew the calling to have patience, i. e., that God's kingdom would not result in a day or short period of time. *Sometimes, the promises of God do not arrive as soon as we expect or wish.* In those times in your life, rather than thinking that God has not kept his promise, you need to have patience and trust.

Note also what Simeon *knew about the Holy Spirit.* There are three references: Verse 25 states that "the Holy Spirit was upon him." Thus, this person was not operating apart from the spiritual realm.

Also, v. 26 says, "it had been revealed to him by the Holy Spirit." Thus, the spirit was operating in his life. This revelation could only have been personal.

And then v. 27 says, "moved by the Spirit." The Holy Spirit was quite active in this man's life.

Would that all believers were moved by the Spirit!

3. Note also: How he responded to the presence of Christ.

Simeon was obedient, and he went to the Temple. Jesus' parents came in, and Simeon praised God as:

- Sovereign, 29a, (*despotes*, meaning master with full control).
- Promise-keeping God.
- Savior (v. 30).
- My eyes have seen *YOUR* salvation. This is all from God, and it is not the salvation of man that brings such joy. "This is the salvation of which the prophets spake, to which all the symbols pointed—the salvation which was hidden from ages and from generations, that it might shine forth like the sun upon this favored dispensation. It is a salvation devised and provided by God, which manifests and glorifies God; a

salvation which is Godlike, being both just and gracious, and beyond conception great; in a word, it is God's salvation. Don't try to invent or contrive a Savior. It won't work. Have your eyes seen HIS salvation?

- Salvation-Preparing God.
- Revelation—this fulfilled the promise from Isaiah 61.
- Glory.

And for some reason, Joseph and Mary marveled (33) about what was said about Jesus. Simeon wouldn't stop, though. He continued and offered a prophecy about Christ, that he would be a decisive stone, over which some would stumble.

Asking "What did he know and when did he know it?" shows us that prior to the birth of Christ, some OT saints knew quite a bit about God and they were very insightful. There are at least five things included (notes Spurgeon) in this utterance of Simeon: *1st here is clear perception; 2nd, perfect satisfaction; 3rd, happy unbinding 4th, dauntless courage; and finally, joyful appropriation."*

Do you know the Lord as Simeon did? Do you respond to him like this?

Next, learn from Anna, the prophetess.

ANNA

Note how different these are. Anna is a lowly widow, whereas Simeon was probably from the upper crust. Both male and female, rich and poor, can see Christ.

Also, note that Luke shows women being at the center of God's work, although not called to the ordained ministry. It's hard to miss that in these opening two chapters: Elizabeth is almost as important as Zechariah (just not a priest), Mary is given much more ink than Joseph, and Anna is presented with Simeon. Again, can we learn that all believers, male and female, can receive callings from the Lord and are called to serve and point to Christ. Only a few things are fenced as off limits for women: to serve as ordained officers in Christ's church.

1. Note, How her piety is described:

- Prophetess (the Holy Spirit was obviously speaking to her and working in her life); she used her spiritual gifts. She wasn't a fortune teller, like Sister Ruby; no, she took God's Word seriously and applied it to the day. She was not making up revelation; she was parroting God's revealed message.

Second, she was from a specific family and heritage. Her family had descended from Asher, and she was the daughter of Phanuel. She had a:

- Long, history of consistent living with the Lord. Pause to ask: how does that happen? What must occur to be a multi-generational Christian? That's a good thing to consider in this first month of the new year. If you have a few moments, what do you need to do to have a spiritual heritage?

For example, at a prayer breakfast, some time ago, a speaker decided to challenge evangelicals. They were all stridently anti-abortion. All were willing to send cards to their representatives and sign up for a march, protesting abortion. The speaker, Charles Colson, asked: how many of you regularly pray with your own children and/or have family devotionals? *We might start there.* Write this down: you won't have a multi-generational witness, if you don't carry it out in your own home. What do you need to change to have daughters that walk with the Lord for 84 years? Maybe it's being at the equivalent of the Temple throughout all their life?

Anna was the product of a godly heritage. And even in a time when others were not looking for God, her parents taught her the true faith. And it was the kind of faith that lasted for a lifetime . . . and for generations. She'd been:

- Faithful in marriage (7 years), and then faithful as a widow for a long time. There was no whisper of immorality, and she devoted herself to the Lord after her husband's passing. Was the rest of her life wasted?
- Continuous worship—night and day. She knew this as a place of comfort and closeness to God. That was more important to her than anything else.
- Fasted and Prayed—great self-denial; she knew that sin needed to be put to death. And she knew that living for the Lord was not always easy; it often required sacrifice.

Note the details, lest any of you think this is made-up. And all of these are common acts that are within the reach of any!

2. What she knew about God:

- God heard prayer.
- God valued intense piety.
- Long-term faithfulness was important.
- God revealed things (prophecy).

Luther noted: "She was a godly maiden, a godly wife, and a godly widow, and in all these three estates she performed her respective duties. May you then do likewise. Reflect on your condition, and you will find enough good works to do if you would lead a godly life. Every calling has its own duties, so that we need not inquire for others outside of our station. Behold, then we will truly serve God, just as Luke says that Anna worshiped with fastings and supplications night and day. But the legalists do not serve God, but themselves, nay, the devil, for they do not perform their duties and forsake their own calling."

3. How she responded to the presence of Christ.

Verse 38 illustrates. There is great comfort in Anna's case. "When you think of the Prince of glory and the Lord of angels stooping so low as this, that a poor woman bears him in her arms and calls him her babe, surely there must be salvation for the lowest, the poorest, and the most sunken. When the all glorious Lord, in order to be incarnate, is born a babe, born of a poor woman, and publicly acknowledged as a poor woman's child, we feel sure that he will receive the poorest and most despised when they seek his face." (Spurgeon) Yes, Jesus, the son of the carpenter, means salvation to carpenters and all others of lowly rank.

If these were Old Testamental, most of us NT saints would do better to return to these folks' piety. Luther noted: "Thus Simeon, as a preacher and lover of the cross and an enemy of the world, in blessing the child, gave a remarkable example of exalting and honoring Christ, who was then despised, cursed and rejected in his own person, and is now treated in the same manner in his members, who for his sake endure poverty, disgrace, death and all ignominy."

To review:

Point 1: True Faith is obedient to the details of Worship.

Point 2: True Faith knows God and responds to him as he is revealed.

Point 3: True Faith knows God is gathering all types, ages, and genders.

We need to be people of the Law, the Temple, the Promise, and Obedience. How well are you doing in these areas? And in the coming year, will you set aside some time to serve God in these areas?

There is also a special place for the seasoned saints to teach us. Young people, learn from those who've weathered many a storm.

The whole of salvation is in Christ. Do not expect to find a portion of it, wrote Spurgeon, "in yourselves or anywhere else. Do you debate this teaching? Then let me ask you, in what point is Christ deficient? What more do you need? Suppose that our Lord Jesus were not perfect as a Savior, what then? Could any of us make up the deficiency? What is there of ours that we could bring to him? If his robe of righteousness were not finished, would any of our filthy rags be fit to be joined to his cloth of gold? One would sooner yoke a gnat to an archangel, and then imagine that you can help your Lord in the work of salvation. Shall a creeping worm be needed to complete the work of him who made the world? Must the Son of God be helped by sinners dead in sin? If Jesus is not able to save you from first to last you are a lost man I have no hope of being saved if Jesus is not the whole of my salvation. I caution any here who are trusting a little in Christ, and also somewhat in themselves, that their hope will be vain. Jesus must be everything or nothing. *If we take Christ we must take the whole of Christ; there must be no picking or choosing."* Simeon and Anna knew this.

To do that, we must, like Simeon, take Christ into our arms and look at him. Give yourselves to him and embrace him. Simeon held that babe in the grasp of love as well as of faith, for I am sure the old man pressed the babe to himself and looked most fondly upon him as he said, "Mine eyes have seen thy salvation." He could not have held it out at arm's length, that would have been impossible in such a case, but he felt that he at length saw the dearest object of his desires and so he clasped him to his bosom. Come, let us one by one do the same. "My Jesus, my salvation, thou art all mine, and I love thee.

This also rules out thinking that you may lose your salvation. The babe would not have been so precious, had that been true. In fact, to the degree that we know that our salvation is all of God and out of our hands, we cherish the Lord Jesus.

- Are we looking forward to the final Advent like these were to the first Advent?
- Would you believe if you were only one of a few who did not give up?

Death to the believer is only a departure from one form of service to another. Same word that Paul uses in 2 Tim. 4:6. To the believer, death is not a thing to be dreaded; he even asks for it, "Lord, now let your servant to depart in peace."

"Now," says he, "I can look death in the face without dread, for I have seen God's salvation." He is not afraid of that tremendous judgment-seat which will be set in the clouds of heaven, for he who will sit upon that judgment-seat is God's Savior to us who believe. The one who looks to Jesus is not afraid of the day when the earth will rock and reel, and everything based upon it will shake to its destruction. He is not afraid of seeing heaven and earth on a blaze. "Mine eyes have seen thy salvation," saith he; and he bears this glorious vision about with him wherever he goes; it is more to him than any earthly talisman could be, it is more powerful than the most potent charm of the mystic or the magician. Such a man is safe; his eyes have seen God's salvation. "He speaks like one for whom the grave has lost its terrors, and the world its charms." (Spurgeon)

Also, there's a time for departure. It is OK to sing, "now let thy servant depart." There is a time to finish our work. I hope we will be able to close the books on previous years, a very fine one in many respects, and say, "now let us depart and leave 2016 in the past. It will soon be time to move ahead."

Grace Even in the Genealogies

Matthew 1:1-17

Most of us read through the Bible like a computer spell check program. My typing on a cell phone is pretty bad. Ask my kids. If not for spellcheck, it would be even worse. I'm thankful for spellcheckers, though. When you're all thumbs, the checker speeds through what you've typed until it finds a word that is misspelled, or not in the dictionary, and then pulls it up. Many of us read the Bible that way—blazing through as quickly as we can, as if a prize were given to the one who finishes first. This "auto pilot" style of Bible reading, in which we zap out the commercials, skips over the hard or the non-sensational.

We chug on along at high speed, crunching the biblical truths, skipping over great portions of gospel until we come to a section that slows us down. In that process we breeze over many timeless nuggets. Some of the most skipped portions in Bibles are the genealogies. Few people ever slow down in those sections. Instead when we get to one of those 'begat' sections, we crank up the reading speed, and in overdrive we accelerate right on past the boiled-down history of entire generations.

Unfortunately, that is true for the Christmas narratives. Most Christians have read these genealogies once or maybe twice in their entire lives. By comparison we usually read about the shepherds, the angels, Zechariah, or Herod, at least once, twice, or thrice in every year. Average Christians probably read all portions of the Christmas narratives 60, 80, or 100 times in their lives, as compared to only 2-3 readings of the genealogies. That discrepancy is hard to justify. As we begin Matthew's gospel, evidently, God did not think the genealogies a waste of Print, with genealogies frequently occurring in gospels that record the birth of Christ. To further underscore this point, the main point of this sermon should be old hat, but I bet it's not too many of us. It is so simple that all Christians ought to know this significance of Jesus' genealogy. If this is new to us this morning, this only proves how biblically illiterate our culture has become.

The genealogy in Matthew, which is the birth line of our Savior, has a central teaching, and it is important for us to know that this, too, is God's Word. Can you guess why, most people don't get a lot out of the genealogies?

Two answers are often given:

(1) Because they don't give me a religious boost by way of personal application to my own life and family now. It's high time that such search for a buzz for self be recognized as an evangelical habit of Me-centricity. According to this school of interpretation, Me comes first. If I don't get a spiritual "buzz" or chills down my spine, then obviously this part of the Bible is not very important. It must 'turn me on' or 'push my buttons.' To hear some talk, it's almost as if the amount of Scripture which folks endorse is dependent on whether or not, it makes one feel good. Is that the standard we want to cultivate . . . that this is God's Word if and only if it lights me up; and if not, don't bother??

(2) 2nd reason, related to this: These are BORING. Imagine, that there are parts of the Bible, or parts of the Christian life that may not be scintillating, pure-Fun, and as thrilling as attending a major playoff game! Where did we ever get this notion that everything in life must be entertaining, interesting, or sensational, or else be rejected as Boring? Other Christians in other parts of the world, say China, or a former Eastern European nation do not hold such prerequisites. I'll tell you where we derived that notion? *Likely from the TV; not from the Bible.* Social scientists tell us preachers not to preach more than 12 minutes because the TV-trained mind, is only accustomed to going 12 minutes between commercials, and our church members are so indoctrinated by the media of the TV, that they cannot even make it without straining to listen to a 20 minute sermon. And 25 minutes pushes the limit, with 30 being out of the question.

Let me hasten to say, that a call to the pulpit is not a license to bore. However, no preacher of the gospel is under a mandate to be a combination of comedian, Shakespearian actor, rock star, and Ryan Gosling. God does not require candidates for ministry to be entertaining. It's hard to miss that one of the leading aspects of why people choose a church, is because the preacher is easy to listen to.

However, if that is the standard, there will be a lot of fine messages never heard. And a lot of drivel will be disseminated; while a number of godly, but not-too exciting preachers will never be heard at the national conference. Is that our goal, to find the most entertaining and witty preachers? If so, many laughs will be chalked up, but there might be very few tearful confessions of sin, accompanied by true repentance—which is not much fun, and certainly not entertaining to the one repenting. Let's not overlook the genealogies, or any other part of the Bible, because it is not accompanied with fanfare, a light show, or a singing Christmas Tree. In fact, many of the light-shows in churches may not have any substance. Can I also give you one observation and warning? Here's the secret. It is not the Liberal churches that have resorted to dramatics, sensationalism, and entertainment for the past 25 years. Look around you. The terminal liberal churches are not hosting contemporary Christian music, nor staging an outdoor drama. The liberals are not advertising Karate Crushers for the Christ, or the Dancing Disco Disciples. It is not the apostate churches which are revitalizing vaudeville in the precincts of their very own sanctuaries. Neither have the liberal churches employed "worship team leaders," which sometimes appear like Emcees, with smooth segues from one portion of the program to the other. It is the conservative, fundamental, and evangelical churches that are doing this, as we sometimes tailor our message to the entertainment mindset of the culture around us. Americans love a good show, but church may not be one of them.

In the same way, these genealogies may not lead to a rush of thrill. But they are God's word. And we best learn how to profit from them. We are supposed to be able to profit from these. These lists are not defective revelation. They are every bit as much the revelation of God as John 3:16. I admit they don't push my buttons as much as John 3:16 or some other verse about salvation. Still they are from the mind of God and for us. Every bit of Scripture is inspired and profit-able for some purpose for us. To ignore these or other parts of the Bible is to deny 1 Tim. 3:16 and also to elevate our own judgment or emotions above the revealed word of God.

All scripture, even the genealogies, are given to us for purpose of doctrine, reproof, or training in righteousness.

So let's look at this genealogy today as preparation for Advent.

Each biblical genealogy has a central theological message to teach. For example, the genealogy in Genesis 5 underscores the message that, arising from sin, inevitably death occurs. The depressing refrain, at the end of each generation is...

___lived ___no. of years, AND HE DIED. (Repeat)

That genealogy and every one had a central theological thrust. There is a message to these 'begats.'

So what is the message of this one in Matthew, leading to the birth of our Savior? The message of this genealogy is that *God uses people of grace, not of merit.* Our God consistently uses the mode of grace to work his plan out in this world. He has never used human ability, moral perfection, nor family inheritance alone to be the chief factor in leading to Jesus' birth or anything else.

Likewise, in this genealogy it is not superior people, although some had become famous by the time of Jesus; it is not categorically superior people who God uses. Instead it is sinners just like you and me that God uses. Some are saints, some are sinners, some are from within Israel, some from without. Let's look at some of them, and have this message of this genealogy imprinted in our thinking this Advent.

I. Males, who were examples of grace; look at some of these males.
  a. Abraham, the very first one in 1:1.

Throughout the bible, he is one of the paragons of grace. His life was a model of grace.

Still, he was not perfect. There were times that Abraham sinned, doubted, and even tried to pass off his wife as his sister, so he could save his neck. Not very becoming for a patriarch of grace—actually very becoming for a model of grace, just not for a model of perfectionism. Abraham too sinned, and was imperfect.

The NT is replete with such references on "By Faith", e.g.,

Rom. 4:11- that Abraham was credited with faith *before*, not after the obedience of circumcision.

Rom. 4:16 ". . . so that it may be by grace."

Jas. 2:23: Abraham believed God . . . and he was called God's friend." Justification by faith!

Gal. 3:6: Abraham believed and it was credited to him as righteousness. By GRACE!

b. Jacob (v. 2); his name means "conniver," struggler, grasper of the heel. He:

- was assisted by a sneaky mom, robbed his brother of birthright.
- fled, while knowingly guilty.
- trekked through life by skirting the rules.
- finally was out-Jacobed by his own father in law, Laban.
- wrestled with the angel . . . but finally refined into a godly vessel.

God can use people like this. Take heart.

c. Judah (v. 3), the father of Perez.

Judah was one of Joseph's brothers. Was he helpful or what? Several episodes in Genesis focus on Judah:

1. At the selling of Joseph.

Gen. 37:26-27: "Judah said to his brothers, 'What will we gain if we kill our brother and cover up his blood? Come let's sell him to the Ishmaelites and not lay our hands on him; after all, he is our brother, our own flesh and blood.' His brothers agreed. So it was not good enough to get rid of Joseph. Judah had the idea to make a profit.

2. Judah and Tamar in Gen. 38.

Here's the story. Judah ran away from home. When he was grown, he was in search for 'greener pastures.' So he rejected his covenantal upbringing, and found a Canaanite for a wife (2). She bore him three sons, Er, Onan, and Shelah. Judah selected a wife for Er, named Tamar—she's mentioned in the genealogy of Jesus. The first son, Er, was wicked, not exactly raised to honor the Lord, so the Lord put him to death (7). Then the next son, Onan assumed this responsibility, but would not have children with Tamar. He too was put to death. Then Father Judah steps in, and after 2 of his sons had bought the farm, he decided to protect the baby of the family, Shelah, and not give him to Tamar. Hence Judah violated the levirate law, in which the family would provide for a widow.

As time passed, Tamar took things into her own hands. These are not perfect saints, just like us today who always wait on the Lord and never take things into our own hands. Tamar hears that Judah is to visit another city. She is really steamed that he's not provided a son to care for her. So she advances to the city, masquerades as a prostitute, and is later picked up by Judah, who thinks she is plying the worlds' oldest trade. Before having sex with him, she asks for some tokens of pledge and that he will give the goat he has promised, so Judah lends her his "seal and cord and staff" (25). They have sex, she becomes pregnant, and a few months later, as she begins to show, she is accused of immorality. Judah confronts her, and then is told [oops] that he is the father (v. 25). He then confesses and gives her Shelah. Judah and Tamar, two of the characters in the line of Jesus. Not by might, nor by power, but by my spirit says the Lord. Not by works, but by grace . . . even in the genealogies.

d. David, in v. 6, is another of those characters. Here is the 'man after God's own heart.' This author of so many excellent Psalms was also the man who conspired to kill another man, so he could have an affair with his wife. David committed sexual sin with Bathsheba.

e. Solomon was the man with 700 wives, and 300 concubines, whose heart was turned away by his wives' gods, the example of perfection?

Solomon, the builder of the Temple, was also the wisest man of his times. However, he was far from perfect, leaving some idols, following after false religion, and being a little short of monogamy.

And consider some of the others listed in this genealogy:

f. Rehoboam—a hot headed rebel, who splits the kingdom.

g. Abijah.

h. Asa -"good but . . ."

i. Jehospephat (v. 8).

j. Jehoram, Uzziah, Jotham, Ahaz, Hezekiah, Manasseh, Jeconiah etc.

This genealogy could also be the Hall of Shame of later Israel history. These were the kings who sold Israel down the river into paganism and idolatry. These kings, in the line of Messiah, were the reason and leaders that led to the Fall of Israel.

Summary: All throughout the OT, God used those who were less than perfect, and who were usable only by Grace. That is what this genealogy is about. These are the characters of grace; hardly perfection. *Secondly, note:*

II. Women, who are especially singled out as exemplars of Grace.

a. You must recall that women were not normally given this high position. It was uncommon to give women any credit back in those days. Thankfully times have changed, and we know better. Still it is striking to see the break with tradition, which here lists 5 women in Jesus' lineage.

The five listed in this genealogy are: Tamar (v. 3), Rahab (v. 5), Ruth (v. 5), Uriah's wife- Bathsheba (v. 6),and Mary (v. 16).

b. All of these had at least one thing in common . . . bad reputation. None of these escaped life unscathed. Each of these in her own way, even though several were pure as the driven rain, were harshly criticized.

c. Further, most were accused of a notorious sin, e. g., sexual immorality.

A thumbnail of each is given below for review and emphasis.
1. Tamar (v. 3).

We've already discussed her above. Simply note that she was known for her deceit, her disguise as a prostitute, her adultery with her own father in law, and would live through life as both the daughter-in-law to Judah, as well as mother of his children. She was associated with trickery and immorality.

2. Rahab (v. 5).

From pagan Jericho, this woman is congratulated for her faith in places in the NT (e. g., James). She was also known as a prostitute. She ran a little full-service hostel, on the red-light "wall" district of Jericho. She wanted to be available to the tourists and visiting businessmen. But something happened to this paragon of vice. Rahab was changed, changed by the Lord, as he interrupted her life. He generated faith in her, and accepted her as righteous. Later she assisted the spies as they prepared to invade Jericho. She had the only believing family, in that city, when it was destroyed. She and her household believed and were saved. The immoral woman is saved, protected, and down the road, Jesus was one of her descendants. Not a perfect gal, this Rahab.

3. Ruth (v. 5).

To begin with, she was a Moabitess—from outside of Israel. She followed her mother-in-law, Naomi. When Ruth's husband died, the mother in law was prepared to return home. But loyal Ruth would have nothing of it. She expressed her loyalty in those famous words, "whithersoever thou goest, so will I." She did, and this young widower, follows Naomi back to her homeland, where she meets the handsome young Boaz—who would become the great grandfather of David. At one point she sleeps at his feet in the barn. Naomi coaches her and tells her to get all dolled up, and put on her best husband-catching perfume. Sure enough Boaz is a little attracted to her. Would anyone hearing this story, think that Ruth was a good little girl, as she pursues this stranger, lays down at his feet all perfumed? C'mon, folks what would you call a lady who did that? *Times haven't changed that much.* Ruth, although a saint, had a reputation problem, and on more than one occasion was accused of immorality. She was in the lineage of Jesus Christ, a woman, who was not totally perfect.

4. Uriah's wife—Bathsheba (v. 6).

It's interesting that here, she is not even called by name, only 'Uriah's wife.' We know about Bathsheba and her undisputed immorality. After all, she had previously even married a Hittite, a definite sinner. Bathsheba was perfect in no one's book. Can God really use frail, sinful people? Yes, the genealogy of Jesus always reminds us of this.

All of Advent is about that theme. God also later used:
Bad Saul and converted him to Paul.
Weak Peter, became a great preacher.
Cowardly John Mark.

Why did God include these in the first chapter of the NT?
a. He could have glossed over this and only mentioned 'good' people. This is another proof of inerrancy. Since included, this must be important.
b. God wanted to show that his purposes were bigger than our frailties. His success does not depend on our perfection.
c. He knew there would be people who needed encouragement from seeing trophies of grace like this.

5. Last of all Mary (16).

She was certainly accused of immorality. Jesus went through much of his life, accused of being an illegitimate son. That's how we treat God-in-the-flesh. Seriously, if your daughter comes to you—and she's been seriously dating a young man—and all of a sudden she turns up pregnant, and tells you, it happened without any sex, how many people will believe that? Mary, the mother of Jesus was accused of sexual immorality. Yet she was in the line of Jesus.

Mary is a beautiful example of how God works by Grace. She was not chosen because she had already earned the favor of God. Mary appears to be a fine young woman but not necessarily the head of any particular class. She may not have been as exceedingly beautiful as many of the books portray; then again she may have been. We don't know.

She may not have been the most intelligent, or the hardest working, although we do see a maturity and dedication in her at an early age, and under a large measure of duress.

Ask "Why was Mary Chosen?" The answer will be the same one, given to that question if asked about any of us . . . or any of these people in this line. Why are any of us chosen?? It is due to God's Grace. It is assuredly *not because:*

> we are the best;
> we are great;
> or we are deserving.

It is only caused by a cause within God himself . . . His great mercy—as Ephesians 2:4-6 says, "but because of his great mercy.

This is true of Mary as well. We really miss the point of Advent, if we look to Mary as categorically superior to other women. She is not, as some believe, in a category different from all women or men. She is one of us. She, too, is an object of God's favor and grace. The angel explained, "You are highly favored" (Lk. 1:28) and "Mary, you have found favor with God" (v. 30). If you don't think so, listen to some of her own words. When it was revealed to her that she would give birth to the Son of the Most High (32) who would inherit David's Throne and reign forever, she responded in amazement, "How can this be? "(34) and "I am the Lord's servant... May it be to me as you have said." There is the obedience of grace.

In Mary's Song, the notes and chords of grace are sung as follows:
- "My soul glorifies . . . and rejoices" (46-47)
- "for He has been mindful of the humble estate of his servant." (48)
- "His mercy extends to those who fear him" (50)

- "He has performed . . . he has scattered those who are proud in their inmost thoughts." (51)
- "He has brought down rulers from their thrones but has lifted up the humble." (52)
- "remembering to be merciful to Abraham and his descendants" (54)

Here is the song of one who extols God for his mercy and grace, for his care of the humble and thwarting of the proud.

This lady knew she was what she was by the grace of God. Do you?

We can even see Grace in Christmas Carols. For example:

- That last triumphant verse of Joy to the World, 'He rules the world with truth and *grace.*"
- "All my Heart This night rejoices" trumpets, "He becomes the lamb that taketh Sin away and for aye Full atonement maketh. For our life his own he tenders, And our race, by his *grace* meet for glory renders."
- "Behold a Branch is growing of loveliest form and *grace*; it springs from Jesse's race.

It's a good time of year to sing Amazing Grace. And at all seasons, it is "Grace, that charms the sinner's ear."

Matthew provides an important side of the story, i. e., that Jesus had a birth. It was a normal birth in some respects, fully human. Jesus had earthly grandparents and great-grands. Mary and Joseph had relatives, too. These are real people in real time, who descended like others; and evidently God thinks that history is important enough to record. This is not wasted print in the Bible. Everything in here is important. And the import of this is that it is the history of grace, the history of God working above and beyond and not tied to human merit.

Do you deserve a merit bonus at this time of year? I think many of you do. Haven't you worked hard this year, accomplished some real gains? Don't you deserve that merit pay increase? You may. But you do not deserve, nor merit the favor or grace of God. It is a pure gift. You have sinned in his sight, and like these people in this genealogy, do not deserve to be in the family of the Messiah. But God has adopted us, he had included us, and incorporated us into his family BY GRACE.

The always-helpful J. C. Ryle's concludes with three lessons in his commentary on this passage.

> We learn, for one thing, from this list of names, that God always keeps His word. He had promised that "in Abraham's seed all the nations of the earth should be blessed." He had promised to raise up a Saviour of the family of David. (Gen. xii. 3; Is. xi. 1.) These sixteen verses prove that Jesus was the son of David and the Son of Abraham, and that God's promise was fulfilled. Thoughtless and ungodly people should remember this lesson, and be afraid. Whatever they may think, God will keep His word. If they repent not, they will surely perish. True Christians should remember this lesson, and take com-fort. Their Father in heaven will be true to all His engagements. He has said that He will save all believers in Christ. If He has said it, He will certainly do it. "He is not a man, that He should lie." "He abideth faithful: He cannot deny Himself." (Num. 23:19; 2 Tim. 2:13.)

> We learn, for another thing, from this list of names, the sinfulness and corruption of human nature. It is instructive to observe how many godly parents in this catalogue had wicked and ungodly sons. The names of Rehoboam, and Joram, and Amon, and Jechonias, should teach us humbling lessons. They had all pious fathers. But they were all wicked men. Grace does not run in families. It needs something more than good examples and good advice to make us children of God. They that are born again are not born of blood, nor of the will of the flesh, nor of the will of man, but of God. (John i.13.) Praying parents should pray night and day, that their children may be born of the Spirit.

> We learn, lastly, from this list of names, how great is the mercy and compassion of our Lord Jesus Christ. Let us think how defiled and unclean human nature is, and then think what a condescension it was in Him to be born of a woman, and made in the "like-ness of men." (Phil. 2:7) Some of the names we read in this catalogue remind us of shame-ful and sad histories. Some of the names are those of persons never mentioned elsewhere in the Bible. But at the end of all comes the names of the Lord Jesus Christ. Though He is the eternal God, He humbles Himself to become man, in order to provide salvation for sinners. "Though He was rich, yet for your sakes He became poor." (2 Cor. 8:9.)

> We should always read this catalogue with thankful feelings. We see here that no one who partakes of human nature can be beyond the reach of Christ's sympathy and compassion. Our sins

may have been as black and great as those of any whom St. Matthew names. But they cannot shut us out of heaven, if we repent and believe the Gospel. If the Lord Jesus was not ashamed to be born of a woman whose pedigree contained such names as those we have read today, we need not think that He will be ashamed to call us brethren, and to give us eternal life.

Learning God's Ways from the Forgotten Man of Advent

Matthew 1:18-25

If you were God and you were sending your Son into the world to save the world, into what kind of family would you send your Son? You might have guessed that God would have picked somebody of prominence, perhaps a priest, a rabbi, a prophet, or a ruler. He would want his Son to be well-cared for, so I would have expected a family that was comfortable financially. Since his Son would need a first-rate education, God would probably pick a well-educated couple. Since the best schools, the best opportunities for meeting the 'right' people, and for having the proper social upbringing would occur in a city, we might have expected the 'right' couple to hail from Jerusalem.

However, God didn't do it that way. He picked an obscure couple, unknown in the religious and social circles of Jerusalem. The man was not a ruler or even a rabbi, but a carpenter of no notoriety. We know that they were poor, because they offered the poor-man's sacrifice at Jesus' birth, a pair of turtledoves or pigeons (Luke 2:24). As far as we know, they were not well-educated. They were common, working people, living in the small, out-of-the-way village of Nazareth in the northern part of Israel known as Galilee.

Mary is usually the Star Parent of the Advent narratives. She is extolled as gentle, faithful, merciful, and because she lived until Jesus' death, she gets more ink than Joseph.

In fact, all we know about Joseph is from these opening chapters of Matt. (or Luke), except for the singular reference elsewhere that he was a carpenter. Yet, Joseph can and should be studied at Advent. For in him, we'll see a model of a faithful father, a man who trusted God in adverse circumstances, and one in whom we see God's Spirit working. Although seldom preached on, there are many of God's way we can learn from Joseph. It won't be wrong to aspire to be like him by God's Spirit.

Joseph is "the forgotten man of Christmas"; that's not an exaggeration. Not much is said about him in the Bible. Not many sermons are preached about him. As a matter of fact, there's just not much written about Joseph at all.

This week I flipped through our hymnal to see how many times his name is mentioned.

– Mary is mentioned by name at least 7 times.

– Joseph is never mentioned–not even one time.

In the great hymn "Angels We Have Heard on High," there is one verse that mentions him–"See within a manger laid, Jesus, Lord of heaven and earth! Mary, Joseph, lend your aid, sing with us Messiah's birth." Unfortunately our hymnal omits that verse, which means that Joseph is left out almost completely of Advent hymns.

Let me briefly list for you the things we know about Joseph:

- His father was Jacob.
- His family hometown was Bethlehem in Judea but he lived in Nazareth in Galilee. That meant that Joseph and Mary had to travel about 95 miles just to register for the census.
- He is from the royal line of David. The genealogy in Matthew 1 makes that clear.
- He was a carpenter by trade.
- He was working class. We know that because when he and Mary presented Jesus in the Temple, they brought the sacrifice of a turtledove, the more affordable option than a lamb.
- He was a religious man, a devout keeper of the Law, a fact we'll see more closely below.
- How old was Joseph? We don't know the answer for sure, but most writers agree that he was a young man and probably a teenager. If we said 17-18 years old, we would probably be

about right, but we cannot be sure on it. Here are a couple of things to learn from him.

1. Not to act in haste

Ryle says that Joseph is a "beautiful example of godly wisdom, and tender consideration for others. He saw the 'appearance of evil' in [Mary]. But he did nothing rashly. He waited patiently to have the line of duty made clear. In all probability he laid the matter before God in prayer. 'He that believes shall not make haste.'" (p. 6)

I wonder: don't we make many, many mistakes because we act hastily? Or we are in such a hurry that we do not consider all prospects. Are you too busy to pray?

The patience of Joseph was graciously rewarded. He received a direct message from God upon the subject of his anxiety, and was at once relieved from all his fears. How good it is to wait upon God! Whoever cast his cares upon God in hearty prayer and found him fail? Prov. 3:6: "In all your ways acknowledge him and he shall direct your paths.

2. Trust in Providence

Joseph didn't spend much time complaining. Although it has become the norm to fictionalize him, and have him say, "Oh, Lord, why did this happen to me; my life's about over now," the Scriptures record no such thing. To the contrary, they show Joseph as a man of obedience who embraces God's providence.

He is called a "righteous" man, and surely he was spiritually mature enough to know that he did not make himself righteous or do things that saved himself. Without expressly saying it, it is true that Joseph was made righteous by the working of God's Holy Spirit.

Matthew 1:19 tells us that *"Joseph her husband was a righteous man . . ."* Other translations describe him as being:

- Just,
- Noble, and
- Godly.

The very fact that God chose Joseph says much about the kind of man Joseph was—and the kind of man God desires to use. Joseph was considerate and kind to Mary—in spite of some very difficult circumstances.

Then too, he provided a home for Jesus, even though the child was not his. In fact, he raised him as his own. After Jesus spoke as a prophet for the first time in the temple of Nazareth, the people took offence at him. They did not believe him. As a way of putting him down, they said: *"Where did this man get his wisdom and his mighty words? Is this not the carpenter's son?"* The people saw him as belonging to Joseph.

And he trusted in God's providence.

3. Looking to God; Joseph at a young age—and he may have been young; it is not automatic that he was a much older guy who had died by the time Jesus reached the cross—but at whatever age, *he looked to God to provide.*

He cared about Mary; and did not throw her under the bus. Compassionate men are considerate of others. When Joseph discovered that Mary was pregnant, he had two options according to the customs of the day: He could institute a lawsuit against Mary for her unfaithful-ness. Although the letter of the law prescribed stoning for an adulteress, Joseph could safely assume that this penalty would not be enforced. But a lawsuit would have exposed Mary to public disgrace and ridicule. Or, he could hand her a bill of divorcement (necessary to dissolve the engagement), dismissing her privately without public fanfare.

Joseph chose the latter because he did not want to disgrace Mary (1:19). Even though he was in pain and he thought at this point that Mary was responsible for his pain, he didn't want to get even or make her pay. He was considerate of her feelings. Biblical love, which we are to have even toward those who have hurt us deeply, seeks to protect and shield others rather than to make them pay.

No doubt, his marriage to Mary was an arranged marriage. The two sets of parents had agreed to give their children in holy matrimony. This is strange by today's standards, but it was the common thing to do back then.

Americans who arrange their own marriages may have a hard time understanding what it said in these verses, without thinking there is a contradiction. Matthew 1:18-20 states: "This is how the birth of Jesus Christ came about: His mother MARY WAS PLEDGED to be married to Joseph, but before they came together, she was found to be with child through the Holy Spirit. Because Joseph HER HUSBAND was a righteous man and did not want to expose her to public disgrace, HE HAD IN MIND TO DIVORCE her quietly. But after he had considered this, an angel of the Lord appeared to him in a dream and said, "Joseph son of David, do not be afraid to take Mary home AS YOUR WIFE, because what is conceived in her is from the Holy Spirit."

Did you notice what seems so odd to us?

- First, it states that Mary was *pledged* to be married to Joseph.
- Then, the passage calls Joseph her *husband*.
- Next we see that he was thinking about *divorcing* the woman.
- Finally, the angel tells the brother not to be afraid to take Mary to be his *wife*.

Judging from Joseph's actions, I have to conclude that he too loved his lady.

- You see, he knew that she was pregnant.
- He knew that he wasn't the father.
- He had every right to believe that she had been unfaithful to him and to their betrothal.
- Then too, there was her story of how she had become pregnant. "God did this to me." Yeah, right! How many of you would have believed that story? Let's face it, this was the only time in the history of the human race that such a thing had happened. Joseph had every reason in the world to think that she had not only cheated on him, but that she was also lying to cover up her sin.

But an angel visited him and confirmed her story. To his credit, in spite of his early doubts, he still did not want to hurt her. He was going to divorce her privately so as to save her from public shame. Again, Joseph loved Mary.

4. He cared more about pleasing God than caring for himself. Or put it this way: "Men of conviction fear God more than public opinion." (S. Cole)

Maybe you've never thought about this before, but Joseph doesn't say a single word in the Gospels. He listens and obeys. We might assume his words are recorded, because we can imagine the conversations he had with Mary, and the Angel Gabriel. He can "hear" him talking to the innkeeper. We can visualize him teaching Jesus about carpentry… but then he fades from the scene. It is widely thought that Joseph was much older than Mary, and when Jesus began his ministry, Mary appears alone, and although the Bible doesn't say she's a widow, we can figure that Joseph has since died.

Joseph probably thought his life was pretty well planned before this birth. His marriage and his vocation were all arranged neatly for him, but then his world came crashing down. He discovered that his bride-to-be was pregnant. We know that Joseph was a man of integrity—he wanted to do the right thing, in the right way. He considered divorcing Mary when he learned of her pregnancy, but wanted to do so without calling attention to the reason, whereas he could have had her publicly disgraced or even stoned to death for adultery. Instead, he risks being questioned about Mary's pregnancy and marries her. In those days, a marriage contract was worked out between families, and the engaged couple continued to live with their parents till their wedding. The townspeople could well have thought Mary and Joseph didn't wait till their wedding. Joseph protected their reputation by moving up the wedding date, and the Roman census took them far away from the town's questioning eyes.

Although Joseph came from the royal lineage of King David (thanks to the Gospel genealogy), we can easily picture him as a humble man. The brief portrait of him in Scripture suggests he was a quiet, unobtrusive man, available when needed, willing to endure hardship and disappointment. Looking forward to fathering his own child, Joseph was faced with being a step-father to a child not his own. He accepted the humbling circumstances surrounding Jesus' birth. He trusted the providential care of God every step of the way. He didn't have any parenting books/classes, any training on how to be a father to the Son of God, but he possessed faith and compassion. Bible scholars portray Joseph as an effective provider and protector of the family.

In all the Christmas pageants performed, Joseph doesn't get a starring role, but his part is so important. His task is to watch over Mary and the baby Jesus. Joseph had the important role of caring for the needs of others.

When our lives take a nasty turn, we cry out, like Joseph must have cried out, "God, how can this be?" But like Joseph, we hear a still small voice from God saying, "Trust Me." *God's ways are not always our ways.* His thoughts are higher than our thoughts, and we may never understand everything that God is doing this side of heaven, but God says, "Trust Me, and all things will work together for good."

It's been said the best thing a father can do for his kids is to love their mother. Joseph's love for Mary reflected Paul's definition: "Love is patient and kind. Love does not envy or boast; it is not proud or rude. Love is not self-seeking or easily angered. It keeps no record of wrongs. Love does not delight in evil, but it rejoices in the truth. It always protects, always trusts, always hopes, always perseveres" (1 Cor 13). Instead of being indignant, Joseph accepted this child as his own. Joseph accepted the revealed will of God. He followed the instructions—journeying from Nazareth to Bethlehem, then to Egypt, then back to Nazareth. Trusting God, Joseph received his son as a gift from God.

Joseph became the Messiah's earthly father, who would teach us all about embracing the providence and grace of God. Joseph is charged with naming their son and thus defining His mission. The name Jesus means "Savior." Archeologists have uncovered the ruins of Sapphoris, a thriving city near Nazareth. It is believed that Joseph spent much time there working as a carpenter, probably with his son and apprentice, Jesus. When Jesus returned to his hometown, the people responded, "Isn't this the son of Joseph, the carpenter?"

Was Joseph a perfect father? No, of course not. We're told that after Jesus was born, Mary and Joseph had children of their own, and those siblings did not become believers in Jesus till after His resurrection. In spite of what their parents tried to tell them of their older brother's miraculous birth, they refused to accept it.

Verses 24-25 are insufficiently celebrated as great Christmas verses. They reveal Joseph's finest qualities: "When Joseph woke up, he did what the angel of the Lord had commanded him and took Mary home as his wife. But he had no union with her until she had given birth to a son. And he gave him the name Jesus."

Every step he takes testifies to his greatness:
1. By marrying her quickly he broke all Jewish custom, but he protected Mary's reputation. She was pregnant and he wasn't the father but he married her anyway.

2. By keeping her a virgin until Jesus was born, he protected the miracle of Jesus' conception by the Holy Spirit against slander by unbelievers.

3. By naming the baby he exercised a father's prerogative and thus officially took him into his family as his own legal son.

While much proper attention is given to Mary, Joseph deserves his credit, too. He is a model of the man of faith, struggling with his doubts, persuaded to believe what God has said and ultimately acting upon his persuasion.

In these days of confusion, Joseph is a wonderful model of what a godly man looks like:

- He was tough when he could have been weak.
- He was tender when he could have been harsh.
- He was thoughtful when he could have been hasty.
- He was trusting when he could have doubted.
- He was temperate when he could have indulged himself.

I pause to ask this question. Men, could those same words describe your life?

- Are you tough-minded, determined to do what is right no matter what it costs?
- Are you tender with your wife and with your children?
- Are you thoughtful, taking your time to make important decisions, or are you quick to jump to conclusions and quick to say things you later regret?
- Are you trusting especially when you think you could figure out a better way to do things?
- Are you temperate and considerate of your wife and her special needs, or do you pressure your wife and your children to perform up to your standard of perfection?

There is one other line of proof about the kind of man Joseph was. When Jesus grew up and began his ministry, he chose one word above all others to describe what God is like. He called him *Father*.

Where did Jesus learn about fathers? From Joseph. Men, the way your children respond to God depends largely on the kind of father you are. You teach them something about God every day–just by the way you live in front of them.

In these verses, we see Joseph's Dilemma, Joseph's Dream (the cause of this conception and the character of this child). We also see clearly Joseph's *Decision*. Joseph's decision was to do what was right, no matter the *cost*, to do God's will even in the face of criticism, even if misunderstood or falsely judged!

Men of conviction develop Godly habits of worship. In Luke 2:22-24 we read of Joseph and Mary dedicating their son at the Temple. In verse 41 we learn that they had the custom of going to Jerusalem every year for the Feast of the Passover. In Luke 4:16 we discover that Jesus had the custom of weekly synagogue worship. Humanly speaking, where do you suppose Jesus learned that custom?

Every family has certain habits and customs. Some develop almost unawares, just by repetition. Others you develop deliberately by deciding that you want it to be a part of your regular family life. Once it's in place, you don't have to debate the matter every time it comes up. You just do it because it's your custom or habit. Joseph and Mary had the custom of worshiping God regularly as his Word commands. In modern parlance, they had the habit of regular church attendance. It wasn't up for grabs. They didn't just do it when there was nothing better to do or when they weren't too tired. They just did it! It was their custom. And why was it their custom? Because it reflected the priority of God in their lives. They honored God by keeping his day set apart for him.

Dads, it communicates loads to your kids if your family only goes to church when it's convenient. The same goes for family Bible reading and prayer. It reflects your priorities. "We're too tired to get up for church today, so we're going to skip it." "We need some time off, so we're just going to have fun as a family this Sunday." Your kids aren't dumb. They figure out your priorities really quickly.

This is what Joseph knew about God (see Ryle, pp 6-8, on), the two names of God. Let us observe in these verses, the two names given to our Lord. One is "Jesus:" the other "Emmanuel." One describes his office: the other his nature. Both are deeply interesting.

The name of Jesus means "Saviour." It is the same name as Joshua in the Old Testament. It is given to our Lord because "He saves His people from their sins." This is His special office. He saves them from the guilt of sin, by washing them in His own atoning blood. He saves them from the dominion of sin, by putting in their hearts the sanctifying Spirit. He saves them from the presence of sin, when He takes them out of this world to rest with Him. He will save them from all the consequences of sin, when He shall give them a glorious body at the last day. Blessed and holy are Christ's people! From sorrow, cross, and conflict they are not saved; but they are "saved from sin "for evermore. They are cleansed from guilt by Christ's blood. They are made meet for heaven by Christ's Spirit. This is salvation! He who cleaves to sin is not yet saved.

"Jesus" is a very encouraging name to heavy-laden sinners. He who is King of kings and Lord of lords might lawfully have taken some more high-sounding title. But He did not do so. The rulers of this world have often called themselves Great, Conqueror, Bold Magnificent, and the like. The Son of God was content to call Himself "Saviour." The souls which desire salvation may draw nigh to the Father with boldness, and have access with confidence through Christ. It is His office and His delight to show mercy. "God sent not His Son into the world to condemn the world, but that the world through Him might be saved." (John iii. 17.)

Jesus is a name which is peculiarly sweet and precious to believers. It has often done them good, when the favour of kings and princes would have been heard of with unconcern. It has given them what money cannot buy, even inward peace. It has eased their weary consciences, and given rest to their heavy hearts. Happy is that person who trusts not merely in vague notions of God's mercy and goodness, but in "Jesus."

The name "Emmanuel" is seldom found in the Bible. But it is scarcely less interesting than the name "Jesus." It is the name which is given to our Lord from His nature as God-man, as "God manifest in the flesh." It signifies, "God with us."

Let us take care that we clearly understand that there was a union of two natures, the divine and human in the person of our Lord Jesus Christ. It is a point of the deepest importance. We should settle it firmly in our minds, that our Saviour is perfect man as well as perfect God, and perfect God as well as perfect man. If we once lose sight of this great foundation truth, we may run into fearful heresies. The name Emmanuel takes in the whole mystery. Jesus is "God with us." He had a nature like our own in all things, sin only excepted. But though Jesus was "with us" in human flesh and blood, He was at the same time very God.

We shall often find, as we read the Gospels, that our Saviour could be weary and hungry and thirsty,--could weep and groan and feel pain like one of ourselves. In all this we see "the man" Christ Jesus. We see the nature he took on him, when he was born of the Virgin Mary.

But we shall also find in the same Gospels that our Saviour knew men's hearts and thoughts—that He had power over devils, that he could work the mightiest miracles with a word—that he was ministered to by angels—that he allowed a disciple to call him "my God,"—and that he said, "Before Abraham was I am," and "I and my Father are one." In all this we see "the eternal God." We see Him "Who is over all, God blessed forever. Amen." (Rom. ix.5.)

If we would have a strong foundation for our faith and hope, we must keep constantly in view our Saviour's divinity. He in whose blood we are invited to trust is the Almighty God. All power is in heaven and earth. None can pluck us out of His hand. If we are true believers in Jesus, our heart need not be troubled or afraid.

If we would have sweet comfort in suffering and trial, we must keep constantly in view our Saviour's humanity. He is the man Christ Jesus, who lay on the bosom of the Virgin Mary as a little infant, and knows the heart of a man. He can be touched with the feeling of our infirmities. He has Himself experienced Satan's temptations. He has endured hunger. He has shed tears. He has felt pain. We may trust Him unreservedly with our sorrows. He will not despise us. We may pour out our hearts before Him in prayer boldly, and keep nothing back. He can sympathize with His people.

Let these thoughts sink down into our minds. Let us bless God for the encouraging truths which the first chapter of the New Testament contains. It tells us of One who "saves His people from their sins." But this is not all. It tells us that this Saviour is "Emmanuel," God Himself, and yet God with us—God manifest in human flesh like our own. This is glad tidings. This is indeed good news.

The December 2005 issue of *Time* devoted a feature to Joseph, (http://www.time.com/time/magazine/article/0,9171,1139838-1,00.html), the earthly father of Jesus. This article tells us:

> Joseph appears in the Nativity story of Matthew and more briefly in that of Luke but is then severely—eventually terminally— marginalized. The Bible never even quotes him directly. Yet

Orlando Pastor Howard Edington extended his research beyond the
New Testament to early nonbiblical sources. In 2000 he published a
slim book called The Forgotten Man of Christmas: Joseph's Story,
which combined biblical analysis with material suggested by his
additional reading, along with brief recollections of his own
family's story. The pastor admits that it may have seemed a strange
project, especially among Protestants, who don't recognize Joseph's
sainthood and whose approach Edington describes as "'We don't
know anything about him? Then just leave him there.'" But he
concluded that "there is great spiritual value to capture, or recapture
in Joseph's story, and if that takes a combination of just good
serious Bible study and some recreative imagination, I think it's a
valid exercise.

That's Just the Kind of God He Is

Matthew 1:22-2:12

Sometimes in conversation, we will find ourselves talking about a great person, and after extolling his/her virtue, it will also be pointed out that this great person has remarkable humility or compassion to supplement greatness. And the compliment will then be stated: "That's just the kind of person he is." I remember on several occasions discussing a great OT professor I had in seminary. Dr. R. Laird Harris knew 7 Semitic languages and was a scholar of immense proportion. He was as insightful as most of us could imagine—an expert in archaeology, science, the OT, and numerous other areas.

However, our family will probably remember him most for another thing he did while visiting. He visited us in April one year. I remember it because it was little Megan's third birthday. And what we remember so vividly about his visit was the honor of having him in our home on that great occasion. But what lasts even longer is this: When dinner was over, Ann and Mrs. Harris cleaned up the kitchen. Dr. Harris and I retired to the living room to talk shop, and those two tiny Hall girls roamed around the house in various stages of chaos, usually with food on their faces or kitchen dishes on their heads. Finally, we cleaned the little critters, and the girls came in to kiss daddy good-night. Dr. Harris, then, wowed my wife by inviting Megan up into his lap, and this absolutely brilliant scholar began to tell my daughter the story of the *Three Bears* with as much feeling and color as I have ever seen. That's the kind of man he is: one who is as caring as he is brilliant. And that episode will always remind us of what a wonderful person he was. This was not for show, he was not seeking to gain something from us, nor was there any advantage to Dr. Harris in reciting the *Three Bears*. He was simply a gracious gentleman who wanted to express some love to a 3 year old. That incident told us a lot about this man's character. It was a snapshot that would remain in our memory.

But I am not so much interested in extolling the virtues of Dr. Harris this morning as I am eager to relate to you that God is like this. We can take snapshots of God at various times throughout the Bible, and each snapshot unfailingly presents him as he really is. Every instance of Scripture is equally a true revelation of the character of God. We see a rich variety of vignettes of God in the Bible. And what I want you to learn today is simply this: *Every snapshot of God, if studied in detail, unveils the heart of his character.* That is as true at Advent and in the Incarnation of Jesus Christ as at any time. This morning, think with me about how the work of God in the birth of Christ—if taken alone—is a reliable revelation of who God is.

The Advent of Christ is typical, typical of God. It has his unique fingerprints on it. If a person's fingerprints are unique and non-repeatable, then all the more with God. His fingerprints are all over Advent. His signature is inimitable.

Christmas is typical of God in the following ways.

1. *It is planned.*
Some pagan religions boast of their worship of chaos. Our God, however, is the God who has a plan and brings it about. Haphazardness and inconsistency are not virtues of God.

a. We should take seriously what the Bible teaches about God's plan of salvation having been covenanted before the foundation of the world. Like all the works of God, the salvation presented at Christmas demonstrates the advance planning of God. Christmas was no afterthought. It was conceived eons ago, before the foundation of the world. Ephesians 1:4 speaks of God's plan designed before the world ever began. In Jesus' high priestly prayer in John 17, he referred to the love between the Father and the Son before the world began. The final book of the Bible speaks of Christ as the Lamb of God, slain for his flock before the foundation of the world (Rev. 13:8). God's plan is an eternal one.

Not only was Advent planned in eternity past, but it was:

b. Frequently predicted in the OT prophecies. The advent narratives show us how concerned God is to note in his Word that the birth of Christ is a precise fulfillment of the prophets. In Mt. 1:22-23, as soon as the angel has announced to Joseph that Mary will conceive Jesus who will save his people from their sins, the Bible tells us: "All this took place to *fulfill* what the Lord has said through the prophet, 'The virgin will be with child and will give birth to a son, and they will call his name 'Emmanuel' which means 'God with us.'" That was a prophecy given by Isaiah some 7 centuries earlier. The prophecy is founded upon the sure plan of God. Advent was no later development. Like all God's works, it is planned far in advance.

c. Several other times, Matthew's gospel makes it plain that OT prophecies are being fulfilled by Christ's birth. When Herod interviews the knowledge class of his day and asks where Christ was to be born, they recall the prediction of an Israeli prophet. Micah 5:2 had predicted that the Messiah would be born in Bethlehem in Judea. Centuries earlier this plan was in place. And Matthew records, "This is what the prophet has written." A few verses later in Mt. 2:15, following the angelic instruction to Joseph that he was to flee to Egypt, Matthew states that this, too, was in fulfillment of OT prophecy, specifically to fulfill Hos. 11:1. Skip down 3 verses, and you'll see another instance of prophetic fulfillment, this time, Jeremiah 31:15 had foretold how weeping would surround the slaughter of the innocents. Still one more time (a 4th time in Mt. 2), Mt. 2:23 refers to Jesus' home in this fashion: "He went and lived in a town called Nazareth. So was fulfilled what was said through the prophets: He will be called a Nazarene."

All this was to fulfill the predictions of the OT prophets. God had a plan, from eternity past, and revealed it through the prophets. God does not act haphazardly; he is quintessentially a God of order (1 Cor. 14:33). This purpose is seen, woven through all his works. That's the kind of God he is.

The birth of Christ models this careful pre-planning. God is not acting randomly in the universe. He is always on schedule and on target.

We should not confuse his inscrutability with irrationality. Inscrutability refers to the fact that often God's ways are not immediately apparent. Humans do not always see how God is working. We certainly cannot always figure him out. That we cannot comprehend the intricacies of God's plan is one thing. However, that is altogether different from the lack of a plan or irrationality. *God has a plan, one that is as excellent as he is.* It is seen in Christmas, as in salvation itself, and this very fact reveals something essential about who God is and how he works.   Next:

2. It involves the Miraculous.

a. The Christmas narrative is saturated with the miraculous, another signature of God. Advent without the miraculous would bespeak a different god. The scriptural account in no way suggests that random forces of nature or normal processes brought all this about. Miracle is at the center of this event. God frequently acts in Scripture through the miraculous.

b. In the birth of Christ, we have an abundance of angels. These angels are not the normal creatures of daily existence. Angels are involved in announcing to Joseph what will happen. They lead him every step of the way. Gabriel appears to Mary, informing her that she will give birth to a son who "will be called the Son of the Most High. The Lord God will give him the throne of his father, David, and he will reign forever; his kingdom will never end." (Lk. 1:32-33) The angel tells Mary that nothing is impossible with God; through a miracle, Messiah will be born.

c. The Virgin Birth is certainly miraculous. In regard to what we know about life, its conception and formation, it would be difficult to create a more miraculous event than a virgin birth. God over-rode the normal processes to have Jesus born. He did not want his son to share Adam's birth defect. God wanted Jesus to be fully human, but he wanted him free of sin's bias. Thus, God provided by contravening the normal biological process of conception. God did a miracle in the birth of Christ that was far from ordinary.

The birth of Jesus was unlike any other birth in history and it has never been repeated. Other religions don't even dare to act as if this happened. Typical of God, he chooses a spectacular, unimagined miracle to bring his son into the world. Mary does not have a sexual relationship with Joseph to begin the life of Jesus; nor was any human father involved. Only the Holy Spirit by a divine miracle.

Thus, Jesus' birth shows God's typical miracle tendency. He's that kind of God.

Other miracles, like the angels' announcement to the shepherds, the guiding star that led the wise men from the East, the divine protection of the newborn Jesus from Herod's ire, and the wise men's discovery of the birth of Christ—all these and more are signs of the miraculous. God shows his power when he trumps the normal processes of nature. Miracle is typical of the kind of God, God is.

3. It employs vessels of Grace.

It is said about some fans in the state where I am from: "His blood bleeds orange." That saying means that a person is a fan of the Big Orange of Tennessee through and through. Cut this person anywhere, and he bleeds orange. Here in this state, it is red and black, or gold and black. God is that way in terms of grace. *Any slice of the character of God oozes grace.* Even in his wrath or justice, there is grace. And flowing from that, God uses vessels of grace. That is to note that God uses grace in his normal operations. Frequently, we see that God uses those that others might not.

In fact, 1 Cor. 1:26-28 notes that God did not choose many people who were wise, powerful, or noble. Instead, he chose the weak things of this world to shame the powerful. He chose "the lowly things of this world" to confound those that trusted in their own ability or accomplishment. God frequently employs methods that do not appear too wise in order to confound the world in its pride of wisdom.

a. Look who God chose in this case. He did not call an aristocratic young man from a fine family and a fine school to be the guardian of Jesus. He called a common carpenter, a man who worked hard and did honest labor with his hands. Joseph, as we see from the narratives, was exactly perfect for the tasks that God had for him. However, he followed God without the support of a large estate behind him, devoid of powerful benefactors, and with an ordinariness of situation played one of the most exalted roles in human history.

Mary was the same way. She did not come from a powerful family. She may have been beautiful, or possibly not. We do know that both she and Joseph had hearts for the Lord, and they were obedient. God used ordinary people for extraordinary tasks. He still does that today, although he may not call us to do the same things that Mary and Joseph did. God's grace is seen in his selection of common people to be the parents of Jesus.

b. The shepherds were also unexpected heroes. This group of vagabonds would not impress any director from central casting. Shepherds were rough, uncouth, and generally looked down upon. They were considered lower class, uneducated and hardly would have been considered to be the first evangelists. But that is what they were. God used unexpected people to be the earliest heralds of the good news. That is typical of his work.

c. Of course, there were some people used in this Christmas narrative who were very wealthy and influential: the Wise men from the East. These God allowed to be in the parade of those who worshipped Christ. God does not exclude a person from the kingdom merely because he is rich or intellectual. Of course, neither do those natural benefits give a person a better standing with God. God employed a range of people to do his bidding in the birth of Christ. He normally does. And that goes contrary to some human expectations.

God's grace works above the principle of merit, utility, or economy. It surprises us in its choices. It confounds the proud and exalts the humble. "The first shall be last, and the last shall be first," would not only be taught later by Jesus; it exemplified his very birth.

4. It defies opposition.

God's work is irresistible. There were definite opponents of God, however, who tried to keep him from completing his plans. God's work is so wonderful and strong, though, it is impossible to prevent him from accomplishing his will. Even the most ardent of human foes cannot keep God from doing his will. That is seen as clearly at Christmas as at any other time.

Consider the enemies of God who tried to thwart his plan.

a. The arch-enemy was Satan. Since his own fall, Lucifer had been the sworn enemy of God. He opposed God at every possible turn and desired to eliminate the work of Messiah. He would do anything he could to prevent Jesus from doing his work.

Revelation 12 presents a figurative scene of this. In that passage, the great dragon (Satan) attempts to devour the pregnant woman and her child. His fury is unleashed as he searched for the child. The enormous red dragon waited in front of the woman who was about to give birth to "a son, a male child, who will rule all the nations with an iron scepter." (12:5) That, of course, is Jesus. However, despite all Satan's opposition, God protects the newborn and his mother and takes her out into the desert where she is safe.

Many rightly see this prophecy's fulfillment in the birth of Jesus.

b. Of course, the nearest villain to Jesus was Herod. When Herod learned of the commotion caused by the wise men, he tried to find where the Messiah-child was so that he could destroy him. Herod wanted to eliminate his opposition, and when he was denied that opportunity, he slaughtered all male children under the age of two. Had our Sovereign God not been in control, the opposition could have triumphed.

c. Another enemy, at least from a human point of view, was Caesar.

In Luke 2, his census could have prevented Christ's birth from occurring if God was not in charge. This only serves to remind us that no human government or governor can thwart God's will. When God wants something done, he is even capable of hijacking a census to get the parents of Jesus exactly where he needs them. Rather than a human governor preventing God's work, they are employed in it— even above their own awareness.

One of the hallmarks of God's works is how powerfully he reduces his opposition to nothing. He wouldn't be much of a God, if these people or demons could alter his plan. No human force or group can prevent God from performing his plan of salvation. At Christmas, he was certainly never in danger of having the opposition thwart him.

5. *The Whisper of God.*

An advertisement for a leading fragrance made its pitch a few years back: "If you want someone's attention . . . whisper." If we hear someone whisper in the midst of an ordinary conversation, we almost instinctively stop and listen. Why, some will even pay more attention if something is whispered.

The birth of Jesus was like a whisper in some ways. It was similar to Elijah looking for God in the earthquake, wind and fire only to find him in the "still small voice." (1 Kgs. 19:12) George McDonald wrote about the contemporaries of Joseph and Mary: "They were looking for a conquering king to slay their foes and lift them high. Thou camest a little baby thing that made a woman cry."

There are many times when we are so noisy ourselves that we fail to hear the soft whispers that should reach our ears. More folks missed than heard the whisper of God in that original Christmas. Most were too busy, too hurried, or too focused on the noisy normal world around them to listen to or even think that God might be speaking to them. Of course, some never hear his voice.

The Bible tells us that God spoke with greater power than previously in the final revealing of his son (Heb. 1:1-2). It began with a whisper as his son was became a small child in a manger. But the whisper cascaded into a shout: "The Word became flesh and dwelt among us, full of grace and truth."

Amidst the clang and clutter and crudity of our Christmases, the birth of the Christ child is still a whisper. God calls out for himself a people who can hear its own tones. For those who are quiet, for those who will listen, the whisper becomes a powerful thunderclap as you hear God whisper your name. Shh, shh, shh, listen to the whisper of God. Do you hear what I hear? It is in the common.

Hear the whisper of God at Advent. It may not be surround-sound with huge sub-woofers. It may not make the floor shake. Typical of our God, he may reveal himself cloaked in the normal, whispered in the common. Do you have ears to hear?

6. *It results in AWE.*

Awe is not the norm in our lives. It is unusual. Indeed, many of us are beyond shocking. Awe results when we are confronted with something out of the ordinary and far greater than ourselves. That is a frequent reaction by characters in these Advent accounts.

The wise men "bowed and worshipped" (Mt. 2:11), bringing their finest gifts. Will you? The shepherds returned glorifying and praising God. Will you reflect the awe?

Each of these things above are like the DNA of God. They point to his identity through and through. They are clearly part of the Christmas narrative, and they are the heart of our God.

The evidence for the event is conclusive: Christmas was committed by God. It is undeniable; it reflects his unique character.

What is it that makes a Christmas classic? There's actually a theme that yokes together the perennial Christmas tales. In Dickens' Scrooge, Ebenezer Scrooge discovers the hard way that he is not alone, that materialism is inadequate as a world view, and that those who have been blessed with much ought to give to those who are impoverished. St. Nicholas was enshrined because he gave gifts to poor children. The other stories that are so worthy of repetition have this theme in common: Stop your normally busy lives, relax the normal search for economic benefit, and give to someone that you would not necessarily give something to. The reason that Christmas will not go out of style is that these acts of giving and receiving are absolutely necessary for enhanced life. Our lives are impoverished if we do not give to others when we are not obligated to give. It is the absence of obligation that makes our giving so rich, so repeated.

That is one of those areas, perhaps, where we show the image of God. God himself gave to an impoverished group—humanity—at Advent. He had no necessary obligation; he was not indebted, nor was it a moral responsibility. He gave, and gave his very best, without calculation as to its inestimable value. He did not buy something external and give it to us. Nor did he build a craft and give it to us. God, in fact, did not donate anything, but gave of himself in the most intimate and personal fashion. He gave his own son.

At Christmas, I want you to know him in all his wonder, praise him for all his majesty, and accept him in his meekness.

That's the kind of God he is. You are invited to know him this Advent for who he truly is! Don't accept any other substitute.

Spurgeon preached: "What human frame was this which could abide the Presence of Jehovah! This was, indeed, a body curiously worked, a holy thing, a special product of the Holy Spirit's power. It was a body like our own, with nerves as sensitive and muscles as readily strained. It was a body with every organization as delicately fashioned as our own and yet God was in it! *It was a frail boat to bear such freight.* How could Christ bear the Deity within himself! We know not how it was, but God knows. Let us adore this hiding of the Almighty in human weakness, this comprehending of the Incomprehensible, this revealing of the Invisible, this localization of the Omnipresent!

God sends an Ambassador who inspires no fear—not with helmet and coat of mail, bearing lance, does Heaven's Herald approach us—

but the white flag is held in the hand of a Child, in the hand of One chosen out of the people—in the hand of One who died, in the hand of One who, though He sits in Glory, still wears the nail-prints. O Man, God comes to you as One like yourself! Do not be afraid to come to the gentle Jesus! Do not imagine that you need to be prepared for an audience with Him, or that you need the intercession of a saint, or the intervention of priest or minister! Anyone could have come to the Babe in Bethlehem."

Can you see God's Plan in your Life?[1]

Matthew 2:1-12

At this joyous time of year, children are happy, and parents are almost exhausted or shutting down. "Mistletoe." But according to Scripture, sometime people are not really that comfortable with God drawing near to them and revealing his plan for their life. This passage in part describes the differing reaction of people toward the birth of Christ. Yet, it is one of those universal instances by which all human beings are tested, not only at Christmas. The eternal principles in this passage test us every day.

On this morning, let me pose a question: "Can you see God's plan in your life? Can you see God's providence and plan in your life?" This is one of the challenging questions for Christians—but not only for Christians, but especially for those who do not believe, or for those who are agnostic, or whatever. Unbelievers expect us to ask about a larger question, and they have been asked, "What do you say about the beautiful order of the universe? If there is no God, how can you account for the complexity, the order of the universe?" For when we look at all the galaxies and stars of the universe, we observe an order, a complexity which is far more organized than the most organized,

---

[1] This is one of those sermons that I heard from another pastor, the Rev. John Sartelle, decades ago while he pastored the Independent Presbyterian Church in Memphis, TN. We heard John preach this, but thought it so nearly perfect that I ordered a cassette tape of it and transcribed most of it. This is John's superb work, but I've adapted it slightly and shared it as such with numerous congregations with his permission. Certain illustrations have been updated, of course, and any mistakes are mine.

efficient computer ever designed. That is hard to dispute and calls for an answer. [for a recent *Answers in Genesis* slideshow, see: http://www.authorstream.com/Presentation/harryd-1585647-creation-or-coincidence/

For example, we would not look at a new iPad mini and say, "That just happened; it is an accident." Imagine if a wife went out and bought the most sophisticated gaming system: sort of ESPN combined with every new Xbox game, and also driven by a virtual reality set of eyeglasses, and then when hubby tumbles down on Christmas morning and shouts, "Where in the world did this come from?" wifey answers, "Oh, it just happened to assemble itself, right here in our living room."

Why, that's absurd. We would say that there is a plan, an architect, chip designers and computer assembly factories. It is all too apparent, and even those who are unbelievers are being faced with a glowing body of evidence about that. So when we look at the universe, we say that ignorance of this order is ludicrous; it is. The question remains: How can one account for the intricate order of the universe?

The non-Christian has become somewhat accustomed to that question in our day, even if they are not asked this as much as in yesteryear. But we have another question to pose that is not asked as often as it should be. I like to ask the people, "What do you do with the plan and order in your own life?" It is observable—not coincidental.

People see how God works in their lives and in the testimony of many, we hear people say that God has been at work in our lives. Many of you would affirm that this morning. It is not all coincidence. You can see God at work in your lives. Perhaps you will look back over this past year. Where were you this time last year? What has God done in your life? Even if one does not attend to the larger question, at least on the personal level, many if asked, "Can you see God at work in your life?" will answer yes. They may not know why, but they do not dispute it.

A young man who was beginning to be quickened to the Spirit of God went to visit the home of an older man, and asked, "How can I see God?" The old man thought. He wanted to answer correctly. The old man said, "Young man, I have a different problem from you. I'm not sure I can help you. I cannot keep myself from seeing God. I can't help but see him. Whether I look at the universe or my own life, the answer is obvious. He's there."

The passage before us reveals the providence of God in a fashion such that we cannot help but see God and his plan in this episode. This passage screams to us about the providence of God. And this is not just a message for Christmas. In fact, we could take this out of the Advent context and still preach the same thing. Indeed, it is possible to get so fixated on Christmas that we miss the real message. Some by now have had enough of the star and the cradle and this and that, but we desperately need to hear about Jesus Christ. That message never tires and don't forget that this really took place.

Here's what sometimes happens. A Sunday School teacher asked children to draw different pictures about Christmas. She got all kinds of portraits. Many were touching, but she got one really weird picture. It was of an *airplane* with odd looking people on it. She asked: "Why did you draw an airplane with those people on it?" And the 6-year old quite modern soul answered, "That's Joseph and Mary's *flight* out of Egypt."

Then he said, there's Pontius, the Pilot. [Behind Joseph and Mary was a little over-weight guy. The teacher asked, "Who is that?" "Round John Virgin."] This year a little girl in our church told Ann, in response to "how do we celebrate Jesus' birthday?" "We go to Chuck E. Cheese."

If we're not careful, as great as Christmas is, it can actually obscure passages like this in the Bible. We think that this is funny, but many of the ideas we have about the birth of Christ are just about as far-fetched. For example, if we asked about the wise-men and what they signify, many of us would be hard-pressed to answer. I believe this story is about the providence of God, the plan of God in individual lives. It is about the birth of Christ, to be sure, but far more than that.

It is not about the number 3, as if wise-men were the focus. Nor is the focus on the star. Some speculate that it was a conjunction or a super-nova. Volumes have been written on this topic, but that is not what this is primarily about. It's about God at work in the lives of people. God was at work in their daily lives as they lived. And some of these people could see that God was at work in their daily lives, while others could not. Some fail today to see the providence of God.

Some will say, "I don't see the providence of God in my life right now." This morning, I want us to highlight some of the principles of God's providence, which are laid out in this passage. I hope that all of us will also take this Christmas message into the coming year.

Principles of God's Providence

The star gave light, and:
1.   *First, you must act on what light you do have. Look at v. 1.*

"After Jesus was born in Bethlehem in Judea, during the time of King Herod, Magi from the east came to Jerusalem and asked, 'Where is the one who has been born king of the Jews'? We saw his star in the east and have come to worship him." We must act on what light we do have. These wise men did not know the entire story. They did not know all the details of the prophecies of Moses, David, Isaiah, Jeremiah, Daniel (concerning Messiah), nor about his lineage, nor the purposes foretold. There was a lot they did not know. But here's what they did have. They did have a message that something about that star was linked to a new Hebrew king. They did not have much light. They did not know much about this Messiah, but they acted on the little bit of knowledge that they did have. Are you? So many of us fail to live up to the knowledge we do have, and most Americans actually know a lot about God and the birth of Christ. *Ignorance is not our primary problem.* They appear to know that a Savior was needed, which presupposes a confession of sin and human limitation. And they were in search of that—not resting in their own strength for salvation.

"They only had a little light of a star in the dark sky, but that was the only light they needed." That's not just poetry—that also describes God's providence. In God's providence, he normally only gives us some part of his plan; he never gives us every detail—at least, not at once. And we must act on the light that he does give.

A young preacher purchased a new set of golf clubs, thinking that his game would surely improve. He went to play with an older preacher. The young minister, thrilled with his new sticks, told the old parson that he might need a new set, too. The older parson duly humbled the younger elder by saying: "John, I'm not playing up to the clubs I have now."

Some of us want God to teach us something new, or show us truths we've never known. Some of us want to see something not seen before, something different. Or we want to be more theologically astute. Some even claim that they want to do more for the Lord. But rarely are we are playing up to the level of what he's already given us. Like the golf clubs, "Are you playing up to what you already know—what has already been revealed about the Lord"?

Here's the principle: If we do not play up to the light that we do
have, God seldom gives more light. Some wonder why our spiritual
lives are in the doldrums. The reason is: God is not going to give us
additional light until we act on the light that we do have and learn to
use what he has given.

I wish church members would do that. We may squander much in
light of "To whom much is given, much is required." Learn about
God's providence, to act on the light that you do have. That's principle
#1 that I wish to stress from this passage.

2.   *"Our sin can blind us so that we cannot see the light that is
there."* Why can't we see the light or know God's will? Some cannot
see it. Consider Herod as an example of this. Listen to v. 3 as it
contrasts Herod with the wise-men: "When King Herod heard this, he
was disturbed, and all Jerusalem with him. When he had called together
all the people's chief priests and teachers of the law, he asked them
where the Christ was to be born."

What disturbed Herod? He was known all over the empire, a friend
of Caesar. He had all that a man could want. He'd built some of the
most ornate and lasting monuments of any Roman King. He'd been in
power for nearly 40 years, since taking over the Roman Senate. He
should have been above some petty rivalry. But that is not what he did.
He sent out for the best of scholars and he desperately wanted to know
what was about to happen. Why?

Because he was motivated by his own sinful condition. He was
owned by jealousy. His own wife's brother (the chief priest), was
drowned by Herod due to his own jealousy. He was jealous of any
rivals. Then he threw a huge funeral, feigning sorrow. He went on to
kill his own wife, because he was jealous of her. He also killed his
mother in law . . . and even his own 2 sons out of fear that they would
sit on the throne. This man was consumed with jealousy. That's why he
couldn't see God's providence. His sin blinded him. Does yours?

Your sin may not be jealousy, which leads to killing others, but
what about some others?"

Do any of the following ever blind you:

- That seemingly incurable trait that never allows you to admit
  that you were wrong? When you cannot admit you were wrong,
  and things compound from there.
- That overcoming urge to control, or be right all the time.

- That powerful lust that drives you to do crazy things, or jealousy of another in the church or at the office.
- Your pride of place or desire for prestige.
- Your desire to get credit or have others fawn over your abilities.
- There are many.

These wise men threatened Herod, for the magi (known as the king-makers and wise men) had tremendous respect. These were the law makers. They didn't come in on a camel or 2, as is often depicted. These were movers-and-shakers, international power brokers. They would be in caravan, accompanied by many soldiers, likely in a procession up to a mile in length. They didn't arrive in stealth; all Jerusalem knew about their appearance.

This shook Herod up, and he wanted to find out who his competition might be. He could not see the plan of God because he was jealous. Why, he could have changed history; he could have sheltered Joseph and Mary. He could have supported baby Jesus. But he did not. He missed it. Some of your friends, this Christmas, will miss it. People even came from a far country and Herod still missed it because he was consumed with jealousy. Some of us cannot see the providence of God in our lives because we are consumed with sin:

Might it be lust?

Maybe desire for power?

Materialism; all you can think of is acquiring what you don't have—morning, noon, and night?

Fantasy marriage to a perfect man/gal, who does not exist?

Desiring revenge on a person for something that happened months ago?

Don't say that none of these apply to you.

Our sins will own us; they will possess us. Just like Herod if not put to death.

Some of us, when I ask the question, "Do you see the providence of God in your lives", have to answer honestly "No." The reason we cannot is because we are owned by someone else, or by some other sin. And we will not see God at work in our lives until we get that right. It does not mean that God is not there, but that we will not see his plan. We won't see his plan until we lay down our lust, or our pride, or our

selfish ambition . . . whatever it is. Herod could not see Jesus, or the
star, if he didn't let go of his sin. Our sin can blind us, so that we do not
see the light.

That leads to a 3rd principle:

3.   *"Spiritual complacency can deaden our sensitivity and
response to God's work in the world around us."* God is doing much
around us, but sometimes we can't see it. Look at v. 5, "In Bethlehem
in Judea, they replied, 'For this is what the prophet has written . . .'"
Then follows a quotation from Micah 5:2. Note this about v. 7: "Then
Herod called the Magi secretly and found out from them the exact time
the star had appeared." Then he sent them out to search for the child.

The Scripture was clear. The OT was clear, they heard the wise
men, but did you notice: Not any of them left with the Magi. No one
even went the 5 miles to Bethlehem to see what was happening. The
Pharisees, the chief priests were spiritually dead. They were
complacent, into their routine—church, week after week, but they were
dead. They were dead to God's plan in the world. Why, people can
even come to church and be that way. One must guard against spiritual
complacency.

Jesus accused the Pharisees of empty complacency. Mouthing
words apart from heart love for God helps no one.

They were not dead orthodox. They were just dead, and did not
know what was coming.

Let me tell you how this can happen in the business world. The
internet began to be popular about 2 decades ago. The rise of digital
communities was a threat to some anti-democratic forces. The internet
actually gave voice to many who would rediscover free expression.
Many oppressive governments could not keep up with the rapid spread
of popular voices. The same is true for print on paper. It was hard to
anticipate, but likely more books have been sold on Kindle or Nook in
2013 than hard copies. That would mean that many publishers or
divisions could go out of business if they did not keep up. Newspapers
have faced the same changing dynamic. Some of the largest and most
respected news outlets went out of business. *US News and World
Report* stopped its hard copy in 2010; then *Newsweek* 2012. Only
TIME is left. Many local papers went under; it may be that only a
fraction of newspapers that were in existence in 1980 will be around by
2020. All broadcast businesses have been impacted by this. And many

publishers and businesses were too complacent; they missed it. Spiritual complacency can deaden our sensitivity and response to God's work in the world around us. God is doing much around us, but sometimes we can't see it.

The same may be true of churches and countries. God is doing some mighty things in our church. One of the great dangers is that we will miss it, with the routine or blindness. We can get caught up in ceremony, and forget our Lord. God is at work here. Don't miss it. I am amazed if a person doesn't see God at work here. They must be spiritually blind. God is doing a lot in our church—why with all the new members and families, with all the gifts he is bringing here, we are making enormous progress. What a joy to worship together and serve God together here. But let's don't make the routine our god.

The scribes knew it all, but they missed the greatest event in human history.

1. We must act on light as we see it.
2. Sin can blind us so that we do not see the light.
3. Spiritual complacency can deaden our sensitivity and response to God's work in the world around us.

4.   Finally, we must not limit God's providence only to our narrow, provincial expectations. Don't limit God's plans only to our own expectations. He's often much bigger. Look at vss. 9-11: "After they had heard the king, they went on their way, and the star they had seen in the east, went ahead of them until it stopped over the place where the child was. When they saw the star, they were overjoyed. On coming to the house, they saw the child with his mother Mary, and they bowed down and worshipped him."

These wise men worshipped. They brought gifts.

You must know that as much as we love this story, many of Matthew's readers who read this story did not like some of it. They said, "Matthew, why did you put the part about those Magi in there?" He probably answered, "because it really happened." And they said well, why did God have those guys in there? Many of us would say, "What do you mean?" These were pagan magi. They had been adversaries of Jews for hundreds of years. These were the Persians who burned Jerusalem to the ground, and carried off the Jewish forefathers.

"And we don't like these guys." said some Jewish reviewer. Does that sound familiar? We have a seemingly incurable desire to tell God with whom and where he can work. It is incredible and nearly unstoppable. Anytime, we have a boundary—whether cultural, economic, national, or what—if we draw the line and say thus far— This is your kingdom and it cannot be much further He will stop over that line and correct our error. He'll say, "Watch me. Watch me. Watch me."

Most of the players belong in this drama. Mary and Joseph belong. Elizabeth and Zechariah belong. Even the shepherds belong, but **not** the pagan Magi. This would be like the British celebrating George Washington's birthday and July 4th.

They just don't do that. Still these pagan magi come and celebrate the birth of the Messiah. This is huge. One can speak theologically about this passage. It is a prophetic picture. In Isaiah 49:6, 700 years earlier, the prophet said: "It is too small a thing for you to be my servant to restore the tribes of Jacob and bring back those of Israel I have kept. I will also make you a light for the Gentiles that you may bring my salvation to the ends of the earth."

The Messiah is to be a light to the gentiles. The dam was going to burst and the faith would spread to the end of the earth.

Daniel 7:13 says the same thing: "In my vision at night I looked, and there before me was one like a son of man, coming with the clouds of heaven. He approached the Ancient of Days and was led into his presence. He was given authority, glory and sovereign power, all peoples, nations and men of every language worshipped him." *All nations*. This should have been known.

It is a universal faith. All people and nations would worship him. The birth of Christ is a completion of those prophecies. God is saying that I am bringing the people. The Persians will come, the Greeks will come, the Africans will come, and the Romans will come. And the Americans will come later. They'll all come. That's what he was saying. The magi are our representatives at the birth of Jesus Christ. The boundaries have been broken down.

God is saying, "Don't limit my kingdom by your provincial expectations. Your view of the Kingdom is not big enough. And it is a subtle reminder and call to each of us to be involved in the world-wide expansion of the gospel. Ira Sankey was a 19th century soloist and song leader for Dwight L. Moody. He was to Dwight Moody, what George Beverly Shea and Cliff Barrows have been to Billy Graham. But let me tell you about Ira Sankey before he led the choirs.

Sankey was a young soldier in the Union army prior to that. Some of us cut off our attention right there. No good can come out of the Union army. He loved music. One night he was standing guard alone. Meanwhile, a Rebel soldier crawled up through the bushes, lowered his rifle, and centered Ira Sankey in his sights. For some reason, there in the darkness, Sankey began to hum. He began to hum "Savior like a Shepherd lead us." Then he began to sing, it grew to a full-throated voice. The confederate soldier sat down in the bushes thinking, "Well he's a dead man any way. I might as well enjoy the song." So he sat down in the cover and listened.

Sankey sang, "We are thine, do thou befriend us, be thee, the guardian of our way. Keep thy flock—from sin defend us; seek us when we go astray. Blessed Jesus, blessed Jesus hear us when we pray. Blessed Jesus, thou hast promised to receive us—poor and sinful though we be."

He finished the song. When he reached the end of the song, the rebel soldier—who could have had no greater enemy at the time—crawled off, but only after wiping his tears away. He understood that God's Kingdom was bigger than our provincial expectations. It even took in the other soldiers—who were both in a greater kingdom. And my, how God used that spared life of Ira Sankey. He was later used to minister to thousands.

God had reminded that confederate soldier how huge his kingdom was.

This Christmas think about how vast God's kingdom is. It includes so many; it is so wide. There are millions today who share the same rejoicing as we do. Might God do something wonderful in China, Iraq and throughout the Middle East? We should be thinking and praying for that. Truly, the child has an adequate grasp on this: Red, and yellow black and white, they are precious in his sight." And it all passes through an undignified cradle. A place fit for animals became the throne of the only living God. Can you see God's providence in your life?

Wise men (and women) respond to God's seeking them by seeking Jesus as their King. Wise men seek Jesus as King in spite of the difficulties of the process:

in spite of the disinterest of others.

in spite of disappointments.

in spite of their own dignity.

Steven Cole wrote in a sermon: "There are three types of people in this story. There are those like Herod who hear of Jesus and are *hostile* toward Him. They want to eliminate Him from their lives because He threatens their running the show. Then there are those like the Jewish priests and scribes who know about Jesus. They can even quote Bible references about Him. But they're *indifferent* to Him. They don't go out of their way to seek Him. And then there are those like the magi. They *responded* to the light they had been given and overcame every hindrance until they found the Savior and fell at His feet in worship. The third group were the wise men; those who sought Jesus as King. Maybe you're not in the third group, but you'd like to be.

What should you do? William Law, an 18th century devotional writer, gives the answer: "When the first spark of a desire after God arrives in [your] soul, cherish it with all [your] care, give all [your] heart unto it. . . . Follow it as gladly as the wise men of the East followed the star from heaven that appeared to them. It will do for [you] as the star did for them: it will lead [you] to the birth of Jesus, not in a stable at Bethlehem of Judea, but to the birth of Jesus in [your] own soul."

Why don't you look back over a few Christmases. It is an opportune time. I used to do that, on Christmas Eve. After the sanctuary was emptied, with only a few lights left burning, I'd sit for a moment and recall where the Lord had led in the past year, and over several years. Can you see God's providence in your Life? I can't miss it.

Most of all, it is clear in his providing the savior, Jesus. Don't miss it, for any reason.

Tackling the Magi: "I finally know who the Wise Men were!" Maybe

Matthew 2:1-2

I've danced around this topic for years and years. Another reason why preaching through books of the Bible is good for all of us is that it forces us to roll up our sleeves and deal with difficult passages. Like many children, all my life I had two questions about these characters in Matthew 2: (1) was it pronounced magi (mag-ae) or maji (ma-ji)? And (2) who in the world were they? So roll up your sleeves and here we go.

a. First, the term: Magi
Most of what we associate with the "Magi" (pronounced Ma-ji) is from early church traditions. Most have assumed there were three of them, since they brought three specific gifts (but the Biblical text doesn't number them). They are called "Magi" from the Latinized form of a Greek word, transliterated from the Persian, for a select sect of priests. Our word "magic" comes from the same root.

As the years passed, the traditions became increasingly embellished. By the 3rd century they were viewed as kings. . . . A 14th century Armenian tradition identifies them as Balthasar, King of Arabia; Melchior, King of Persia; and Gasper, King of India. Rembrandt even painted: The Adoration of the Magi.

These are interesting traditions, but what do we really know about them?

The ancient Magi were a hereditary priesthood from what are known today as the Kurds; they are credited with profound religious knowledge. After some Magi, who had been attached to the Median court, proved to be expert in the interpretation of dreams, Darius the Great established them over the state religion of Persia. It was in this dual capacity, whereby civil and political counsel was invested with religious authority, that the Magi became the supreme priestly caste of the Persian empire and continued to be prominent during the subsequent periods.

The Role of Daniel

One of the titles given to Daniel was *Rab-mag*, the Chief of the Magi. His unusual career included being a principal administrator in world empires—the Babylonian and the Persian Empire. When Darius appointed him, a Jew, over the previously hereditary Median priesthood, the resulting repercussions led to the plots involving the ordeal of the lion's den. Daniel apparently entrusted a Messianic vision to a secret sect of the Magi for its eventual fulfillment.

Political Background

Since the days of Daniel, the fortunes of both the Persian and the Jewish nation had been closely intertwined. Both nations had, in their turn, fallen under Seleucid domination in the wake of Alexander's conquests. Subsequently, both had regained their independence: the Jews under Maccabean leadership, and the Persians as the dominating ruling group within the Parthian Empire.

It was at this time that the Magi, in their dual priestly and governmental office, composed the upper house of the Council of the Megistanes (from which we get the term "magistrates"), whose duties included the absolute choice and election of the king of the realm.

It was, therefore, a group of Persian—Parthian "king makers" who entered Jerusalem in the latter days of the reign of Herod. Herod's reaction was understandably one of fear when one considers the background of Roman-Parthian rivalry that prevailed during his lifetime.

When the Magi arrive, Herod who was ultra-sensitive that someone might try to de-throne him, he thought that they were there to anoint a

Persian king, a new rival. He was allied with Rome, but Persia to the east was a danger. So he took careful notice.

In Jerusalem, the sudden appearance of the Magi, probably traveling in force with all imaginable oriental pomp and accompanied by an adequate cavalry escort to insure their safe penetration of Roman territory, certainly alarmed Herod and the populace of Jerusalem.

It could seem as if these Magi were attempting to perpetrate a border incident which could bring swift reprisal from Parthian armies. Their request of Herod regarding the one who "has been born King of the Jews" (7) was a calculated insult to him, a non-Jew (8) who had contrived and bribed his way into that office.

Consulting his scribes, Herod discovered from the OT prophecies that the Promised One, the Messiah, would be born in Bethlehem. Hiding his concern and expressing sincere interest, Herod requested them to keep him informed.

In those ancient days all men believed that they could foretell the future from the stars, and they believed that a man's destiny was settled by the star under which he was born. It is not difficult to see how that belief arose. The stars pursue their unvarying courses; they represent the order of the universe. If then there suddenly appeared some brilliant star, if the unvarying order of the heavens was broken by some special phenomenon, it did look as if God was breaking into His own order, and announcing some special thing.

b. Time: The visit of the Magi took place after the Presentation of the Child in the Temple (Luke 2:38). No sooner were the Magi departed than the angel bade Joseph take the Child and its Mother into Egypt (Matthew 2:13). It was "in the days of king Herod" (Matthew 2:1), i. e., before the year 4 B.C., the probable date of Herod's death at Jericho. It was *probably a year, or a little more than a year, after* the birth of Christ. Herod had found out from the Magi the time of the star's appearance. Taking this for the time of the Child's birth, he slew the male children of two years old and under in Bethlehem and its borders (v. 16). Some of the Fathers conclude from this ruthless slaughter that the Magi reached Jerusalem two years after the Nativity. Art and archaeology favor this view. Only one early monument represents the Child in the crib while the Magi adore; in others Jesus rests upon Mary's knees and is at times fairly well grown (see Cornely, *Introd. Special. in N.T.*, p. 203).

From Persia to Jerusalem was a journey of about 1000 miles. Such a distance may have taken any time between 3 and 12 months by camel. Besides the time of travel, there were probably many weeks of preparation. The Magi could scarcely have reached Jerusalem till a year or more had elapsed from the time of the appearance of the star. St. Augustine (*De Consensu Evang.*, II, v, 17) thought the date of the Epiphany, the sixth of January, proved that the Magi reached Bethlehem thirteen days after the Nativity, i. e., after the twenty-fifth of December. His argument from liturgical dates was incorrect. Neither liturgical date is certainly the historical date. In the fourth century the Churches of the East celebrated the sixth of January as the feast of Christ's Birth, the Adoration by the Magi, and Christ's Baptism, whereas, in the West, the Birth of Christ was celebrated on the 25th of December. This latter date of the Nativity was introduced into the Church of Antioch during St. Chrysostom's time, and still later into the Churches of Jerusalem and Alexandria.

That the Magi thought a star led them on, is clear from the words which Matthew uses in 2:2. Was it really a star? Rationalists, in their efforts to escape the supernatural, have elaborated a number of hypotheses:

- The word *aster* may mean a comet; But we have no record of any such comet.
- The star may have been a conjunction of Jupiter and Saturn (7 B.C.), or of Jupiter and Venus (6 B.C.).
- The Magi may have seen a stella nova, a star which suddenly increases in magnitude and brilliancy and then fades away.

These theories all fail to explain how "the star which they had seen in the east, went before them, until it came and stood over where the child was" (Matthew 2:9). No fixed star could have so moved before the Magi as to lead them to Bethlehem; neither fixed star nor comet could have disappeared, and reappeared, and stood still. Only a *miraculous phenomenon* could have been the Star of Bethlehem. It was like the miraculous pillar of fire which stood in the camp by night during Israel's Exodus (Exodus 13:21), or to the "brightness of God" which shone round about the shepherds (Luke 2:9), or to "the light from heaven" which shone around about the stricken Saul (Acts 9:3).

c. Let's spend the rest of our time on Application.

1. God can call believers to himself from all over, not necessarily from the lineage that is closest. We are asking for trouble when we suggest that only certain families or certain tribes or races have God's blessings. Even a mangling of the OT is not convincing that God only and always wanted to work only with Jews. There are too many non-Jews in the OT to disprove that.

And often, as with the apostle Paul, God takes some who were once enemies and he brings them home to Christ. In this case, God brought folks from a long way off and they were not Jewish in background.

Ryle comments (*Expository Thoughts*, pp. 10-13): These verses show us that there may be true servants of God in places where we should not expect to find them The Lord Jesus has many "hidden ones," like these wise men. Their history on earth may be as little known as that of Melchizedek, and Jethro, and Job. But their names are in the book of life, and they will be found with Christ in the day of His appearing. It is good to remember this. We must not look round the earth and say hastily, "All is barren." The grace of God is not tied to places and families. The Holy Ghost can lead souls to Christ [in many ways]. Men may be born in dark places of the earth, like these wise men, and yet like them be made "wise unto salvation." There are some travelling to heaven at this moment, of whom the Church and world know nothing. They flourish in secret places, but Christ loves them and they love Christ.

These verses show us, secondly, *that it is not always those who have most religious privileges, who give Christ most honor.* We might have thought that the scribes and Pharisees would have been the first to hasten to Bethlehem, on the slightest rumor that the Savior was born. But it was not so. A few unknown strangers from a distant land were the first, except the shepherds mentioned by St. Luke, to rejoice at His birth. "He came unto His own, and His own received Him not." (John i.11.) What a mournful picture this is of human nature! How often the same kind of thing may be seen among ourselves! How often the very persons *who live nearest to the means of grace are those who neglect them most*! Familiarity with sacred things can have the awful tendency to make men despise them. There are many, who from residence and convenience ought to be first and foremost in the worship of God, and yet are always last. There are many, who might well be expected to be last, who are always first.

These verses show us, thirdly, *that there may be knowledge of Scripture in the head, while there is no grace in the heart.* We are told that king Herod sent to inquire of the priests and elders, "where Christ should be born." We are told that they returned a ready answer to him, and showed an accurate acquaintance with the letter of Scripture. But they never went to Bethlehem to seek for the coming Savior. They would not believe in Him, when He ministered among them. Their heads were better than their hearts.—Let us beware of resting satisfied with head-knowledge. It is an excellent thing, when rightly used. But a man may have much of it, and yet perish everlastingly. What is the state of our hearts? This is the great question. A little grace is better than many gifts. Gifts alone save no one; but grace leads on to glory.

These verses show us, next, a splendid example of spiritual diligence. What trouble it must have cost these wise men to travel from their homes to the house where Jesus was born! How many weary miles they must have journeyed! The fatigues of an Eastern traveler are far greater than moderns understand. The time that such a journey would occupy must necessarily have been very great. The dangers to be encountered were neither few nor small.—But none of these things moved them. They had set their hearts on seeing Him "that was born King of the Jews;" and they never rested till they saw Him.

It would be good for all professing Christians if they were more ready to follow the example of those men.—Where is our *self-denial*? What pains do we take about means of grace? What diligence do we show about following Christ? What does our religion cost us?—These are serious questions. They serve serious consideration. The truly "wise," it may be feared, are very few.

These verses show us a striking example of faith. These wise men believed in Christ when they had never seen him; but that was not all. They believed in him when the scribes and Pharisees were unbelieving;—but that again was not all. They believed in him when they saw him a little infant on Mary's knees, and worshipped him as a King. This was the crowning point of their faith.—They heard no teaching to persuade them. They beheld no signs of divinity and greatness to overawe them. They saw nothing but a new-born infant, helpless and weak, and needing a mother's care, like any one of ourselves. And yet when they saw that infant, they believed that they saw the divine Savior of the world! 'They fell down and worshipped him.'

We read of no greater faith than this in the whole volume of the Bible. It is a faith that deserves to be placed side by side with that of the penitent thief. The wise men saw the young child in the home of a poor woman, and yet worshipped Him, and confessed that he was Christ. Blessed indeed are they that can believe in this fashion!

This is the kind of faith that God in which delights. We see the proof of that at this very day. Wherever the Bible is read the conduct of these wise men is known, and told as a memorial to them. Let us walk in the steps of their faith. Let us not be ashamed to believe in Jesus and confess Him, though all around us remain careless and unbelieving. Have we not a thousand-fold more evidence than the wise men had, to make us believe that Jesus is the Christ? Beyond doubt we have. Yet where is our faith?

2. *The Magi took seriously two things: Prophecy and Miracle (they followed a star).* They were also obedient to how much they knew, not crippled by how much they did not know.

3. *They became evangelists; changed hearts want to tell this news to others.*

4. *They knew that gifts were appropriate, and they brought expensive gifts.*

5. *Briefly, contrast the Magi and chief priests/Herod,* who had been given much but rejected gospel truth and also the similar contrast between Pilate and chief priests in the Passion Narrative.

At the end of Jesus' life, the religious leaders who should have known accuse Jesus of being the Messiah (which they do not believe), giving him an opportunity to assent and establish that testimony. Then the chief priests stir up the crowds to demand Jesus' crucifixion. Then they remind Pilate of Jesus' prediction of resurrection (which they do not believe) so he will post guards and thus lend even more credence to Jesus' resurrection. Then after Jesus' resurrection, the chief priests make up a cover story and also prevent Pilate from disciplining guards who supposedly were sleeping. In short, by saying things that they do not believe, they further the purposes of God in Jesus' Passion.

Similarly, in Matthew 2, the chief priests also tell Herod where the Messiah would be born—which they also do *not* believe! This statement also enables the Magi (Gentiles) to see and worship Jesus at his birth, just as the chief priests' urging of crucifixion made it possible for the Roman centurion to acknowledge Jesus as "a son of God" at his death.

Perhaps the chief priests in Matthew 2 may be seeking to protect their own interests and divert Herod away from Jerusalem to the sleepy village of Bethlehem. At any rate, there is great irony in chief priests who in seeking their own interests (even in saying things that they do not believe) actually further the purposes of God and His Messiah—from start to finish.

Larry Swain: "The role of the magi is as a foil which condemns Herod and the chief priests for their blindness—if the Magi are to be understood as Gentiles this only increases this role—that God has revealed truth to Gentiles and not to those who serve in His temple."

6. Perhaps they were starters of churches in Persia upon return. Let us learn not to take for granted what we've been given, and the privileges of being exposed to God's Word. I am glad to refer readers to See Matthew Henry's *Commentary* and applications below.

> Nothing will awaken those that are resolved to be spiritually dead or obstinate. We may lament the amazing stupidity of these Jews! And no less that of many who are called Christians!
> These Magi were Gentiles, and not belonging to the commonwealth of Israel. The Jews regarded not Christ, but these Gentiles inquirers found him. Note, many times those who are nearest to the means, are furthest from the end. The respect paid to Christ by these Gentiles was a happy preview and specimen of what would follow when those who were afar off should be made nigh by Christ.
> What induced them to make this inquiry? They, in their country, which was in the east, had seen an extraordinary star, which they took to be an indication of an extraordinary person born in the land of Judea, over which land this star was seen to hover; this differed so much from anything that was common that they concluded it to signify something uncommon. Note, *Extraordinary appearances of God in the creatures*

should spur us to inquire after his mind and will; Christ foretold signs in the heavens. The birth of Christ was announced to the Jewish shepherds by an angel, to the Gentile philosophers by a star: to both God spoke in their own language.

IV. So, They came from the east to Jerusalem, in search of this prince. They might have said, "Let's just wait here, comfortably at home, until this Savior comes to us." But they were impatient to be better acquainted with him, and they took a long journey to inquire after him. Note, *Those who truly desire to know Christ, and find him, will not regard pains or perils in seeking after him.* Then shall we know, if we follow on to know the Lord. Their question is, Where is he that is born king of the Jews? They do not ask, whether there was such a one born? (they are sure of that); but, Where is he born? Those who know something of Christ cannot but covet to know more of him.

They call Christ the King of the Jews, for so the Messiah was expected to be: and he is Protector and Ruler of all the spiritual Israel, he is born a King.

To this question they had a ready answer, and went to find all Jerusalem worshiping at the feet of this new king; but they come from door to door with this question, and no man can give them any information. Sadly, there is more ignorance in the world, and in the church too, than we wish to admit. Many that we think should direct us to Christ are themselves strangers to him. They have their answer ready, We are come to worship him. They conclude he will, in time, be their king, and therefore they will start serving him. Those in whose hearts the day-star is risen, to enhance the knowledge of Christ, must make it their business to worship him. Have we seen Christ's star? Let us study to give him honor.

V. When Herod heard this he was troubled. He was not a stranger to the OT prophecies about the Messiah and his kingdom, and the times fixed for his appearing by Daniel's weeks; but, having himself reigned so long and so successfully, he began to hope that those promises would not occur, or that his kingdom would be perpetuated in spite of them. It did not cheer him at all to hear talk of this King being born, now, when the time fixed for his appearing had come! Note, carnal wicked hearts dread nothing so much as the fulfilling of the scriptures.

Further, it seems that most of Jerusalem, except the few there that waited for the consolation of Israel, were troubled with Herod, and were apprehensive that the consequences of the birth of this new king would involve them in war, or restrain their leisure; they, for their parts, desired no king but Herod; not even the Messiah himself. The slavery of sin is foolishly preferred by many to the glorious liberty of the children of God, only because they anticipate some present difficulties attending that necessary revolution of the government in the soul.

Matthew Henry is helpful again in his view of **The Christmas Gifts.**

The gifts of gold, frankincense, and myrrh were also prophetic, speaking of our Lord's offices of king, priest, and savior. Gold speaks of His kingship; frankincense was a spice used in the priestly duties; and myrrh was an embalming ointment anticipating His death.

(i) Gold is the gift for a king. In Parthia it was the custom that no one could ever approach the king without a gift. And gold, the king of metals, is the fit gift for a king of men. So then Jesus was "the Man born to be King." But He was to reign, not by force, but by love; and He was to rule over men's hearts, not from a throne, but from a Cross. Remembering that Jesus Christ is King, *We can never meet Jesus on an equality.* We must always meet Him on terms of complete submission and complete surrender.

(ii) Frankincense is the gift for a Priest. It was in the Temple worship and at the Temple sacrifices that the sweet perfume of frankincense was used. The function of a priest is to open the way to God for men. The Latin word for priest is Pontifex, which means a bridge-builder. The priest is the man who builds a bridge between men and God. That is what Jesus did. He opened the way to the presence of God; He made it possible for men to enter into the very presence of God.

(iii) Myrrh is the gift for one who is to die Myrrh was used to embalm the bodies of the dead. Jesus came into the world to die. Jesus came to give for men His life and His death.

Gold for a king, frankincense for a priest, myrrh for one who was to die—these were the gifts of the wise men, and, even at the cradle of Christ, they foretold that He was to be the true King, the perfect High Priest, and in the end the supreme Savior of men.

1. Once they found the King they sought, they presented themselves to him: they fell down, and worshiped him. We do not read that they gave such honor to Herod, though he was in the height of his royal grandeur; but to this babe they gave this honor, not only as to a king

but as to a God. All who have found Christ fall down before him, adore him, and submit themselves to him. It is the wisdom of the wisest of men, and by this it appears they know Christ, and understand themselves and their true interests, if they be humble, faithful worshipers of the Lord Jesus.

2. In the eastern nations, when they paid homage to their kings, they gave them presents; We must give up all that we have to Jesus Christ; and if we be sincere in the surrender of ourselves to him, we shall not be unwilling to part with what is dearest to us, and most valuable to him and for him; nor are our gifts accepted, unless we first present ourselves to him living sacrifices. The gifts they presented were gold, frankincense, and myrrh. Providence sent this for a seasonable relief to Joseph and Mary in their present poor condition. These were the products of their own country; what God favors us with, we must honor him with. Some think there was a significance in their gifts; they offered him gold, as a king, paying him tribute, to Caesar, the things that are Caesar's; frankincense, as God, for they honored God with the smoke of incense; and myrrh, as a Man that should die, for myrrh was used in embalming dead bodies.

In the future, he will also receive the gifts of gold and frankincense; but no myrrh: His death was once and for all. What gifts are YOU going to give Him this year? How will you worship him?

The Battle for Christmas: Virgin Birth!

Isaiah 7, Matthew 1, and Luke 2

No dad would believe it. Sure, dads are gullible at times, but if your teenage daughter came to you and said, "I'm carrying a child, and I have had not relations," you'd be furious. That, however, was the exact predicament of Mary's father. She was a Virgin.

The Virgin Birth (VB) is a concept that is beyond/contra to all nature we know. God wants us to believe in and embrace it.

A. The Virgin Birth is taught in the Bible.
1. It's OT prediction occurs in Isaiah 7.
        This is not speaking mainly of Israel; nor of anyone else, if we allow the NT to be our main commentary on the OT.

2. The NT confirmation occurs in Matthew and Luke, and I've been helped by a sermon by my friend, Terry Johnson, on the verses in Matthew. He points out the following.

Matthew says that the work of the Holy Spirit in Mary took place in order to fulfill the promise recorded in Isaiah 7:14. Notice Matthew's view of inspiration. What Isaiah the prophet said God said. The prophecy was "spoken by the Lord through the prophet." Isaiah, the prophets, and the apostles did not write their own words. The Lord spoke and still speaks through them. What Scripture says God says. Scripture is trustworthy because what God says is true, always. What God says in Scripture is true, always. It can be relied upon. What it predicts happens. What it promises and warns occurs. This is why you can build your life on this book. When someone asks you why you live as you do as a Christian, here is your answer. *What the Bible says God says.* What God says is true. When God speaks we listen. You may not want to listen to your mother or dad or teacher or boss or the IRS. But when God speaks, you better listen. The Bible is true. What it says about Jesus is true. If you are not yet a Christian this is worth pondering. You can depend upon what this book says. What it teaches you can believe. What it commands you can obey. Not only can you safely build your life on what it says, but you cannot safely ignore what it says. God himself is speaking to you in his word. He is telling you what is true and what he wants you to believe and do. You cannot afford not to listen.

Matthew's point: *The Child in her womb was conceived apart from human procreative activity.* No male seed was involved. The Holy Spirit-made birth of Jesus will be a virgin birth, in fulfillment of the Messianic prophecy of Isaiah 7:14. A "virgin" (*parthenos*, the technical term for virgin, as in the LXX), he says, "shall be with child, and shall bear a son." In other words Mary, in fulfillment of Isaiah 7:14, has conceived a child apart from sexual activity. The Child has no human father. A human paternity test will yield nothing in this conception.

Clearly the Bible teaches the supernatural, virgin birth of Christ. Matthew repeats this four times:

1. Mary was "with child" before she and Joseph "came together" (v 18).

2. That which was in Mary's womb was "conceived . . . of the Holy Spirit" (v 20).

3. A "virgin" would be "with child" (v 23).

4. Joseph "kept her a virgin" until Jesus' birth (v. 25).

Parthenos means virgin in Matthew. Likewise Luke proclaims the same in equally unambiguous contexts (Lk. 1:34, cf. vss. 27, 35). Mary for example, is responding to the announcement that she will conceive and bear a son by asking, "how can this be, since I am a *parthenos?*"

Yet it remains a dogmatic article of faith among skeptics that this could not have happened. Previous liberals scoffed at the idea. They identified it as myth, similar to pagan stories of mating between humans and the gods. They were answered by the Scottish scholar

James Orr and then supremely refuted by J. Gresham Machen in *The Virgin Birth of Christ* (1930). Machen's work (Used copies available for $7.50) has never been answered by the liberals, yet they continue to jeer. Even today they will roll their eyes and chuckle at the mention of it. Why? Not because the Bible is unclear in what it is teaching. Not because it can be historically disproved. Not, one would think, because this is something God cannot do. Rather, it is because of the skeptic's assumptions, bias, or presuppositions. They don't believe because of their philosophy.

    1. First, there is *their view of Biblical authority*. The Scripture is only trusted in matters "religious" (narrowly defined). For them, the Bible is an important source of religious wisdom but limited by the cultural biases of its day and riddled with errors in matters of historical detail. This is really the crux of the matter. What are we to say when the Bible asserts something as true that contradicts one of the cherished assumptions of our day? The doctrine of the virgin birth contradicts the tenets of naturalism. Some so-called evangelical Christians have found the pressure to conform to the culture so great that they have advanced a theory of a "limited inerrancy," limiting the Bible's infallibility to those areas which are strictly "religious." The problem is that this puts me in the position of defining what is "religious" and isn't, what is true and what isn't, and what is believable and what isn't. *I become the authority*.

    Let me give an example. Is the virgin birth religious truth or historical? It's both, isn't it? How do you separate them? The virgin birth is rich with religious meaning. But it is also about a girl named Mary who conceived and gave birth to a boy named Jesus while remaining a virgin. If the "history" is not true, if she in fact was not a virgin at the time of his birth, then no religious significance can survive either. Christianity is a religion rooted in history. Christianity claims to be historical. God reveals himself in history. The Exodus happened in space and time. There was a land named Egypt, a man called Pharaoh, another named Moses, and so on.

    Likewise there was a Joseph, a Mary, and a baby Jesus. Remove the historical events of the gospel from the gospel message and the whole thing falls to the floor. You end up with no virgin birth, no teaching ministry, no healings, no crucifixion, and no resurrection. The Christian religion is interwoven with and dependent upon historical events. Paul says that if there is no resurrection, for example, our faith is "worth-less" and we "are still in (our) sins" (1 Cor 15:17). Ultimately, one cannot separate historical details from religions. The attempt to do so will rob Scripture of its authority. Why? Because if it errs in the historical bits that are open to verification then how can it be trusted in the religious bits that are not? The Bible is either true and authoritative, or it isn't. It is not for us to pick and choose. If you start down that road, time plus logic will eventually take the Bible right out of your hands.

2. Other skeptics avoid the Virgin Birth because of *their view of the supernatural.* Is our world an open or closed system? If it is closed, then the intervention of that which is beyond the natural, is impossible. If as one leading theorist said at the outset of his TV series, "the universe is all that there is or ever will be. . ." if that is so, if he and other naturalists are correct, then miracles by definition never occur. There can be no virgin birth, no resurrection, in fact, no inspiration of Scripture. God does not act within this world. All we have is us. Liberal theologians, for example, say a resurrection from the dead is absolutely absurd. It is impossible. They say this not because of careful evaluation of historical data. They did not sit down and look at evidences and arguments for the resurrection. They reject it categorically because of a philosophical bias against the supernatural.

So much for open-mindedness. They see miracle stories as ways in which the gospel writers made concrete for others the fact that an encounter with Jesus made them feel better. They created stories to explain their faith, they would say. But is there evidence to support this assertion? Not a shred. All that we know points to men who wrote as they did because they were absolutely convinced that the things about which they wrote actually occurred. Matthew writes of a virgin birth because he believes, as did all of the early Christians, that Christ was truly born of a virgin. It is arbitrary and indefensible to exclude supernatural explanations of events merely because of a bias against them.

It is a serious error, involving the rejection of clear scriptural teaching. Some church leaders have made the mistake of thinking that this is not a doctrine worth having a fight over. It doesn't strike at the "vitals" of the Christian faith they have thought and so have made peace with unbelief. But when the doctrine of the virgin birth is compromised, much more is lost as well.

First, the doctrine of Scripture is compromised. If it errs here, how can it be trusted elsewhere? If it is robbed of its authority here, how can it remain authoritative anywhere? Surely this is the history of the last century of church history. When denominations and educational institutions abandoned the virgin birth, they lost much more. They were left holding an impotent Bible in their hands, and have seen one orthodox doctrine after another fall.

Second, the supernatural nature of the Christian religion is compromised. Are we to assume that God cannot miraculously bring about a conception in the womb of the virgin Mary without the male seed? If this is something that God cannot do, then it calls into question all the supernatural elements of the Christian religion. We may be left with ethics, but little else. Indeed ethics will not be preserved either, as the events of the past 100 years prove as well. Too much is given up when one gives up the virgin birth. The same anti-supernatural bias will next reject the inspiration of Scripture, then the atonement, then the resurrection, then the regeneration of sinners. One is left with a god who cannot speak, cannot act, cannot answer prayer, and cannot be known. Little is left.

Third, possibly the dual nature of Christ is compromised. If the supernatural dimension of Christ's origins is compromised, then it is hard to see how his full deity and his sinless humanity could be maintained. Is he truly God? Then the divine "seed" must have been present from the beginning. Is he truly man? Then how could he have two human parents and still be exempt from human guilt and corruption? In the virgin birth we have the union of the human and divine that is the root of Christ's dual nature. He must be truly human if he is to be one with us and atone for our sin. He must be truly divine if he is to be without the guilt and corruption of sin and able to endure the infinite wrath of God against sin. The virgin birth is the necessary foundation upon which this doctrine is built.

This is not a side issue. In the virgin birth we see the foundation of the whole gospel. We see the supernatural intervention of a gracious God who brings his Son into the world, uniting him to human flesh, that he might save us from our sin.

So, this is taught in the Bible.

B. The Virgin Birth is also confessed in creeds and throughout Christian history.

1. It is professed in numerous creeds and denied by none.
2. It was held and embraced throughout history—the early church held to this. Only modernity has blushed over it.

C. If the Virgin Birth is REJECTED it is because:

1. It is not in our experience; or
2. It requires miracles.

Note, however, that true Faith embraces miracles and is not limited to our experience.

What is at stake? Simply put:

a. Throw out miracle, and your throw out our faith.
b. This affects the deity of Christ: This was God's method of combining human and divine nature in the Messiah.

Below, I want to highlight four things that are at stake this Christmas related to the Virgin Birth. And these will be at stake every Christmas. Yes, we are in a war.

We also live in a day of "cafeteria Christianity," where folks go down the line and say, "I'll have some of this, but I don't want any of that. I don't like it." They pick and choose what suits their fancy, as if they are free to take whatever they like from the faith and disregard the rest. Coupled with this is the prevailing notion that doctrine is at best a bizarre hobby, and at worst intolerant and divisive. According to this view, it really doesn't matter what you believe as long as you're loving and accepting toward others, no matter what they believe.

All Christians enjoy the story of the birth of Jesus. The familiar narrative of Joseph and Mary, their trek to Bethlehem, no room at the inn, the humble birth of Jesus in the stable, and the adoration of the shepherds and the magi, makes for a story we never grow tired of repeating. But there is one part of the story that many professing Christians would just as soon leave out: the virgin birth of our Savior. A majority of Protestants long ago ceased believing in this In its Sept. 11, 1970 issue, *Christianity Today* published a survey that revealed that the virgin birth is denied by 60 percent of Methodists, 49 percent

of Presbyterians, 44 percent of Episcopalians, 34 percent of American
Baptists, and 19 percent of American Lutherans.

Perhaps that part of the story sounds just too incredible for the
modern mind.

And besides, what difference does it make? Isn't the important
thing that we believe that in Christ God was present among men?
Why is it necessary to believe in the virgin birth? I want to answer
that question in this message. I want you to see that:

Belief in the virgin birth of Jesus Christ is essential.

A few doctrines are "fundamentals" of the Christian faith. Sincere
Christians   may   differ   on   their   understanding   of   the
nonfundamentals—such areas as prophecy, spiritual gifts, and views
of baptism. But to deny the fundamentals of the faith is to depart from
the core of what it means to be a Christian in the historic sense of the
word. The virgin birth is a fundamental doctrine of the Christian faith.
To deny it requires that we deny the authority and truth of the Bible,
the deity and sinless humanity of Jesus Christ, and that he is the
Savior as taught in Scripture. Or, stated positively, to affirm these
essential doctrines, we must affirm the virgin birth.

*1. Belief in the virgin birth is essential to affirm the truthfulness of
the Bible.*

Since the Bible clearly teaches the virgin birth of Jesus, one cannot
consistently claim to believe anything else the Bible says and at the
same time deny the virgin birth. The main reason skeptics reject the
virgin birth (or the virgin conception of Jesus) is that they assume
naturalism and thus reject miracles as being mere fables passed down
from a time when people were not as scientifically knowledgeable as
we are today.

But the Bible begins by assuming the fact of God: "In the
beginning God created the heavens and earth" (Gen. 1:1). It teaches
that the reason men reject God is not intellectual, but moral: they
suppress the truth because they do not want to turn from their sin and
submit to the Lordship of the Creator (Rom. 1:18-21). The fact of an
intelligent Creator is evident in his creation. To think that anything as
complex as life on this earth could have evolved by sheer chance plus
time is a leap of faith that runs counter to the principles of the
scientific method. When we examine any complex mechanism,
whether a watch or a computer, we do not assume that given enough

time, such a thing could happen by chance. We know that an intelligent designer put these things together for a purpose.

Which is more logical: to conclude that something as complex as plant and animal life on this earth, and the conditions necessary to sustain it, interdependent as it all is, happened by sheer chance over billions of years, with the parts that needed the other parts hanging on for a few billion years until the other necessary parts evolved; or, to conclude that an omniscient, omnipotent Creator designed it?

If a supernatural God is the source of creation, then miracles are not a problem. He can interrupt the normal laws of his creation and perform supernatural deeds if He chooses. The angel states this to Mary when he announced that she would bear the Savior. She was puzzled as to how she could have a child, since she had not had relations with a man. He explained, "The Holy Spirit will come upon you, and the power of the Most High will overshadow you; . . ." He concludes, "For nothing will be impossible with God" (Luke 1:35, 37). It was a miracle.

Critics say that the virgin birth is just a myth similar to other ancient myths, where influential men were said to have been conceived by the gods having relations with human women. It's not surprising that Satan would invent many such counterfeit stories to confuse and cloud the facts surrounding the birth of the Savior.

But invariably such mythical stories sound like fables, whereas the biblical accounts read like factual history.

Matthew was one of the twelve, and we can assume that his source was either Jesus or Mary. Luke states that he made a careful investigation of the facts and talked with eyewitnesses (Lk 1:1-4). It is probable that he talked directly with Mary. Matthew's and Luke's accounts are independent of each other, yet both men report the same miraculous event. Thus to reject the virgin birth a person must reject the word of two independent historians who lived at that time and whose writings have been accepted as factual history by thousands of scholars.

If a person rejects the historicity of the virgin birth and claims that it is only the "spiritual lesson" of the story that matters, then he has effectively cut himself off from the necessity of believing any of the history of the gospels. The by-now notorious "Jesus Seminar" is a group of supposed scholars who vote on their opinion of how likely each sentence and story of the gospels reflects what Jesus really said or did. The basis for their voting is subjective opinion.

Using the same method, we could establish that Plato or Shakespeare or any other author was not authentic, because it doesn't "sound" like that author—*in my opinion*! We would have to reject the accuracy of all written history. But such fools are arbitrarily rejecting, on the assumption of naturalism, the historical research of credible sources.

In addition to the historical factor, Matthew 1:23 asserts for his Jewish readers that the virgin birth of Jesus was the fulfillment of Isaiah 7:14: "'Behold, the virgin shall be with child, and shall bear a son, and they shall call his name Immanuel,' which translated means, 'God with us.'"

Some Bible scholars may debate the exact interpretation of Isaiah 7:14, but however you interpret Isaiah 7:14, Matthew is stating that its ultimate fulfillment meant that a woman who had not had relations with a man would bear a son and that this child was none other than God with us, God in human flesh. Mary was that woman and Jesus was her child, the promised Messiah of Israel.

I might add that there is no biblical basis for the view that Mary remained a virgin all her life. That teaching is based on the unbiblical view that sexual relations in marriage are impure. Other Scriptures (Matt. 13:55, 56; Mark 6:3) show that Mary had other children. If they were Joseph's children by an earlier marriage, one of them, not Jesus, would have been heir to the throne of David. Matthew 1:25 implies that Mary and Joseph had normal relations as husband and wife after Jesus' birth.

The virgin birth of Christ was only one of numerous prophecies written hundreds of years previous to his birth which he fulfilled. Together with the historical accuracy of Matthew and Luke, these prophecies affirm the truthfulness of the Bible. You cannot really believe the Bible if you deny the virgin birth. The truth of Scripture is one thing at stake at Christmas.

2. Belief in the virgin birth is essential to affirm the deity of Jesus Christ.

If Jesus Christ is the son of a human father and a human mother through natural biological processes, then he is not God in human flesh. It's that simple. He might, under those circumstances, be a man indwelt by God, a man upon whom God's Spirit rested. But he would only have been a man. His existence would have begun at conception. He would not and could not be the eternal God in human flesh.

The Scriptures repeatedly affirm the full deity of the Lord Jesus Christ. "In the beginning was the Word, and the Word was with God, and the Word was God. . . . And the Word became flesh, and dwelt among us, and we beheld His glory, glory as of the only begotten from the Father, full of grace and truth" (John 1:1,14). "But of the Son, He says, 'Your throne, O God, is forever and ever, and the righteous scepter is the scepter of His kingdom'" (Heb. 1:8). Jesus himself told the Jews, "Truly, truly, I say to you, before Abraham came into being, I AM" (John 8:58). When Thomas saw the risen Lord Jesus and cried out, "My Lord and my God," Jesus didn't correct him for blasphemy, but rather he accepted and commended such worship (John 20:28, 29).

Alexander Maclaren observed, "Christ takes as his due all the honor, love, and trust, which any man can give him—either an exorbitant appetite for adulation, or the manifestation of conscious divinity." "Either he was wrong, and then he was a crazy enthusiast, only acquitted of blasphemy because convicted of insanity; or else—or else—he was 'God, manifest in the flesh'" (ibid., sermon on John 14:1, p. 257).

No natural union of a human husband and wife could ever bring God into this world. That is the core truth of the Christmas story, that the baby of Bethlehem is uniquely, "God with us." The means God used to take on human flesh was the miraculous conception of Jesus in the womb of the virgin Mary. To affirm the full deity of Jesus Christ you must affirm his supernatural virgin birth. The full deity of Christ is at stake in the Virgin Birth at Christmas.

3. Belief in the virgin birth is essential to affirm the sinless humanity of Jesus Christ.

If Jesus was born of natural parents, then he was born a sinner like all other human beings, and he would have needed a Savior for himself. If he had sin of his own, he could not have died as the substitute for others. The Scriptures clearly teach that the whole human race, from Adam onward, is born under the curse of sin (Rom 5:12; Eph. 2:1-3). To redeem that race from sin, Christ had to be identified with us in our humanity, and to be sinless himself. Just as the Scriptures teach the full deity of Jesus Christ, so they clearly teach his full humanity. He was not a hybrid God-man, half of each. He is undiminished deity and perfect humanity united in one person forever.

Jesus had to have at least one human parent or he would not have shared our humanity. But through the superintendence of the Holy Spirit in the virgin birth, Jesus was able to be born as fully human and yet as sinless. The angel tells Mary that because the Holy Spirit will come upon her and the power of the Most High will overshadow her, "for that reason the holy offspring shall be called the Son of God" (Luke 1:35). Mary herself was not immaculately conceived. Luke 1:47 makes that plain where Mary refers to "God my Savior." You don't need a Savior unless you're a sinner.

The angel asserted that because Mary would conceive miraculously through the Holy Spirit, her offspring would be the holy Son of God. The virgin birth is necessary to affirm the sinless humanity of Jesus Christ. Thus, belief in the virgin birth is necessary to affirm the Word of God; the deity, and the sinless humanity of Jesus Christ.

4. Finally, belief in the virgin birth is essential to affirm that Jesus Christ is the Savior.

Christmas isn't just a story to make us feel warm and fuzzy about family, friends, and peace on earth. At the heart of the Christmas story is that the human race is lost, alienated from the holy God because of our sin. The angel told Joseph, "You shall call His name Jesus [= Jehovah saves], for it is He who will save His people from their sins" (Matt. 1:21). Today you are either in your sins, alienated from God, facing his judgment; or, Christ has saved you from your sins, so that you are reconciled to God through faith in Christ. If you are lost, your greatest need is for a Savior. The virgin-born Jesus is the only Savior.

To be our Savior the Messiah had to be a man, because only man could die for the sins of the human race. The wages of our sin is death (Rom. 6:23) and that penalty must be paid either by the sinner or by an acceptable substitute. But that substitute must Himself be without sin. Furthermore, He must be more than a man to die for the sins of the whole human race. He must be God in human flesh. Bishop Moule once said, *"A Savior not quite God is a bridge broken at the farther end."*

In his classic book, *The Virgin Birth of Christ*, J. Gresham Machen wrote, "How, except by the virgin birth, could our Savior have lived a complete human life from the mother's womb, and yet have been from the very beginning no product of what had gone before, but a supernatural Person come into the world from the outside to redeem the sinful race? . . . A noble man in whom the divine life merely pulsated in greater power than in other men would have been born by ordinary generation from a human pair; the eternal Son of God, come by a voluntary act to redeem us from the guilt and power of sin, was conceived in the virgin's womb by the Holy Ghost." (Machen, 395)

"Late in time, behold him come; offspring of the virgin's womb." The virgin birth is a picture of the new birth that God wants to bestow on every sinner. The initiative and power are totally from God. It also defies human parentage. Mary could do nothing except passively receive what God would do for her. She couldn't offer her best efforts, she didn't need to promise to try hard to bear the Messiah. All she did was to say, "Be it done to me according to your word" (Lk 1:38). God did it all. You can't try to save your-self or get into heaven by your own efforts. All you can do is receive what God has done in Christ.

Let this stunning biblical truth lead us to:
> Wonder
> Praise
> Respect for MIRACLE: Nothing can Stop God
> Liberation.

Conclusion: Radio commentator Paul Harvey told a memorable parable of a man who did not believe that God had taken human flesh in the person of Jesus. He was a kind, decent family man, but he was skeptical about the message of Christmas and couldn't pretend otherwise. So on Christmas eve, he told his wife that he was not going to church with her and the children, because he just couldn't believe. So they went without him.

Shortly after the family left, snow began to fall. As he sat in his fireside chair reading the paper, he was startled by a thudding sound against the house, then another, then another. At first he thought someone must be throwing snowballs against the living room window. But when he went to investigate, he found a flock of birds, huddled miserably in the snow. They had been caught in the storm, and in a desperate search for shelter, had tried to fly through his window.

He didn't want to leave the poor creatures there to freeze. He thought of the barn where his children stabled their pony. He put on his coat and boots and tromped through the deepening snow to the barn. He opened the door wide and turned on the light. But the birds didn't come in. He went back to the house and got some bread crumbs and sprinkled a path to the barn, but the cold creatures ignored the food and continued to flop around helplessly in the snow.

He tried catching them and shooing them into the barn, but they scattered in every direction, frightened by his well-meaning actions. As he puzzled over how he could help save these frightened creatures from sure death, the thought struck him, "If only I could become a bird and speak their language, then I could show them the way to safety in the warm barn." At that moment, bells from the church rang out through the silent, falling snow, heralding the birth of the Savior. The message of Christmas suddenly made sense, and he dropped to his knees in the snow.

It is possible to believe in the virgin birth and incarnation of the Savior and yet not be saved. Salvation does not depend upon affirming the creeds. "The demons also believe" (James 2:19). Salvation depends upon personally receiving the free gift of eternal life which God offers to you through His eternal Son who took on human flesh through the virgin Mary on that first Christmas, who offered Himself as the substitute for sinners on the cross. If God is truly with us in Christ, then we must come to God only through Christ.

Advent: God in the Commons

Matthew 1:18-25; 1 Corinthians 1:26-29

Most of us, if we were invited to serve on a planning committee to introduce the Messiah to the world, would try to make as big a splash as possible. We'd hire PR firms with all the trappings of glitz and glamour; we'd try to spin the press and have sensational pyrotechnics; we'd have crowds ready—paid for if need be—and we'd look for huge endorsements and celebrity power. We might even try to book our Messiah on a leading TV show. And we'd mean well in all that.

The Jews thought similarly and had done so for centuries. They awaited a dashing, handsome, ripped Messiah, who would courageously swoop in on a white stallion and lead the Jews back to their glory days. This Messiah would be the envy of the world, perhaps the first international Superstar.

We'd do all we could for optimal product placement: we'd try to place our Messiah amidst celebrities, with fans, wealth, radiance, and loyal followings. We'd seek headlines, bright lights, big cities, and pizzazz, wouldn't we!!

But God did not. He did not wrap Christ in the dazzling.

God placed the Messiah amidst the most common of circumstances, in the outback, and born to less than stellar parents at the point of conception. This year instead of seeking the grandiose, how about we look behind the amazing portrait of the birth of Christ in Scripture to see how many small details, how many common things show us the Lord. God may best be found in "the Small Stuff at Christmas" (a small book by Bruce Bickel and Stan Jantz—

Uhrichsville, OH: Barbour Publishing, 2007), and it all matters. As such, he is accessible to any who believe, and does not, thankfully, require any grandiose props.

Maybe we should begin with the OT prophecy's reminder that the Messiah would originate in Bethlehem of Judah, the LEAST.

The OT prophet Micah (5:2) predicted, "But to you Bethlehem . . . though you are small among the clans of Judah," the Messiah would come forth. It was not a large clan, but a small one from a small country. God chose to work through the least.

First of all, make sure you note that God's love is seen in the common gift at Christmas. God's love was not merely an idea or an intention—it is an expression of his character. "When we understand that God is love, we come to realize that it is in God's nature to give of himself. He gives to bless us, though that idea flies in the face of a prevalent belief that God is a vengeful or grumpy deity who delights in creating misery for us poor humans. Nothing could be further from the truth." (25) Of course, most of this bad view of God stems from the idea that we should blame him, instead of ourselves, for all the world's problems. Still his love is at the epicenter of Christmas as noted by the 19th century poet, Christian Rossetti:

> *Love came down at Christmas,*
> *Love all lovely, love divine:*
> *Love was born at Christmas,*
> *Star and angels gave the sign.*

Love is something very common and often known in the little details. Know God's love this Advent.

Second, God predicted this event for centuries—and these predictions were public knowledge, not secret or shrouded. Bible scholars recognize that there are dozens of OT prophecies. These, too, became so widely known that even Herod inquired about them. The birth of Christ was a sign of love; and it was a token that accidents do not govern history.

One mathematician put the odds of all OT prophecies converging on Christ this way: "Suppose that the State of Texas, some 267,000 square miles, could be covered 3 feet deep with silver dollars—7.5 trillion cubic feet of silver dollars. Only one of those silver dollars would be marked with a red X and buried randomly in that gigantic pile. Finally, a blindfolded man would be dropped from a plane anywhere over Texas and allowed to stumble around for days, knee deep in silver dollars, before he would be allowed to select just one coin. The odds that the man would select the silver dollar with the red X are the same odds as one man satisfying all the prophecies of the Messiah." (32)

Advent was not a secret; it was not hidden, or revealed only to the intelligentsia. It was broadcast for a long time and in public.

Advent is about the arrival of a person. If you're not familiar with the term advent, it comes from the Latin *adventus*, to arrive. Have you ever looked for a loved one to arrive—maybe as young children you knelt on the couch and looked out the window for grandpa and grandma or as a fiancé looks for his future spouse to get home from a long trip? The expectancy builds. This is all very common and normal.

So Advent is the looking for the arrival of Jesus Christ. This Christmas, will you slow down a bit to see this? Will you be home, waiting by a fire, to welcome the Lord when he comes? Will you jump up and run to the door when you see the signs of his approaching? God is known in things that common at Advent.

Glory to God is another big part of Advent. However, in practice we give God the glory "when we make God look good by our lives, our words, and our actions." (87) "Seeking glory for yourself is human; giving glory to God is divine." Mary knew and practiced this.

The birth of Christ also symbolizes something as normal as human 'hope.' Jesus is the hope of the nations, and hope is a human emotion known to many and needed if you've lost it.

- The child hopes for a particular gift and parents try their best to nourish that hope.
- A wife hopes for the return of her husband's affection—a common thing.
- A worker hopes for a year-end bonus.

Christmas is all about hope, the hope that God has not forgotten his promises and that he will save us. The sending of Jesus, so common in many ways, was God's way of renewing and rewarding hope—a needed ingredient for life. Our deliverer came in a diaper instead of with power and prestige. So, God gives hope that he can conquer even with the commonest of instruments. This Christmas, you can have hope in the future because of what God did in the past? And God may give you what you need in a package that is wrapped contrary to your expectation. "The hope of Christmas is the confident assurance that God is in control and knows what he's doing." (57)

The Lord Jesus also had a past like everyone else. He had ancestors who are listed in Matthew 1 (traced from Abraham, through David, Josiah, and Joseph) and Luke 3 (traced via Zerubbabel, Levi, Judah, Joseph, back through Noah, to Enoch and Adam). He did not arrive from outer space, nor from a test-tube concoction but just as every other human did. Jesus had a family, and that reminds us that God works through ours. Something as common as a family and a maternal birth shows us the full humanity of the Messiah. 'The humanity of Jesus means that he understands us; the deity of Jesus means he can save us.' (63)

Some of his ancestors even reacted like we commonly do. When God first announced to Elizabeth and Zechariah that John would be born, they reacted with so much trepidation that God has to say, "don't be afraid . . . God has heard your prayer.' God even appears amidst a case of infertility here and he provides. Joseph and Mary also reacted in fear from time to time, and with understandable worry. "Christmas is a time of miracles, so don't doubt that God has the ability to perform one . . . he may leave you speechless. (69)

And when Jesus was born to a virgin, God did not remove that virgin from the normal circumstances (complete with scorn) that would occur. She would be mocked—that happened—her family would have a hard time believing her—happened—why, Joseph would even have doubts. Done. This is what you'd expect if a 16-year old girl told you that she was pregnant with the messiah but had not had relations with a man. *The Bible does not fantasize—it realizes.* Her conception seemed preposterous, the gossip mill in Nazareth went into overdrive—blogs were filled with comments, Twitter messages were flying—and all she could do was trust God and trust her husband. Yet Mary neither complained nor failed to obey and follow God. She was the Lord's servant. She accepted difficult circumstances—that, too, is part of the common experience in Christmas. Are we ready to accept whatever it is that God brings us? You'll miss out on the Advent joy, as Mary would have, if you cannot see God in the details of difficulty as well as in the majesty of his miracles. Yes, we can have a rich and joyful Christmas with very little prosperity; Christ can be found in the common. For we, too, can carry with us—not physically as Mary did—the Messiah, and give him to all.

Joseph was an ordinary guy. He wasn't seeking notoriety or a place in history. He was a regular Joe (pun) who had few qualifications for greatness—he never expected to go down in history; he lacked the credentials of Zechariah, and as a tradesman and common laborer, he wasn't very successful or prosperous. His town, Nazareth was a crossroads on a trade route *enroute* to somewhere else. His family was poor, and his education was unspectacular.

"But in God's paradigm, credentials, qualifications, and past accomplishments are basically irrelevant. That's what God is looking for: ordinary, common people who simply obey when he calls them."

God cares more about your attitude than your aptitude.

- We should be more concerned about hearing God's call than the consequence that may befall.
- If you think that you are worthy to serve God, your ego probably disqualifies you from doing so.
- When you know you are incapable without God, then there is little argument about who should get the credit for the accomplishment.
- God often leads you to a destination you can't see from your current location. You'll only get better idea of where he is taking you after you start moving." (93)

At Christ's birth, God has the perfect PR opportunity—it was the celebrity birth of all eternity. . . . If God had wanted worldwide attention for his Son's birth, he could have picked the center of the known universe—Rome—the hub and commercial nucleus, or even Nazareth. But Bethlehem, why in that sleepy, little country town? Because God delights in bringing accomplishments into the small places and small details of life; it shows his power.

The shepherds were pretty common, too. God chose the shepherds to receive the greatest announcement of all time. By telling these who were so unsophisticated, he let it be known that no elitist education or exalted social status is required. Thus it is good news for all people. But the shepherds were unlikely candidates for carrying such news.

Thankfully, they were not shrewd enough to pull off a scam. "God delights in using people we consider less deserving. The good news of God is so simple you have no excuse for not believing it or sharing it. While the shepherds returned to work, they were still praising God for what they had seen and heard. Why do we stop praising God for what we've seen and heard by the time we get to our car in the church parking lot?" (154)

Christmas is also about a simple thing like joy. Joy overflows, by its nature, and it is so much longer lasting than momentary happiness.

Gift giving is also a common thing. We do this for birthdays, anniversaries, and many other occasions. At Advent, gift giving is a great token of love, and the wise men did this. At Advent, we see that God's gift exactly meets our deepest need. It cures our sin disease, and yet God's gift was not what we were expecting. That is part of the beauty of God's supreme gift—it's not what the Jews were expecting but it was what humanity needed for spiritual life and freedom.

And part of the richness of gift giving is that sacrifice was involved. This was not a gift that God hastily grabbed at a store on the way to the event. It wasn't cheap—it was infinite in value; and it was uncommon. That part of Advent was NOT COMMON: "That, O My God wouldst die for me." The best gifts are those that require a costly sacrifice. You might want to keep these in mind as you finish your shopping.

While it is true that 'it's not the gift but the thought that counts,' it is also true that most gifts illustrate the amount of thought involved. "A gift of your time and attention is more valuable than anything that can be wrapped. An inexpensive gift is irrelevant if the gift was thoughtfully chosen. A high price is meaningless if there was little thought involved." (201)

Matthew 1:21 reports that he was given a common name, a name that reminded people of Joshua, but his name Jesus fit in with those around him. It hardly stood out, but it meant, "he will save his people from sin." Our Lord was given a common, human name—not a divine name, although at his name, every knee shall bow tongue confess.

This year, look for God among the common: things like routines, regular shopping, regular church services, family traditions. There'll be several more days, many chances to get lost, and tons of opportunities to see how God comes into our common history and enriches it with his presence. It may not be the sensational or the spectacular that incubates the Lord of glory.

A Christmas devotional says: "God is in every detail of the Christmas season—the big and the small, the familiar and the obscure. You'll find him there encouraging you, challenging you, loving you. You'll find him invite you to slow down, stop stressing, and start living. You'll find him in Christmas" (for he designed it that way).

If that is true, why don't you:

(a) slow down this year to make note of it;
(b) After making notes of some things, seek to share these with workers and friends;
(c) By all means join us to worship and celebrate.

While some of our Puritan forebears did not celebrate Christmas—mainly because the Roman Catholic traditions had obscured Christ in the holidays, losing him in the details of various celebrations—it has always seemed hard for me to resist the urge to point to Christ in every way possible at this time of year, especially if the secular world awards us a month to do so. Yes, there is shopping, yes there is more traffic and more parties, there are pageants and gift wrapping, but most importantly, there is Christ, nestled in:

Common hay in a
Common stable, born to a
Common couple, with very little, made of fully human
Common DNA, surrounded and discovered by
Common workers.

Rather than being born in palatial grandeur to a power couple, our Lord was given to a lower middle-class family in an undistinguished part of Palestine at a time of great oppression, while taxes just kept going higher and higher.

The nativity scene, found in many homes, is a small, common piece of furniture—often used for year to year and stored. But it seeks to depict the baby Jesus who was God's eternal son, who'd resigned from heaven to take a celestial demotion to come to earth, assuming human form to save us. "Despite its comparatively bland appearance, the nativity scene is the premier Christmas decoration. It stands for the moment when God directly intervened into time and space to give us his Son. You don't get that kind of significance with a candy cane." (20) Yet the decorations in your house are not nearly as important as having Christ in your hearts.

Something small like a crèche can have that meaning. No wonder rebellious folks don't want to see its message.

God presented all this as a simple story in a very old book, which is easy to obtain. God didn't make a movie, a thumping soundtrack, or plan a weekend sports or film festival to introduce the Messiah. He told a story—one that is true and powerful, one that does not grow old, and one that has more impact than a legend. It's power is that, generation after generation find that it is true—that is describes us, that it shows us our need for redemption and who our Redeemer is. It is a story with great news.

Conclusion: 1 Corinthians 1: 26-29 clues us in to the mind of God. His plan was not to resort to the easy methods of using the wise, the influential, those of noble birth. In fact, God is so powerful as to be able to use the foolish, weakest, and most lowly things to humble the world, to nullify great powers so that no one can boast. *It's as if he spots all other leaders infinity, and still wins.* Bringing Jesus into this world in such commonality was how God chose to arrive. And it is typical of his greatness and grandeur. Let's not despise the day of small things, nor the common. Let us pray together that this year, we will see the God of Advent in the common things of life—not demanding stupendous signs.

All kinds of people went and told the story. Might you be one of those??

Are you already overstressed, behind on shopping, overspent, exhausted, tired, and wondering if you can make it to Christmas? And when the season is over, will you have anything good to remember about this year? Are you already frenzied, and your calendar filled up, with double bookings from today on? Do you feel like something is missing, an emptiness? It may be so because in this sacred time, you have no room . . .

> No room in your schedule
> No room for quiet and reflection
> No room for solitude
> No room to include someone around your table
> No room for Jesus . . . or others?

That's not the way you planned it.

No room in your schedule means no opportunity for Jesus to do something surprising in your life. No room for quiet and reflection means no chance for you to hear God's still, small voice in your thoughts. No room for solitude means no place for you to be alone with God. No room in your resources means no possibility that you will enjoy the blessing of giving to God's work. No room for Jesus means no way for you to truly appreciate Christmas.

In the midst of this flurry of activity, many of us try to remember the reason for Christmas. We do our best to stay focused on . . . the fact that Christmas celebrates the birth of Christ. Keeping Christ in Christmas can be difficult—not just because of much secularism. All cultural and political arguments aside, we simply live a fast paced life . . . and God often gets moved to the background. None of us plans that; it just happens. (8-9)

Maybe our prayer for each other might be that our hectic pace will be tamed so that we can see God in the details of this season. Remember his presence around you in the common things—slow down and peer into those, and you may find Christ more at the center of your holiday and more beautiful than ever. The details and common things of Christmas are rich.

Let's close with a Christmas favorite, "One Solitary Life" by James A. Francis.

> Here is a man who was born in an obscure village, the child of a peasant woman. He grew up in another obscure village. He worked in a carpenter shop until He was thirty, and then for three years He was an itinerant preacher. He never wrote a book. He never held an office.
>
> He never owned a home. He never set foot inside a big city. He never traveled two hundred miles from the place where He was born. He had no credentials but Himself.
>
> While still a young man, the tide of popular opinion turned against Him. His friends ran away. One of them denied Him. He was turned over to His enemies. He went through the mockery of a trial. He was nailed upon a cross between two thieves.
>
> His executioners gambled for the only piece of property He had on earth while He was dying -- and that was His coat. When He was dead, He was taken down and laid in a borrowed grave through the pity of a friend.

Twenty [Nineteen] wide centuries have come and gone and today He is the centerpiece of the human race and the leader of progress. I am far within the mark when I say that all the armies that ever marched, and all the navies that ever were built, and all the parliaments that ever sat, and all the kings that ever reigned, put together have not affected the life of man upon this earth as powerfully as that One Solitary Life."

God was in the commons. *"Let every heart prepare room." Then heaven and nature will sing.*

And store this away: "Christianity, if false, is not important. If Christianity is true, however, it is of infinite importance. What it cannot be is moderately important."-- C. S. Lewis

The Prophetic Names of Messiah

Isaiah 9:1-7

The words of Handel's *Messiah*, one of the greatest proclamations of the Gospel in music, echo with these words: Wonderful Counselor, Mighty God, Everlasting Father, the Prince of Peace.

These four terms echo in our ears the message of who Christ is and what he does. The OT predicts this is what his name will be called. And we should know him as such.

This is one of the oldest Advent prophecies. Coming from Isaiah who prophesied in and around Jerusalem around 730 BC (before the fall of the Northern Kingdom in 722). By the way, St. Augustine called Isaiah the 5th Gospel. So this points our attention to the Lord Jesus, and we see the good news in this passage. The gospel shines so brightly because Isaiah was speaking into such darkness and impending gloom. The brutal, inhuman, aggressive Assyrians were about to take over the promised land. And Isaiah sees the distress and suffering that was about to occur.

Isaiah spoke and ministered in a time of spiritual darkness. It was a time when truth was scarce (8:16) and superstition abounded (8:19). The distressed and hungry were to be found everywhere (8:21).

When the prophet Isaiah looks at the world he lives in, he sees so much darkness. He observes that the people of God have been infiltrated by heathen influences and no longer keep themselves pure and undefiled. He sees men, women, and children who refuse to serve and obey God. The people have lost God's way (vs 20); they consult mediums and spiritists (vs. 19). They either have made a deliberate decision to do without God in their lives or they have chosen to ignore Him. Whatever the case may be, these men, women, and children live in sin and in rebellion against God and his ways.

Isaiah also looks at the darkness in the public institutions of his day. He sees kings, rulers, priests, and prophets who are supposedly leaders in righteousness become the first to sin against God. He sees injustice and evil on the part of the rich and powerful against the poor, the widow, the orphan, and the alien. He sees false prophets and teachers that lead thousands astray with their lies and heresies. He sees that the land of Israel has been invaded and conquered by the hated, heathen Assyrians.

Isaiah sees a world filled with darkness, and he knows about Satan and his host of evil spirits and demons. He knows how they oppose God and His kingdom at every turn. He knows how they rejoice in lies, prejudice, arrogance, wrongs, and every form of sin.

Isaiah also knew the heart of man. He sees that darkness is there as well (Is 6:5). He knows that within himself, as within you and me and all people, there is sin, evil, and all sorts of desires that run counter to the will of God.

Darkness. Darkness everywhere. Deep darkness. Darkness that many times throughout history has threatened to prevail. But into this darkness comes a light.

For this prophet sees in the distance how God will bring the Savior who would deliver the people from this darkness and death. Isaiah saw that the need was not for a national or political Savior, for the real problems of humanity are not political or social. The real problem, from which we need deliverance is because we labor under sin. We are, as Isaiah knew, people of unclean lips and hearts. We have a darkness within us that is incurable from within us. We need God to come from outside and to change us.

Isaiah sees ahead to the Savior, over the present horizon. He will save us. And four descriptions of the Messiah are given to us here.

1. The Lord Jesus is our *Wonderful Counselor.*

He gives the wonderful, supernatural counsel. His advice is the very best.

a.   Jesus reveals himself as our Wonderful Counselor.

Isaiah 11 tells us that Jesus did not judge by what he viewed externally, but he peers into our hears. As John 2 told us, Jesus knew what was in man. Jesus saw inside the heart of Nicodemus, THE teacher of Israel who needed a savior. He had seen Nathaniel under a fig tree before Philip retrieved him. Then our Lord sees the deepest need of the woman in Samaria, who was offered living water, and he sees the deepest needs of a man who had been paralyzed for over 38 years.

Jesus is a wonderful counselor. This is as clear as anywhere with Simon Peter. Peter often said, "I don't need you," but he clearly did. And after his resurrection, Jesus asked Peter, "Do you love me?" Our Lord asked him this three times, and then, finally Peter answered, "Lord, Jesus, you know all things." Isn't that a sign of a wonderful counselor? Do you know Christ in this fashion?

Our wonderful counselor knows all things.

b.   Jesus is also a wonderful counselor in that:
He was trained to be such by his heavenly father. Later Isaiah sees God's child being trained. In Isaiah 52, Isaiah hears the Lord speaking about how God has trained his servant. Isaiah saw that the reason that Jesus is such a wonderful counselor to his people is because he has been where his people are. Jesus has known the struggles, the sufferings, the darkness of his people, and the father has been training him to be a counselor, who is wonderful—in the sense that he understands us from the inside and his counsel is not cold, metallic— he is not counsel-at-law but counsel, full of grace. He's been there.

- A person who has lost a loved one is such a counselor.
- A person who has been through by-pass surgery.
- A person who struggles with child-rearing can sympathize with another parent.

Long before the Child was ever born, long before the Son was given, Isaiah foretold that God was planning to send a Counselor for the brokenhearted people of the world. And long after Jesus' entrance into the world we can see that he personified the kind of counsel that will go out from Jerusalem in the last days.

- "He will teach us His ways, and we shall walk in His paths. For out of Zion shall go forth the law, and the word of the LORD from Jerusalem" (Isa. 2:3).

- ". . . the Spirit of wisdom and understanding" (Isa. 11:2).
- ". . . the LORD of hosts, who is wonderful in counsel and excellent in guidance" (Isa. 28:29).

It's appropriate, then, to ask ourselves whether we are as astonished at the wonder of a counselor as Isaiah was. Are we captivated by his insight and practical genius? Where else can we go to learn how to love, how to feel, how to live, and how to die? Where else can we be so assured of the acceptance and forgiveness and comfort of God? Where else can we look into a face that is the face of our Creator, Savior, and Counselor?

    c.   Jesus also continues to be a wonderful counselor through the ministry of his Word.

God's Word is brought to us here in our worship. What a precious fellowship when we forget the human voice and hear the voice of the Lord counseling our own hearts from the message. Our hearts may even burn within us.

During a sermon, we have this conversation with the Lord, as we say, "My, I had no idea; You mean you advise such-and-so?" And the Word of the Lord speaks to our hearts. This is what we need to look for together and to search for. If you're here today, searching for counsel, God provides!

Jesus Christ is that counselor. Isaiah knew this, and part of the promise of God is that Christ will be our wondrous counselor. Christ was born to be that Wonderful Counselor, and you should look to him today.

- A counselor is someone we can talk to about anything, and at any time.
- A counselor is there to help us make decisions.
- A counselor helps us confirm godly ideas and directions for our lives.
- A counselor is also there to help get us back on track, when we have lost our proper direction.
- And Jesus Christ is our Wonderful Counselor; He doesn't make mistakes like the rest of us.

Next Isaiah tells us that Christ is:

2. The Mighty God.

John (1 Jn. 3) tells us that the Son of God appeared in order to destroy the works of the devil. In order to be the Wonderful Counselor, the Everlasting Father, it is essential that our Lord also be able to deal with, overcome, and defeat anything that might thwart his purposes for our lives. All of nature, all that might destroy or mar us must serve Christ.

Isaiah saw this and knew that the Messiah would be mighty enough to deliver his people from their spiritual bondage. No mere political leader, nor a therapist does this; but the Mighty God.

God breaks all those bonds, he takes captive (as 9:4 shows) the Midianites and confiscates the boots and garments (9:5) of those who are conquered and casts them into a fire. This God shatters the darkness with light, and he overcomes powerlessness with his mighty power.

Isaiah knew that human beings are in such a state as to need this kind of Savior who can mightily change our lives—not merely instruct or lecture us, nor cheer us on, but One on the horizon who would inhabit and transform us.

He overcomes all that might stand in the way. His saving grace is MIGHTY.

Isaiah 9:4 speaks of the yoke that is removed from our shoulders. We are depicted as under a burden that crushes us. And Jesus comes to remove that burden. He knows that you need more than your own efforts, too.

Only Christ can remove sins. He is mighty in that regard; for there is a bondage that has been destroying and crushing us. God's people need Christ to break the power of reigning sin.

When this savior comes, as v. 3 notes, Joy breaks out. The Messiah, according to these verses, frees us from darkness (via counsel) and from bondage (via his might).

This is the way it was in John with Nicodemus: unless you are born from above, you cannot see the Kingdom of God. In his blindness, Nicodemus did not, at first, admit his own spiritual bondage. But he was like one of those defeated with Midian, their yoke was shattered and they were delivered. Messiah did that. He was mighty; and that produces freedom, peace, and joy.

Jesus healed people and told them to rise up and walk. That required power!! The Mighty God deals with my sin problem.

Psalm 24 asks, who is the king of glory? The answer: He is the king of glory, the Lord strong and mighty. He is able to overcome everything necessary for saving his people. Isaiah saw the coming of Jesus and he told us that he is the mighty God.

The yoke of sin burdens us, and the staff is heavy. Our sinfulness is a heavy burden that crushes us. Later, Jesus will invite: Come to me, you who are heavy burdened. You cannot keep the commandments by yourself. As such, you will stand crushed. However, if you've become conscious that you don't merely need better instruction but you need to receive his rest, there is hope.

When Jesus forgave the paralyzed man, let down through the roof, our Lord said, "Son, your sins are forgiven." That infuriated some people because they heard a claim of divinity. Who can forgive sins but God alone. Yes, Jesus can. He is the Mighty God, come to deliver us from the heavy yoke. And Jesus not only set the man free, but he also cured the paralysis and said, "take up your bed and walk."

Isaiah also knew that a bondage oppressed us. A staff has been laid on the people's shoulders. And the power of this sin must be broken by Someone else. And when that happens, people rejoice (see v. 3). The Mighty God is a complete Savior, who also destroys our bondage to darkness and gloom.

That bondage formerly blinded us to that grace in Jesus. That is our natural bondage. And it required a Mighty God to do away with this.

Isaiah also gives a hint about how Jesus saves us in the words, "The Lord will break the rod of the oppressor on the day of Midian." And particularly, "to us, a child is born, a son is given."

Midian's defeat refers to Gideon. Gideon's army was reduced from 32,000 to 10,000, and eventually to 300. And that small army overcame the military might and organization of Midian. The Lord demolished this powerful army with an army that had weak weapons. God uses things that may be small or weak to do his work. He used a child, a baby—with soft flesh, eyes wet from crying, and God conquers through this. The Lord uses the weak, the humble to overcome the proud, the smart, and the strong.

In the weakness and foolishness of our Lord, Jesus died in humiliation of the cross, bearing the judgment of the holy God against our sin. And he broke the power of cancelled sin.

And later when Jesus died, God showed his MIGHT. By his death, Christ accomplished atonement. The glory of the salvation of the Mighty God is seen on the face of the dying Savior and by the resurrection of the Mighty One.

The focus of Isaiah's prophecy is *El Gibbor*, the Mighty God who is our true Hero. What this prophet in the eighth century BC anticipated, the New Testament confirms. Because the Messiah would be God, He would have God's power. But to Isaiah, the amazing thing was that the Messiah would not only have the power of God, He would be the God of power!

To US a child is born. Martin Luther said, 'being a Christian means using personal pronouns. Do you know his birth for you?

3. The Everlasting Father.

Isaiah knew that the coming Savior would come first as the son, but would be the Everlasting Father.

To be the Wonderful Counselor, the Mighty God, and the Prince of Peace, as well as the Everlasting Father requires the Trinity! Christ is one with the Everlasting Father.

How can the eternal son also be called the Everlasting Father? Isaiah knew a little of this, although it was foggy at best. But Isaiah knew that our Savior was also our caring, comforting, providing Savior.

The paradox of the Savior who is the Son of God is that the offspring of the woman also is our Everlasting Father.

a. The Lord Jesus becomes to us as an everlasting father because he has been sent to father a new humanity.

Adam was our father; and his entire family has failed, is broken, and carries death. But Jesus sires a new family, a new race, and Jesus is not bankrupt like Adam.

The virgin birth signifies that Jesus is beginning a new race. And as John has already taught: to those who received in him and believed on his name, to them he gave the right to be the children of God, born not of the flesh, of the will of man, but of God.

The Everlasting Father came into the world to birth a new family.

b. As the Everlasting Father, he has promised never to leave us as orphans. In John 14 . . . Jesus promised to never leave his little family as fatherless. Once we're born again, we look to our Father who satisfies and provides.

If you love me, you will obey what I command. And I will ask the Father and he will give you another Counselor to be with you forever—the Spirit of truth. The world cannot accept him, because it neither sees him nor knows him. But you know him, for he lives with you and will be in you. I will not leave you as orphans; I will come to you." (John 14:15-18)

When we trust in Christ, we cease being orphans. Isaiah saw that the Messiah would adopt us into his family, and provide a home for us.

G. K. Chesterton said that the stable reminds us that God became homeless so that we might have a home and an everlasting Father, who not only starts a new humanity in the church, but also who will never cast us off like orphans.

c. Jesus is the continuing, everlasting father who will never leave you. He is the One who brings us into the family, and it is a blessed family.

Hebrews 2 has Jesus saying, "Here am I and the children have given to me." He takes his children and gives them to the father.

Are you at home with Jesus this Christmas? Is he your everlasting Father?

4. The Prince of Peace.

Many people long for peace at this time of year, but it is often a peace that does not flow from the manger. The angels originally announced Jesus' birth in association with peace. They, and Isaiah, knew that it was in Christ that true, lasting peace is found. He is called the Prince of Peace. The name "Prince of Peace" is the Hebrew *Shar Shalom*, which means "the one who removes all peace-disturbing factors and secures the peace." This automatically sets him apart from most human rulers whose reigns often depend on bloody conquest. His rule rests on a bloody sacrifice!

a. This name is given to remind us of our great need: that we need peace with God. We need to have hostilities cease between the Lord and sinners.

All the human hopes for peace, however, will not come about by the efforts of man—for we are bankrupt. When Jesus is announced as the Prince of Peace, that title reminds us that in and of ourselves, we cannot produce what we most deeply long for.

We have turned away to hatred, warring, hostility. Peace is not in our nature; it must come from outside of us. In our heart of hearts, we cannot produce peace by ourselves.

b. If the title reminds us of our deepest need, his birth announcement tells us that he can meet our deepest need. The angels sang of this, and reassure us that such peace is not found from our own resources but from the Prince of Peace. If there is to be real peace in our hearts, we must have: a Savior. And the sign is that the Savior will be born in poor, primitive cloths. The Prince of Peace came as a common baby.

c. His royal title reassures us that he will bring peace. Of the increase of his govt and of peace will see no end. The Lord is bringing peace to this world by bring folks to himself. Not only did he bear God's judgment but he also has the authority to rule over our lives and give them true peace.

We also need to have a Master to reign over us if peace with God is to remain.

Christ comes in humility and meekness, and he promises to take away our warring tendencies—which no one else can do—and bring peace.

Have you asked him to be your king, the king of peace? Those who trust Christ as their Mediator and Savior are given by God an assurance that flows out of a right relationship with Him. Once we are in Christ, the Prince of Peace shows us that He can bring peace wherever He rules. He can bring:

Peace in life's trials. "Peace I leave with you, My peace I give to you; not as the world gives do I give to you. Let not your heart be troubled, neither let it be afraid" (Jn. 14:27).

Peace in life's maturing process. "Now may the God of peace Himself sanctify you completely; and may your whole spirit, soul, and body be preserved blameless at the coming of our Lord Jesus Christ" (1 Th. 5:23).

Peace in life's victories. "The God of peace will crush Satan under your feet shortly" (Rom. 16:20).

Peace in life's relationships. ". . . endeavoring to keep the unity of the Spirit in the bond of peace" (Eph. 4:3).

Peace in life's witness. "The fruit of the Spirit is love, joy, peace, longsuffering, kindness, goodness, faithfulness, gentleness, self-control" (Gal. 5:22-23).

What a treasure is ours in Isaiah's predicted Messiah.

Now there are at least two lessons in this for us today, and those two lessons are this. First of all, Isaiah is reminding us that the salvation of sinners always produces joy in the hearts of God's people, because we ourselves are sinners who have been saved, and those who are sinners who have been saved rejoice when we realize our own salvation, and we take joy in the salvation of others.

What do you take most joy in? Well, Isaiah's reminding you that those who have been shown mercy take the greatest joy in God as they see Him work salvation in sinners, as sinners are converted to Him. Do we take joy in that? Is our deepest joy in God, and in the salvation of sinners?

And if so, how does that show itself in our living? How will it show itself as we celebrate this holiday season? Will we celebrate this season of the year in sharing the gospel with others . . . friends and family who don't know Jesus Christ? Will we share the gospel with neighbors and fellow workers? Will we have a deep joy and concern when we see those who were lost found by Jesus Christ, and enfolded into His family and pardoned for their sins? Will we celebrate our own redemption, whether it was this year or last year, or fifty years ago, with joy in our hearts? Do you remember when you first knew the forgiveness of your sins? Do you remember the joy that dawned in your heart when you realized that you would stand before God acquitted and accepted, not because of anything in you, but because of what the Lord Jesus Christ had done for you? Do you remember that joy? Do you experience that kind of joy in seeing others come to Christ? And thus, do you invest your life and your resources so that they might?

- These four names are four ways in which Christ *is known and to be made known.*
- In each name one of the two words always emphasizes the human side of the Messiah's rule and the other the God side.

Wonderful Counselor is a GUIDING name.

Mighty God is a POWERFUL name.
Everlasting Father is a TIMELESS name.
Prince of Peace is a COMFORTING name.

Why all the Joy?

Matthew 1 and Luke 1-2

Missionaries Wayne and Amy Newsome were here recently. They talked about how Christmas was celebrated in Japan and among Muslims. Even there, folks sing "Joy to the World" and "Silent Night."

There are many possible moods and emotions that Christmas might produce. Some of us associate Advent with our childhood, it's excitement and joy. We think back to those good times, those times of surprise and love, the times when our parents stunned us with joy because of their love, and we love God for all the memories. It's really quite nice to do as Mary did, and treasure up things in our hearts to ponder. A time of reflection as another year draws to its close is in order, and some people are already moving, at this time, into a new year. Others react to this holiday with an understandable sadness; a dear loved one or a spouse has been taken away, and no holiday is the same. Still others, react with an irritability that shows that they have too much to do and have not gotten it done. And there are many other possible reactions to the birth of Christ, including a loathing of the Incarnate Son of God, as Herod exemplifies.

But most people find that one of the most persistent emotions for Christmas is joy, a simple human release and reaction to goodness or blessing. Not incidentally, the Advent narratives in Matthew 1 and Luke 1-2 turn up a large number of references to joy. Perhaps it will help all of us to review these briefly and see why joy is so appropriate. That may also help us appreciate all the celebration and song.

Why did these various persons or parties have such joy? Let's survey these in order.

It may help to have a short review of where Malachi left off (see sermons below from Malachi) to appreciate the context better. Israel had been straying for a long time. She sought to argue with God that she was really faithful. He knew better and brought a lawsuit against her to prove his case. That is followed by over four centuries of silence. Then, the gospels burst onto the scene.

The first characters introduced in the Advent narratives are: *Elizabeth,* Mary's cousin, and *Zechariah.* In Luke 1, the theme of joy is introduced when the angel reveals to Zechariah that his wife will have a son. Elizabeth had been barren, and now God was going to open her womb in an unexpected way. The angel of the Lord appeared to Zechariah as he was serving in the Temple, and told him that Elizabeth would bear a son and that he should be named John. In Luke 1:14, that same angel said, "he [John the baptizer] will be a *JOY* and delight to you and many will rejoice because of his birth. The joy was not merely because this couple would start their family, it was because John would be "great in the sight of the Lord" (1:15) and "bring back many to the Lord their God. And he will go on before the Lord in the spirit and power of Elijah to turn the hearts of the fathers to their children and the disobedient to the wisdom of the righteous—to make ready a people prepared for the Lord." (1:16-17). Zechariah was amazed, and like Abraham of old, he did not know how all this could happen, and he even doubted a little.

Later, however, the birth of John would unfold just as the angel said, and Zechariah would note the following—as soon as his tongue was untied for his doubting—in his psalm at the end of Luke 1, he said, "Praise be to the Lord, the God of Israel (1:68). God has redeemed his people, shown mercy to our fathers, remembered his covenant, rescued us from our enemies, and God "enables us to serve him without fear in holiness and righteousness." Surely, those truths evoke and produce elation.

Why the joy in this psalm? Because Zechariah knows that God is at work, he never forgets his promises, and the joy that God gives is superior to any of life's difficulties or challenges.

The next people to express joy are: *Mary and Joseph,* particularly Mary; cf. her psalm in Luke 1.

An angel reveals to Mary that God is supernaturally working in her, too. She goes to visit her relative, Elizabeth. As soon as Mary enters, Elizabeth's babe leaps in her womb, and the Scripture tells us that John was filled with the Holy Spirit from that moment, certainly a comment that indicates that children can be touched by God early on. Elizabeth seemed to know that Mary was the "mother of my Lord," (1:43) a pretty stunning term to use for any family member. God had obviously revealed much of his plan to her, and not only does she react in joy, but even her babe "leaped for **joy** in her womb" (1:44)

That gives rise to Mary's psalm in Luke 1:46-55, which begins with a reference to her soul glorifying the Lord and "My spirit *rejoices* in God my Savior."

Why does she express such joy? Because she understands God's plan of salvation and knows what he is doing, she affirms that life is more than the events of this past week. She knows that eternity is real and waiting. Mary praises God that he cares for the humble who seek him. She rejoices because the son that she will nurture, the baby that she will cradle and sing to, is the Savior of the world, the one who will bless all generations (v. 48). God performs mighty deeds (51)— and that gives rise to the believers' joy. Even with the difficulty ahead, Mary's spirit rejoices, she rejoices in God my Savior. Few of us will have a more difficult nine months than young Mary.

And don't forget how Scripture portrays the: *Shepherds.*

These were the first to hear the announcement that Christ had been born. The glory of God accompanied the heavenly messengers as they brought greetings to these humble shepherds. They reacted in understandable fear. Then note what Luke 2:10 tells us: Don't be afraid—the spectacle of heavenly messengers itself was enough to produce a fear-overload among these shepherds—the news the angels bring is "good news of GREAT joy." Once again, the joy is great, even for the humble in society, and it also bore promise to be good news for many people. The Savior, born in the city of David, produced *joy.* It told the working class and societal outcasts that God's love was large enough to embrace all of them. God's love was so great and deep that it reached the lost.

The *Angels* themselves were the bearers of joy. We tend to think of these as super-humans, but the angelic messengers are really quite different in nature. These spiritual beings rejoiced in the good tidings of God, but for reasons different than our own. These angels were not fallen. They do not need a Redeemer. Thus, their joy was not personal or related to their eternal destiny. The joy of the angels stemmed from their fellowship with the Triune God. They had long been preparing to serve God. For centuries the various angelic messengers had been announcing, intervening, and assisting God's saints. They had, to some degree, some idea about what was coming. Now, after all the previous history, they were giving the long-awaited herald. The angels brought these glad tidings of great joy, and they realized what a boon this would be for the world. They rejoiced not only over the glory of God—which was their highest concern—but also over the peace that God was bringing to those on earth on whom his favor rested.

There's another part of this cast that is not always associated with joy, but there had to be some thrill dwelling in them. Consider the: *Wise men.*

What are these guys? I wish I could tell you for sure, and commentators are divided as to who they are. Some think they were Babylonian astrologers, others think they were followers of the Zoroastrian religion, and still others think of these are petty-rulers, who followed the zodiac on the side. Most likely, all the various legends can't be true at the same time. This much, though, we can say: they were non-Jewish believers— [perhaps Arabs]. Note what they did?

They travelled, they took the OT seriously and interpreted the prophecies, and they were looking for the Messiah.

What is their reaction: it is 3-fold, (a) overjoyed, (b) worship, and (c) gave gifts.

God is also a character who rejoices.

Of course, by speaking of God as a character, I do not mean to insinuate that he is a human character. Still, he is the animating force behind all this. God sent his son, as I shared last week, at just the right time. And as he did so, there was commitment to fulfill his eternal covenant. But this was not a pure act of drudgery. Even the Incarnation betokened some joy on the part of God the Father. Why joy? Because he would be reunited with the Son from the Easter Resurrection onward and because Christ was dying for the people loved by the Father. There was joy in knowing that the effective power to save was great enough to conquer any and every fear. God was, somehow even though incomprehensible, joyful in this birth.

Jesus; took on our flesh not due to compulsion but voluntarily. John indicates that no one took his life from him but he gave it up for us freely. Jesus laid down his life as a sacrifice and there is always joy in serving God, even if it is very painful. Also, recall that Heb. 12:1-3 explains, "for the *joy* set forth before him . . ."

The Rev. Bill Harrell's Dec. 2002 Newsletter observed: "The NASV uses the word joy 182 times. Most of those references are in the OT, where physical exuberance is prominently associated with joy. The fewer NT refs to joy are remarkable for their lack of association with such demonstrative exultation. . . . The Apostle Peter describes the Christian's joy as inexpressible and full of glory (1 Pet. 1:8). By the word, inexpressible (or unspeakable in the KJV), we usually understand that the cause we have to rejoice in our salvation is so great that no amount of laughing, clapping, leaping in the air, or shouting could fully express it. This understanding, of course, is true. Yet, I suggest that it is a fuller understanding of the words inexpressible and unspeakable when we acknowledge that for the Christian, there are silent depths to the glorious and substantial joy he has in Christ.

It is often remarked that there is no account in Scripture of Jesus having laughed, but that hardly implies a joyless Jesus. For Jesus speaks of his joy being in his disciples, thus making their joy full (Jn. 15:11). He prays in his high priestly prayer that his disciples may have his joy made full in themselves (Jn. 17:13). The writer of Hebrews speaks of Jesus having endured the cross for the joy set before him, meaning not a distant carrot dangled from a stick but rather that Jesus was filled with joyful anticipation at every moment and juncture of his earthly life.

The fact is that Jesus contained within himself the fathomless source and immeasurable substance of true joy. Those in Christ who possess the genuine joy of the Savior will not [necessarily] be given to glib laughter and giddy excitement. They will maintain within themselves a quiet and strengthening joy, which is a fruit of the Spirit (Gal. 5;22), whereby they may find delightful dimensions in their pleasures as well as in their trials (Jas. 1:2). True Christian joy is a deep taproot that anchors the soul through the storms and calms of life in the glorious victory of Christ.

We should not mistake shallow and transient happiness, which depends upon pleasing circumstances, for the enduring joy of the Lord that gives us enduring strength in the most severe trials. . . . The true joy of the Lord imparts to us a nobly serene and humbly grateful deportment, indicating our confident assurance that we are possessed by divine grace and are bound for indescribable glory, because our God has provided the salvation he had for ages past promised."

In conclusion: Who had no joy?

Herod, the king who was so taken with his power and who feared all rivals could not enjoy the birth of the Messiah.

Herod had no joy. He did not believe and refused to embrace God's will. What an example of bitterness within the narrative of Christmas. With all the singing, the rejoicing, yes, it is possible for some to be so despondent, so self-absorbed that they cannot rejoice in God's goodness and provisions. If you ever find yourself tempted in this direction, don't let the Herod syndrome get you.

This year at Advent, know *The Joy of Deliverance.*

Part of the robust meaning of Christmas is that God has provided a way out. Much of the OT is filled with the symbolism of the Exodus. When baby Jesus was whisked away to Egypt after his birth, there is another deliverance. We are delivered from our sin. When Christ was born, that gave us liberation, freedom, our chains were snapped off. The feeling of that, almost like a narrow brush with death, brings joy. It is far better than a deliverance after final exams, better than an exultant athletic victory, more serendipitous than receiving a great gift.

Think of the feeling of escaping something bad coming your way. The joy of deliverance should be fully enjoyed at this time of year. Don't rob yourself of this joy that God intended you to have.

The joy of Christmas is not totally different from the joy that Abraham had when he got back his son Isaac. Israel at the time of the Exodus flew away from the evil, and sang praises to God.

You and me? Should we not slam on the brakes to know God's joy at this time of year? Should we not put some things aside, reprioritize and rediscover the simple joy that was shared by folks like these shepherds, this impoverished young couple, and the angels in heaven?

God seems to think that we need to stop, and gaze at an infant, to see how humility is blessed and how ordinary weakness conquers. God is that strong!!

The Christmas season affords an opportunity to rid the heart of sadness and gloom. Hope brightens and whitens all that it touches. The Bethlehem manger is much, much more than a historical milestone; it is an unfolding promise to all who believe. Jesus is the Gift who keeps on giving. The Christian can rejoice in things eternal, even when temporal circumstances are difficult.

The joy of Christmas is to be found in a spirit of generosity. We need to reaffirm the sacred foundation that supports the gift-giving tradition of the Christmas season. While we should not be carried away to excessive debts and pride-driven spending, we should exercise generosity in deed and spirit as a true celebration of Jesus. Remember that the gift is always a token of the heart. Most gifts are soon broken, used and forgotten, but a loving, giving heart endures the tests of time. Shouldn't we give the gift of joy at this time of year?!

Unless we reinvest Christmas with its glorious message and meaning, the holidays will pass like a pagan festival. Unless we truly celebrate Christ, the greatest story ever told will be lost amid the bells, bows and baubles. Make your holiday a holy day. Add another seat or two at your table. Set free whatever grudges or ill will you would hold on to. Sing the carols at the top of your voice. Tell Christ's story with thanksgiving and awe. Wrap every present in love. You are the reason Jesus came. No one has more cause to celebrate than you do. Rejoicing is definitely in order.

Counting the Miracles of Christmas

Luke 1:37

Christmas is nothing if it is not miraculous. The preponderance of miracles is at the center-stage of Christmas. Miracles are so central to the Christmas texts that if one subtracted all of the miraculous passages, there would be very little left to the birth narratives.

That is, in fact, what some theologians did about 100 years ago. Let me tell you a very, sad Christmas story. It is about the Miracle-Less Christmas.

When vintage liberal theology was in its inception, it denied that the biblical miracles were true. "Surely," this skeptical theology said, "these accounts were written by pre-scientific, mythological people, who don't know as much as we moderns. Why, we, living after the dawn of modern science, know that there could be no such thing as a genuine miracle. Every occurrence has a natural explanation," therefore these verses that speak of miracles must be discounted because of their superstition.

These are the theologians who cast a green bead if they believe the verse is authentic, a red bead if they deem it not to be a saying of Jesus, or a yellow bead if they wish to view it as partially true but helpful.

The result is that there was very little reckoned to be true and authentic in the biblical test. So Christmas was stripped. This method, when applied to the resurrection narratives, led one famous theologian (R. Bultmann) to say, "We know very little about the first Easter."

Why, the normal reader might ask, when there are 8-10 chapters in the Bible on the Resurrection, can we know very little? The answer is because a particular theological approach takes an unauthorized red pen and arrogantly slashes out any miracles from the outset. When all this hacking and cutting is done, there is very little left.

That approach has also been used toward these Nativity narratives. These same theologians and their disciples said from the outset: "There can be no miracles. Therefore, excise any miracle verse from Luke 2 and Matthew 1. Hence all of the angelic appearances, the miraculous conceptions, the Virgin birth itself, the guiding star, the Magi, the Shepherds, Mary and Joseph had to be summarily edited out. All because the Liberal Faith honored the status quo of man's limited knowledge more than God's Revelation. And Christmas became empty. Emil Brunner, a mid-20th Century theologian said, "The doctrine of the virgin birth would have been given up long ago were it not for the fact that it seemed as though dogmatic interests were concerned in its retention." (Cited in Berkhof, 336). In place of the miracles of God, the Liberal Faith substituted good deeds, stories of philanthropy, and an emphasis on 'Peace and Good will to all.' Rather than the focus being on the miraculous birth of our Savior-Redeemer, all this skeptical sect—which by the way fills the majority of pulpits in America and the democratic West—had was a slim hope, a very slim one, that people would just happen to be nice at some season and cordial to one another, out of the phantasmic innate goodness of their heart. Hence, the miracle-less Christmas, stripped of its essence, focused on human peace and good intentions.

Subtract the miracles from Christmas and you have almost nothing. Here's what the anti-miraculous NT would say about the Birth of Christ, in place of Luke 2:1-21:

> There was once a Roman ruler, named Caesar Augustus. He may have taken a census, while King Herod was the Jewish Ruler. It is possible, though not definitive, that there was a young man named Joseph (a common name) and a young maiden named Mary. She was pregnant and had a baby who may have been placed in a manger because poverty was great in the area at the time, and the Jews were oppressed. And, being in a pastoral region, there were probably shepherds living out in the fields in the vicinity, keeping watch over their flocks.

And the naturalistic Christmas, devoid of miracles, ends abruptly. That's about it—No miracles, No supernatural occurrences, No divine birth; No Savior, and No redemption that comes out of that.

All that is left to the Nativity narratives is to express valuable lessons in mythical form. For example, Zechariah and Elizabeth are represented in the narrative as older folks because new ideas supposedly come up only when the ideas from which they sprang are old and powerless. Zechariah was dumb because the priestly wisdom of Israel was dumb in the failure to believe in Christ. The Magi are the crown of the mythical representation, symbolic of the role of giving in the new religion. Herod was the symbol of worldly power— corrupt and immoral.

Not much to get excited about, huh? Much less enough to sustain a tradition of worship.

Subtract the miraculous from Luke 2 or any other passage, and you remove not the peripheral but the *central* message of the Bible.

In this chapter and at this Christmas I hope you'll review the Nativity narratives with me and apprehend the miracles like you've never seen them before. I want you to run through these familiar opening chapters of Luke and Matthew and count the miracles of Christmas.

#1. Make the first miracle of Christmas all the fulfilled prophecies of the Messiah's Birth. There are over 20 separate OT prophecies about Christ's birth.

It was prophesied that he would be born of a virgin; that he would be from the tribe of David; that he would be born in Bethlehem; that he would be known as Immanuel, etc. The odds of these happening regarding the same person are astronomical.

Open you Bibles and turn to Luke 1 to count the miracles that preceded Christmas. Make a list sometime if you wish.

#2. In Luke 1:13 an angel appeared to Zechariah, Jesus' uncle. Angels are not every day occurrences. They don't just become visible and speak to us each day of the week. We believe in the unseen and that angels are real, but it is a miracle anytime one appears to a person. An angel appeared to Zechariah and spoke to him.

#3. In the next verse is the 3rd miracle. The angel said to Zechariah that Elizabeth would carry a child. Zechariah and Elizabeth were advanced in years, possibly not as old as Abraham and Sarah in the OT, but still past normal child-bearing years (1:7). The announcement was given that Elizabeth would bear a son and that he would be named 'John.' (1:13)

#4. The next miracle is that John the Baptizer would be filled with the Spirit from birth (1:15). This does not happen to most newborns—at least none of ours. We pray that our children will be filled with the Holy Spirit, but John was from birth. This human life in the womb was capable of this.

Zechariah was a little befuddled. Was this true of just his imagination? Was he really going to have a child or was this just his 'wish.' He asked God for a sign of authenticity and God gave him one in v. 20 that will be the 5th miracle.

#5. God said that Zechariah would be dumb until John is named. Zechariah could speak but God miraculously stopped his speaking ability. Usually we think of miracles as only that which is good, but Zechariah loses his speech. Now some might think that to be a good miracle for a preacher, but God did this to give him a sign.

The scene in Luke 1 now shifts to Mary. In Luke 1:28 an angel appears to Mary. That's a separate Angel and a separate visit and we won't even count that. In v. 30, the angel tells Mary that she will give birth to a son named Jesus and that he will be the Messiah.

#6. Mary had not had relations with a man and this prophecy is that her son will be "son of Most High" and "heir of David." This is a sheer miracle.

#7. The next miracle is in Luke 1:41-42. When Mary greets Elizabeth the Babe in Elizabeth's womb jumps and Elizabeth was filled with the Spirit. The miracle is that Mary's simple salutation can have such impact. God was surely and miraculously at work here in the infilling of Elizabeth with the Holy Spirit.

The key verse of this chapter is 1:37: "For nothing is impossible with God." God can overcome any natural barrier or any obstacle to work his plan. He can do a miracle whenever he needs to. He can make a virgin pregnant or strike a speaker dumb or whatever. He can even cause the 2nd person of the Trinity to be born of human flesh. God works miracles at Christmas.

#8. The next miracle is when Zechariah's speech is restored in Luke 1:63. When asked the name of his son, Zechariah wrote, 'John.' The people were amazed. Why not Zechariah Jr. or some other good family name. What is this John business? At least he could have been named John the Jew or John the Presbyterian instead of John the Baptist. The miracle in all this is that God fulfilled his word prophesied back in 1:13.

#9. The final miracle of this chapter is the Holy Spirit in-filling Zechariah in 1:67 which led to the prophecy in vss. 68-79.

#10. With these miracles briefly noted in Luke 1, turn over to Matthew's gospel, which focuses more on Joseph. Again, we see the presence of Angels. In Matthew 1:20, an angel of the Lord appears to Joseph in a dream. This angel speaks to him by name, explains the miraculous conception and tells Joseph about Jesus' birth. This angelic appearance is the *10th miracle* of the birth narratives.

#11. The next miracle is that God leads the Magi from the East to Jerusalem via miraculous astronomical phenomena. The Guiding Star deviated from any normal manifestation to lead these wise men. That miracle doesn't happen every day. First of all, stars don't move out of their place; secondly, if they do that, they don't stop over a manger. This star led the Magi and guided them to Christ's birth place, and there they worshipped and gave gifts.

#12. They then were miraculously warned to avoid Herod and go back by way of a different route.

#13 The miracle is that another angel comes to Joseph and tells him to flee to Egypt to escape Herod's wrath. Joseph obeys and this miracle removes Jesus from the Slaughter of the Innocents. Then after Herod dies, the angel again tells Joseph to return to Nazareth. Angelic and miraculous leadings pervade the Christmas history. Angels, by the way, appeared 3 times to Joseph, and also to Zechariah, Elizabeth, Mary, and the shepherds—totaling 7 times in these verses.

#14. Back to Luke 2. The Virgin Birth itself is recorded there. This is undoubtedly the greatest of Christmas miracles. Every Ob-Gyn today will tell you that a Virgin Birth is a biological impossibility. Naturally speaking, that is true. But God the Author and Creator of Biology may supercede his own laws at his own command. Regardless of what anyone says, or what the current state of obstetrics is, God's Word says that Jesus was born of a Virgin. Believe it. Machen said: "As a natural phenomenon the virgin birth is unbelievable; only as a miracle, only when its profound meaning is recognized can it be accepted as fact." (218)

#15. The 15th miracle involves the shepherds. They were tending their flocks and here comes another angel. An angel appears to them and tells them where they can find the Messiah. They go to Bethlehem and sure enough they find the baby. God has miraculously told them the great news and led them to the manger. They then go to tell others this good news.

#16. Finally remember that not only were there several individual angels involved but at one point (2:13) there is a great army of angels who gather together to sing Glory to God in the highest.

There are at least 16 separate miracles in these chapters, probably more if you go back and scrutinize.

All around the birth narratives, we see angels, prophecies, the miraculous, the Holy Spirit's infilling, the Virgin Birth, and untold signs and wonders. Miracles are at the heart of Christmas. Christmas is saturated with the miraculous. The only sensible conclusion is that God desires to use miracles to draw attention to the paramount birth of our Savior. In 1923, J. G. Machen noted, "When we examine the narratives in themselves, one fact . . . stares us in the face. It is that the content of the narratives is strikingly supernatural; the NT accounts of the birth and infancy of Jesus are suffused with the miraculous . . . the miracles are really central." (VB, 210-211)

With God nothing is impossible. He may and did use any number of miracles to accomplish his purpose.

This is not only historically true, but it is also true today. We don't have to experience these personally in order to benefit from them. Let me suggest four applications of this.

(1) First, accept the 'miraculous' as part of your theory of knowledge. Do not rule out the miraculous. Every scientist studies the natural, but the scientist who is a Christian is also convinced of the supernatural. Normally, this scientist makes conclusions based on what occurs in nature but a biblical view of the world means that God can intervene and work miracles. Christianity is fundamentally supernatural and presupposes the miraculous. Don't ever adopt a theory of knowledge that excludes the miraculous from the outset.

Norvel Geldenhuys writes: "He who believes that God is really the Almighty Creator and Preserver of the whole creation will have no difficulty in believing that He has intervened miraculously in the course of human history. Such a person realizes that, although God as a God or order will not act 'contrary to nature,' or violate His own laws, nevertheless, where it is necessary for His glory and for the spiritual well-being of mankind, he acts in a supernatural manner by bringing into play higher laws than those with which we are human beings are familiar. Especially with the coming of Christ into the world it is the most natural thing that God Almighty should by these supernatural means announce and display the greatest of all events in the history of mankind—the incarnation of Christ for the salvation of the lost." (on *Luke*, 72)

(2) Second, don't surrender Christmas to the naturalists or secularists. Christmas is radically supernatural . . . or it is nothing. Don't let the message of Christmas be kidnapped by non-Christians. Depend on its miraculous nature and publicly speak up for these miracles. Don't be silent, passive, nor retreating under the onslaught of those who disbelieve in miracles. Christmas carols, for example, can be widely played and if you choose sound ones, they proclaim the gospel. Think: We don't play, "Up from the Grave He arose" in April in the malls, but we do play "He rules the world with Truth and Grace," in those same public sectors in December. How might you help in gospeling by carols?

At Christmas time, seize the opportunities to include the miraculous in your explanation of Christmas. Don't abandon the miracles at the heart of Christmas, and don't let your family have a secular Christmas.

(3) Third and positively, witness to the miracles of Christmas. Tell your children and families about these miracles. When you hoist the little ones on your shoulders to see the passing parade, tell them this is about Jesus who changed everything and who is miraculous. Don't assume they know all there is to know about Christmas. Also, at a family gathering, raise the question about miracles. And challenge your non-Christian friends to explain the origins of Christmas or to explain its meaning apart from these miracles. Use this season to plan a doubt in the unbeliever's mind. Hold up and champion these true miracles as a platform to point people to Christ. That's why God designed these miracles in the first place.

(4) Fourthly and finally, make sure that you remember what great lengths God went to in order to provide our Savior. God hurdled countless natural barriers to send our Redeemer. He overcame inherited sin by the Virgin Birth. He overcame Herod's sabotage with Angelic miracles. He overcame Joseph and Mary's reticence to believe. He hurdled all the natural law which supposedly prohibit the Infinite from becoming the Finite. He shattered the categories and human limits and natural laws . . . all for one purpose, i. e., to save his people. *For God so loved that he sent.* And he used miracles to go to extreme lengths to provide the Atonement and save his people. Appreciate our Great God's un-necessary but free condescension to reach us—while we were still sinners. And God is still doing the miracle of changing the human heart.

Count the miracles this Christmas. Add them up. If they are myths, then dismiss Christ and Christmas. But it they are true miracles then listen to God's Word this Christmas like you never have before. Count the miracles this Christmas.

The excellency of God in Advent was expressed in this hymn by Ambrose of Milan (340-397):

Savior of the nations, come, Virgin's Son, make here thy home!
Marvel now, O heav'n and earth, That the Lord chose such a birth.
Not of flesh and blood the Son, Offspring of the Holy One;
Born of Mary ever blest God in flesh is manifest.

Wondrous birth! O wondrous child of the virgin undefiled!
Though by all the world disowned, Still to be in heav'n-enthroned.
From the Father forth he came and returneth to the same.
Captive leading death and hell, High the song of triumph swell!
Thou, the Father's only Son, Hast o'er sin the vict'ry won.
Boundless shall thy kingdom be; when shall we its glories see?
Praise to God the Father sing, Praise to God the Son, our King.
Praise to God the Spirit be Ever and eternally.

The First Christmas Carols

Luke 1:46-55, 67-79

Music is a large and normal part of the Christian life. If Scripture is accurate—and it is in every instance—our singing of praise will continue into heaven, and angels and elders fall down around the throne and continue to praise God.

In general some people underestimate the power and role of music, thinking that it is insignificant as a matter of worship or praise. It is not. When God's Word is annexed to music, the message and song are both enhanced. Some of our moments of highest worship are those in which we sing God's praises from the very depths of our hearts. When heart, mind, and voice combine, powerful praise results.

During Advent, that is very important. We listen to our Choir's special music, and we sing those great carols. The practice itself of singing praises in honor of Christ's birth dates all the way back to the biblical narratives themselves.

Today, as we continue to reflect on the attitudes we should have at Advent, I want to point out to you the earliest carols in the NT. Without going into a lot of details, there are two lyrical pieces in Luke 1. And although the literal word "sang" does not occur in either of these, it is clear to anyone who knows the least bit about Hebrew poetry, which this is, that these could be sung and, in fact, carried a unique Hebrew rhythm.

Note: the earliest songs were those which were used in praise of God. The entire collection of the 150 psalms is the Hymnal of ancient

Israel. God not only wants us to sing to him and sing his praises mightily, but as in so many other areas, he did not leave us without direction as to how to do that. God left us a self-contained hymnbook within the scripture, if we would see it aright. The Psalter is another token of God's loving-care for his church, as he did not leave her without musical expressions of praise. He guides us even in that.

God wants music to glorify him, and to build up his people. He did not leave that to chance, nor fail to reveal how we should worship him in this important area.

Today, let's remember these two hymns, and distill from them the attitudes we should have at Advent. The first hymn is in Luke 1:46-55, with the second (by Zechariah) in vss. 67-79. And they have some parallel features, each stressing similar themes. If I were arranging these, I'd classify the five stanzas, which are common to both hymns, as follows:

I. Awe/praise at the attributes of God.

a. 49-51a. As for her song, Mary praises God for being "The Mighty One who has done great things," the holy one (49). He is characterized by mercy (50), and he performs mighty deeds (51a)

b. Likewise, Zechariah praises God as the redeemer (68), merciful (72), faithful to his covenant (72-73), the Most High (76). These psalms of praise focus on the attributes of God. They are written to honor and praise God, not the sentiment, opinion, nor achievement of man. They ascribe praise to our great God. That is the hallmark of any hymn acceptable for worship, and it is a characteristic of the best of Christmas carols. Note, as we see them, how frequently they praise the attributes of God. The earliest and the best Christmas carols are songs in praise of the character of our God.

A second theme contains a twist of irony. God is always doing the unexpected, as far as worldly expectations go. Contrary to the standard operating procedure of the world, he does not always work with the strong, the powerful, or those who believe they have a right to honor. In fact, in both of these two earliest Christmas carols we see:

II. Reversal of worldliness: humility.

a. Mary, in vss. 51-53 sings praise to God for how he scatters the proud, particularly those who are proud in their inmost, secret thoughts. Those today who are secretly proud must fear the Lord in light of this. God has brought down rulers, those who thought their thrones immune from the scope of God's sovereignty (52). Instead He has lifted up the humble. Also, in v. 53 of Mary's carol, God has sent the rich away empty, but filled the hungry with good things. This is more how God works, than to think of him as going along with the proud-but-powerful.

That may be the way the world does things. It may be the normal operating procedure to cater to the "best and the brightest," but God works according to a different plan. He's not impressed by the best or the most splendid of human power. It is nothing to him. And he consistently opposed the proud, but lifts up the humble. Mary praises him for this, and counts herself as an object lesson in the way God works. God did not choose an earthly princess, nor a daughter of prominence to bear his own son. He did not choose the accomplished, but the humble. He's working in our lives that way as well.   Maybe you're one of those humble.

b. Zechariah, now cured of his doubt learned the same thing. In his carol, he counts himself blessed to be among those to whom mercy is shown (72) and sings of the God who rescues us from the hand of our enemies (74). This Advent, become more personally convinced of and familiar with how God works to reverse worldliness and promote humility. As exemplified by the birth of our Savior, the first shall become last, and the last shall become first. In fact, we would do well to recall that year-round. I hope you'll find a way to express that great reversal this week.

The third stanza of both these hymns is praise to God for:

III. The continuation of the Covenant, a theme worthy of song.

a. In vss. 54-55, this hymn praises God who remembers to be merciful to Israel, by keeping His covenant promise, the promise he made to Abraham and his descendants forever. God made a promise to the fathers, and he will not forget it. Even the best of our human counterparts make promises and renege. But not God. His promises never fail, and that aspect is most worthy of our praise in Christmas music.

b.   Zechariah, too, praises God for the continuation of his covenant. He sings that God has remembered his holy covenant (72) and the oath he swore to Abraham (73). The birth of Christ is the outworking of that oath God swore. Moreover the keeping of God's promise enables us to be rescued from our enemies (74), to serve God without fear (74b), and to walk before him in holiness and righteousness all our days (75). . . all our days. If we knew God as we ought, as Mary and Zechariah did, then we, too should praise God for these same things.

Another refrain in these hymns is:

IV. Praise for salvation.

a.   Mary rejoices in God her Savior, while Zechariah praises God as his redeemer (v. 68). Also Luke 1:69 sings of God who is the horn of salvation, and v. 71 praises God for his salvation from our enemies. God, the Savior, is the focal point of these carols.

Finally, and most fittingly, these hymns express a commitment or:

V. Desire to live the rest of our lives for him.

a.   Focus especially on vss. 77-79. From these moments on, Zechariah will walk in the knowledge of salvation (77a), live in the forgiveness of sins (77b) and know the tender mercy of our God by which the rising sun will come to us from heaven to shine on those living in darkness and in the shadow of death, to guide our feet into the path of peace?. Don't you want those things at Christmas? Are your hearts hungering for that guidance, that peace, those blessings of mercy?

Then come to Christ, in your hearts. If never before, or if all over again in deeper and deeper ways. And do sing. Unleash those inhibitions. Join together and make a joyful noise. Join with angels and archangels, and all the company of heaven to praise our God, who is worthy—now and forever more—of any praise we can utter.

All the News Fit to Print

Isaiah 52:7, Luke 2:8-10, Matthew 2:1-12

Think about the day you were mesmerized by a scrolling news ticker that screamed, "Breaking News." Of course, no one saw any of those 30 years ago. Even when President John Kennedy was assassinated, arguably the largest single news event of the 1960s, networks could only break in. And back then most TV sets were black and white, no color. Newspapers, by their very nature, cannot post updates—they simply wait until the next day. It was only after the 1970s that scrolling announcements began to pop up on TV screens. Even then, it was largely the advent of CNN 25 years ago that led to "breaking news" becoming a familiar part of our vocabulary.

Breaking news: that's what Advent is all about.

When are you glued to your TV set for "breaking news"? For some, it is to learn of a sports score or to see how the stock market did for the day. Or maybe you have to travel or have loved ones arriving, and you want to see if the weather will work. Maybe it's a murder, a kidnap on a vacation island, a Middle-eastern attack by US troops, or a presidential scandal. Most of us were glued to our TV sets or radios as 9/11/01 unfolded, weren't we. Sadly, but almost hypnotically, we watched those World Trade Towers fall over and over again. On-the-spot-reporting drew all 250 million Americans into the chaos and tragedy. News is important to everyone over 22—and to a few business majors under that.

The press plays such a large role in our life. The internet has only enlarged the world of news. Now, everyone's a commentator or a citizen blogger. Think about how much we depend on news, either print, televised or electronically delivered on some computerized device. I still like newspapers—they bring a world into one's living room. Of course, one should also read critically—neither believing everything that is written, nor trusting every journalist to be strictly objective. We live more by news than you think.

Some people greet one another, with "tell me some news" or "what's up?" or "what's happening?" We expect others to tell us news of some sort. That is part of human dialogue and interaction. And it is normally interesting.

As I said, I like news. I used to watch a late-night news show that would display the next morning's newspaper headlines from major daily papers in its final 2-3 minutes. I found it interesting. Now, you can log onto the internet and pretend you live in a dozen cities and see the daily news at the finger click of a mouse.

But no news is more important than our good news. And it is news. God on the first Christmas morning brought news—news that would change the world forever. Something was different from that time on, and people needed to know this news. The angel said, "I bring you good tidings, good news of great joy, which shall be for all the people." (Luke 2:10)

The Christian faith, in fact, steals . . . or redeems the category of news. The evangel comes from good + announcement, or good news. Last year, I ran across a "Sermon for Christmas Eve" by a Hungarian pastor, Abraham a Sancta Clara (1644-1709) [in Hughes Old, vol. 5). Although I had never heard of him, I am borrowing from his idea with a considerable updating. If that's the case, and we take this at face value, how would the breaking news of Christ's birth have been handled, especially from different angles? This morning suppose four various editorial boards met on Christmas Eve and planned their newspapers for the first Christmas morning. How would they approach the news of the day? Let me give you what I think each above-the-fold lead story would be for each.

Below are four different news reports—sure, there's a little editor's license involved, but I do so to treat the history in these accounts as real. First from:

(1) The Jerusalem Post

HEADLINE: "Shepherds as Reporters? C'mon."

Last night, another ruffian-led commotion disrupted a peaceful Bethlehem night. Claims have been made that angels and bright lights—even some kind of solar flare or meteor shower—announced the birth of the Messiah.

We have been unable yet to verify these reports, and some of the sources are questionable, but to give you the first news from God's city, below is what one reporter found. Abraham ben Judah reports that a lower-class couple, with some moral questions surrounding their marriage already, was traveling from their home in Nazareth to register for the new Dictatorial tax in Bethlehem. Joseph of Nazareth was to register there because he was a descendent of the great king David.

While the couple was traveling, the young woman—who claims not to have had previous marital relations—delivered a baby. The young son of the covenant had to be born in a stable outback, because no lodging preparations had been made. All of this, press reports can verify.

However, then the ruffian shepherds—with no journalism training—come into play. They wanted in on the press and tried to claim some responsibility as well. They claimed that an Angel appeared to them, complete with the *shekinah* glory and light. According to these shepherds, who now seem to be roving throughout the town spreading this gossip, this angel announced that in Bethlehem, the Savior was born, and that he was the long-awaited Christos-messiah, the anointed one.

None of the leading religious authorities, however, place any credence in these reports. When asked for a comment, the leading rabbi, Hillel said that they would be the first to know if Yahweh were raising up any Messiah. Also, any such Messiah would probably arise from their own well-trained corps of scribal scholars.

Rabbi Hillel assured *Jerusalem Post* reporters that no such Messiah had been born. God would most assuredly only work in concert with them, and they would be the conduits for any positive steps for the Kingdom of God. The Sanhedrin would release a full statement and study later today.

When asked, what to make of the angels and miracles, the rabbi sniffed: "That says about enough about the sources, which are disreputable. None of our well-educated rabbis believe in outdated ideas like miracles and angels anyway. This is peasant folklore, rest assured. Plus, the Romans are clasping our necks so tightly that the Almighty himself probably could not liberate us. We need another Moses, not a Messiah.

Still, as we were filing this report, one shepherd returned from Bethlehem. And he reported that he'd seen Joseph, Mary, and a Baby. These shepherds promised to pass on the breaking news to other neighbors, regardless of press coverage.

(2) The Roman Tribune

"Yet Another Liberator-Messiah" read the headline. The Roman governor had little comment yesterday on the claim that another Messiah had been born. "Yes, and taxes will rise, too, he said, wryly. For six centuries, the hapless Hebrews have expected some Messiah to come. They thought that the Maccabean brothers would deliver them almost 200 years ago, but look who still rules. Not them but Rome's finest."

Then a short time ago, they expected a fellow named Judas of Galilee to lead a political revolt. He was hung, as any opponent of Rome's power would be. This would be the latest of a string of disappointments.

Of course, the glory of our Empire is Supreme. No one would or could topple our wise Caesar, who is about as divine as one gets. Our military is stronger than ever, our people love their leaders because of our improvements in roads, granting some vote [admittedly on minor things], and for the civility we have ushered in.

The *Pax Romana* is unparalleled. No other govt has ever given so much to its people. They will, in exchange, reward us with years of governance. It is inconceivable that Rome could ever fall.

Markus Aurelius III, chief negotiator for Caesar, today, confirmed with customary Roman confidence when told that some kind of Jewish King had been born. "They've always been a runt nation, always will be. Perhaps a baby would be a fitting leader for those desert dogs."

The *Rome Tribune* staff found reactions ranging from mockery to non-interest when its reporters asked Rome's senators what they thought of the breaking news. One tenured senator said, "It's hardly good news, in fact, it's not news at all. That's rumor. The more important story of the day is this: we've just approved a massive road expansion project, the world's first public/private agreement. The plan is to sprinkle Rome with roads. Private funds will be taken by taxation and the public will benefit. Rome's politicians have found a genius way to have new roads and it won't cost us a denarius. All we'll do is tax everything that moves outside of Rome—let this new king defy our tax revenuers in Judea if he thinks he is powerful— we'll tax all our conquered people so much that they'll never think of rebelling again, and we'll bring all that money to Rome. Not only will we enhance our beautiful city, but we'll provide arteries for our military to move faster."

Rome is, as all know, entering a time of consolidation and world domination. After over a century of keeping this empire running and growing, as well as providing peace to our far flung empire, we will soon run the world from Rome. No child emperor can dethrone Rome. Whatever the rumors in Judea, a pretend ruler will not be in the news long, and our throne will be eternal.

Rome is strong, glorious, affluent—sure there's a little immorality but our people deserve it—and if we put our resources to work and use our native genius, we'll continue our empire.

As far as religious leaders in Rome, none were concerned about claims that a Jewish messiah would arrive and lead the way to peace.

There is, in short, no need for a new king. Only the poorer class, dispossessed Jews, who think they deserve more than they have would dream of such a thing. Sure, they wish they could rule their own land, but they've shown themselves to be miserably inept. While they might pine for a Golden Age, that is simply outdated and no longer needed. The modern world wants efficient government, good education, and safety from criminals. People would rather pay taxes than have a rag-tag Jewish Messiah.

Rest assured, Rome: this is but the latest rumor mongering of mongrels.

In other news, taxes were raised and Governor Quirinius of Syria reported that some were slow to comply. He would, thus, require subjects to register by the town of their fathers' birth.

(3) The Babylonian Journal

Arab leaders fired arrows into the air as they heard that both the Romans and Jewish regimes might be overthrown. The tribal leaders from Babylon were thrilled at the prospect that Israel would finally be obliterated. Several leading sheiks boasted that their mortal enemies the Jews could now be removed from the face of the earth. They saw this as a sign that Allah hated the Jews and wished to replace them.

Babylonian leaders also considered sending an army to attack Bethlehem while she was in a weakened state. King Darius the 14th thought it might be a good time both to sack Israel and perhaps to transfer her to Babylon's empire, taking a prized pawn from Rome.

On another front, an ancient group of priests gathered gifts—a very large and sudden withdrawal of gold roiled the middle eastern commodities markets—packed up and traveled to Bethlehem. Their journey was an interesting one, as they followed a star from Kirkut, following the ancient highway, toward the capital of Israel.

Our reporter from our Jerusalem bureau eventually interviewed one of these priests, who said: "we've long believed that God would send his divine Messiah to rule on earth. The old prophets, dating back to the time of Jeremiah indicated that he would be born in Bethlehem of Judah, and that the child would be from the lineage of King David, the greatest Monarch of Israeli history. All the signs had been gathering for some time, pointing to this, and this event is of such importance that we had to leave our country and travel to honor this king. If he is who we expect him to be, he will rule the world and he will be the only governor to have an ongoing reign.

The moving, celestial star merely confirmed that we were on the right track. As we headed west, the star led us, and upon arrival in Bethlehem, we were warmly received by King Herod. We did not anticipate that he would be a friend of our interests, and we later learned that he was plotting as he characteristically does to eliminate any possible competition. Oddly, he did not even seem aware of the ancient prophecies, and we had to tell him where we expected this anointed one to be born. We informed him that the prophet Micah had written, "But you Bethlehem, in the land of Judah, are by no means least among the rulers of Judah; for out of you will come a ruler who will be the shepherd of my people Israel." And we understand that shepherds were involved in spreading the first reports. Neither does that necessarily surprise us.

So, you see, our search was not as mysterious as previously thought.

Meanwhile, Darius the 14th proposed other programs to . . .

4. How sad, though, the fourth paper: *Hell's Herald*, whose slogan is: *All Bad news, all the time. Your source for unfairness and prejudice.*

Headline: "Humbug Squared."

Satan was unusually downcast today as news reached his dark lair. Despite his best efforts to prevent Christ from being born—he'd initiated as early as in Patriarch Joseph's day by trying to snuff out the line of Judah—recently even by using Herod as a pawn, apparently Satan has been unsuccessful—but only to this point—in eliminating baby Jesus. "What could a baby do to me anyway," growled Lucifer. His last-ditch effort led him to so inspire Herod that Herod slaughtered every male boy under the age of two. "If we cannot triumph by removing baby Jesus of Nazareth, then we'll sow so many versions and perspectives that truth itself will be obscured. Either way, we'll conquer the world and dominate the interpretation of the news from now on."

The underground newspaper, which was catching on with so many who lost their connections to their family, expected a surge in readership as it planned to include graphic pictures that would ensnare future generations.

Hell's Herald editorial board also was just returning from a Long Range Strategic Planning Conference, in which they adopted a multi-pronged strategy to debunk Christmas. The board decided to use every weapon in its arsenal to try to obliterate this holiday—and as a last resort, they decided to concede the notion of holiday because a vacation day would often lull the people into leisure and distractions.

Christmas didn't really happen—that would be a great way to spin the news. Why not, Satan cheered himself, do as we've done so many times in the past, especially with so many agents, and take the good news and turn it by our own interpretations. Why I can even make forbidden fruit look appealing. Or worse/better yet: here's a superb idea. Why not encourage all the nonbelievers to take over this birthday and give to it nothing but secular importance. Then later, we can try to convert it into a multicultural bazaar.

By 2005, we can have a Christ-less-mas Spirit (December 14, 2004 WSJ, Review and Outlook).

> We'll start in Europe with a "manger makeover at Madame Tussaud's wax museum in London [2004]. Standing in for Joseph and Mary are soccer star David Beckham and his pop-singer wife, Victoria, hardly a beatific couple.
>
> [Then] It's also Christ-menos in Barcelona, where the city council approved a modernized crèche dreamed up by local art students. Even the baby Jesus is missing in this setup, which replaces the holy family with a businessman on a mobile phone, a delivery man with a gas bottle and a blind man—figures the students somehow found "more emblematic" of the city known for the soaring towers of Gaudí's *La Sagrada Familia* cathedral.
>
> Perhaps the lesson lies in a third example of multiculturalism gone wild. A teacher in Como, Italy, tried to accommodate her non-Christian students by allowing them to substitute "this is the day of virtue" for "this is the day of Jesus" in a carol. The change sparked outrage throughout the town—except among the students, who chose simply to sing the original lyrics and move on.

We'll circle the globe, and finally target America. There we'll turn the holiday into a winter holiday and raise up lawsuits by the thousands to intimidate folks into diluting the reason for the season.

Hell's Herald knew that with craft, deceit, and enough reiterations of the lie, that many people would gradually lose any history of Christmas. In the process, they would lose Christ. Editor Lucifer Diablo said, "and the world would finally be freed from tyranny."

Thus, the Breaking News of the birth of Christ.

All of these make the following plain:

(1) The birth of Christ was a real event. Contrary to some religions (the Book of Mormon, Quran, etc.), no one could verify most of their religious teachers. There were many eyewitnesses (see Luke 1 and Acts 1), who could have filed their own dispatches. Abundant sources, from all classes/from different countries, were present. The birth of Christ was a historic event.

(2) Also, it was so real that the normal enemies of God would react as described above. Herod tried to remove the newborn power. Rome would not, if it knew what was

coming, condone a competitive power. All the enemies of Israel would probably rejoice.

(3) The news could be reported from different angles, each with vested interest. As another token of reality, any event like this can be reported in different ways and still be true. Shepherds, Magi, Angels, Joseph/Mary, Herod, Inn-owner, citizens of the area would all have slightly different angles on this same event.

(4) This news did not rule out the supernatural but contained it. It would be a perversion of this news to strip away all miracles.

(5) And this news set the hearts of believers to praise. It should set your heart to Joy.

The good news is as old as the OT. A verse in Genesis 3 foretold it long ago—that a time was coming when the seed of woman would conquer the seed of the serpent. Later the Prophet Isaiah 52:7 would announce. "How lovely on the mountains are the feet of him who brings good news, Who announces peace And brings good news of happiness, Who announces salvation, And says to Zion, Your God reigns!"

From the earliest breaking news alerts "in the Old Testament, the good news *is the message of God's reign, His sovereignty.* No doubt the people of God were expecting this good news because it is used here in Isaiah 52:7 of the message of the messenger that is bringing news of the victory and the reign of God on behalf of his people.

The good news was also identified with the Messiah himself. When Jesus went to the synagogue in Nazareth to explain to them who he was, he quoted from this passage. This is what is says. "The Spirit of the Lord God is upon Me because He has anointed Me to bring good news to the afflicted. He has sent Me to bind up the broken hearted, to proclaim liberty to the captives and freedom to the prisoners." When people at Jesus' home-town synagogue heard that, they knew that the good news announced that their bondage was about over.

At the time of the Roman Empire, the term, good news, had a common meaning. When Roman generals would win victories for the nation, the victories would be announced in Rome and all the provinces as good news. It was a technical term attached to celebrations of victory. Furthermore, it was also used interestingly, of what the Romans believed were communications from their gods, especially through the oracles. As the Roman people would go and visit an oracle, looking for a word from their gods, they would often refer to those words as good news. It's interesting, because God is really going to speak the word of good news in contrast to the false words from the false gods of the Romans, and yet he uses that language that would have been understandable to anyone in the Roman world; they would recognize that God is communicating a revealed word to his people.

Christmas is always and invariably about good news. And this news event would affect many people. On Christmas Eve of 1982, Ted Koppel signed off his ABC's *Nightline* program this way. "Those of us who work at this profession of journalism are rarely at such a loss for words as when someone asks us to define the nature of news. Usually we mumble something about the importance of an event—or its relevance or timeliness; hoping all the while that no one will ask 'important or relevant to whom?' As for timeliness, all that means, of course, is that something happened recently.

Well, the event that Christians around the world celebrate this [day] did not, of course, happen recently. It was relevant (at the time) to only the tiniest handful of people; and as for its importance, I think most of us in the news business would have to concede that, had we been there [2005] years ago in Bethlehem, we would probably have overlooked the event. Which says something about what's news—and what's important." (Source AJC, 12/24/04, p. A 11 in "It's OK to say 'Merry Christmas'" by Gary Lawrence) Would you or someone you love dearly miss out on this breaking news? Or would you love it?

The Savior of the world, God's Son born!! That's headline stuff, unless you are numb to spiritual matters.

A Scottish theologian (John Murray) put it better than most, once when describing the glories of the great mystery of godliness: "the infinite becoming finite: the eternal and supra-temporal entering time and becoming subject to it: the immutable becoming mutable: the invisible becoming visible: the Creator becoming created: the sustainer of all becoming dependent: the Almighty becoming weak. God became man." Earlier, Milton the poet said that the Son left the courts of everlasting day, and chose with us a dark house of mortal clay. *The Ancient of days became an infant of days.*

That's good news. May every heart this morning love this good message. It's news, it's heralded. And it will not pass out of relevance.

The Birth of Jesus: In Time and Over Time

Galatians 4 and Luke 2

The title may seem a little abstract or philosophical, but time is vitally important to all of us. And as we consider time and its use today, we'll see that God uses that as one of his tools. The Elizabethan poet, John Milton, spoke of time in these words:

> *"Fly envious Time, till thou run out thy race,*
> *Call on the lazy leaden-stepping hours,*
> *Whose speed is but the heavy Plummets pace;*
> *And glut thyself with what thy womb devours, . . .*
> *So little is thy gain,*
> *For when as each thing bad thou hast entomb'd,*
> *And last of all, they greedy self consum'd,*
> *Then long Eternity shall greet our bliss,*
> *With an individual kiss,*
> *And Joy shall overtake us as a flood, . . .*
> *When once our heav'nly-guided soul shall clime,*
> *Then all this Earthy grossness quite,*
> *Attir'd with Stars, we shall forever sit,*
>   *Triumphing over Death, and Chance, and thee O Time."*

Time will ultimately be retired. That is a majestic Christian doctrine.

And if any of you think that time is not very important, wait until it runs out when you've not completed your shopping list or when it ultimately runs out on that day when God calls you home. The older we all grow, the more important time is for us. And timing is as much a part of our lives as oxygen.

Time is both inescapable and part of God's creation. It is the web that God weaves around and through our lives. As the hymn affirms, "Time like an ever rolling stream bears all its sons away, they fly forgotten as a dream dies at the opening day."

Some view time as an ill constraint or as a negative. But this morning, I want us to return to the Advent narratives, chiefly in Luke, along with one other important epistolary reference, and learn how important time is and how God uses it. In so doing, we'll be directed to profound truths that focus on Jesus Christ.

As we do so, I hope you will note:
- o   How unlikely the characters are in the Advent narrative;
- o   How thoroughly God works in all of this;
- o   How totally Christ-centered all this is.

1. First, consider several things about the overall concept of time itself in the birth of Christ. Begin with me by reviewing Galatians 4. The context is this: Paul is making a point that an heir is a child, even the heir of a great estate is under tutors. So, we were all, at one time, in slavery to the basic principles of the world." (Gal. 4:3)

Then verse 4 turns to an exalted theme. Amidst the slavery and sin of the human race, God—and this is the message about Christmas— did something about that despair-causing situation. When the time had fully come, God sent his son. God waited for the right time, one that he had planned for millennia, and then he acted for good in keeping with his eternal and perfect plan.

Please learn from this something that rests at the heart of our faith, and something that also sounds like a paradox: *not every moment is equal or the same.* Not every second is a second; not every hour is the same. I know that sounds odd and may go against certain quantitative maxims, but time, according to this and other passages, has a ripening quality, an inherent unevenness. If you take the best fruit in the world but pluck it too soon, it will be hard. Or if you harvest things too late, they may have become soft and rancid. Fruit ripens and is best when ripe.

There are two different Greek words for time: *kronos* and *kairos*. The first refers to blind sequence or chronology; the second denotes a special moment of greater value.

The Scriptures treat time sort of like ripening fruit. To pluck certain things too soon will harm the effect and vice versa. And it is a terribly difficult thing, in so many cases, to know what is best on matters of exact timing. I occasionally disappoint friends and family by either plucking things too soon or waiting too long.

In this passage, though, it is not a matter of human timing or our discernment that is discussed. What is considered in vss. 4-5 is how God determines time, especially how he knew the time was right to bring Jesus into the world. Fortunately, in his case in contrast to any human being, he is always perfect in his assessments of timing. This very verse demonstrates that. God sent his son—that's why we celebrate Advent—at just the right time, when the time was fully ripe. It is no accident that God did not send Jesus at the time of Abraham, Moses, or Elijah. Nor did he wait until the Middle Ages or the 18th century to do so. God sent Jesus at the exact right moment of human history; not a nanosecond early or late. He could have chosen other time schedules, but he did not. The Lord Jesus himself was keenly sensitive to his rendezvous with destiny. Several times in the gospels, he avoided a conflagration with the Pharisees, because the time was not ripe. He threw a bucket of cold water on those disciples who wanted to rush in and anoint him king too soon. He knew that timing was part of God's work. And our Lord himself honored that timing, loved God's sense of perfection revealed in it, and yearned to fit in with the divine sense of timing.

For centuries, those who had been brought up on the OT wanted to see their Messiah. They waited and waited. Think about how long the Jewish people and all the faithful waited for the Messiah.

They longed and yearned . . . Abraham wanted to see that day, but he only saw a prefiguring of it when his only son, Isaac, almost became a vicarious substitute. Moses, wanted the people to leave Egypt and march not only into Canaan but right into heaven. When David spoke of "The Lord said to my Lord," he would have loved for the Messianic kingdom to be a reality in his lifetime. Any believer in the goodness and power of God wants to see his kingdom come in his own lifetime. Those fiercely courageous OT prophets longed for God's plan to come about in their time, but it never did.

As year succeeded to year, and particularly as the Jewish people were forced into Babylonian exile—their iconic and ornate temple destroyed—many people wondered if God would EVER send the Messiah. Godly, prayerful widows would pray and pray, and live and die—but no Messiah. Hard-working fathers would toil and toil, but still no Messiah. And on the rise, each successive pagan empire seemed more and more ruthless and increasingly brutal. The trend of human history to the believing eyes that loved God's ways seemed only downward all the time. Had God forgotten? Either he had, one might justly conclude, or else there was a huge and largely invisible timing factor.

Jewish history offered dim consolation for the 500 years preceding the birth of Christ. Would the fullness of time ever cry out its first breath? The yearning for salvation was not satiated, and people continued to attend the synagogues in large numbers, even in Roman-occupied territories.

A sense of expectancy, a waiting for the Messiah, could not be squelched. These active synagogues would later provide excellent first-meeting places for the missionary Paul.

So, first in terms of anticipation, God prepared OT history for a long time, a very long time. From that first reference to salvation in Gen. 3:15 until the birth of Jesus had been thousands of years. Don't you know that people were tempted to say, "this religious stuff is all interesting mythology, but the idea that God will decisively and definitively act in human history to save us . . . right! 2 Peter reflects that skeptical sentiment, present even in his century.

But God was not asleep; he just works on deeper levels than most of us realize. He was preparing the way, he was leveling the paths and straightening the highways. He is still at work in that way.

But the fullness of time would only come about, not only when Jewish religious events culminated but when God used even secular powers to broadcast the good news.

Consider some of the following Roman political developments. *By the time of the birth of Christ, Rome was at the zenith of her power. It spanned from the borders of India to Britain. Rome assimilated several other nationalities and regions into its empire. They also muscled foreign opposition into submission.* Following the Greek empire, the Romans built the first western empire. By the time of

Christ, the following had been developed, things that we take largely for granted:

Language: The Greek language itself, an assumed custom that many would not value, under God's providence became an excellent transmitter of the gospel. Drawing on earlier philosophic and literary terms, it was both universal and highly nuanced. It was perfectly suited to present the Christian message; fine shades of meaning could be expressed by its wide vocabulary. Already, Greek philosophers had raised questions about origins, moral norms, self-control, truth, and thus John's gospel begins powerfully with a Greek term: "In the beginning was the *Logos*, the Word. And the *Logos* was with God and the Logos WAS God." Peter, Paul, Luke, and John would use this language to spread the good news. God had prepared a culture, a language, a pre-existing literary, artistic, and philosophical situation and in the fullness of time, Jesus was the Lord over all that.

Military: The Roman army, unwitting servants of the Savior to be sure, served to pave the way for the spread of the good news is two key ways: (1) first, they precluded external interference from other national agents and they enforced the Roman law. That gave Christianity a cradle of stability and peace within the empire. Moreover, the *Pax Romana* brought a civic stability, formerly unimaginable, that allowed the events of Christianity to unfold without disruption from gangs and anarchy. God was conducting this entire symphony and it was a wonderful work.

After Christ's birth, several converts came from the military. They became witnesses, and used the discipline of the regime to quickly touch many lives. Not all were converted, but many witnesses in the Scriptures came from the military, certainly another one of those thorns in the flesh of pacifism.

Roads and Public Services (to allow the spread of information and the gospel). Citizens traveled freely, unrestricted by political barriers. Shipping was at a new height. The Roman highway system allowed commerce, itineration, and the exchange of ideas in a way that was heretofore unprecedented. The Romans even pioneered early forms of postal service that would later convey Pauline epistles. The way was prepared for messengers of Christ to take the message of the birth to the ends of the world.

Justice system (for Paul's appeals): With the rise of Roman democracy, another branch of government also characterized the beginning of the modern age: an ordered system of justice. The Romans broke down their government into small, governing regions—their legal system, too. Roman citizens had certain rights; they could avail themselves to fixed legal procedures, and in Paul's case, citizens could even appeal to Caesar. God was preparing an infrastructure that would support the spread of Christ's good news. All things were working together for God's good, including secular developments on many levels.

And of course, **taxation** to provide for all of this. Certainly, it was a bracing amount to pay to Gentile dogs, as the Jews saw it, but the confiscatory policies of the Roman government led to the trek from Nazareth to Bethlehem. Why, when these things are considered, one almost is assured that an all-wise God is planning all these events, nurturing his plan, which culminated with the birth of the Messiah.

Amidst all of this, at the right time, God sent his son, born of a woman, born under the law to redeem those under the law that we might receive the full rights of sons." (Gal. 4:4-5) The timing was perfect, as perfect as all God's other works and virtues. Lesser deities might panic and attempt to force things before their time, but God sits in heavens, unmoved . . . unthreatened . . . never rushed or frantic like the latest Christmas shopper . . . he is above all, perfectly orchestrating the birth of the Savior. The time was right, and God brought about salvation through his son, born of woman, born under the law to redeem his children.

2. Next, move your attention to some of the characters involved. Luke sketches these with a historian's sense of detail and perspective.

Of course, Luke 1-2 is the fullest portion of scriptural narrative that deals with the birth of Christ. The first chapter provides these historical markers or clues.

- "In the time of Herod." 1:5. Note carefully the emphasis on sequence and chronology throughout the entire first chapter of Luke.
- **1**:10, "And when the time . . . came."
- "Then" v 11.
- 1:23, "When his time of service was completed." (Zechariah)
- 1:39, "At that time." (Mary)

- 1:57, "When it was time for Elizabeth; then "on the 8th day" (59).

Then chapter 2 opens with a reference to a concrete historical era.

Kings and the powerful were going about their business. A government was exploiting the people who could not stand up for themselves and confiscating their money for its own ends. Great and small were operating on a one-dimensional plane, giving little thought to God, the fullness of time, or the Messiah. Think about Caesar Augustus. He didn't wake up one morning and think, "How can I serve God, today—perhaps by issuing a decree that a census should be taken to raise more tax revenue"? He was not conscious of God at all.

Notice how all the details assume the normal operations of history and time. Caesar was doing his job, Quirinius was a specific governor, who history has verified as ruling in this period, and this takes place in the jurisdiction of Syrian, in which Nazareth lies.

God is clearly working in history here. He is using and ordaining the details. This plan of salvation is not happening only in the heavenly realms or outside of time, but right smack in the middle of history. And the good news is that God is so incredibly ABLE.

The Point: God uses history and many different characters both to describe who Christ is and to point us to him. In this inspired narrative, God works with a wide-ranging cast. It involves malicious rulers, humble shepherds, three odd mystical characters from the knowledge class of first-century Babylon, a lower-class girl, facing stigma from her community, and no partridge in a pear tree.

However, what is far more important is how God acts in all this. That is far more significant than the sum total of action by the various bit part players. Not to denigrate human activity—sure, human action is important in both long and short run, but these verses remind us, again at Christmas as most everywhere throughout sacred writ, of the glorious and dominating influence of God in the world and in our lives. What God does, changes human history. What God does alters the courses of lives and of presumed governors. It is his activity that is important, his doings, his plans, and of course his time.

Every character in this drama is introduced but influenced by God—even the bad guys. The sovereignty of God ever works that way. No one of these characters is permitted to do its worst, not even Herod. Sure, he may slaughter infants—and how evil can one be! But, notice this: when evil men attack God's anointed, they do not succeed. There is an incredibly powerful message of victory and assurance, woven throughout these verses. If you're down about something at this holiday, go back and read these texts, for they provide powerful relief and profound insight. Instead of "Yes, Virginia, there is a Santa Claus," the message of the gospels is, "Yes, Virginia, God is at work and in charge—of all of human history and of all of your days and hours."

Although believers struggled for years and had to fight off the darkness with everything in them, the light was dawning. The people had walked in great darkness, but the light was appearing. In the midst of human history and time—certainly the strongest forces we know—God was interrupting and bringing the Messiah. God's plan of salvation was and is bursting onto the world as surely as Mary was giving birth.

And the Prince of Peace was coming, despite any opposition or any forces. God is greater than time, greater than the flow of history—which to us and to every idol is unavoidable. God, the creator of time, has also designed time in a fashion that the Divine can still break in; and he is still doing that. Yes, he is; don't ever doubt that. If God could not interrupt the flow of time, the world would be ruled by the false-god named "Sequence." Cause and effect would box in God. If history confined God, then the Angels certainly would not have sung "glory to God in the highest," but "glory to *Chronos* in its trivialest." Praise the Lord at this Christmas that God is not a slave to external forces, he is working out his plan.

And all of human history is defined by three unmovable focal points: (1) the creation, (2) the advent of Christ, and (3) the Judgment of God at the end of human history. Is this humbling? Yes, it is. To embrace this article of faith means that we do not control the levers of life nearly as much as we wish to tell ourselves. We get so ginned up about certain things that either seem so irreparable or we voluntarily place upon our shoulders burdens that are too large for our own shoulders, and we get very frustrated. Sometimes it feels like we are feverishly swimming upstream against a mighty current. But it is precisely when we realize our own impotence, our own spiritual inability as the theology of the Reformation states it, that we begin to look upwards and with the empty hands of faith, we join the likes of

Mary and others, who say, "May it be unto me as you have said. I am the Lord's handmaiden."

It humbles us to see how truly ineffective we are at changing the courses of our own families, our own nation, and many other things. But that is designed by our Creator/Redeemer also to show the majesty of his grace. His work is superior to all our efforts. If you want to control things, that reality may irritate you; if, however, you want to survive, you will eventually find comfort in trusting things to God.

Indeed, one of the great dynamics of these Advent narratives and of all of Scripture is that we must confess how much we need and depend on God and how out-of-control our lives are. I know that may sound like I'm preaching a doctrine of CHAOS, but on the contrary to the Greek notion of fatalism, I am actually preaching that old Christian message of surrender and submission to the wise will of God. How God works is what we need to be attuned to this Christmas.

Go back to the opening of Luke 2 to review how this works. God works in time

And, in keeping with what I stated earlier, if the focus of these chapters is not on time and human characters, just who is the center of all this: why it is the humble Jesus of Nazareth. He is at the center of all this, and God surely wants you and me to re-arrange our focus and gaze a little more at Christ-child.

"Come adore on bended knee."

What/how is God working in our midst today? I can't read hearts and internal matters, but I can tell you this: He is at work, and like the wise men, we'd be wise to look to the heavens and seek to understand how he is at work, for he most certainly is. And God is able to work in our own historical situation. Don't ever doubt that the birth of Jesus signifies these two things:

- "Greater is he that is in you than he who is in the world."
- "If God is for us, who can be against us."

God is Sovereign over human history; there is no inch of the universe where the Sovereign does not claim, "mine." Even the stable, the Roman palaces, the back rooms of religious malice that conspired against the Lord and his Anointed, do not escape the all-sovereign eye and hand of God. He not only sees, but he also acts. You can trust that in the coming week.

In Luke 1:38, Mary said, "May it be to me as you have said." Surrendering to God's overshadowing will is a good thing. There is rest in it, there is peace. We do not carry a load that God has not intended for us; we fit into his scheme. What a gift to give, if we could only give that gift to those around us: the peace that passes all understanding, when a world looks—and it is only appearing to be— spinning out of control.

Let me conclude with this other verse that has stalked me this week as I've thought about this topic. Romans 5:6 also tells us that something happened at a *kairos* moment: "at just the right time," while we were still sinners, Christ died for us. This is stated as the grand demonstration of the love of God. While seldom will anyone give his life in exchange for another, occasionally we will do so for one that we love or for one that we deem to be a good or deserving person. But hardly ever will we give our life for one who is a criminal, a user, a hater, or undeserving. Yet, God, at the right time gave Christ for us—while we were powerless, enemies, and sinners, incapable of helping ourselves. Thus, do we see clearly God's love, over and above time, but also born into time.

On the Incarnation

John 1:1-5, 14, 18

Before we get into our subject this morning, let me render two Latin phrases into common English, since some have asked about them.

Advent = *ad* (to) + *venire* (to come); thus Advent is the coming to earth of Christ. It speaks of his leaving heaven to come to earth and be our Messiah/Redeemer. Folks in the OT waited and waited on the Messiah; they prepared for him for centuries. Thus, Advent is a time of preparation, when we focus on Christ. This season is often accompanied by wreaths and the lighting of candles, each of which point to some aspect of OT prophecy looking for Christ.

The second term is Incarnation. It also is derived from Latin, and it means to become infleshed. That term, although not in the scriptures themselves, refers to how Christ left behind the glory of heaven and took our flesh on him. He not only wore it for 33 years, but he was in the flesh.

Irenaeus wrote: "The Son of God became the Son of Man in order that the sons of men might become the sons of God."

Now these two concepts conjoined to create a massive stumbling block for two groups in the ancient world. *First*, to the Jews; they fully expected God to send a human Messiah, raised up out of Israel. What they did not expect and could not accept, however, was that this Messiah could also be fully God. As staunch believers in monotheism they did not think this possible. The *second* group was the Greeks.

For them, God was pure idea or spirit and could never be mixed up, as their ancient mentor Plato had taught, with bodies or flesh.

So, these two dominant groups in first century Palestine had a major headache, whenever anyone suggested that Christ was God in the flesh. And it remains an intellectual stumbling block still.

Many people have philosophical reasons for rejecting God in the flesh. They believe that certain things are impossible. Numerous unbelievers claim something like this: God, if he exists at all, is incapable of becoming a human. Should he ever do that, he would cease to be God, for the very categories of humanity and deity cannot co-exist. After all, we've never observed, and cannot point today to, a human who is also fully God. Or if God were to become human, then he would suffer all our frailty. If oil and water cannot mix, if square pegs cannot be crammed into round holes, if suburban, European Presbyterians cannot sing African-American spirituals, if 2+ 2 cannot equal 5, then surely God and man cannot dwell in the same body.

And those criticisms should, perhaps, be dealt with. However, they are not always the show stoppers imagined. Let's agree to deal with some of those at some time, but before we do, let's first hear what the Christian Scriptures teach about the incarnation, and see if it helps or hinders the entire Christian theology.

First, there were certain OT expectations, surrounding the Messiah. Although the Jews did not expect God to take on the flesh of men, they did expect Messiah to be so close to God as to be virtually indistinguishable. As early as Isaiah 7:14, the prophet predicted that a virgin would conceive and give birth to a son, who would be named "Immanuel," which means God with us. So this Messiah-Immanuel would be known as God with us, God inseparable from us. A few chapters later, that same "child is born . . . son is given, and the government will be on his shoulders and he will be called Wonderful Counselor, Mighty God, Everlasting Father, Prince of Peace." Those are pretty exalted titles, fitting I admit for God alone and not for any human. The root of Jesse in Isaiah 11 also has divine attributes.

Then Isaiah 40:3 had a Messianic prophecy. It predicted that the forerunner to the Messiah would call out, "Prepare the way for the Lord, make straight in the wilderness a highway for our God." That was the Messiah pointed to, and you can see how closely associated he is with God.

So, even the OT prophecies should have led Jews to be open to this prospect, but they were not.

We also have some other OT precursors of this curious mixture of human and divine in Jewish belief. Jews thought that God incarnated himself in several ways. Wisdom is God-Incarnated in Proverbs 8. The Law was divine, as well as presented to Moses, and the Temple was where God dwelt.

So, several OT texts prepare the Spirit-enlightened mind to embrace Jesus as fully God. There was enough information to lead several disciples and many converts in Jesus' own time to see him as the predicted Messiah. But hardness of heart and the creation of wrong and unbending theological categories kept them from doing so.

But more importantly, several NT texts claim that Jesus was God in the flesh. Turn to the opening words of John's Gospel to see one of the most impressive.

Let me lift five short points from this section in John 1.

1. *"Word" was chosen because it was the most apt expression of mind and intent.*

Speech is an open window to the soul. Sometimes words slip out that show our real intent; at other times, we think long and hard and carefully select our phrases which reflect the passions of our hearts. In this case, Christ is the Word of God. He is the authentic commentary from God on himself. Christ the Word perfectly expresses what God wanted to convey to us.

When God issued this Word, that means that we are no longer in the dark. We are not left clueless. We know what God has in mind.

Thus, when Christ came to earth, as the spoken word of God, from that point on, God is no longer totally mysterious. He has revealed himself and made himself clear. God did not hide and remain only in heaven; he has shown himself. He has spoken, and Christ is the defining expression of who God is. There are no other words similar, nor is there any, later, better word.

2. *This "Word" was not only close to God but **WAS** God.*

This word was also as old as God. There was nothing before this Word existed. He was in the beginning, before creation and he witnessed, as well as cooperated with, all acts of creation. There is no other object that comes between God and his Word.

Note the three aspects in v. 1 of how the Word is related to God. He was (a) in the beginning—so he is as old as God; and (b) he was also with God. The term is literally translated as "in the bosom of God," that means the Word was in the nearest possible proximity to God. This Word was not some distant agent or process, he was in the lap of God. The Word and God are inseparable, both expressing the same mind. (c) But also absorb the third claim in v. 1—that one which shatters all cults: "The Word was God." Or God was the word. Cultists try to avoid the strong language in the Greek NT, but sensitive translators for centuries have clearly seen this: The Word is not only close to or longstanding with God, but the Word is divine. Somehow, though distinct, the Word is also united with and equally divine as God. The Word was as divine as God.

No other religion in the world has or does claim that for its earthly manifestation of God. Only Christianity has the inspiration or originality to invade the world with this claim: Not only is Christ close to God, he is more than Immanuel (God with us), he is God inhabiting the manhood of Jesus of Nazareth. Compare that to other religions, and it is mind-boggling.

One may not believe that, but that is what John's Gospel claims for our faith.

Wright notes that Jesus, in fact, is God with a human face: "This, moreover, is a God who became human without doing violence to his own inner essential nature. The true God is the God of sovereign love; and it's a contradiction in terms to suppose that love will remain uninvolved, or detached, or impersonal. The true God isn't a vaguely beneficial gas. He wears a human face, crowned with thorns." (N. T. Wright, *The Original Jesus* (Eerdmans, 1996), 82.)

Next:

3. *The "Word" was the instrument of God's work (3-5).*

As John, who observed Jesus personally, wrote later, in vss. 3-5, this Word was also involved in the major works of God; indeed, he was the agent. Through Jesus, the Word, all things were made. That, by the way, is one of the reasons why creation is so important. Creation is not removed from our Savior—to the contrary, Jesus was the instrument involved in creating. And it is not some things, but all things that were created through him. As v. 3 continues to note, "without him nothing was made that has been made."

Jesus also possessed life itself. In him was life, and that life was the light of men. Only God gives life. And when John, a few chapters later says that the Father has life in himself and has "granted the Son to have life in himself," (5:26) he is making the strongest possible assertion of the deity of Christ.

Jesus gives light and life.

4. *The Word became flesh and, in the process, retained glory, grace, truth (14).*

Now drop to v. 14, for vss. 6-13 provide an interlude and an introduction to John the Baptist. The theme of Jesus as the Word, however, resumes in v. 14. There we are told that the Word became flesh, that is, the incarnation. This Word did something that other speech-acts cannot do. He took on life, not only verbal status. The Word miraculously crossed-over categories and he became flesh.

In the process, though, it is key to note: he lost none of his goodness. Verse 14 continues to state that this Word emitted glory. "We have seen his glory." That glory was not disputed; John thought of it as a known act. Glory means a weight or heaviness that makes an impression. Jesus, thus bore the glorious impression of God; and it was not a light impression, but a strong one.

His glory was unique: it was the One and Only. No other possessed this.

Furthermore, two other divine attributes are listed at the close of v. 14: Grace and truth.

Jesus had grace, the overcoming quality which gives mercy and forgiveness to those who do not deserve. Jesus was no petty deity. He was so great that he could afford to give grace and forgive, while losing nothing.

He also was full of truth; there was never any lie or deceit in our Lord. He was as fully truthful as God the Father is. All that he taught, said, and modeled were truths of God. The Word was not wrong.

So when we hear about Jesus, the Word taking on our flesh, make sure that you understand that he lost no deity in the process.

Finally,

5. *The word tabernacled with us. He took on our tent, as one literal translation might read. He did not camp away from us, but was God-embodied. Jesus took on the tent of our flesh and dwelt with us. We do not journey, in other words, where he has not been. He knows our flesh.*

Remember that in the Jewish Church its greatest glory was that God tabernacled in its midst: not the tent of Moses, not the various pavilions of the princes of the twelve tribes, but the humble tabernacle in which God dwelt, was the boast of Israel. They had the king himself in the midst of them, a present God in their midst. The tabernacle was a tent to which men went when they would commune with God, and it was the spot to which God came manifestly when he would commune with man. To use Matthew Henry's words, it was the "trysting place" between the Creator and the worshipper. Here they met each other through the slaughter of the bullock and the lamb, and there was reconciliation between them twain. Now, Christ's human flesh was God's tabernacle, and it is in Christ that God meets with man, and in Christ that man hath dealings with God. . . . The glory of the tabernacles was the Shekinah. What does our text say? Jesus Christ was God's tabernacle, and "we beheld his glory, the glory as of the only begotten of the Father." Jesus is not the tabernacle without the glory; . . . The apostle however points to a surpassing excellence in Christ the tabernacle, by which he wondrously excels that of the Jewish Church. "Full of grace and truth."

Later, Jesus would say, "If you have seen me, you have seen the Father." Also John 5:23 says, "all [are to] honor the Son just as they honor the Father. He who does not honor the Son does not honor the Father, who sent him."

And Thomas reacted this way in Jn. 20:20, "My Lord and my God."

Colossians 1:19 adds: "God was pleased to have all his fullness dwell in him and through him to reconcile to himself all things, whether things on earth or things in heaven, by making peace through his blood, shed on the cross." Also, "He is the image of the invisible God." (Col. 1:15)

Acts 20:28 refers to "the church of God . . . for whom he shed his blood."

Titus 2:13: we "wait for the blessed hope—the glorious appearing of our great God and Savior, Jesus Christ."

Hebrews 1 further describes Jesus as the exact replica of God's radiance.

The Christian faith revolves around this fact: God came and took on our humanity in the person of Christ, who was the Divine word. G. C. Berkouwer wrote (156): "[T]he heart of the Christian religion pulsates in the confession that in Jesus Christ, in the Incarnation of the Word, God truly came down to us. The church continually sensed and understood that the pivotal difference could not and might not be reduced to a variation or nuance in formulation, but that it concerned a confession of which it is as true as of the confession of a sola-fide that the church stands or falls with it."

Third, note that all of these possible rejections are fundamentally doubts about the power, ability of God. They join together to teach us that God is not limited and he can do anything he plans, even possess a human body. He can overcome all things. Do we wish to worship a God who cannot overcome human flesh? What a predicament that would land us in.

If, and we are on good grounds to assume the truth of Christianity, if God can inhabit the flesh, think what else he would be able to do:

Creation by his mighty word. Small miracles and large miracles depend on the same kind of God. If he cannot do the one, he cannot do the other. But a God who can create this entire, elaborate cosmos can certainly produce the incarnation.

He may also work many other miracles. Start with the next chapter of John—water is changed to wine. The God of the Incarnation is the God who reverses the course of nature. Since he made it, he can change it.

The miracles like the divine healings make more sense after we see the incarnation.

- Miracles like those at Christmas.
- Miracles like the resurrection.

If God cannot become incarnate, then I suggest he cannot do any of these other miracles. If he is unable to hurdle that barrier, he may not hurdle others. On the other hand, if he is the God of the incarnation, if he can take on the flesh and still remain fully God, then he is much bigger than many people think, and he is able to do exactly what Scripture says he can. If not, he is no God.

At Christmas, we celebrate the mastery of God over his creation. He did not create and then become a slave to his creation. He is ever over it all.

This is why Alfred Edersheim called this, "the world's greatest event" [p.185].

We Christians get too easily used to the most astounding claims and assertions rolling off our tongues as though they were mere commonplaces. The eternal God, God the Son, the second person of the Triune God, taking to himself a human nature and living forever after as a man—God and man together in a single person. This is more exciting than any adventure, more perfect than any fairy tale we have ever heard or read. Hollywood in its wildest imagination—even with the third part of the *Lord of the Rings* trilogy out in 2 days—cannot improve on this! A visit from heaven to earth; God appearing incognito; coming to endure the most horrible trials to win salvation from his people who have been enslaved to the cruelest of masters—the Devil and their own sinful hearts. We can call the incarnation, the birth of God the Son as a human infant, exhilarating or we can call it devastating, or, we like many other people, can call it a myth or fairy tale; but if we call it dull or uninteresting then words have no meaning at all.

And, let there be no mistaking this: the incarnation is the central fact of the Christian faith, its central doctrine, its central proclamation. Without it there can be no Christianity. That's certainly why God began Jesus' life as he did. Now you will certainly hear folk say that Christianity does not need this miraculous history, that its spirit, its teaching can continue whether or not you believe the Bible's account of the incarnation and the virgin birth. But the man in the street knows full well that this is rubbish. Christianity without the incarnation is not Christianity at all.

That is easy enough to demonstrate. Not only is the incarnation so clearly taught in the Bible, not only does it lie beneath all the central assertions of our faith, not only is it essential to the gospel, the good news of Christ as the Savior of sinners, but *it explains, it accounts for, it answers the great objections that unbelievers have against the Christian faith.*

Take for example the miracles that are reported in the four gospels. Can we who live in a modern century really believe that Jesus walked on water, or that he fed 5,000 with a little bit of food, or that he gave sight to a man blind from birth, or that he rose from the dead on the third day? Still today many people find these accounts simply incredible, impossible to believe in a scientific age. Of course, these events were incredible to the folk who witnessed them; the gospels make that clear. But, don't you see, all of the difficulty in believing accounts of the miraculous simply disappears if you accept the incarnation, that Jesus Christ was both God and man, that he was utterly unlike, in this most profound way, any other man who has ever lived or shall live in the world. If the incarnation is real, the difficulty does not lie with Jesus' rising from the dead—that goes without saying—the real problem is that he suffered and died in the first place! That God should stoop so low for us!

Or, take the Bible's teaching about man's sinfulness, his guilt before God, God's wrath against sinners and his impending judgment of them. Probably this is the central objection of most people who turn away from Christianity. They do not care for what it says about man being so great a sinner and they do not like the notion of a God of judgment and vengeance.

But, accept the incarnation and this objection disappears. Accept that God became a man, underwent a thirty-three-year course of humiliation at the hands of his own creatures, endured their scorn, suffered and died at their hands for the sins of the world, and it is no longer possible to doubt that sin and guilt are gigantic things. If it took God himself coming into the world as a man, to suffer and die so cruelly for his people's salvation, if it took *this* to secure man's forgiveness, then man's sin must be a terrible thing indeed! One measures the sickness by the cure: so great, so expensive, so painful a cure leads us back to a very sinister and deadly disease. And if God himself endured his own wrath—for our salvation—does that not make it impossible to doubt that God is in fact holy and just as well as abounding in love?

Or, take the very common objection to Christianity heard nowadays that it requires the belief that there is but one road to God and heaven, that Christianity alone is true and that the other religions and philosophies of the world are false. This is *so* politically incorrect in our pluralist day, so unwelcome, so offensive to modern taste. It strikes so many as intolerant, arrogant, proudful. "You say you have the truth and everyone else is in darkness. Where do you get off?"

But, accept the incarnation and this objection too vanishes in an instant. For if the living God who made heaven and earth came into the world as a man to save men from their sins, then it goes without saying that *this and this only* is the way of salvation! If God did **that** for us, no one could continue to think that religions and philosophies that left this fact entirely out of account could direct men and women safely to God.

Or, finally, take the very practical objection that so many have to Christianity, viz. that it asks too much of its adherents. It is one thing to have to perform certain religious rites from time to time, even briefly every day; it is one thing to be asked to live according to a not very demanding ethical system; it is one thing to be able to practice one's religion and keep largely intact one's high view of himself and independence of judgment. But Christianity asks, no it demands, the surrender of one's pride *and* of one's independence. It demands absolute subjection of one's will to the rule of God. It demands that its followers strive to practice an ethic, a way of life, that even the most ardent Christians have found exhausting and deeply frustrating. It sets standards that are so high that they cannot be achieved in this world yet Christians are required to strive to achieve them regardless of obstacles. And what is demanded is invariably that which human beings are, by natural instinct, least inclined to give: the denial of self and the love of enemies above all.

Ah, but what if God really did come into the world as a man? What if he really did live incognito among men for those thirty-three some years, suffering abject humiliation at the hands of his own creatures and, finally, gave himself to death on a cross to pay the price of our sins? What if salvation really cost so much and took so much. Well, then, as C. T. Studd so memorably put it: "If Jesus Christ be God and died for me, then no sacrifice is too great for me to make for him." Set the bar as high as it can be set, the incarnation makes entirely reasonable whatever demands a holy God may make of his sinful creatures and, especially, of his sinful children, whom he has saved by the sacrifice of his own son!

A real incarnation means that we can no longer fit our Christianity into the rest of our life, but must fit the rest of our life into our Christianity. It means that being a follower of Christ must be the all-consuming passion of our existence.

In all of these ways and others like them, the incarnation is the explanation of the Christian faith as well as its core doctrine. This is the gospel, the good news, that God has become a man for man's salvation, that nothing short of God becoming a man to live and to die in man's place would do and so God did it, sending his own Son in the likeness of sinful man to be a sin offering, which is how Paul puts it [in Romans 8:3.]

As the great 17th century theologian Francis Turretin beautifully put it: "The work of redemption could not have been performed except by a God-man, associating by incarnation the human nature with the divine by an indissoluble bond. For since to redeem us, two things were most especially required—the acquisition of salvation and the application of the same; the endurance of death for satisfaction [of God's justice] and victory over [death] for the enjoyment of life . . . our mediator [had] to be God-man to accomplish these things: man to suffer; God to overcome; man to receive the punishments we deserved, God to endure and drink it to the dregs; man to acquire salvation for us by dying, God to apply it to us by overcoming. . . . God alone could not be subject to death, man alone could not conquer it. Man alone could die for men; God alone could vanquish death."

As Rabbi Duncan, a 19th century Scottish Presbyterian, admitted, "We make far too little of the incarnation; the Fathers knew much more of the Incarnate God. Some of them were oftener at Bethlehem than at Calvary; they had too little of Calvary, but they knew Bethlehem well. They took up the Holy Babe in their arms; they loved Immanuel, God with us. We are not too often at the cross, but we are too seldom at the cradle; and we know too little of the Word made flesh . . ." [Moody Stuart, *Life of Duncan*, p. 167; several paragraphs above are taken from a sermon by Dr. Robert Rayburn]

Well, brothers and sisters, let it not be so this year! Not this Christmas. Not among us! No matter what the circumstances of your life. No matter what your trials, what your sorrows, or what your joys at this moment of your life and this time of year, the incarnation throws all of that into the shadow, makes all of that comparatively nothing. God entered this world as a man. And if you know that and believe that and have ordered your life in keeping with that fact, then you are in living touch with the very center of reality. All that matters most and matters for ever is yours for you understand "the only thing that ever really happened." Or, as John puts it, "he who has the Son, has life, and he who does not have the Son of God does not have life." And, if you do not have the Son of God, remember what he himself said: "The one who comes to me, I will never drive away."

Benjamin Warfield in an essay, "Imitating the Incarnation" (*Person and Work of Christ*, 564-5), put it this way. Christ, "with no pride of birth, though he was a king; with no pride of intellect, though omniscience dwelt within him; with no pride of power, though all power in heaven and earth was in his hands; or of station, though the fullness of the Godhead dwelt in him bodily" came and took on our flesh. Thus Augustine asked, "Why are you proud, O man? For God became low for you."

A much earlier saint, Athanasius, wrote a powerful work, *On the Incarnation.* Some of his insight, beginning with chapter II, might be refreshing.

> For He alone, being Word of the Father and above all, was in consequence both able to recreate all, and worthy to suffer on behalf of all and to be an ambassador for all with the Father.
>   (8) For this purpose, then, the incorporeal and incorruptible and immaterial Word of God entered our world. In one sense, indeed, He was not far from it before, for no part of creation had ever been without Him Who, while ever abiding in union with the Father, yet fills all things that are. But now He entered the world in a new way, stooping to our level in His love and Self-revealing to us. He saw the reasonable race, the race of men that, like Himself, expressed the Father's Mind, wasting out of existence, and death reigning over all in corruption. He saw that corruption held us all the closer, because it was the penalty for the Transgression; He saw, too, how unthinkable it would be for the law to be repealed before it was fulfilled. He saw how unseemly it was that the very things of which He Himself was the Artificer should be disappearing. He saw how the surpassing wickedness of men was mounting up against them; He saw also their universal liability to death. All this He saw and, pitying our race, moved with compassion for our limitation, unable to endure that death should have the mastery, rather than that His creatures should perish and the work of His Father for us men come to nought, He took to Himself a body, a human body even as our own. Nor did He will merely to become embodied or merely to appear; had that been so, He could have revealed His divine majesty in some other and better way. No, He took our body, and not only so, but He took it directly from a spotless, stainless virgin, without the agency of human father—a pure body, untainted by intercourse with man. He, the Mighty One, the Artificer of all, Himself prepared this body in the virgin as a temple for Himself, and took it for His very own, as the instrument through which He was known and in which He dwelt. Thus, taking a body like our own, because all our bodies were liable to the corruption of death, He surrendered His body to death instead of all, and offered it to the Father. This He did out of sheer love for us, so that in His death all might die, and the law of death thereby be abolished because, having fulfilled in His body that for which it was appointed, it was thereafter voided of its power for men. This He did that He might turn again to incorruption men who had turned back to corruption, and make them alive

through death by the appropriation of His body and by the grace of His resurrection. Thus He would make death to disappear from them as utterly as straw from fire.

Chapter III:

(17) There is a paradox in this last statement which we must now examine. The Word was not hedged in by His body, nor did His presence in the body prevent His being present elsewhere as well. When He moved His body He did not cease also to direct the universe by His Mind and might. No. The marvelous truth is, that being the Word, so far from being Himself contained by anything, He actually contained all things Himself. In creation He is present everywhere, yet is distinct in being from it; ordering, directing, giving life to all, containing all, yet is He Himself the Uncontained, existing solely in His Father. As with the whole, so also is it with the part. Existing in a human body, to which He Himself gives life, He is still Source of life to all the universe, present in every part of it, yet outside the whole; and He is revealed both through the works of His body and through His activity in the world. It is, indeed, the function of soul to behold things that are outside the body, but it cannot energize or move them. A man cannot transport things from one place to another, for instance, merely by thinking about them; nor can you or I move the sun and the stars just by sitting at home and looking at them. With the Word of God in His human nature, however, it was otherwise. His body was for Him not a limitation, but an instrument, so that He was both in it and in all things, and outside all things, resting in the Father alone. At one and the same time—this is the wonder— as Man He was living a human life, and as Word He was sustaining the life of the universe, and as Son He was in constant union with the Father. Not even His birth from a virgin, therefore, changed Him in any way, nor was He defiled by being in the body. Rather, He sanctified the body by being in it. For His being in everything does not mean that He shares the nature of everything, only that He gives all things their being and sustains them in it. Just as the sun is not defiled by the contact of its rays with earthly objects, but rather enlightens and purifies them, so He Who made the sun is not defiled by being made known in a body, but rather the body is cleansed and quickened by His indwelling, "Who did no sin, neither was guile found in His mouth."[7]

This year at Advent, be sure to worship the risen Christ for his Incarnation.

Pretty Good Privacy; Excellent Advent

Galatians 4, Hebrews 1, John 3:16

Some of you are aware of my transformation from liberal arts slog to internet wonk. Of course, I could try to blame all this on the elders, as in Flip Wilson's: "The elders made me do it." But you probably wouldn't believe it. Actually, we are beginning to see a little pay off from our internet ministry. More people read these sermons now, than hear them. We believe the Lord has provided us with an amazing and affordable broadcast tool. The information highway holds much promise.

Indeed, you can expect to hear more and see more about the ministry uses of the internet in the years to come [Note: one can quickly sense that this sermon was written in the mid-1990s]. Living in this community, filled with computer hacks and wonks, has provided us with an ideal climate in which to seize the ministry opportunities.

I know a lot of people are afraid of the internet. To some degree, I don't blame them. To hear some people talk, it is nothing but an electronic emporium for pornography and perversion. No doubt those elements do exist, but I can't find any sinful vice that is more available on the internet than it is at the corner store. Another chief concern for some has been security: How can a person make sure that his private transactions remain private? Along with that has come the desire to have a form of economic exchange which will not be stolen. That is proving to be one of the more difficult tasks for the internet. Fortunately, our ministry and use of this electronic medium does not require that we have solutions to these problems. Being a non-profit organization, in some ways, makes life simple.

In response to that need for proper security, a software package has been developed called "Pretty Good Privacy." Perhaps you've heard of it. By the admission of its own title, it does not claim to be perfect, or infallible; just *pretty* good. Of course, surrounded by a world of advertising hype and exaggeration, it is nice to hear a modest claim rather than a product advertised as the greatest ever. And to tell you the truth, for this stage, that is normally adequate. Pretty good privacy is for the serious person who wants to make sure that their communications and exchanges are private—from Big Brother—and also secure—from Big Burglar. Here's from the latest release:

"Pretty Good Privacy [PGP], is a public key encryption package; with it, you can secure messages you transmit against unauthorized reading and digitally sign them so that people receiving them can be sure they come from you. Security is only as strong as the weakest link, and while the algorithms in PGP are some of the strongest known in the civilian world, there are things outside the program's control which can weaken your security as assuredly as forgetting to lock a vault door. Even if you are already familiar with public key cryptography, it is important that you understand the various security issues associated with using PGP."

This program, therefore, depends on the following:
1. That your beginning package is secure—always a threat to those who are concerned about privacy.
2. That you "lock the vault door."
3. That no stronger external forces interfere.

In sum, you must do your part, and there must not be any greater external force to conquer you. If those things are true, then you'll have pretty good privacy.

I have heard this topic discussed so much recently that I could not resist thinking about pretty good privacy and advent. One is pretty good, and the other is excellent. Do we have a "pretty good Advent?" As you might expect, God does not do many things "pretty well." He does all things very well. Let me point out a few to you this morning, just from the Advent narratives.

How Advent shows that God's work is more than Pretty Good:
 1. God sent his Son.

According to the Scripture, God had a plan from before the foundation of time. And this plan to save his people was centered around Jesus Christ, the eternal Son of God. For centuries people awaited the coming of the Messiah. He had long been predicted. Finally, when the fullness of time had come, God sent his son (Gal. 4:4) into the world to save us.

This very idea, this grandest of plans is not "pretty good." Many plans in our day and age are pretty good; and many religious ideas throughout history are pretty good. But God's plan is wonderfully excellent in every way, so much so that it leads us to sing and praise at this time of year. We can hardly keep ourselves from praising God, if we try. The reason is because of the excellencies of God's plan. It is greater than any work of art; more perfect than any other design— beautiful and effective in all it does.

God's plan is not pretty good. If it is only pretty good, then it might be fortunate to receive some modified or pretty good allegiance from us. But you realize that God's plan is better than that. It is superb. The advent makes the angels sing. As they gaze onto what God does, they cannot help but burst out into song—a couple of times. Indeed, all through Jesus's ministry, the Son of God is seen as better than Pretty Good.

"The Love of God illustrated" is seen from this quote from Charles Spurgeon. "Truly you might say there was nothing in you to make him love you, but he left heaven's throne for you. As he came down the celestial hill, I think the angels said, 'Oh, how he loved them!" When he lay in the manger [as] an infant, they gathered round and said, 'Oh, how he loves!' All throughout his life even when the angels saw him sweating in the garden, when he was put into the crucible and began to be melted in the furnace, then indeed the spirits above began to know how much he loved us." (Spurgeon, on Jn. 11:36)

God gave us the very best gift possible—in the sending of his son. He did not give a pretty good son, but a perfect one:

2. The Son is Perfect, not merely 'pretty good.'

When John 3:16 talks about God's Son being given for us, that also makes it clear that God's love is so great that it can only be expressed in the giving of his Son. As that most memorized verse is read, all too often the emphasis is placed on the second half of the verse, the "whoever believes." In that process, while it may be noble to exult in human faith, on the other hand it obscures the real emphasis—"the so-great love of God." God's love is not pretty good love, but he "so-loved," to the greatest extent that he gave his Son, the center of Christmas, as well as Easter.

Jesus was sinless and perfect in all ways. He never had a single flaw, nor moral failure. He never had a blemish, nor weakness. He never thought an impure thought. Although he was like us in all human ways, never once did he sin (Heb. 2)

God's Son is perfect; not merely pretty good.

It is the mistake of modernity to speculate that Jesus was only one of several supreme prophets. If Jesus was only a good moral teacher, or at best, an exemplary religious prophet, then the best that Messiah might bring would be pretty good salvation. The Gospel of Liberalism believed that Jesus was not fully divine, but only a good and insightful prophet. Accordingly, pretty good religious standing was the best that that religion could confer. The weakness is in that view of the Savior. He is not pretty prophetic, or pretty exemplary, nor substantially worthy of imitation. Jesus is not a little omniscient, nor occasionally omnipotent, *nor pretty god-ish.* He is fully God at all times.

The opening verses of the Book of Hebrews inform us about the character and moral perfection of Jesus: "The Son is the radiance of God's glory and the exact representation of his being, sustaining all things by his powerful word . . . [the] heir of all thing, and through whom the universe was made." (Heb. 1:2-3)

In terms of his moral perfection, he is thoroughly and totally perfect in all that he did and all that he undertakes. He is benevolent and benign—always working in concert with the Father. From the perfection of the son, therefore, flows a perfect salvation. Jesus kept all the law that Adam did/could not. Jesus was perfect man, as well as perfect God. Jesus was our covenant-keeper, who perfectly executed the requirements of God in our place. As a result, the salvation he brings is as perfect as his character. Find a flaw in the character of the Savior, and you'll find a flaw in the manner of his salvation. However, the flawless Savior also gives flawless salvation.

3. The miracles surrounding Advent are more than 'pretty good.'

At this time of year, amidst much of the hoopla that modern fanaticism has created, we see nothing that parallels or supersedes the miracles of Advent. The set of miracles surrounding the Advent are as stunning as possible. Rivaled only by the Resurrection narratives, the Advent miracles were not pretty good, but supremely excellent.

Review a few with me to see the point.

First, there was the miraculous birth of the Baptizing forerunner. Elizabeth had been barren, and Zechariah was "well along in years." While Zechariah is serving in the Temple, an Angel appears to inform him that he will have a son. Zechariah cannot believe it, and to show the seriousness, the angel strikes him mute, until the birth of the baby baptist. Once John is born, Zechariah gives him the name John (not Zechariah, Jr.), and onlookers are amazed. Zechariah also has his speech restored.

Then an angel appears to Mary to foretell the virgin birth. Even though some would dismiss this out of hand—mainly because they had never seen one before—the Scriptures use this to magnify the birth of Christ. His was no normal birth. Indeed, there have been none others: Not pretty good miracle, but unparalleled.

As Jesus is born, other angels summon the shepherds and announce the glad tidings. The Star from the East is another incredible miracle. I barely need to remind you that this star was not a pretty good celestial phenomenon; but it was an awesome astronomical feat. Further, after the wise men arrive, and Herod seeks to kill the Christ-child, God—by miraculous means—delivers Jesus and his family. If not for the miracles, Jesus would have been one of those many male children who were cruelly slaughtered.

One can study the individual miracles, but even more impressive, if viewed together, the excellency of the incarnation is underscored by the strength of these miracles. The miracles were not pretty good human efforts.

4. Our need is huge, not 'pretty big.'

Another wrong calculation by many people is that they do not recognize their spiritual need as great. Some people may go so far as to admit that they are spiritually hindered, but they hold out hope that something may happen to restore them to earlier or greater spiritual capacity.

However, the Bible does not portray us as fairly sinful, or pretty fallen. According to Scripture, we are so fallen, that we are "dead in our sins and trespasses." We are unable to pull ourselves out of the pits. Despite the best of unregenerate efforts, prior to Christ's invasion of our life, we do not think correctly; we do not view things as God wishes, our emotions are out of whack, and we are unable to ignite our own spiritual fires. We are not just fairly fallen, but utterly wracked with sin and its attendant miseries. We must cry out with the apostle Paul, "Oh, wretched man that I am. Who can deliver me from this body of death?"

I think most of you know that I am a sinner. If you don't, just take my word for it. Unfortunately, I have no questions about my own depravity. It is very real. What amazes me, though, is to watch how many Christians seem to believe in "Pretty Good Depravity." Pretty good depravity is the idea that humans are sinful in several or a great many of their efforts; perhaps even a majority. But that is different from the biblical teaching of total depravity. According to Scripture, it is not the case that some parts of the human personality are fallen, while others are unstained by the Fall. Nor is it the case, that our minds calculate correctly most of the time, as if one can admit to being fallen, but not too fallen. I do not believe in Pretty Good Depravity, but that Depravity is total.

Hence, the need we have for salvation is not pretty big, but huge. It is true that we stand, as it were, on one side of the Grand Canyon. If all of us leap our best, and all the Olympic long jumpers leap their best, all will result at the bottom of the Canyon. We'll not get close.

5. *Justification is more than 'pretty good.'*

According to the scriptural testimony, the act of justification is a thorough one. Justification is a legal declaration by God, the Judge, in which he commutes our sentence, saves us from condemnation, and pronounces us "Not Guilty" in view of the law. The effect of justification is that we are freed from our sin, and no longer under the guilty sentence of God's law. We stand, then, in the presence of God "just as if I'd never sinned." God does this entire work, quite without any help or contribution from us.

How can God do this and still be just? The answer is that he does this through the work of Jesus Christ who as full man, suffered in our place and died in our place. He was born to die in our place.

When God justifies a person, that person is in the very best of spiritual conditions. He /she is not pretty well justified; but thoroughly justified. Our sins are forgiven as far as the east from the west. The distance between the skies and the earth is a drop in the bucket compared to the remission of our sins. God saves to the uttermost.

Justification, and every other work of God, is perfect, and never pretty good. So is sanctification, so is the way God keeps us until the very end. God's plan to give us new glorified bodies at the last resurrection is equally perfect. His providence—day in and day out—is not "pretty good" providence, but holy, perfect, majestic, and divinely sovereign providence. His guidance of us is excellent; so is his care—even during affliction.

How great a salvation! One may compare to themes of the Book of Hebrews. Hebrews 2: 3 speaks of "such a great salvation." This salvation is beyond comparison, better than anything else. It is not just one among the many. It is the only that is "so great." Later that same chapter compares Jesus to angels and their ministry. He is far superior—not just a pretty good angel. Hebrews 3 instructs us to fix our eyes on Jesus, who was superior to Moses. Jesus is not depicted as one who was a pretty good prophet, when compared to Moses; no he was infinitely superior. Jesus was greater than all the high priests; he was greater than Melchizedek. He far exceeded the highpoints of the OT priests and prophets.

He is even better than the OT sacrificial system.: "But the ministry Jesus has received is as superior to theirs as the covenant of which he is mediator is superior. . ." (Heb. 8:6) The salvation that Jesus brings is so perfect that it never needs repeating. It cannot be improved upon. Rather than continually performing sacrifices, when our Priest gave himself on the cross, "he offered for all time one sacrifice for our sins and sat down at the right hand of God." (Heb. 9:12).

God does all things excellently. That is the key word to remember. It may help to remember it this way: The very best, at our optimum effort, is for human beings to do pretty good. In fact, to claim more is to participate either in exaggeration or self-flattery. Pretty good is the best we can do.

God, on the other hand, does nothing in "pretty good" fashion. None of his works are fairly awesome. All are superbly grand.

1 Peter 2:9 tells us what to do in light of this: "But you are a chosen people, a royal priesthood, a holy nation, a people belonging to God, that you may declare the [excellencies] praises of him who called you out of darkness into his wonderful light." Older versions translated this as "excellencies." "So excellent is that state in which sinners are

advanced by believing in Jesus Christ, that the sharpest sighted in the world, the longer they look upon it, will still see more and more of the excellency and privileges thereof." This is especially helpful during affliction: to know that God is excellent in all his ways.

Have you a difficulty? God is excellent in it; learn to see his hand.

Have you cause for rejoicing? Then praise God in his excellency.

Do you look at Advent? Then see his excellency.

"That which is the Lord's end in bestowing all these privileges upon believers, and which they should make the great end and business of their life, is that they may show forth the praises of the Lord . . . or by their prudent and seasonable commending to others his properties, such as his wisdom, power, terror, sweetness, faithfulness, etc."

The message of Advent is that salvation is superb and excellent—not pretty good. A pretty good salvation would not deserve our worship, but the longevity of Christmas shows that we have so great a salvation!

A Real Christmas Service

Philippians 2:1-11

Advent is a season of celebration and anticipation of victory. We do not go about bemoaning our sin and stressing our sinfulness. That is reserved for Lent, which we Protestants have eliminated. Advent is not the time of year to have frowns on our faces. Its message seems removed from solemn scowls or anything less than cheer.

The sights and sounds of Christmas are focused on the shining star, the worship given by the other kings, the adoration of the shepherds, and in all, the exaltation of Jesus our Lord. Though he was born a babe, that is quickly overlooked, as we resume our triumphal celebration. Indeed, it is more fun to enjoy those aspects. And although I don't want to be a killjoy, I do want us to make sure that we do *not* overlook one very significant aspect of Christ's person and work, which of necessity must come before our celebration of Him. That is the aspect of service. Christ came to serve. As Matthew 20:28 states, "The Son of Man did not come to be served, but to serve, and to give His life as a ransom for many." And the manner of his coming shows real Christmas Service as much as anything else. Too often the glimmer of the Christmas ornamentation blinds us to the truth that Jesus came as a lowly, unpowerful infant. He did not come as an accomplished military General on a White Stallion.

We live in such a success-oriented world, that one can never stress too often that Christ does not work in that way, nor by the methods of this world. Our Lord was above power and success-plays. He never needed to rely on His power, because the contest was never in question- not even close. There was no rival Potentate, who was close to defeating Christ, even if Satan has yet to get that message. *He just doesn't get it!* In that Christ was never threatened, He was free to conquer by the opposite of human force. He used the weapon of humble sacrifice. As the well-known title reflects, Jesus truly stoops to conquer.

But the more I think about it, the more I can see why some looked for a "white Stallion" Messiah. It helps to recall that the Jewish legends which had grown up around the coming Messiah, had by the first century depicted *Messhiach* as a conquering Liberator, who would sweep into Palestine and free the captive Israelis. Sure this was pretty self-interested, and sure this was not exactly supported by the OT, but it certainly played well in local politics. So through the centuries the home team began to look for a Messiah who would destroy the Romans, exact vengeance for the ills of the past 6-7 centuries of disgrace, elevate Israel back to the top of the heap of International politics, and establish the geopolitical center of gravity right in downtown Jerusalem. This messiah would, of course, be dashing, brave, eloquent, a graduate no doubt from the finest schools, and from impeccable lineage. He would likely be a Levite, a descendant from the Priestly line, an expert in the Jewish law, and most importantly, a sort of Caesar-abinowitz—a proven military man, crafted after the image of the Roman conquerors of that time, only rabidly pro-Zionist. This would totally benefit one people, and would advance their interests only.

I can see why the people had crafted this Messiah after their own wants and image of success. Isn't it funny how we still do that today? And it is very close to idolatry to craft our expectation of God after our wants, needs, and even national interests. The more I think about it, and most people would do the same thing, If I were drawing up a job description for a Messiah, we would have it read like the above description.

    WANTED:
- proven leader of battles of conquest.
- willing to slaughter at command; no problem with ulcers or conscience.

- strategic genius to work with a few to overcome many.
- conversant with Latin; well-educated.
- miracle-working ability.
- undaunted bravery and limitless courage.
- expert in all martial arts and combat.
- experience in government, as well.

So just prior to the First Christmas, that is what the Jews and most others were looking for in a Messiah, if they were looking at all. Some, no doubt, had grown weary like some moderns, and given up hope even looking for God to work above this history.

Yet God, according to Philippians 2 befuddled the 'conventional wisdom' by sending what seemed on the surface to be a most unlikely Messiah. It did not start with a great Inauguration, nor festive celebration. It was not accompanied with the ticker tape of conquest. Instead, God sent the Messiah, in the lowliest of circumstances, and chose the route of humility over raw power. That is a lesson for us at the Advent.

As with many other passages, follow the Divine Logic in this passage. Although the order of these verses begins with our attitude and how we are to be servant-followers of Jesus, we'll begin first with Christ as our Model, as our Accomplisher. Next based on that, and *not in reverse order*, is the command that we follow our Leader. Finally, I wish to tie this in with this Sacrament we'll receive today, and make a few suggestions for our Advent preparation.

I. The humility of Christ.

Verse 5 contains the command that we should have the same attitude as Christ. Then the next 3 verses proceed to lyrically describe how Christ's attitude of "coming not to be served, but to serve" was acted out in his life and ministry. Instead of being a great leader who demanded an adoring procession, and the best seats in the house, our Lord was born in a manger—even without any prepared baby clothes, not to mention royal robes. Although he was as far as his very nature, fully God (v. 6), Jesus did not consider the equal standing or recognition as God as something to be grasped.

Have you ever seen someone of great stature, be so at home in that, that when faced with a challenge, they did not even resort to an appeal to their power? Occasionally we see an example in athletics. I think especially of the Special Olympics. On more than one occasion a leading athlete will be helping with the Special Olympics. For example, Carl Lewis will race against some handicapped racers. And when a Downs Syndrome racer comes up to the Fastest Human Alive and says with Downs Syndrome braggadocio, "I'm gonna beat you Mr. Lewis," Carl Lewis does not reach down and call up his strongest resolve to run his best race ever. It is quite alright if the handicapped racer wins. In fact, that is preferred. Carl Lewis can walk away from that fame and glory. It is not necessary for him to prove himself in this race. That is a partial measure of his greatness. In some small way, that is the way it is with Christ here.

He does not have to prove his God-ness on the human stage. He can walk away from that. He is not striving to be equal with God. He'd seen how disastrous that was in the past. The last one who seriously thought he could be equal with God was Lucifer. Jesus, on the other hand, who was fully God and who was a person within the Triune God, did not act as though equality, the same recognition, nor glory was something to be pursued. He could have, sure. But he did not. And that's part of why so many power-seekers missed Him. Still do. That's also at the heart of this Christmas and this Advent.

Consider this fictional dialogue.

The Conversation that Didn't Take Place

Do we even dare to glimpse into what Christ gave up to come to redeem his people? Can we fathom? Advent is a good time to reflect on that. What if Messiah had looked out for No. 1, his own interests? What if Christ had been unwilling to come to earth and die for his people? What if he'd wanted service, instead of to serve? Bear with me, as I suppose, only for illustration's sake, that the following conversation took place.

> *God*: "Jesus, do you want to go down to earth and redeem my people? Someone's got to do it."
>
> *Jesus*: "Not any time soon, Father. You know I'm really tied up in this project and with a few other primary sectors. Plus we've got the Long-range task force due in the near future. After that, there's some stored-up leave time I want to get to, as well. But really I'd just prefer to not get involved."
>
> *God*: "Well I have promised, and we did covenant accordingly."

Jesus: "Yes, I recall, that all sounded good back then, but times have changed, and I honestly had no idea that the human race would get so out of hand. Still I know I made a commitment. Perhaps, I could grudgingly pencil in a few days somewhere along the line. OK, What will it take? Also perhaps, you could refresh my memory, what we stand to personally gain or lose?"

God: "It is an expensive proposition to be sure. I knew full well how costly it would be. Redemption always is. You'll have to leave behind most of the comfort and glory here."

Jesus: "Not the Complex! I'd be lost without it and would have a difficult time adjusting to new environment."

God: "That's not insuperable. We could overcome that."

Jesus: "But the planet of men is so grungy. It is so filled with hatred and violence. You know they don't respect the values we hold as Holy. It is like throwing a pearl before swine. If only we could either delegate this matter to someone else, recruit one of their own, or maybe even teleconference this. Can't we use some other method, than the hands-on one?"

God: "Also don't forget what it involves. The Messiah will be unpopular, not recognized for his greatness. You'll begin in humble beginnings and go down from there. At the low point you'll be rejected by those closest to you, led through that false hoax of a trial, and finally nailed on a cross."

Jesus: "Yes, it'll get pretty dirty down there. And another thing, it will be truly painful, for I (or whomever) will have that human flesh which attracts pain. Are these people really worth all this? Things are going so nicely up here. No problems, no traffic, no personnel problems, and all the glory goes to the proper center. I'm truly fulfilled up here."

God: "Do you want me to order you?"

Jesus: "Oh no, that is not necessary. Let me first remand it to one more study commission. It's so comfortable up here. . . and so wretched down there—There'll be no thanks you know—and let this commission have a few millennia, then we'll get right on it, after we hear their informed report. Doesn't that sound good?"

God: "It has to be done now. What are you afraid of, or hesitant to leave behind?"

Jesus: "Well that may be the real issue. It's just so great up here. I share the glory with you. We have no problems. Even the 24 Elders are constantly falling down to worship us. Anything we want, we can instantly have. Our streets are paved with gold, we have unending food, no sadness (not even any weeping), we have sufficient precious metals and luxurious clothes. The Throne here is superb, and the last interloper has already been dispensed. Besides no one else down there truly understands me. And those people! They are vile, rebellious, exceedingly proud, and who wants to give his life in exchange for theirs? To top it all off, do we really have to start off in that smelly stable, without even a proper reception? Maybe the White Stallion approach, with a quick wrap-up might be better. After all, some of the Israelis are still looking for that."

Well fortunately that conversation never occurred, nor ever would. That is not the Jesus of the scriptures. That could be the Jesus modelled after our own human or corporate images. Thank God, that this was not the conversation. On the contrary, it was the opposite. Jesus never balked at the Incarnation. He did not hold back. He did not seek to hold on to the equality with God. Our Lord Jesus *did* come to this earth, and he did waltz around in the mud and grime of this sinful planet. He did die on the cross for us. And wonder of wonders—He left all the comfort, glory, and accomplishment of heaven to do this for us.

Not only did he leave this all behind, and more than any of us could ever know, but moreover, He made himself of no standing (v. 7) and "took on the very nature of a servant, being made in human likeness" (7b). He <u>servanted</u> himself. He still, of course retained his full deity. He could not put that aside; he merely added another nature on top of that—overlaid Deity with humanity. And "being found in appearance as a man, he humbled himself and became obedient to death- even death on a cross!" (Phil. 2:8). That's how Advent was launched . . . in SERVANTHOOD.

Praise God at Advent, that this was the conversation which never took place.

Such is our Lord's model to us. And we must take this to heart in Advent. To ignore this, is to minimize the greatness of our Savior's love and mercy for us. We must see something of his servanthood in his birth in the stable. He was born in a smelly stable, with not proper regal robes, and without the fanfare so richly deserved. This is real service at Christmas. Christ came down at Advent.

And likewise, God Himself will not allow us to lose the imitation which is also required of us. Not only are we to know this as a theological fact, but God calls each of us to follow this example—We only can, of course, if we're made new, and animated by the grace of God—and there is no better time to hear this, than at Christmas. It was Christ's beginning of service, and should be ours as well.

II. Go back now to vss. 3-5, for they tell us to imitate Christ—if you know him—in this life of service. The command is clear in v. 3: "Do nothing out of selfish ambition or vain conceit, but in humility consider others better than yourself." The command is that we are not to allow ourselves to be motivated by ambition to be NO. 1, nor by vain conceit which tells us that we are best and most deserving. Instead, we are to follow our Master, and lay aside any earthly glory we dare to claim.

That is what Christ did. He did not operate out of selfish ambition, nor vain conceit. If anyone ever deserved to do so, it was Him. But Christ did not. Rather in humility he *did* and we are to "consider others better than yourselves" (v. 3). How do we do this?

Try a couple of things this Advent.

In the *home*, try to anticipate what the other family members would want to do. Put their interests first this year.

In the *shopping malls* try this: If push comes to shove, back up and give the other person the right of way. Try to see how many chances you might even have to share the good news, by letting others go first, if you're racing for that check-out register or scurrying.

In *Church* let us make a covenant this year, that we will not seek our own interests. How often it is that we demand a suggestion or create/tailor make a service to fit our own interests, schedules, or wants. Why not, have the Spirit of Christ reign at our church activities this year? We won't all get our way, but let's be on the lookout to see how we can put forth the interests of one another.

Further, "Each of you should look not only to your own interests, but also to the interests of others." (v. 4). That is exactly what Christ did at Advent. Will you? This path of Christian maturity is painful; it calls for self-sacrifice, but none greater than our Lord.

Finally, in this passage, it clearly spells out that "Your attitude should be the same as that of Christ Jesus. . ." That's why we've looked at that first. So how manifest will:

- humility
- service
- others' legitimate interests

be for you and your family this year?

Ask it from the other side. How manifest will:

- selfish ambition
- vain conceit
- pride
- own interests be for us. (That list hurts doesn't it?).

This is real service . . . to follow Christ and be a servant. That's this passage calls this congregation to this Advent. Not merely to take care of our own, but to seek to serve others' interests. Be on the lookout for selfish ambition . . . in planning.

Watch out for vain conceit.

Beware of pride. Let's all slow down just a little bit, be a little more self-reflective, and ask, more frequently, "Is what I want my will, and in my interests? Or is it what God wants and in the interest of His people?? Whose will is it? Ask, "In whose interest is this?" Before we fight, or quarrel, or get all steamed up, first calm down, and ask whose will are you pursuing?

Every year, I try to warn people about PRESBYTENSION, that malady that strikes high-end, successful people, who are accustomed to being bosses, more than others.

Whose interests are you championing? I imagine we'll be saddened to realize how much of our own will we try to get.

Instead, we are called to service. And not a single one of us will be called to greater service than our Master. He came and served. While everyone else was feasting at the dinner, he was taking off his nice clothes, putting on a servant's apron, and washing not the dishes, but the disciple's feet. He started this in the stable. No Jesus wasn't a famous conqueror, nor was he a well-paid Lord. He had nowhere to lay his head . . . except on the cross. And that was OK with him. He was a servant. Are you? Are you? Will you forget this in the hectic pace of Christmas?

III. In case you are prone to do just that, as I am, perhaps you need a sacramental reminder of the sacrificial service of Jesus. That's what this sacrament is for today. It, too, has the central meaning and symbolism of sacrificial atonement.

It tells us that if left to our own interests, or in our own merit, we would not have salvation. In fact, we are so sinful that we need a drastic atonement. We needed the perfect God-Man to come down and die in our place. No other sacrifice would take care of that. We required a most costly redemption. So costly that it interrupted heavenly glory. Jesus left all his accomplishment behind him. He descended, a *definite demotion*, to be born in an outback room. He was mocked all of his life, as being born out of wedlock. He never was brought up in a court of royalty, only the hearth of humility. He then was rejected by his own, trampled on as a common political criminal, and finally killed. Never once did he sin, or deserve that punishment.

Yet through it all he remembered that he loved his people, and loved them to the uttermost he did. The Babe born on Christmas was the Savior who would die 33 years later at Easter. This sacrament is a tangible reminder and seal of that. As you take it today, do so especially in remembrance of his humility and service. And renew your covenant with God to be a servant, not to be served. That is Christ-like Communion. That is real Christmas service.

A Christmas Fruit Basket for Pastor

Galatians 5:19-26

"All I want for Christmas is my two front teeth." What a simple request from a child. Many of us recall that part of the Broadway song. Perhaps some of your own children have sung that. Well my request is similar. It is simple. I bet you didn't know you were coming to church to hear the wish list of the Pastor this morning, did you? Well you are about to. Could you boil down your Christmas wants to one line. Here's mine: All I want for Christmas from the Congregation is a basket of fruit. That's all; but a special kind of fruit.

Most of us know how delightful it is to have the UPS van slow as it passes the front of our houses at this time of year. If it stops in front then we normally (regardless of age or sophistication) stop what we're doing and intently peer from that spot which we've chosen long ago to be the vantage from which we spy (for we'd want no one to know) to see if the Parcel is bringing a gift for me. And sure enough the man in the chocolate-brown suit rings your bell, you answer it with a fabricated, "Oh my, what a surprise," and zoom to read the label. It is a basket of fruit, like the one sent in a previous year. You open it, and begin immediately to enjoy that gift. At this time of year, with all the rich goodies, and elaborate dishes, hardly anything is as refreshing as fresh fruit. Many people even give a mixed assortment of fruits, in expensive fruit baskets.

Just this past Thursday evening, Ann and I enjoyed one of the best pieces of watery fruit, since this time last year. It had been a hectic day.

Papa had spent the day in ecclesiastical luncheons—you know how old that mash-potato circuit gets. Then after a rushed afternoon, the family sped out to buy a Christmas Tree. We brought it home, only to hear father's annual vocabulary outburst, and finally had it standing—for the first time. We gobbled down a snack, discovered that all the strings of lightbulbs had conspired to go out in the same year . . . as they do every year, and snacked some more. Meanwhile, the helpful elves helped pull the tree down once . . . twice . . . and nearly a third time, before we locked the cat in the washroom, and poured up a victorious of toast of Egg Nog with peanut butter-brownies to top it off. After baths, and prayers, my wife and myself, felt strangely exhausted, and yuck from all the junk. Then she said, "How 'bout a grapefruit"? And it was lovely. Why, after the grapefruit, I was even able to beat Andrew to sleep. Fruit this time of year, is wonderful.

That's all a pastor wants for Christmas this year. Of course, if you've baked chocolate goodies, don't withhold those. Of course, I'll eat those as well. But all I'm asking for this year is some fruit. In just a moment, you'll see what kind.

To be honest, I feel a little embarrassed asking for anything from you. You're always so generous to us. But I feel compelled to ask for this fruit this year, not only for my own good, but for your spiritual good as well. The kind of fruit basket you can all give me, is one filled with the Fruit of the Spirit. It will cost you no money, and will last longer than anything else. In fact, while you're at it, you might want to assemble more than one fruit basket.

This passage of Scripture describes for us the Fruit of the Spirit. It is a well-known section, and I hesitate to repeat it. However, I'm convinced that it holds much for us, especially at this time of year. In fact, we may need to hear it at this time of year, more than any other time, for this reason. This is the season of *Presbytension*—the time of year, when church members are most tense, and most apt to inflict lasting damage on each other. We may need a sign hung over our heads, this time of year: "Beware of Church-Goers."

When I was a young pastor in Georgia, every Christmas was filled with controversy over the Choir. There was an underlying staff problem, and year after year, oh quite predictably, it would break out and spill over an incredible amount of bitterness into the church. People all just got so steamed up over things which really did not have much (if any) eternal significance. Seldom could the church enjoy Christmas because the leadership, along with their respective loyalists, were fighting. Tis the season to be jolly. To top it all off, then we had to have a Staff Christmas party . . . where some of the staff weren't even speaking. As a young minister this made quite an impression on me. I resolved to avoid, if at all possible, such hectic pace, as to be so tense as to be unable to enjoy Christmas. Watch that Presbytension. Maybe the Baptists and Methodists have the same kind of tension or higher, but I'd have to see it to believe it.

One of the things we can do about this—and this lasts not only throughout the year, but throughout eternity—is to have the Fruit of God's Spirit living in us. View this passage this morning with me, as descriptive of two different kinds of fruit. All I want for Christmas is the Fruit of the Spirit to be exchanged in our congregation.

Compare first with me, what the opposite Fruit basket contains. This is *not* what I want for Christmas. In fact, I urge you to avoid the vices of vss. 19-21 like the plague. These are the fruit of the flesh. I want you to be sure to notice, that the Scripture is clear, here and elsewhere that our real spiritual beliefs do manifest themselves. They will not remain invisible. Paul has already noted (in v. 17) that the sinful nature desires what is contrary to, or consistently the opposite of, the Spirit. Likewise, the Spirit is in direct opposition to the flesh or carnality. There is no in between; one or the other. The Christian will avoid what follows in vss. 19-21. List those briefly with me, as rotten fruit, which is to be avoided.

I. 19-21 provides a list of the *obvious* acts of the sinful nature. Again, these are not disguised.
- sexual immorality;
- impurity;
- debauchery—All of the first three deal with the area of sexual unfaithfulness;

These are obvious, and not possibly from the Lord. Also, the fruit catalogue continues to list:
- idolatry;
- witchcraft—These two deal with violations of the 2nd commandment;

Then follow a number of interpersonal sins, to be on the guard against in this season:

- hatred;
- discord. How many times will we see these at our church, in the next weeks?
- jealousy—Are any of you? About anything?
- fits of rage; This is the kind of anger, which is nursed like a glowing ember. In fact, it is stoked occasionally, and leads to rage. It is consciously kept glowing; it is intentionally fueled.
- selfish ambition—Any in the church?
- Dissensions . . . factions—groups which form around individuals and elevate the small uniqueness over the larger Christian unity. Beware of those who are super-pious.
- envy—the same as the 10th commandment. Does any here covet their neighbor's house, tools, spouse (your neighbor's wife), or anything else which the Lord has not provided for us?
- drunkenness—Some believe there is a special "allowance" at this time of year' for this.
- orgies, and the like.

These make up the Fruit basket of the flesh. These are the evident works of one religion . . . the way of mankind apart from Christ. These are the fruit of the sinner, pursuing his own way and own desires. Do these show up in your life? At Christmas, if a video of our lives were replayed in January, would you appear Christian at all?? Which fruit is in your life?

The accompanying warning is a stern one: "that those who live like this will not inherit the Kingdom of God." That is unambiguous. Neither is this unique. There are several passages in the NT, which list habits of the flesh and warn that such will not inherit the Kingdom of God (cf. I Cor. 6). That Fruit Basket, is the Fruit, which tempted Eve, so long ago. It is a reckless and damaging gift to give. Please don't give it for Christmas.

II. Contrast this with the fruit to bring at Christmas. These are the fruits to work on this year in vss. 22-26.
a. LOVE

This morsel is the consideration of the other and their needs. At Christmas time, cultivate this fruit as first and foremost. It is at the head of the list. What kind of love is called for? I Corinthians 13 probably paints a portrait of this fruit best, if you'd like to review it.

Let your love be expressed in gift-giving. Although my wife will tell you that I'm not good at this, neither am I one of those "bah Humbug" monastery-type Christians, who think all material things are inherently bad, and sinful in themselves. Evidently Our God himself did not despise material things, as he took on a very physical body. He did not float around as a hover-craft spirit. Nor did he command us to assume the most frugality possible. Materialism is sinful, but godly and proper use of the material is fine. I think it's perfectly appropriate to give nice, even lavish gifts to those we love at Christmas. It's OK for your love to be expressed in gifts. It might even be OK to splurge occasionally for those we love so dearly. But most importantly give your love.

Whatever you do, or give, do it with love. Let us restrain that impulse to get even, or to inflict harm, in this Advent. If we'll be loving toward one another, in this season, that is one of the best gifts you could ever give this Pastor.

. . . It takes love to anticipate what the other person will truly enjoy.
. . . It takes love to save all year to sacrifice.
. . . It takes love to seek and find that special gift.
. . . It takes love to endure the others' quirks and foibles.

Do that at Christmas. As Colossians 3:14 says, "Above all put on love, which binds all these things together in perfect harmony.

b. JOY

Isn't it wonderful to see the joy on children's faces at Christmas? Why my children started rejoicing in October. How 'bout giving the gift of joy this Christmas.

Joy is that overflowing happiness, which goes beyond the bounds of normal contentment and pleasure. Joy spills over into praise. There is satisfaction . . . then pleasure . . . then happiness, and finally joy. Joy results when the pre-occupation with self and its ambitions is downplayed long enough for us to marvel at what God has done. It is that kind of joy at the birth of our Savior, which should normally overflow in several ways.

One way you can include joy in your fruit basket, is to enter into the singing of these Christmas praises to the best of your ability. For Christmas, give your pastor joyful singing at worship time. I'll make a once a year deal: If you'll all sing and worship, I'll even pick songs that you know—at least 90% of the time. Let's joyfully gather around our Savior and sing joyfully.

Another way to express joy is to work on your faces. Let me explain what I mean by that. Plastic surgery is certainly out of the question. What I mean is to ask you to not go around quite as heavy-hearted. A smile can lighten up a lot of things. Isn't it about time we smiled a little . . . perhaps even engaged in a few belly laughs? Is our burden to carry really that uncommon to the human race, or are we not perhaps taking ourselves too seriously? And when someone asks, "How's it going?" before launching into all the tribulations of your day, consider correcting that attitude, and speaking about your joy. It's nice to hear some good news.

Likely the greatest way to show your joy, however, is a way which is befuddlingly difficult for some. The best way to share our joy at Christmas, is to tell someone about Christ. Many Christians have a strangely difficult time doing that. We can talk about all kinds of subjects, but we avoid that one. Well don't do that at Christmas. This is our holiday. Its very meaning is about Jesus Christ, recognizing him as Messiah-King, and his work of salvation. If you rejoice in that, tell someone this month how much you love Christmas and the "Reason for the Season." I'll make it easy on you. Don't anyone tell the good news to a total stranger, and don't go up to anyone on the street, with whom you have no relationship at all. Instead, talk to a friend, someone you work with, and be sure to plan ahead, to tell them why you especially have joy at Christmas. And then invite them to church, or give them a small piece of Christian lit. That's one thing to do with your joy.

Also consider giving that extra gift, to the person *not* on your list and not expecting a gift from you. That's fun.

Joy is seen in our faces, on our lips, through those common gestures. It is a fruit of the spirit. I want it in my fruit basket. Do you have any?

c. PEACE

This peace, "which passes all understanding" comes in several shapes and sizes.

1. The first kind of peace you can give me is peace with God. The most basic and needed kind of peace is peace with God. We can have peace within a nation, inside our homes, and our streets can be free from violence, but those are not the most basic kinds of peace. Peace with God is what we all need. What I'd love to have, is a fruit basket which is filled with the knowledge that each one of you, I mean every one, has that peace with God. This fruit is the work of grace in your hearts. It is the absence of war with God. He is no longer at war with you and you've become his friend. Are you one of God's friends, or are you a declared enemy of God? For Christmas, do as the people in Paul's time did for your Pastor. Give yourselves first to God, and then to us (2 Cor. 8:5) . If you have peace with God, sometime this month, express that to me.

2. We also need peace with one another. Now I haven't seen any good fist fights at church lately. But I do know this. I've seen Pastors carted out on ambulance stretchers, never to return to a pulpit in some church fights. I've seen people mortally wounded, and I've known of good people getting real hurt in good churches at Christmas.

I'm not aware of any declared wars in our church at this time. But I do know this. There have been some in the past, and there are still some walking wounded. Why not use this time of year to make peace. It would be for your own good, but if for no other reason, Do it for your Pastor. Make it my Christmas gift, to make peace with someone here in this church. Some of us are capable of carrying around old battle-axes which are 5, 10, 15, 25 years old. Can you recall those old battles?

Don't you think it's time to bring those to the cross? Let's be at peace with one another. And as soon as the truce is made, it will be broken, so be prepared to forgive 70 x 7. But do have peace . . . peace with one another. That is the Fruit of the Spirit. Its opposite is discord and factionalism.

We need to stop intentionally irritating some people. We don't need to go out of our way, to look for reasons to anger each other. Let us do anything we can to decrease tension and genuinely help one another. Give peace at Christmas. Give it not just to me, but to those in your church, and those in your family. Is there one family member that needs forgiveness, that needs to have the hatchet buried? Isn't 20 years long enough to bear that grudge? The fruit of the spirit is peace.

d. PATIENCE

As you are probably aware, this word in its original sense was translated, "long-suffering." It indicates the patience which is required while we wait, or suffer for an extended period of time. Ongoing-suffering, or patience, is one of the most needed presents. It may be at the top of our list. Somehow, things just don't seem to happen as fast as we would like them to. What do we do? We usually get mad, stomp off, grumble a good bit, and in the end turn up very impatient.

I know I need patience. If you could give me that, you'd do the world a favor. I must need patience more than any pastor. Things always seem to go to slow for me. I'm always in a hurry, and then impatient. You could give me patience the hard way, but I hope not.

I had a very good friend in the ministry some time ago. He had one lady in his congregation who came up to him, and said, "Dr. Knox, you're going to be a pearl when I get through with you." At first he thought that was a nice compliment. However, as the lady went on, she reminded him how pearls were made. A grain of sand, of some foreign matter slips inside the shell of an oyster. It irritates the oyster, and begins to collect more secreted matter. As the concretion occurs, soon the pearl becomes calcified, polished, round, smooth, and hard. It all begins with an irritating grain of sand. This lady saw her calling in life to be the irritant. Now please, don't give me patience by that method. Tribulation does work patience, but I'd just as soon do without that bitter fruit. Don't enlist to be the Designated Irritant.

Instead, give the sweet fruit of patience. We need to be patient when others don't catch on, or understand as fast as we who are cerebral wizards. I ask you all to have patience with your Pastor who still has a lot to learn and much improvement. I ask you to be patient with your church. It is not perfect yet, like the one created in your imaginations to be perfect, or the one we used to attend. We are a learning, growing body. Please be patient with the various imperfections of your church and staff. Give me the fruit of patience.

Patience calls for each of us to keep the willingness to have *my* schedule interrupted by the other. It calls for my surrendering of some "To Do lists" which may not get finished. Patience means that everything will not be completed by the deadline. Patience is a good antitoxin for the ubiquitous *deadline-itis*, which is going around this time of year. Please be and give patience. There are few fruits any sweeter. And its sweetness is further enhanced, when you don't add "Oh, and by the way, it only out of the goodness of my heart, and to satisfy the Pastor, that I'm *so* patient with you, as to extend your deadline.

e. KINDNESS

Kindness is needed in the fruit basket. It is the positive effort at satisfying the other.

Kindness, is hard to define, for we all seem to know what it is, when we see it.

Kindness goes out of its way to be helpful. It goes the extra mile, gives the unexpected, the uncalled for. Kindness seeks to anticipate, or look ahead for ways to do good.

That short note, that flower, that little home-baked goodie . . . all of these are ways to express our kindness. Take this year, to try a little kindness. Care to shoot for one a day?

. . . It takes kindness to attend to the wishes of the shut-in.
. . . It takes kindness to help the slower person.
. . . It takes kindness to touch that life which is ignored by everyone else.

f. GOODNESS

Goodness has long been recognized as relating to the sphere of morality. It has definite moral overtones, and its opposite is bad. The fruit of goodness is grown in our lives as we are rooted into God. As Psalm 100:4 says, the Lord is fundamentally good. He is good in all that He does, and all aspects of his work are divinely and perfectly good. There is nothing in him that is not good.

When a person comes to Christ, that seed of goodness is implanted in him. We are then to progressively grow in accord with his character. Goodness is the work of the Holy Spirit in our lives and it is a fruit to give for Christmas.

g. FAITHFULNESS

How can you give faithfulness at Christmas? First make sure we understand what this word means. Faithfulness means to be *full to the faith*, or to measure up to the faith we profess. That works its way out in our lives in a number of ways. This word is akin to the word for "trustworthy." Hence for us to be faithful is to be trustworthy, trustworthy under stress, or dependable. What a gift to give, dependability. I'd rather have 10 dependable people than 1,000 undependable ones. It is always good to give faithfulness, or trustworthiness to another Christian.

Faithfulness is often the missing component in an age where commitments are quickly and easily broken. I invite you to use this Advent season as a time to renew your various commitments. Have you been faithful to them? For example, have you been faithful to give as the Lord has prospered? I ask you to be faithful in that. I was so impressed this week as one person called and asked what their Faith Promise commitment was. They'd forgotten the amount and wanted to be *faithful* to that. I told them the amount they'd promised was $4.8 million. Faithfulness. Have you been faithful to your membership vows? Why not review those sometime, and see if there are glaring areas of unfaithfulness? What about other vows? Are you faithful to those other major commitments of life?? The fruit of the spirit is faithfulness. If you have not this fruit, where is the Holy Spirit? Who is growing the fruit of your life if there is no faithfulness?

We could do with some good old-fashioned consistency of character. Year in and year out, not in a fair-weather kind of way, but through the thick and thin, that is what is needed. Give to your church, to those in your family, to your Pastor, or to anyone, some plum called faithfulness. It is one of the sweetest fruits.

PAUSE to note that fruit coming to bloom is quite natural. It may not be quick. It does not grow overnight (So if any of you have to wait a year, that'll be alright with me, as long as you do the planting now). Nonetheless, when fruit grows, it grows quite naturally.

In fact, Jesus expects fruit to grow in the Christian's life.

Do you realize that fruit-bearing is not the exception, but instead, the rule of the Christian's life? Jesus, would be quite surprised to hear some folks who seem to think that they can be Christians, but live as bad fruit. He actually discussed this thoroughly in Matthew 7:16-20.

h. GENTLENESS

This is especially needed in times of rush and harshness. We especially need to be reminded to be gentle with children. It takes gentleness to not bite the head off of someone, who doesn't please us. Gentleness is the opposite of that biting, retaliatory strike. It is matured beyond overpowering. The fruit of the spirit is gentle. Its opposite is in the catalogue above.

i. SELF-CONTROL

The piece of fruit to include in my basket—all I want for Christmas is the fruit of the Spirit—is the fruit of self-control. I need that desperately at times myself. *Somebody please give me self-control.*

We need self-control in terms of food consumption, don't we all. We need self-control in terms of our budget. It may not be wise to drastically exceed our realistic dollar amounts. Perhaps we need to reign in our "wants" and discipline ourselves to give to others.

That is a large part of this self-control. It is self-disciplined, it is not run wild by emotion or passion. It is passion in check. There are many areas we need this self-control. In anger, in zeal, in our attempts to move forward. The fruit of the spirit is to be seen as we are controlled by the spirit, and our passions in line. This self-control is needed to keep our priorities right during this distracting season. It is needed to maintain family and personal devotional patterns. I remind you to keep those devo times alive and constant. Other things will wait.

Share some self-control with me. I'd love a huge heaping of this. For this is a gift I truly need. In the basket, it will look like the fruit of moderation, instead of unbridled passion.

This chapter concludes with Galatians 5:24-26. There we're told that those who are truly Christians, those "who belong to Christ Jesus" have "Crucified the sinful nature with its passions and desires." That is the Christian life at Christmas, a life crucified and serving, not a life seeking its own. And the scripture continues, "Since we live by the Spirit, let us keep in step with the Spirit. Let us not become conceited, provoking and envying each other" (Gal. 5:25-26).

III. I learned an interesting thing this week about this list of 9 graces. They are primarily interpersonal. They mainly can be seen in the context of person-to-person relationships. They are seen on the horizontal level of the way we treat one another. Yet they also have a vertical dimension as well. They also, if we'll notice, illustrate how God treats us. In these 9, we furthermore, see the very heart of GOD unfolded at Christmas. God gives each of these to us at Christmas, and expresses his gifts in these ways.

For example, he at Advent, God gives:
Love - cf. John 3:16 and 15:13.
Joy - Lk. 2:10.

Peace - Lk. 2:14.

Complete this list at home. Study these to see how God exhibits these toward us.

All of these can come only by the Divine Gardener, who plants these fruits in our lives and gives these graces to us. We can't manufacture them in our own flesh. They are actually contrary to the flesh. Do you need these? Do you want these, as I do? Then draw near to Christ at Christmas.

All I want for Christmas is . . . Fruit of the Spirit among us. So does God.

The Birth of Jesus Triumphs Over Satan

Revelation 12

These Scripture verses may seem odd for a Christmas sermon. Who'd have thought we could turn to the Book of Revelation, with all its apocalyptic symbolism and surrealistic word-pictures to inform us about Christmas. Yet Revelation speaks to us in every age and any season, at all times in life. One of the things we learn from a sermon series on Revelation is the timeless application of the message of Revelation. It is most appropriate, and I cannot pass up the opportunity, to mine this final book for an Advent sermon.

This book and particularly these chapters have more relevance than just at the end of time. Even though we usually associate the message of the Revelation with the Second Coming of Christ, it also tells us much about his First Coming at Christmas.

This passage in Revelation 12 teaches us about the birth of Christ. It particularly portrays by a vision a cosmic conflict of the ages in which Satan tried to destroy and annul the Incarnate One's entrance into this world. Satan, symbolically described here as a dragon (12:3, 4, 9), tried to annihilate the Christ child before he was ever born.

Chapter 12 describes in symbolic terms both the heavenly warfare and why Christians face such satanic evil and persecution. Throughout, it stresses that God has decisively defeated Satan and assures us that he is already defeated. "Satan's power on earth is, to be sure, terrifyingly real to believers. But this is not because he is triumphant. It is because he knows that he is beaten and has but a short time." (L. Morris)

The dragon tried to destroy both the woman (who signifies the church) and the Messiah (the male child) who would rule all nations with an iron scepter (Ps. 2:9 fulfilled). But this highly symbolic vision encourages us that through the Messiah's incarnation on that First Christmas, Satan's effort was thwarted.

This passage in the Revelation depicts the continuous struggle between God and Satan's forces. Yet miraculously, God delivered the Messiah from extinction and provided the triumph for Messiah. Before we go further make sure you have the main picture before you. Don't get bogged down by the details yet. There are three main characters in this passage:

- Pregnant Woman — not Mary. This is a sign according to 12:1.
- Dragon — clearly identified as Satan according to verse 9. This one is not hard.
- Male Child — who can only be Christ "who will rule all nations with an iron scepter." That was predicted long ago in Psalm 2.

So this vision is about the invisible spiritual warfare surrounding the birth of Christ. Don't get side-tracked on the sun, moons, stars, number of crowns and heads right now. Just for now keep the conflict between these characters before you. Ask: of what central event and character does this describe? It is this Triumphant Messiah, who was born into the humblest estate, that we worship today.

His triumph appears all the more majestic and worthy of worship if we recall the most intense Satanic efforts to eliminate the coming of the Messiah. From the Garden of Eden until the First Christmas, Satan was not sleeping, but was at work with all his might trying to exterminate the Messiah who would come. But he never did. God was triumphant on that First Christmas day and avoided the dark tyrant's threat. This morning I'd like to review some of Satan's efforts and God's resulting victory. In doing so, we will see the Bible's triumphant philosophy of history which comforts us at all times. Messiah triumphs every time.

Think of an arch-enemy, or a rival who tries year after year to defeat another one. This arch enemy gets close, but never quite wins.

After years, he is seething, and resorts to more and more devious methods. He will do anything to stop the Messiah.

Accordingly, this is a great and continuing drama. At Christ's birth he triumphed over his deadly arch enemy's violent efforts. The Revelation speaks to this and gives us an unveiling of the cosmic significance. "Thus viewed the entire Old Testament becomes one story, the story of the conflict between the seed of the woman and the dragon, between Christ and Satan. In this conflict, Christ, of course, is victorious." (Hendriksen, p. 163[2])

So this morning let's review how Satan tried to defeat Christ in the Old Testament epoch and up to the Birth. And this Christmas let's better appreciate and worship our triumphant Messiah.

The first skirmish and hint of perpetual warfare between Christ and Satan is found in the Garden of Eden. Genesis 3 records the temptation, sin and fall of Adam and Eve. After this, God exacts appropriate judgments on Adam, Eve and the Serpent. In Genesis 3:15, God's judgment pronounced on the Serpent (Satan) is that he will bruise the heel of the child of the woman (Messiah), but that child will crush (destroy) his head. This is exactly what happened at Calvary's cross. The Serpent (same as the Dragon in Revelation 12) thought he'd won the victory by putting away Christ. But No!

So then the conflict is announced (as early as Genesis 3) that the Serpent would repeatedly try to destroy the Champion Messiah. But the Messiah will triumph or crush his enemy. Revelation 12 and Genesis 3 both have the same characters in mind (Messiah - Woman - Satan) and proclaim the same message: Messiah is triumphant.

In time, children are born to Adam and Eve: Cain and Abel. But Cain slays Abel. Then Seth is born. Does Satan realize that the family of Seth has been predestined to bring forth the promised seed, the Messiah? One is inclined to think so, for the devil now begins to do all in his power to destroy Seth. He whispers into the ears of Seth's sons that they must marry the daughters of Cain. He tries to destroy Seth's generations in order thus to annihilate the promise concerning the Messiah. Does the dragon succeed? It looks as if he might, for the

---

[2] Much of this sermon is adapted from William Hendriksen's commentary, *More than Conquerors*. It is a superb biblical theology approach, and it is and should be widely shared. His chapter is almost impossible to improve on, and thus is largely reproduced, with ever-so-slight modifications here.

whole world has been corrupted. Satan has triumphed . . . no, not entirely. Among the families that descended from Seth there is one which fears the Lord, that of Noah. God saves this one family, while the Flood destroys the rest. In this one family the promise is continued. The line of Messiah is triumphant and Satan cannot exterminate it. God whisks the woman and child to safety.

The next stage of conflict is after the Flood. Again the dragon stands in front of the woman in order to destroy the child. The promise concerning the Messiah is now given to Abraham and Sarah his wife. Humanly speaking, however, that promise will never be fulfilled, for Abraham is old and Sarah is barren. The dragon has almost triumphed, when the miracle happens and Isaac is born! The promise is now given to Isaac. But the Lord orders Abraham to offer Isaac as a burnt-offering! And Abraham stretched forth his hand, and took the knife to slay his son . . !" What now will become of God's promise? Surely, now the dragon triumphs. But does he? You know better. The Angel of the Lord appears and says to Abraham, "Do not kill the lad. Now I know that you fear me, because you haven't withheld your only son from me. . . and in your seed all the nations will be blessed." Who was this seed to bless the nations? Not just Isaac but Jesus. The New Testament tells us in Galatians 3:16: "The promises were spoken to Abraham and to his seed. The scripture does not say and to seeds meaning many people, but and to your seed, meaning one person who is Christ."

The Messiah would be the triumphant blessing to all nations and people who believe. Revelation 12 teaches us this angle of persistent warfare throughout the Old Testament where Satan tries to kill and destroy.

The seed that was going to destroy the serpent's head would be born from the generations of Isaac and Rebekah, but Rebekah was barren! Again Jehovah, the God of the promise, performs a miracle, and Rebekah conceives so that the promise is continued in the line of Jacob.

And we cannot overlook Satan's attempt to terminate the Messianic line in Joseph's time. I believe that Satan inspired jealousy in Joseph's brothers and motivated them to sell him into slavery into Egypt. The line of the Messiah was about to come about and the dragon waits, ready to pounce and destroy it. But God whisks Joseph away to safety.

Satan was behind all that. You remember how that account goes:

- Joseph was sold into slavery; his brothers were jealous of him;
- Raised to prominence in Potiphar's court;
- Accused of fooling around with Mrs. Potiphar;
- Thrown into jail; it looks like he will die out in shame;
- Interprets dreams; one of which later leads him to interpret Pharaoh's dreams;
- Then becomes second in command in all of Egypt;
- Meanwhile famine strikes Israel;
- Joseph's brothers come to Egypt in search of grain;
- Joseph provides;
- If he'd not been there, the twelve tribes likely would have starved.

But Joseph shows his knowledge of God's purpose as he says in Genesis 45:8, "It was not you who sent me here, but God. He sent me ahead of you (v. 7) to preserve for you a remnant on earth and to save your lives by a great deliverance."

Genesis 50:20 reaffirms: "You intended to harm me, but God intended it for good to accomplish what is now being done, the saving of many lives." In this, God provided a beautiful example of harmony. All throughout Scripture this conflict and attack is present.

You see, Satan tried to use slavery, moral accusations, imprisonment and famine all to stamp out the tribes of Israel so that Jesus would never be born. That was his goal: to devour the son before he could be viable. But in all this our Triumphant Messiah is victorious. Hear Revelation 12:4b: "The dragon stood in front of the woman who was about to give birth so that he might devour her child . . . she gave birth to a son, a male child who will rule all the nations with an iron scepter." This is a fulfillment of Psalm 2:9 concerning the Messiah.

Next the Dragon tries to devour the child of the woman by tempting Israel to become a part of Egypt's religion. After Joseph, the Jews were enslaved by the Egyptians. Before the Exodus, the Jews were nearly acculturated into Egyptian cult worship. But Satan does not triumph! Pharaoh tries to extinguish the line by murdering all males at birth. God sends a deliverer—Moses, who leads the people out and away from the Satanic inspired religion of Egypt. But Satan dogs their tracks in the wilderness. He immediately seduces them into idol worship of a calf and rejecting Moses' leadership. Yet God protects, refines, and disciplines this people as they head toward the Promised Land. The Messiah of Triumph is coming. Satan is not more powerful.

The whole of the Old Testament is the story of Satan's unsuccessful attempts to prevent Christ birth. God is sovereign. Throughout the period after Moses' death (during the time of Joseph and the Judges) the Messiah's stock is often seduced away from Yahweh by other false religions. But the dragon is not effective in consuming the seed of the woman. There is always a remnant of faithful followers, looking for the Messiah, who did not capitulate and receive the mark of the beast on their forehead. The promised Messiah would still be born and triumph over Satan.

Again history moves on. Out of the tribe of Judah God chooses one family, that of David. The promised Messiah will be born as the Seed of David. So the devil now aims his arrow at David. David must be destroyed! We read in the Book of Samuel, "And Saul had his spear in his hand; and Saul cast the spear; for he said, I will smite David even to the wall." Saul did this because an evil spirit (an agent of the Dragon) came mightily upon him. Did the dragon succeed? No, for David escaped out of Saul's presence twice. The Christ even during the Old Testament is at work on earth, safeguarding the promise concerning himself!

O, Glorious and Triumphant Messiah who will be the shoot coming up from the stump of Jesse (Is. 11:1).

Later in Elijah's time, the Dragon nearly succeeds in conquering the seed of the woman. In the late 9th Century B.C. Israel has virtually given up its worship of Yahweh in exchange for Baal worship. But God sends Elijah to confront this evil and he triumphs over the Baal prophets. He (Elijah) thinks he is alone. Although small in number, God assures Elijah that there are 7000 more who haven't bowed the knee to Baal. This remnant will result in the Triumphant Messiah . . . unless Satan can first terminate it.

Lct's shift to another scene, a century later. Athaliah, the wicked daughter of wicked parents—Ahab and Jezebel—is reigning. In order that she may have absolute power she conceives in her heart to destroy all the seed of David. Thus again the coming of the Mediator in human form is threatened. The dragon stands in front of the woman; his wrath is directed against the child. And now, finally, Satan is successful. At least, so it seems. Read in 2 Kings 11: "Now when Athaliah the mother of Ahazia saw that her son was dead, she arose and destroyed all the seed royal." Destroyed all the seed royal! Of course, if ALL the royal seed is destroyed, then the Christ cannot be born as the legal son and heir of David. Then God's plan is frustrated. Then the promise has failed. Athaliah destroyed ALL the seed royal. That is, she thought she did! Read the next line (2 Kings 11:1, 2ff.) "But Jehosheba, a priest, took Joash, the son of Ahazia, and stole him away from among the king's sons that were slain, even him and his nurse, and put them in a bed-chamber; and they hid him from Athaliah, so that he was not slain."

How wonderful are God's ways. How marvelous his providence!

Soon we see Joash again six years later. And upon his head there is a crown. We hear people shouting: Long live the king! Again the promise is saved. Christ will be born of David's line.

Isaiah witnessed God's triumph in even more extensive manners. Amidst the imminent oppression of the Assyrian military machine, poised to slaughter Judah he prophesied that the young virgin would conceive a "Sign of Hope." Isaiah 7:6ff says, "Therefore the Lord himself will give you a sign: behold, a virgin shall conceive, and bear a son, and shall call his name Immanuel." God's purpose must stand. Immanuel must be born . . . from the family of David!

This Messiah would be a sign of God's assured triumph. Still later, Isaiah saw God deliver Hezekiah and Judah from the Assyrian horde. Isaiah envisioned the coming of the Triumphant Messiah and knew that God would safeguard the Messiah's parentage. Yet by the time of Isaiah's successor, Jeremiah, Satan appears to have all but triumphed. The darkness of the Babylonian captivity clouded Israel's horizon. The people had been taken from the land. Ah! the land, the birthplace of Abram's seed was stolen. Humiliated Judah was exiled from the ash-heap of defeat and carted off in exile to Babylon. Isn't this the end of this Messiah's people? How can he come from a tribe cut off at its roots?

Now hasn't the Dragon conquered? No more than before. God forbid! God's people will be kept in exile and even return to yield God's own Messiah. For God used men like Daniel in exile, still to preserve the remnant. Even in captivity God's purposed plan for the

Messiah from the Jews could not be thwarted. The Dragon will not triumph by devouring the woman's child who'll rule all nations with an iron scepter. This son is safeguarded by God's throne.

A little later, King Ahasuerus is reigning. It is the fifth century B.C. At the request of Haman, the king now issues a decree that throughout his vast domain all the Jews should be put to death, Esther 3:13. This decree is sealed with the king's ring! This promise could not be broken. But Jehovah's promise concerning the Mediator, to be born of the seed of David, was sealed with the oath of the King of Kings! Need I relate what happened? Read the book of Esther. The Jews, again, were saved! The Messiah would come!

Even in the period between the Testaments, when Greece and Rome tried to exterminate the pestiferous Jews (as Herod called them), God preserved these people for the particular purpose of producing the Messiah. Satan seemed to triumph, but what empty victories, if any were his. Praise to our Triumphant God!

Clarence Larkin (a leading dispensationalist) wrote: "The history of the Christian Church [indeed all of human history] is but one long story of the 'Irrepressible conflict' between Satan and God's people." The lesson is clear: The OT is the chronicle of warfare between the seed of the serpent and the seed of the woman. The serpent and his agents constantly try to knock the child of the woman off the throne that is so rightly is. But he is never successful. That's why the NT says, "Greater is he who is in you than he that is in the world."

This drama was played out once again at the birth of Jesus.

If you have your Bibles turn with me to Matthew 2:1-18 for what seems to be the final act in this mighty drama. Yet it is not really final. The scene is Bethlehem. There in a manger lies the Christ-child. But although he is now actually born, the Dragon tries to destroy him. Remember Revelation 12 covering with one stroke of the pen the entire previous history of Satan's warfare against the Christ, applies also to the events that took place in connection with Christ's birth. Remember v. 4 "And the Dragon stand in front of the woman who is about to be delivered, that when she is delivered he may devour her child."

Hence in Matthew 2 we see wise men from the East. We see them in the audience-chamber of Herod. They ask about the location of the coming royalty (vss. 2:2-5a). "Be sure," says Herod, "to report to me as soon as you shall have found the child, that I also may come and worship him. The record in Matthew 2:7-8 states his intention was to kill the child. The Dragon used Herod to try to quench God's plan. But the wise men, warned of God, returned to their country another way after they had found and worshipped the Christ (v. 12). Still, the Dragon refuses to admit defeat. The infants of Bethlehem and surroundings, two years old and under, are slain. Notice how Satan indiscriminately murders infants in his attempt to kill the Messiah (cf. 2:16). But God triumphantly and miraculously provided. And Herod failed. So did the Dragon. The Christ-child was safe in Egypt. God's purpose can never be frustrated, not even by human choices. Christ's birth in Bethlehem is God's victory over the Dragon. The Savior's death on the cross for his people is his further victory. Christ triumphs!—And the angels sing: "Glory to God in the highest."

The Bible is a marvelous unity. Revelation is tied into Genesis, and that is all on display at Advent. One might even suspect that this book had a unity of authorship, or that the plan was written in advance by a all-knowing God.

This passage in Revelation 12 applies not only to the spiritual significance of Christmas but is also relevant to our everyday struggles with Satan. It is not just end-time material. And if God can triumph like this over such an enemy in such dire circumstances, know that he can still triumph over any enemy and any circumstance through Jesus our Messiah. Messiah came and triumphed over Satan's wiles. He still does that at Christmas.

Sometimes, you wonder if the Messiah will triumph. At this particular time as some of us face sadness, loneliness, doubt, a first Christmas without a loved one, a disappointment, or a crisis, you may feel . . . it may seem that the Dragon is about to consume and that the Messiah can't possibly triumph over these circumstances. Despair seems to envelope the whole of our existence. But remember he has triumphed and he will! Today, in his own way Messiah is and will triumph over Satan. The Dragon will not triumph. You can rest assured of this because God is faithful and never once in history of the record of Satan vs God has Satan really triumphed.

The birth of Messiah is God's majestic triumph over the powers of darkness. In this historic event the child of the woman predicted in Genesis 3 escapes the attack of the Dragon and conquers. Hallelujah!

For this, at Christmas we should truly celebrate. Hence this Christmas celebrate the Triumph in which God provided by safeguarding the birth of Messiah. What a Triumph. What a Messiah. Born at Christmas to overcome Satan. Indeed, Good News! The best of news. Messiah of Triumph has come. Let us all celebrate his Triumphant birth in our hearts with Great Joy!

Also remember that his Word is always true. "The death struggle of a defeated foe will bring severe tribulation, but the outcome is certain—God will come in judgment to destroy his enemies and reward his own." (Mounce, loc. cit., 234)

"Joy to the World!" is appropriate for "He rules the world with truth and grace; and makes the nations prove the glories of his righteousness and wonders of his love."

The Incarnation Vs. Selfishness

John 1 and Luke 2

The incarnation opposes selfishness at every turn. I'm sure by now that everyone has thought a great deal about Christmas and probably some don't want to hear another homily on the subject. However, if we look at the First Advent with clarity, we'll see more about Christ. And at this time of year, as at every other, there is nothing more important than to do as the wise men did: stretch every nerve to see Jesus.

As we see him in the cradle, we see his selflessness—a lesson never out of season. The incarnation stands opposed to selfishness.

In fact, nearly every character in the First Advent drama is faced with an ethical and personal decision before dealing with Jesus: Will they seek their own end/glory or another's?

First, Zechariah and Elizabeth had opportunities to be disciples of selfishness instead of trust in the Lord. They had one of life's crushing blows. They were unable to have children. They could have despised God or cursed him. But they submitted to his will, and continued to worship him. Zechariah served as a priest, and an angel announced the good news to him about a coming son. A selfish parent would have gathered up a long-awaited son, and shared that prize with no one. Yet, the angel predicted, "Many of the people of Israel will he bring back to the Lord their God." (Lk. 1:16) Zechariah and Elizabeth would have to share their son with others; ultimately, they would have to share his head with a martyr's sword blade.

How would you like it if you waited for years to have the most precious thing in the world, only to have a fine, strong young son, beheaded? Many would become embittered, but these folks knew God's plan. They loved God over self.

Joseph could have been selfish had he wanted. When he was faced with the most important decision about his life, he could have opted for a number of measures that would not have put God first. Sure, they would have put him more at ease.

The first option available to Joseph was to selfishly ignore God; to *act like an atheist*. In his case, he could have forgotten about the appearances from the angel. He came from a fine Jewish family—probably was taught from the time he was on his parents' knees. He could have acted the part of a materialist. He could have denied spiritual reality altogether.

Ebenezer Scrooge did that. I don't know if you've viewed or read that entire masterpiece by Charles Dickens, but the reason it has such enduring quality is that it shows us the end of selfishness, and how a life can deteriorate under the spell of avarice. In Scrooge's case, his selfishness was interwoven with his materialism. It was a specific kind of materialism, too.

The new philosophy of his day was "empiricism." That life-philosophy—still with us under many later names—believed that nothing could be true, unless it could meet certain definitions of a fact. And, conveniently, the definition ruled out miracle, much of morality, and eternity. Only that which a person could see or feel was true. A human perspective became the criterion for truth. That world-system is present in Dickens' "A Christmas Carol."

When Marley's ghost first appeared to Scrooge, he could tell that Scrooge did not believe in him. The ghost asked, "What evidence would you have of my reality, beyond that of your senses?"

"I don't know," said Scrooge.

"Why do you doubt your senses?

"Because," said Scrooge, "a little thing affects them. A slight disorder of the stomach makes them cheats. You may be an undigested bit of beef, a blot of mustard, a crumb of cheese, a fragment of underdone potato. There's more of gravy than of grave about you, whatever you are!"

Scrooge, you see, was a good follower of David Hume. He thought that nothing beyond the senses existed, or ever would. There was no such thing as the spiritual; only the material. So, in order to explain the specter, Scrooge had to conjecture a material cause. Perhaps this was a sleepless night, filled with apparitions because of indigestion. Materialism.

Later, he even thinks he can extinguish the spirit, if he snuffs out the candle. Of course, the Ghost of Christmas past reminded him of his idolatry. When he was taken back in time, he sees his young love who accuses Scrooge of replacing affection for her with the cold clink of currency. Although, he feebly denied it, she knew a golden idol replaced love. Scrooge was selfish enough, as he rationalized that "There is nothing which is so hard as poverty." His love answered, "You fear the world too much. All your other hopes have merged into the hope of being beyond the chance of its sordid reproach. . . . Gain engrosses you."

Scrooge had changed as he grew in love with money, security, and sought to protect himself from the unseen which he denied with things seen and counted. He was too selfish to love.

Interestingly, when Scrooge is delivered from his materialism, he also loses his selfishness and praises heaven.

Joseph, had he wished, could have been a selfish materialist. He could have successfully united those two philosophies of life, and he could have:

- Rejected any belief in God or duty;
- He could have disbelieved any revelation by an angel;
- He could have acted like there is nothing else but what we see, hear, touch, taste, and smell. That theology could have justified his selfishness. But he didn't; he was open to God.

But there would be other opportunities to choose selfishness, and don't you believe Satan stood, crouching like a ravenous lion; to tempt him? Satan would have triumphed if he could have gotten Joseph to worship selfishness instead of God.

Then again, he could have—and did consider—quietly divorcing Mary. To do so would have been the route of expedience, and who could have blamed this young man. He was permitted under Jewish divorce laws to divorce Mary. Sure, the law counted them as married, or in the espousal period, but upon finding that she was not a virgin— certainly pregnancy would prove that—Joseph could have filed for a divorce. He would be on solid grounds if all looked as it did.

Why have his life ruined at this point? Why, he could find another fine woman in due time; he could have a happy family, and he could avoid the social stigma that would surely arise. Wasn't it in his own best self-interest to dump Mary? It seemed that way. He was, as the Scripture says, "a righteous man," and his reputation shouldn't fall into disrepute merely because of some fluke—that's assuming Mary's story was true.

He had a construction business to run. He wondered if it is was good to let God interfere with his vocation. It wasn't good business for neighbors to do business with Joseph if he was married to the . . . you know what. He could be selfish or God-centered; and God gave him the strength to do the right thing.

Of course, had Joseph lived in our world today, he might have looked for yet another ethical compromise, and might have sought an abortion. Surely, he could have with little effort justified that act, and convinced himself that this little mass of tissue would be more of an inconvenience than a convenience. Why, he was only little more than a teenager himself, with a lot of life ahead. Did he really want to limit his future options?

Can you, after seeing some of this, pause with me for a few moments and see where you are selfish? Where has your selfishness been driving you? Can you think—I can—of times when your self-drivenness has made you unbearable? Even ways where you can justify yourself? If selfishness rules us, we are contrary to Christ. He did not allow it.

Do any glaring areas stare back at you? They do me.

Mary, of course, could have easily persuaded herself to flee to another country or do something disastrous. How could a young lady face her friends if she went through with this?

However, look to Luke 1 to see how Mary reacted. Instead of responding in belief, Mary could have checked herself in for psychiatric treatment. If miracles were impossible, then she must have been losing her mind when the Angel said, "Greetings you who are highly favored! The Lord is with you."

Mary was troubled; she could have run away. What occurred to her was a biological impossibility. But with God, all things are possible. He can even take a frightened, young peasant girl, and transform her into the mother of grace. Rather than insisting on her own rights, rather than thinking that she should have been consulted before anything happened, she responded: "I am the Lord's servant. May it be to me as you have said." She cared more for God than for her own petty universe.

She praised God, and you would do well to re-read her whole song in Luke 1:46-55.

Then later in Luke 2:19, "Mary treasured all these things and pondered them in her heart." Mary knew God. He had vindicated her and was vindicated to her. She trusted him. For years to come, she would reflect back on this and know that the Lord was mighty. Mighty enough to overcome her desire to pursue selfishness. God would not let these characters be selfish. Maybe we need to be constrained similarly—even against our will and desire. That is God acting lovingly toward us at times.

Minor characters, too . . . had the full range of self-centered options before them.

The Magi could have stayed home in Arabia. They traveled a long way, and they didn't come from a strong biblical community. They were a little odd in Judea. It would have been easier for them just to be quiet or stop that religious stuff. Had they been selfish, they would not have sought a king, nor honored him with gifts.

As soon as they met Herod, they likely figured out that he was a bad apple. It wouldn't be hard to guess what he was up to. They could have done a few favors for him, made some money, or lobbied for ambassadorships. Or, had they been selfish, they could have returned inconspicuously to their own land, fleeing from Herod.

Instead of selfishness, they chose truth, and they followed God.

All of what I said of the others above—including the temptation to be practical atheists could have been true of the Shepherds. They were not afforded the wealth or luxury of spending much time on religion. They were also outcaste, low-class workers, who were notorious for their untrustworthiness. They, too, could have ignored God and his revelation.

They were simply going about their business one night, when an
angel appeared to them. God's glory was all around them—a
convincing sign—and to indicate that this was a real appearance from
God, instead of a product of the human imagination that frequently
flatters itself, they were terrified. They used to be sore afraid.

The angel announced good news of great joy that was to be for all
people. A Savior, the long-awaited Messiah, was born. He is Christ
the Lord.

They could have run off, acted as if this miraculous event had not
happened, or they could have tried to turn that revelation into a road
show and make money from it. Surely, they could have fattened their
wallets by opening a religious shrine, beginning a TV ministry, or
selling relics. They could have immortalized their own little hovel,
beneath where the angel first appeared, but they were too busy
following God to be concerned for themselves.

That seems almost to be a law in this passage: Those who busy
themselves with God's truth and following him, do not have as much
time for selfishness. Humble service takes precedence over self-
interest. Indeed, we serve God, at Christmas or any other season,
when we are consumed with his glory, rather than our own.

The shepherds followed the instructions; they went to Bethlehem,
and responded in faith. Maybe, although they are not often described
this way, maybe they were honest, righteous, and obedient servants of
the Living God, who could have done otherwise, but obeyed the Lord
and his command. Will you, as he speaks to you through his Word?

Simeon/Anna (I can't go into detail here), but these could also be
included in the Hall of Fame of selflessness. Simeon has been waiting
for the dawn of the Messiah for a long time; a real long time. This
saint was not selfish; he was waiting and worshiping, when the Holy
Spirit fell on him. He had been told that he would not die before the
arrival of the Messiah. He believed the message and did not depend
on selfish sense.

When he saw Jesus, he blessed him, and prophesied about him.
Also, Anna, was an old lady, a widow of 84, who constantly
worshiped, prayed, and fasted. She, too, saw baby Jesus and praised
God for him. Simeon and Anna were not self-centered, but God-
centered. Their plans were on hold and they worshiped as a priority.

So, are you beginning to feel a little bad about yourself? Many
preachers want you to feel guilty this time of year about all the money

you've spent, and how you've not given to the church. I'd rather you face your selfishness, and I have to also do that, to more fully appreciate what the Lord has done for us at Christmas.

It is a pretty apparent theme, isn't it.

This consistent choice faced each character in the biblical narratives: To follow God, do something difficult, and serve the Lord's will OR to serve and glorify self. Not only will one lifestyle or the other prevail in your home, but it will also manifest itself in daily life.

- Are you too busy to be kind this time of year?
- Are you to self-absorbed to care?
- Are you seldom willing to forgive or understand?
- Are you not courageous enough to stand for God's truth, lest others might make fun or not understand?

Even Herod was faced with an opportunity. Of course, he cared only for his own political survival. He would do anything, eliminate any young lives to insure he retained the crown. He thought his own privilege as ruler was even more important than human life. So, he resorted to murdering all the young males under the age of two in Bethlehem.

He tried to press the Magi into service, and doubtless made many of his servants accomplices to murder and mayhem. He worshiped self. That was a hostile enemy of the incarnate babe born in a manger. It is no accident.

However, who had the greatest temptation to opt for selfishness? Jesus himself.

Philippians 2 tells us something very important about the Incarnation and how it opposes selfishness. Christ was in very nature God, but he was not consumed with ambition to be equal with God. Jesus did not selfishly cling to his glory, privilege, or demand the honor that was so rightly due him.

In his coming to earth, he chose the polar opposite of selfishness. He transformed himself, complete with all the deity that none of us have, into a servant. He humbled himself and assumed the form of humanity. He did not cease being God; he added humanity to that divinity.

There were many opportunities to escape coming to earth. Even then, he could have opted for self-interest, but he became obedient. Jesus suffered insults, beginning with his Birth. When even the best man would be tempted to resort to his power sometime, the Lord of Glory stooped. He came into the lowliest of circumstances, he willingly confined himself to all that God had for him.

The Incarnation was a body block on privilege and selfishness. Jesus, gave himself, rather than insisting on receiving praise and comfort. He had the raw power and authority to get out of this; but he didn't. He chose to serve.

Another verse says similarly: "For even the Son of Man did not come to be served, but to serve, and to give his life as a ransom for many." (Mk. 10:45)

William Barclay commented: "The Christian should have only one ambition—to be of use to the Church of which he is a part and the society in which he lives. The chance he dare not miss is not that of a cheap profit but that of being of service to his God, his church, and others." (*in loc*. 2 Tim. 4:6-8)

This Advent will you focus on selfishness or Christ's selflessness?

On the Day after Christmas

Luke 2:21-35

Before I get into the exposition of this text, I want to make three prefatory remarks. *First,* I realize that for many, in fact for most— nearly all of those 8 or under—this day is the most depressing day of the year. One of the best days has just ended, and it is a full 364 days until next Christmas. Some adults feel the same way, and have a distinctive let down following Christmas. However, for the Christian, it is good to be together for worship to know that life goes on, worship goes on, Christian joy and service continue uninterrupted. Rather than viewing Christmas day as one gigantic thrill which is over and done with, we can walk with God every day, some with even higher joy. We are as joyful as ever, knowing that every Sabbath is a celebration of the resurrection of Jesus.

Second, the passage I'm about to speak on contains one of the oldest hymns in Christian history. Last week we talked a little about the song of Mary and Zechariah. Today we'll look at the short but pregnant-with-meaning song of Simeon, which begins with the words, "Now let thy servant depart." The Latin is *"Nunc demittis,"* or literally, "Now demit (depart) thy servant." Many are familiar with Mary's *Magnificat* ("My soul magnifies"), but far fewer know Simeon's *Nunc demittis*. Yet this song was in many ways, in the early church considered nearly equal to Mary's own song. As far as we can tell, the earliest churches, when they considered what songs to use in worship, went straight to the scriptural wording, and selected their songs of praise from the inspired Word of God. We could learn from that in our own age.

And this was one of the earliest and most used portions of scripture, set to song. It is rich in meaning, now as then.

Thirdly, these two characters, Anna and Simeon, teach us great examples of patient faithfulness, or what Eugene Peterson has called a "quiet obedience over a long time." However, Simeon is in no one's Hall of Fame. He may have been a great Christian like you, but seldom recognized. For example, have you ever heard an Advent sermon on Simeon? Few have. Falling in the biblical narratives as he does, he is seldom recognized as a hero.

Simeon is one of those offensive linemen of spirituality. You know how all the running backs and quarterbacks receive most of the favorable press, while the mammoth linemen work and grunt and move other heavy weights, seldom receiving MVP awards, or rave reviews. Still they are necessary. Ask any quarterback.

The same is true in any sport and in every church. Simeon is like the batter after Mickey Mantle and Roger Maris. Can you remember his name? Or can you recall who batted after Babe Ruth? 20 years from now, who will remember the other guard for the Chicago Bulls in their 3-peat years, besides Michael Jordan? A lot of people in history who have done fine things are not remembered because they fall in life, just after a climax. You may be one of those people, and likely many of you are. As we complete a year together, I want to encourage those of you who will never be famous. For all those who follow someone who has been larger than life, or if you've been faithful, but still are not listed among the famous, I want us on this morning after Christmas to consider the lives of two who are normally overlooked in Christmas celebrations. These are some of the regular people, who happened to be in the right place at the right times.

Simeon and Anna are only mentioned here in the Scriptures. Following the tremendous narrative about the Shepherds, the angels, the glorious birth of our Savior, comes the next chronological bit of information about our Savior. On the 8th day he is taken to the Temple to be circumcised and this is where we meet Simeon and Anna. On the day after Christmas, let's look at the passage after Christmas.

Let's look one more time (before we leave these verses) at:

I.   *Joseph and Mary's quiet, but consistent faithfulness.*

I've already pointed out to you, how faithful and obedient Joseph and Mary have been. I want you to see, though, how this is consistent in their lives. In fact, from their example, we might even conclude that faithfulness, by its very nature, is something that is consistent. If obedience is the exception rather than the rule, that's not normally called faithfulness. Faithfulness is the consistent obedience, or good faith, to God's word. Joseph and Mary were not *just occasionally* faithful, as are all too many of our contemporaries. They were *consistently faithful*. Are you?

Simeon was. On the 8th day, Joseph and Mary gave Jesus the name the angel has pre-assigned. They didn't, a week later, name him Joseph Jr. or some family name, but the Savior. And on this 8th day, they kept the law as it had been previously given. They went to Jerusalem. These people did not wait a long time to have the covenant seal applied to their children.

Mary, a mere eight days earlier had given birth to her first child. She was probably still a little uncomfortable to make the journey to Jerusalem. Nevertheless, there was no question about obedience, just faithfulness. Long ago the OT has prescribed that the firstborn male should be circumcised on the 8th day, as a sign that this child was included in God's covenant. Parents were not to wait for some imagined age of accountability, or for the child to make their own decision. The normal expectation was that the child would grow up and share the strong, vibrant faith of the father. It was not an option for the child to postpone spiritual development and covenantal duties/obligations.

Circumcision was a symbolic recognition that God is gracious in giving life. Every child is a precious, undeserved gift from God, lent by God for a season. God gives us holy seed, and they are to be brought under the covenant by believing parents.

Nor should anyone think from this passage (or any other) that mere dedication is in view. This was a sacrament, the older cousin of our sacrament of baptism, the symbolism being the same. Joseph and Mary were not merely dedicating Jesus; they were obeying God and following what He'd said to do. Too frequently parents either leave too much to the child, or do too little themselves in regard to their precious covenant seed. But not Joseph and Mary. They presented Jesus for the only infant ceremony, the sacrament of circumcision. They obeyed God quite precisely, and we could all do with a little more of that.

Surely they presented him to the Lord (22), but the act was circumcision. Parents, if you would be obedient to the Lord, bring your children for the God-ordained sacrament of covenant baptism. Times and standards haven't changed.

Evidently Joseph and Mary were poor, and could only afford to sacrifice a pair of young pigeons. They could not afford the full expense associated with a firstborn. But they were faithful with all that they did have. Just because they had little, they never sought to use that for exemption. They were faithful, consistently so, even as they knew the haunting insecurity of poverty. So much so, that the final comment on their parenting at this state is in v. 39: "When Joseph and Mary had done everything required by the Law of the Lord (Note this is not some human law which can be ignored at will.), they returned to Galilee to their own town of Nazareth.

Note: To harmonize, with Matthew 2, the Wise men, evidently came some time later, as the angel of the Lord tells Joseph to flee to Egypt as the wise men meet Herod. Since they return to Nazareth at this time, it must not be the same time as their flight to Egypt.

The parents of our Lord were faithful. Let us pray and strive to be so.

II.   SIMEON
a.   His spiritual status, before meeting Christ

We see in Simeon another of those characters in scripture who is more OT than NT. However, Simeon shares the character traits of a NT saint, just as we do. Once again, if we take the Scripture seriously and don't impose some artificial division on the text of scripture, we see that Simeon was just as redeemed as we are. Even though he was very Jewish and very OT, he was included in the one church, just as we are. There is not evident here, an alleged Jewish plan of salvation separate from a Gentile plan of salvation.

Simeon was quite spiritual, and inwardly so. According to v. 25 he was righteous and devout. Take that first word first. The word righteous means to meet up to God's standards. If Simeon or any other person does this, it is not because of their own inherent right standing. To be righteous means to be declared righteous in God's sight. A person at any time is declared righteous in God's sight only by the undeserved grace of God which comes to us when it is not owed. It is not because of our faith, nor because of our lineage that any is declared righteous. It is because God is well-pleased to shed that grace on us. Simeon was "graced," or declared righteous the same way we are. He was justified by God.

Next he is described as "devout." The word is used only here in Luke (but in Acts 2:5; 8:2; 22:12) and means "careful about religious matters" or cautious. And Simeon is praised for this, not mocked. The precision and care he exercised regarding his faith was commended. We would do well to pursue the same care and cautiousness about holy things.

As the verse continues, Simeon was actively seeking God's will. Two descriptions make this clear. He was "waiting for the consolation of Israel." Israel for some generations have been under the thumb of the Romans. She was a puppet state, controlled by a Rome-appointed Governor, who was a traitor and oppressor. She was heavily taxed. Why, the census might even have been an opportunity for retroactive taxation, an idea with some renewed popularity. Israel had little hope; in fact the only hope was in her long-promised Messiah. But the years passed, and there was no divine deliverer, just a succession of evil and tyrannical rulers. Israel's only hope and consolation would come with the Messiah. While many others had given up, while the faith waned, not so with Simeon. He was anticipating, awaiting the consolation, in the person of the Messiah. His spiritual life and faithfulness were not dependent on good times, nor smooth sailing. Even in hard times, like those greatest and most common of saints, Simeon waited faithfully, not giving up on God, knowing that he would keep his promise.

Also "the Holy Spirit was upon him." For those who think that the Holy Spirit was a new invention at Pentecost, this and other verses put that idea to rest. God did not just begin to dispense his Spirit after the resurrection of Christ. He gave his spirit to any and all those in the OT who were saved. In fact, the only way we can be saved, is to first have the Holy Spirit come into our hearts and melt away that old nature, substituting in its place a new spiritual nature. Simeon had the Holy Spirit.

Just as much as you and I. Just like you do when you are really feeling the presence of the Spirit, Simeon had the same. He was filled with the Spirit. The minuscule difference in phraseology between the Spirit being "upon" him, as contrasted with "in" him is insignificant, both pointing to the real operation of the Spirit which is always internal.

Simeon was justified as we are, filled with the spirit (sanctified) as we are. He walked with the Lord as we do. And he was also seeking the Lord's will, as we do. In v. 26, his seeking of the Lord's will is hinted at in these words: "It had been revealed to him by the Holy Spirit that he would not die before he had seen the Lord's Messiah." So he was walking with the Spirit. On that particular day, he was "moved by the spirit" (v. 27) and went into the Temple Courts where he met Joseph, Mary and Jesus. He was to "do for [Jesus] what the custom of the Law required" (27).

You see from all this, that Simeon was faithful, not occasionally, but consistently. And he'd waited a long time for this. Most of us can be fairly faithful if the Lord does something in a pretty short time period. It's hard to be quietly faithful for a long time, isn't it? Why, most of us consider ourselves super-saints if we remained faithful to the Lord for a year. Simeon and others had been faithful for years, decades, generations. They'd seen fine people die in faithfulness, still not receiving the consolation of the Messiah. How well have you done at remaining faithful for a long, arduous wait? To do so develops deeply sanctified people. Such was Simeon. He'd learned to wait on the Lord, even when the Lord did not act quickly. But God's time did not diminish Simeon's desire. He loved the Lord, and trusted the lord. He knew it was all in God's hand, and so he waited. But he believed all the time, and was faithful.

From that heart and experience of faith came a great song.

b. *His song: The Nunc Demittis.*

As I've already said, this was one of the earliest and greatest of songs. Simeon erupts into praise of God. As he takes the 8-day old tiny lad into his arms, as he feels the flesh of the incarnate Messiah, he cannot do business as usual. He praises God, and the words of his hymn of praise are too good to pass over.

First, he does not praise God as "moderator, or president." The biblical idea of God is not that he is a glorified chairman of a committee, who builds consensus. That may work in certain corporate contexts, but not in heaven. God is a divine monarch. He is the Sovereign, the one who rules unilaterally without seeking permission or referendum form his subjects. Simeon knows this, perhaps better than many American Christians who grow up in a democratic context. Simeon was ahead of some of us, and realized that God was to be praised as Sovereign; there were some things which weren't voted on. God is Sovereign, and those who are consistently faithful, know Him to be.

I must admit that I take a kind of contrarian joy in this word and this teaching of scripture. For all of us who so want to control our lives, who work so feverishly to be in charge, we are thwarted by this teaching that God is . . . do you know what the Greek word is? It's *Despot*. Now normally we think of a Despot as an evil ruler, but there is no evil in God. He is an all-wise, all-good, perfect Despot, and a Despot, who by being a Despot is not evil. He is that sovereign, and in the strongest possible terms, as elsewhere in scripture. God wants to make it clear to us, if we'll only listen that we should know him and praise him for controlling our life. In sum, that he is the controlling Despot, and not we ourselves, is the cause of Simeon's praise that is raised here in connection with Jesus. Can you praise God as the Sovereign Despot yet, or are you still holding out for human control?

When God's sovereignty is recognized in every sphere of life there is consolation for life and death.

Simeon is so filled with gratitude that his life can now be dismissed. He praises God as Sovereign, and then pleads to be dismissed in peace. For all these years, he'd held out, perhaps even on occasion praying to be healed or spared just until he can see the Consolation. He is now fulfilled and having seen that is ready to be dismissed to heaven. There is nothing any longer to await, and Simeon dies that Christian death, the kind that is ready to be dismissed in order to be at home with the Lord. Now he can go, released from his bondage. But the wait was worth it.

He prays to be dismissed in peace, because now—at last—his eyes have seen God's salvation. there it is, wrapped in the soft flesh of an 8-day old baby. That is the salvation of God. And note what Simeon says about this salvation, other than it is wrapped in the flesh of a baby. This salvation was not an after-thought.

It had been "prepared" or planned in advance. The salvation came about just as God had pre-ordained. Praise him for this forethought. And it is most public, prepared 'in the sight of all people".

Furthermore, this salvation includes and has effects on the whole world, including both Jew and non-Jew. To the non-Jews, the salvation through Jesus was described as a "light for revelation to the Gentiles".

That may seem like a curious phrase. It didn't actually originate with Simeon, dating all the way back to Isaiah.

Thus, Jesus was the light that led the way to salvation for the Gentiles. He was also the salvation for Jewish people, described as the Glory to your people Israel. Either way, Jewish or Gentile, Jesus was the Savior, and the only means of salvation. There were no others, and not separate plans of salvation.

That was Simeon's song, a song which has been used throughout the years. We'll have it sung in a few minutes, and you'll quickly be able to tell how ancient it is. It sounds almost like a Gregorian chant, yet the words of Scripture pulsate through it, in whatever meter it is sung. Christians sang this in the catacombs, they sang it at early Christian worship services, throughout the middle ages, and at the Reformation was rediscovered. It has fallen out of favor, due to its unusual tune (but certainly not more unusual than say Rap, country-twang, or blues), but probably more likely because without glamour, as this song focuses on the very words of scripture and not the frill of human aggrandizement and entertainment, it appears to be a strain of unadulterated piety. The words lend themselves to praise, worship, and a reminder of Who/What God does.

Now I couldn't help but notice":

c.   *The intriguing reaction of Joseph and Mary in v. 33.*

This is one of those places where we should not read too fast in the Bible. Luke's gospel has already told us a great deal about what Mary and Joseph knew about Jesus. Mary knew the following:

* Elizabeth's miraculous conception;
* Zechariah's testimony;
* Name of Jesus would be filled with spiritual symbolism;
* Miraculous virgin birth (which angels explained to Joseph);
* Shepherds came to worship, after the glorious angelic announcement.

Luke 2:19 adds, "But Mary treasured up all these things and pondered them in her heart."

One would think that they had things pretty well figured out. But perhaps that is only because we can see so much retrospectively. It might not have been so clear, if you were going through this yourselves, or for the first time. Remember there is no precedent being followed here. This is virgin territory—in more ways than one. Now 8 days later, when Simeon gives this song, the Scripture says that Mary and Joseph "marveled at what was said about him." That may strike us as curious, if we minimize the faith-trek of Mary and Joseph.

We've heard the Christmas story so frequently that we tend to think of this as routine. It certainly was not for Mary and Joseph. It was difficult, and fraught with uncertainty. Mary and Joseph were following this one step at a time. It was unknown. And they had little confirmation. Perhaps by now, they even wondered, as many of us do after a great spiritual plateau, if what they'd experienced was really true. They had now had eight peaceful "regular days. Perhaps this wasn't real. Maybe Jesus was a regular little boy.

But not with Simeon going on like this. He praised God for this lad, as he did for no other. This was a unique baby, the one who was identified with salvation. So Mary and Joseph too, marveled. And I'm sure they were thrilled. But there also comes some disconcerting news.

d.   Finally we come to Simeon's *prophecy.*

This inspired message about Jesus is typical revelation. Like the covenant itself, this message has a component of covenant blessing and one of covenant cursing for disobedience. The prophecy was startling, and it is possible that Mary did not comprehend it until 33 years later, at the death of her baby son. Still Simeon's prophecy is amazing in what it reveals.

Look at vss. 34-35. After Simeon blessed this family he spoke, and he spoke about the future. First he noted that Jesus, the child, was destined—he had a certain future—to have a two-fold effect. He would cause the falling and rising of many in Israel. Simeon is keenly sensitive to how there is no neutrality, nor middle ground regarding Christ. There is no true equilibrium in regard to a relationship to Jesus. We are either for Him or against Him, and as a result, we will either rise or fall based on that. God does bring judgment; that is not an outmoded concept.

Jesus, the babe born at Christmas, was the Great Divider in history. He did not come to unite all mankind. He separates:

The sheep from the goats;
The righteous from the unrighteous;
Those who acknowledge Him and those who deny Him;

Those who rise and those who fall on his account.

It was God's plan, God's decree, the destiny of Jesus to part the waters of human soul.

Jesus would also be a sign—much of his life was caught up in symbolism—that was spoken against. It is certainly true that many spoke against him and reviled him. Sad, but accurate, Jesus was not universally loved. He was spoken against.

He also served to reveal the very inner and unseen thoughts of many hearts. Jesus is the divine diagnoser of hearts, even if other humans don't see. He goes behind the human heart, which he and Jeremiah knew to be "deceitfully wicked. who can know it." Still those hearts would be uncovered by Jesus. There would be no coverups, no disguising our true hearts.

And finally, Simeon brought the sad news that Mary too would suffer, suffer that awful pain that a parent does when the parent outlasts the child and has to bury their son. Mary would have her own soul pierced, wracked with sadness at the death of the baby she now held so securely and lovingly.

All This Simeon predicted years before it happened.

III.   ANNA

Anna (whose name means grace) was also a waiting, faithful believer. She may have even waited longer than Simeon. According to Scripture, this prophetess from the tribe of Asher was "very old." When the Bible calls a person very old, they must've been old. I prefer the translation of vss 36b-37a as "she had lived with her husband 7 years after her marriage and then was a widow for 84 years. If she'd been married at say 16 (younger back then) that would mean that at the tender age of 23, her husband was killed, and she with no children was left all alone. Her only solace was the Temple and the life of the believers. She devoted herself to the service of God, using the gift of prophecy for 84 years and even stayed there night and day, "Fasting and praying." She well could have been 107 years old.

She was a real godly lady, a role model for older ladies, and for younger women to aspire. She sees Jesus and breaks out into thanksgiving. Following that she too predicts that the child was the key to redemption.

As we close out a year of worship together, as we put all our Advent things back, be sure to remember these saints "before the altar bending, keeping watch o'er . . ." May they be remembered for their constancy in faithfulness. And you, too.

The Shepherd Boy: The First Gift

Luke 2

Christmas is a great time of year, isn't it? Of course, we all know that the reason is because God gave us a great gift at Christmas, Jesus Christ. However, it's still kind of nice to get other gifts isn't it? I bet some of you like gifts.

Our family received some gifts this year, and it's really great. One of the nice things about gifts, is that they are more than we deserve. That's what a gift is; not something you earn.

Gift-giving to Jesus at Christmas began back in Bible times. Do you know who the first person was to bring a gift to baby Jesus? Most people think it was the wise men, who brought gold, frankincense, and myrrh. But according to the Bible that was just a little later.

Without getting into all the detail, here's the order:

- Joseph and Mary to Bethlehem to be taxed.
- They couldn't find any room and had to stay in a stable.
- Mary gave birth.
- Then we're told about the first people who learned about it: The Shepherds.

They came that night to see Jesus, and went out from there praising God. Mary and Joseph then went up to Jerusalem 8 days later to have Jesus circumcised. Only later did the wise men arrive and Jesus' family fled to Egypt to avoid Herod.

So the first people to see the newborn baby were some shepherds. We don't actually know who brought gifts before the wise men, but I want to tell you the (fictional) story about:

Jacob the Shepherd boy

The fields were full of sheep. As many as a dozen flocks would huddle together in some areas. The sounds of the sheep-choir, with all their unison "baah-ing" became well known to shepherds. Most of the shepherds were kinda rough, like cowboys. They weren't always clean, didn't always shave, and they didn't always act perfectly. They were even looked down on by some people.

And sheep were gentle animals, even if they were sort of dumb.

A shepherd's job was fun at first for 9-year old Jacob, but sometimes it got kinda boring. Keeping sheep was OK; but he wondered if other kids his age didn't have things a little nicer. Maybe they even had their own homes. All Jacob had was a tent, which moved wherever the flock was.

Jacob didn't have a mom. She'd died before he really knew her. His father took care of him as best he could. Jacob's father was a shepherd, and he'd given him a special Junior-size shepherd's crook for his 9th birthday. Jacob felt like a real grown-up now. The crook didn't cost much; in fact his father made it. Jacob was proud of it, and used it a lot. One night, when he was 9, he was on duty all alone. This was the first time, he'd been trusted to guard the flock alone. He felt like a real shepherd. Like all the grown-up shepherds he played a soft hollow-branch flute at night to occupy his mind. It sounded about as good as the sheep baahing.

Jacob wasn't timid, but suddenly he heard some noises. The noise, which at first sounded like a swishing of branches, or like rushing of wings, maybe a flock of geese, grew louder, until it was nearly deafening. Then a brilliant explosion of light.

The sheep were spooked. A couple almost fainted. Jacob didn't know what it was. But as he listened on, this was a night he would never forget. At first he saw a lead Angel, then others, maybe a thousand. They seemed to fill the sky, and blocked out the midnight blue with bright white. They sang thunderously; the ground shook:

"Glory. . . Glory. . . Glory to God in the highest.

Peace. . . Peace . . . Peace to men who are favored on the earth."

Jacob had never heard a more beautiful or wonderful song.

The head Angel flew over to him. By now all the other shepherds were awake, but none had a more star-gazed look than the youngest shepherd. Nor were any of the adult shepherds any more astonished. Jacob, being a quizzical young lad, asked, "What's happening? What's this all about?"

The Angel responded, "We are here to sing and announce the birth of the Son of God. Jesus, the child of the great Heavenly king who made the whole world and every living thing, has come to earth. You will find him in a stable in Bethlehem. He will be the one wrapped in assorted rags. He is born as the poorest of the poor, but is the Savior of all. You are the first to learn about this. Go now and worship God in the flesh." All the shepherds took off running without even speaking to one another, nor even looking after the sheep. They were happy, combined with a little fear.

After learning about this, Jacob thought he would take the newborn a gift, or two. He knew how nice that would be, because he hardly ever received any gifts. There was only one problem. He didn't have any presents, or any money. He was kind of poor and shabby. And he didn't have any baby toys. He'd only kept one little stuffed sheep made from lamb's wool, which was very soft and cuddly. He didn't mind parting with it, although secretly he slept with it every night he could.

He thought that would be a good present. He could also give baby Jesus his flute. He thought he'd like a whistle. And also he thought. Why don't I give Jesus my very most valued thing. He looked in his hand at his Junior Shepherd's Crook. That was all he had of real value, and that was a lot. But if this was the Son of God, then He deserved the very best. Jacob decided to take his best and give it to Jesus, even if it meant having no staff. He'd do his work with his hands if he had to, and fend off attackers some other way.

So he tagged along with his father and the others. He could barely keep up with them. Fortunately, it wasn't too far. When they arrived at the stable, no one had thought to bring baby gifts. Shepherds didn't go to baby showers very much; so they didn't know the custom. Eventually as they gawked on Mary and the newborn, stunned by the workings of God, the grown shepherds felt uncomfortable and wanted to give something. Do you know how that feels when you want to give somebody something, but don't have anything to give?

At that moment, up stepped the 4'7" shepherd. He spoke to Mary in a 9-year old voice. "Uh, m . . . miss . . . . We've brought something for the baby. It's not much, but it might help. Here's a . . . a little stuffed animal for him to sleep with. Even boys need something to hold onto. And here's a little flute-whistle for him to blow. He can pretend like he's a real shepherd. And for when he grows up, here's a Junior Shepherds' Crook. My dad made it for me, and I've about outgrown it. I'm ready for a full-size one now and won't be needing this much longer. Maybe your son will be a shepherd. He could guard the sheep and fight off wolves. He could use this to guide them."

Mary managed the first smile since she awoke. Groggy, but deeply touched, she smiled so sweetly and thanked Jacob. It was her first baby gift. She would cherish it always.

Later that night, Jacob was given a full-size crook. His favorite uncle was so impressed that he gave him his own 8-foot long crook. Jacob would always prize it and keep it until his death.

Much later, about 30 years later, when Jacob had his own herd, he met Jesus again. Jacob still had his crook that his uncle gave him, and he met Jesus one day, as He was talking. Jesus was speaking, and when he saw Jacob walk up at a distance, he immediately remembered him. Jesus knew everything.

It almost seemed as if Jesus changed his talk in mid-stream, and he said these words looking straight at Jacob:

> I tell you the truth, the man who does not enter the sheep pen by the gate, but climbs in by some other way, is a thief and a robber. The man who enters by the gate is the shepherd of his sheep (1-2). . . . I am the good shepherd. The good shepherd lays down his life for the sheep . . . I am the good shepherd. I know my sheep and my sheep know me . . . and I lay down my life for the sheep . . . They, too will listen to my voice, and there shall be one flock and one shepherd (11, 14-16). . . . My sheep listen to my voice; I know them and they follow me. I give them eternal life, and they shall never perish; no one can snatch them out of my hand. (Jn. 10)

After he finished, Jesus went up to poorly-dressed Jacob and said, "You were the first one to bring me a gift. I remember your kindness. Before anyone else, and no one even knew about it. I always loved that crook. By speaking these words which will go down in history, I dedicate them to the first giver of gifts at Christmas, a little shepherd boy. I did grow up to be a shepherd, like you said. The Good Shepherd. And I do use a crook to guide the sheep and protect them. I started out with the one you gave me as my first present. I still have yours and want to return it so you can give it to your son. Keep passing this down, and tell your son these things.

I will die one day, but I will always raise up more shepherds, shepherds like you, who give their best, and do it without thanks. Those who remember me will always be remembered.

After Jesus died, Jacob went to visit Mary. She remembered him, and returned his Junior crook to him. He gave it to his son as she watched on.

Won't you give your best to Jesus this year. Your best is to give him your love, to love him with all your heart, mind, and strength. That is a gift we could all give to Jesus this year. Won't you? One of the last times Jesus talked with his disciples on earth, he said "if you love me take care of my sheep."

Advent with an Attitude

Luke 1

Luke, the author of this gospel was a medical doctor, but also a well-trained scholar. He writes this gospel to a Roman man, Theophilus, possibly a ruler who was a new convert, in order to sustain his faith. Luke admits that others had undertaken to write such accounts of the life of Jesus (1:1), and that those accounts can be verified by contemporaneous eyewitnesses (1:2). Still he wants to "carefully investigate" the life of Christ, and he has set out an "orderly account" (another phrase for historical writing), with a purpose in mind: "So that you may know the certainty of the things you have been taught" (1:4). Thus Luke's gospel, from the very outset takes on a historical slant, to a degree not matched by others. He begins with the birth of Christ, but first with the events which lead up to that, events which are fraught with miracles, and packed with instruction.

In the Sundays remaining before Christmas, my sermons will focus on the attitudes apparent in these Advent characters.

This is not merely to see what their attitudes were as a matter of historical curiosity, but also to see how these typify the Christian life.

Today, as we prepare for the Lord's Supper, I want to lift out—from the life of Zechariah and Elizabeth—two attitudes present and to be imitated.

a)   Love for righteousness (v. 6) (also in 8-10).
The first attitude to be imitated from Zechariah and Elizabeth is their love for righteousness. Righteousness, is a term that is not used

that frequently anymore. It means the condition of being right or correct in God's sight. According to the Bible, Zechariah and Elizabeth were upright in the sight of God" (v. 6). The word used here is the same one used throughout all the OT for a righteous person. These two were right in God's sight. And that last part is very important.

After all, it is God's view of things which is most important. We may be right in a lot of other people's eyes, but if we're not right in God's sight, then all of that does not matter. I'd rather be upright in God's sight than admired by all the greatest of the world. Is that your attitude at Advent? Have the things of this world taken a dimmer sheen, in comparison to the things of God? Is it your main agenda item, day in and day out, to be reckoned upright in God's sight? If so, then you'll not only have a blessed Advent, but a blessed eternity.

This week I read a devotional that made a keen observation about righteousness. R. C. Sproul pointed out how the Bible never commands us to be "spiritual," but merely to be righteous. Yet much of modern religion is the pursuit of being Spiritual, while ignoring God's call to be righteous. The difference is great and observable. If our desire is to be spiritual, then we will focus on inner experiences and strive for things which can never be measured. On the other hand, if we pursue righteousness, we will seek to please God's objective standards, and it will become apparent regardless of intention or motivation, whether we are pleasing God or not. In this sense it is better to pursue righteousness than inner experiences of spirituality. After all, Jesus said, "Seek first the Kingdom of God and his righteousness (not for you to be spiritual), and all these things will be added as well." Join together at communion and at Advent to be seekers of righteousness, of God's will and way. Let our pursuit, our agenda, to be what God says is right.

Zechariah and Elizabeth were upright in God's sight, and they observed all the Lord's commandments and regulations blamelessly. The word "blameless" is significant. It means not convictable of a crime in a legal forum, or innocent. Some people mistake this word to mean absolutely "perfect" in all ways. That is not what it means. Instead, it is a reference to the outcome of a trial, in which the accused is found innocent. That is to be blameless. The word does not mean that we never have anyone who accuses or blames us; for what human could ever meet that. Even the best are accused.

But blameless means "not convictable of the crime; if tried then vindicated.

Now this raises an issue for some people. Didn't Zechariah and Elizabeth live before the resurrection of Christ? Actually, not only before the resurrection, but before the birth of Christ. These were OT folks, weren't they? Well, could OT people be righteous and blameless in God's sight, before the sacrifice of Christ was accomplished? And if so, how?

The answer is the same was any of us are today: That in God's *sight* we are upright and blameless. None of us ever is, or was, upright or blameless on our own. That is something that we could not accomplish in any Testament. Know as you enter Advent, that we may be upright with God only if he sees us that way, only if God charges our sin to Jesus Christ, and then in turn credits Jesus' righteousness to us. That is the only method of being upright in God's sight, now, or 4,000 years ago.

God is the one who saves, and even the amount of information we have about Christ is not a final barrier to the work of God in our lives. He can take those who knew very little of the details about salvation, and work salvation in their lives. The signs of that are clear throughout the Scripture and no less in the birth narratives.

Count the people alive at the coming of Christ who manifested the Fruit of the Spirit, and ask how did this get in them.

Mary = humble, submissive, obedient, joyful amidst disgrace, trust the miraculous.

Joseph = obedient, righteous.

Wise men = faithful to what they know, hungry to know the King, believed in prophecy.

Shepherds = glory, joy, peace, and grace.

Simeon and Anna in Luke 2 = fasting, prophet, loves Messiah.

People have these fruits in them only due to the indwelling Spirit of Christ. These are not native to human nature. If Christ's Spirit is not in us, then we will not have these traits. And since they do not come naturally, we will only have them if we are possessed with the powerful Holy Spirit.

Righteousness is a key theme of scripture, even if largely lost in today's world. Consider just a few Psalms.

Consider what a brief review of this term in the Psalter shows us about the value in loving righteousness:

- 5:12   O Lord, you bless the Righteous.
- 11:7   For the Lord is Righteous.
- 34:15   The eyes of the Lord are on the Righteous.
- 37:25   I have never seen the righteous forsaken.
- 55:22   God will never let the Righteous fall.
- 119:137 Righteous are you, O Lord.
- 140:13 Surely the Righteous will praise your name.
- 145:17 The Lord is Righteous in all his ways.
- 103:6   The Lord works Righteousness.

As we approach Advent and the Lord's Table, do you love righteousness? Is that your heart's goal and love? If you do, then you will confess both that you have not been righteous by yourself, nor can you. Also that you hunger and thirst for the righteousness which comes through this sacrament.

The 2nd attitude we should have as we approach Advent is a:

b)   *Yearning for Revival.*

Zechariah and Elizabeth were not merely going through the motions in their spiritual lives. They sincerely loved the Lord, worshipped him, and wanted to please him. They also sensed a need to have a deeper spiritual walk with the Lord. Each of us should have that.

Zechariah and Elizabeth were sad that they had no children. Once, when Zechariah was serving his turn as priest, an angel appeared to him. Zechariah was alone and the angel appeared on the right side of the altar (11). Zechariah was scared out of his mind. He hadn't planned on seeing an angel that day. He never had before. He'd simply got up, shaved, read the *Times*, and drove on into church. All of a sudden this angel appears, and tells Zechariah who was gripped with fear and startled: "Do not be afraid Zechariah, your prayer has been heard, your wife Elizabeth will bear you a son, and you are to give him the name John. He will be a joy and delight to you, and many will rejoice because of his birth, for he will be great in the sight of the Lord. . . ."

Zechariah is stunned, but the angel won't slow down. He proceeds to tell Zechariah something about a turning back, a revival of sorts that will come from his son, John. I want you to see the effects of true revival which would come from John's ministry, and which are preparatory to Advent.

Before I do, let me clarify something. By 'revival' the Scripture does not mean an imitation of revival, nor as a recent speaker expressed a "restaging" of the Great Awakening's effects. But true revival. All too often we think of a Revival as a time of the year, as if God's work occurs each Spring or Fall. Then again, some people foolishly think we can schedule these things in advance, and then if we'll only use the right methods, we can produce the right effects. That is not what the Bible presents as Revival.

Revival is aptly described here as a turning back to God. That is revival, not a one-time occurrence, nor an emotional outpouring. True revival re-orients our whole course of life. Nothing else.

Many Christians are beginning to pray for this, although we should pray for it to come in God's way and at his own time, too. Even true revival is dependent on the sovereign will and timing of God. It might not be God's will to bring a national or church-wide revival in our times, although we all hope to see such.

Let me point out to you four aspects of true revival, the kind we should be yearning for at Advent, in vss. 16-17.

1. Being "brought back to the Lord" v. 16

First, as I've mentioned, it is a bringing back of people to the Lord. Have any of you wandered far from the Shepherd? Have you veered away from his precepts and plan for your life? Then if you love him, turn back. Even in little areas. Come home, repent. That's the first step in revival. John, Zechariah's son would be used of God to bring back many people of Israel to their God.

I think we need this too. Aren't there many ways you should turn back? Can't you think of some specific things, use of time or money, ungodly involvements, that God has been nudging you about? Yes, you've heard that still small voice calling you back, urging you to give up, but you've not? Let the revival begin today, with your resolve to let God have his way with you, whatever it may involve. However, he will lead. Whatever it will take. That's the beginning of revival.

For many of us, that may entail a returning to our (Rev. 2) first love. *Frequently we have to go back before we can move forward.* At Advent and at the Lord's Table, come seeking revival, turn back to your God.

2. The spirit and power of Elijah.

A second part of this pre-Advent revival is that John the Baptizer would go forth in the spirit and power of Elijah. Elijah, the 7th c. BC Israelite prophet still cast a large shadow over Israel by the birth of Christ. He was remembered for his miracles and power. Elijah, by the power God gave him, worked many miracles.

John the Baptist would continue in that train. We may not be able to work miracles on demand, but this revival is the kind in which God works above normal means. Sometimes that may be the miracle of conversion, in which God changes the sinner's heart. Or it may be powerful in bringing repentance and change in people's lives. This Advent, look to God for the spirit and power of Elijah.

Another part of that spirit was the manner in which Elijah stood for truth and righteousness among those who did not always follow the ways of God. Elijah was not a prophet for profit. His views and proclamation could not be bought. He was a man of moral courage, righteous, steadfast, and bold in the face of opposition. We need more Christian leaders like that. That's part of the spirit of Elijah. Pray that God would revive us by raising up fearless and courageous preachers, throughout our land, who will so greatly value the holiness and righteousness of God that they will care not what man can do.

Notice a third sign of true revival in v. 17. The agents of revival will:

3. Turn the hearts of the fathers to their children.

Dads, I'm going to call you to do something radical this Advent. Moms, you too, but I'm going to single out dads, because God does here. Sometimes moms are saddled with the major responsibility of Christian nurture. But at the end of the OT, fathers are called on to concern themselves primarily with the nurture of their children. And we need a revival of father-led spirituality in the home.

At the end of the OT, in the final book, Malachi speaks of the coming of Messiah. And one of the signs in conjunction with that is that the coming prophet would turn the hearts of the fathers to their children. That prophecy is mentioned again here at the beginning of John the Baptist's ministry.

One of the greatest and surest signs of revivals is when dads put aside some of their other concerns and seek to disciple their children. God has designed the home to be the training ground for Christian nurture. Every dad is to lead in the spiritual nurture of their children. Fathers, are you?

Let me give you four quick conclusions about that, too.

1. If you're not very good at this, or not too experienced, join the club and learn as everybody else had, by mistakes. I know of no instant manual for this. It takes the love for God and our children that translates itself into the will to do this.

2. If you haven't been as faithful in this as you should have been, join the club. But let's don't stop there.

3. If you're honest, likely the real reason you don't do this is due to you doing other things, and pursuing other interests. You must sacrifice something to do something. In all likelihood, you must stop something, to carve out time for this.

4. This will be one of the most valuable things you'll ever do.

Dads, will you be a part of this revival? As the world goes by in a crazy season, as we all party too much and spend too much, and watch too much football, will you prioritize your children, to try to nurture them. We have less than four weeks, will you set some time aside each week for your children? Maybe God will turn your hearts toward your children.

In Advent, will you give up 2-3 extra hours a week, cancel something, some commitment, some opportunity, some big sale or project to give part of your heart and attention back to your children.

It's the busiest time of the year. We're most tempted to postpone the spiritual needs of our children, thinking that gifts will satisfy instead, I challenge you to take spiritual opportunities, and disciple your children.

This would have an evangelistic overflow. You'd have a great witness.

4. Turn the disobedient to the wisdom of the righteous.

The final part of this revival, is that not only will fathers turn their hearts toward their children, but will also seek to turn the disobedient to the wisdom of the righteous. There is an accompanying moral reform associated with revival. And we should see some sign of this in our Advent preparation, as well as in our receiving of communion.

The goal in all this: To make a people prepared for the Lord.

Will you recommit yourself to these this morning at communion?

Advent with an Attitude: An Explanation of the Reaction

Luke 1:26-38; Matthew 1:18-2:8 and 2:16-17

It's still something that intrigues me. As long as I work with people, it continually amazes me how different people can react to the same event or circumstances differently. Some of you like classical art and music; others of you can't stand it. The same is true of religious speakers. Occasionally we will have a guest speaker in, and some of you absolutely love the guest, while others do not. The same person will often evoke two opposite reactions.

Two couples listening to the same CD may have totally different reactions. That is true with a lot of people and a lot of life's moment. It's also true of the birth of Christ, then and now. As wonderful to us as the Birth of Christ is, some people are less than thrilled with it. In the late 20th century, we probably have as many Scrooges per capita as any society since Dickens's classic, featuring the original Ebenezer Scrooge. Millions of Americans grumble about Christmas, seem grumpier than normal, and act as though they despise Christmas, all that it stands for, and the birth of Jesus. Perhaps they do. That's how some people react to Christmas.

Others, can't wait until Thanksgiving is barely retired to drag out every sliver of Christmas tinsel imaginable, and celebrate to the hilt. Some love Advent, appreciate its richness, rejoice in the Lord over his birth, and revel in gift-giving. It is an excuse to be generous. That's how some react to the birth of Christ.

But why the difference? Don't you wonder sometimes? How can some love Advent, while others hate it?

Well, in just a moment, we'll see how the same was true 2000 yrs. ago. In the original Christmas narratives these differing reactions were evident. Joseph, Mary and others are presented as heroes, as mighty examples of true Christian response, while evil Herod (we can hardly say his name, without the expectation of a "Boo. Hiss" arising) reacted to the same things oppositely. What accounts for this? If you wonder, let's first note the responses as recorded in the Bible.

I.   Look at Matthew 1-2 with me. And let's focus on attitudes.
       A.   Joseph = obedient (Mt. 1);

The key attitude in Joseph that is most worthy of our imitation is his obedience, even when he faced ridicule and in the face of abnormal operating procedures. Joseph, perhaps was not as heroic and immediately malleable as Mary, but in the end his steadfastness is a lesson to us all. He was trained in obedience, the obedience of faith.

Pull out the strands about his attitudes from Matthew 1. First we note that he was morally pure. There is nothing in this narrative to indicate that it was even possible that the child in Mary's womb was a result of pre-marital sex. If it had been even a bare possibility, then Joseph would not have shown the genuine confusion and bewilderment that he did. He was obedient to God in the area of sex, and it was just as difficult back in the first century to be chaste as it is today. Yet throughout all of this, he was morally pure. Joseph was a godly young man.

According to 1:19 Joseph was a righteous man. That's the word we dwelt on last week. He was in right relationship to God, and lined up with God as he was supposed to. He met God's standards, and was righteous through the work of Christ in his life. That righteousness—as any true righteousness—worked itself out in treating others rightly. Despite all the social stigma and embarrassment associated with an out of wedlock birth, still Joseph cared about Mary, her reputation, and her future. He loved her. Not knowing what was going on, he'd originally planned to quietly break off the betrothal (19). Yet even in that, he did not want to expose Mary to disgrace, and sought to quietly put her away. His righteousness is seen in how he treated Mary.

Then an angel appeared to him and told him to take Mary home, that the child in her womb was conceived by the Holy Spirit (v. 21).

The son born to her was to be named Jesus because he will save . . . save his people from their sins." This was to fulfill the prophecy long ago of Isaiah.

Now you have to pause just a minute here to wonder why Joseph reacted the way he did. This was a pretty unusual dream. It was not often that a chaste betrothed young bride showed up pregnant, especially with the explanation that the Holy Spirit supernaturally implanted the Messiah in her womb. Joseph, had never heard of such a thing, and could be forgiven for not quickly jumping at this explanation. It is highly unusual, and requires more than a little faith and obedience. Joseph rose to the occasion and remains a superb example of following God's revealed will, even at times when it does not seem to line up with our sight. Joseph operated by faith, not by sight. He was a true believer.

After the dream, Joseph got up and did exactly as God had commanded (v. 24) and took Mary home as his wife. Just to be safe, he still had no sexual union with her until she delivered Jesus (v. 25). Joseph was obedient at every turn.

Luke 2:4 also tells us something about Joseph's character and example: "So Joseph also went up from the town of Nazareth in Galilee to Judea to Bethlehem the town of David, because he belong to the house and line of David . . . to register with Mary . . ." Joseph was obedient, even to an oppressive law of a government that was far over-reaching, and hostile to the true faith. Yet he showed the humility and obedience that is fitting of a true saint.

After the birth of Jesus, once more we see Joseph obeying God's will. In Matthew 2:13 Herod desires to slaughter all lads under the age of two in and around Bethlehem. The Angel warns Joseph and provides safe flight for Jesus' family. The angel appears to Joseph and orders him to escape to Egypt, stay there, and return only when told. This would be hard to do. Joseph obeys; he follows God's orders and typifies Christian obedience. Never once do we see Joseph express: "But Lord, I've got to have a few questions answered and a few concerns satisfied before I follow you." No, he acted in obedience . . . consistently, and when it was not popular, difficult, and perilous. That's Advent with an Attitude.

How's your obedience?? Are there some things in the Bible that you don't want to obey? Let me ask it this way: Joseph operated based on what God had revealed. He did not selectively obey some things, and disregard others. He obeyed all that the Lord had commanded. What about you? Is that the way the Lord finds you at Advent? Willing and eager to obey all that the Lord has revealed? Or tight-fisted with your obedience, chincy and only obeying some, or that which is comfortable?? Is there some difficult thing the Lord is calling you to obey? Joseph obeyed, consistently—even if it meant re-locating his fragile family; and you should also. And that is his attitude at Advent.

Where he got that attitude, or why he had it we'll see in just a second, but first a contrast. This is one of those cases with two people reacting exactly opposite to the same set of circumstances.

Parallel to Joseph, is another character, who really has an attitude, this time not so positive, King Herod. Why did he react so differently to the birth of Christ?? First, look at his reaction.

B.   Herod = furious.

Interestingly, Herod does not show up in Luke's account, only in Matthew's. We first meet him in the opening verse of Matthew 2. He seems unaware of what is about to happen. It is not until he is rudely awakened to the possibility of a rival king by the visit of the wise men, that he even realizes that the Messiah is about to be born. Herod reacts in a manner that it totally keeping with his nature. He looks out only for his own interests, and is selfish, threatened with the birth of a new king.

His first reaction is to be disturbed (2:3). Then he begins a mad search to find out where is rival is, so that he might destroy him. That is his only thought, to kill or eliminate the God-child. He only wants to protect his own turf. He summons the chief priests, those who should best know from the scriptures what is going on. They inform him that the OT prophecies point to Bethlehem. Herod, then begins to narrow his search down. He is frantic as he goes. He calls the Magi in. They'd tipped him off in the beginning; perhaps now he could use them.

He squeezes a little more information out of them, about the exact time, and tells them that it is his desire to worship this newborn king. He sends them on their way, and tells them to let him know as soon as they find the Messiah. They go and find him, but God warns them later in a dream (v. 12) not to go back to Herod. Then Joseph flees to Egypt, barely avoiding a disaster.

When Herod realizes that he's been out-connived by these men, note his reaction in v. 17: He was furious and Herod gives the order to swing throughout Bethlehem and find all Jewish males less than two years of age. The blood-dipped swords of the Romans who indiscriminately murder thousands of young male blossoms, accomplish the devilish will of Herod. He is a child of his father, who was a murderer from the beginning.

Herod illustrates the hatred for the gospel that Jesus spoke of. It was not a mild hatred, or a little dislike for the things of God, but instead as Edmund Burke once said of Atheists, "Those who do not love God with all their heart, soul, mind, and strength, *hate* him with all their heart, soul, mind, and strength." Maybe you know some people like that. That is Herod's reaction, one of bitterness, jealousy, envy, strife, hatred, violence, murder, trickery.

Why does he have that reaction to the same events of Joseph and Mary?

Now I said I would attempt an explanation. Turn with me to Galatians 5; for I think there's one in that passage. It speaks of the fruit of the flesh as being self-evident and clear. Those are the blossoms of Herod. It is clear from that passage that the fruit of the flesh is manifest. It makes its presence known, as in Herod's case. It is characterized by:

> sexual immorality
> impurity
> debauchery
> idolatry
> witchcraft (Herod consulted every medium that moved.)
> hatred
> discord
> jealousy
> fits of rage (Herod)
> selfish ambition
> dissensions, factions
> drunkenness, orgies and the like.

These will not inherit the KOG. This is the reaction of Herod, and the attitude of all those who despise the birth of Christ. These people react the way they do to the birth of Christ because they do not know or love God. No one on earth, now or at the time of Jesus' birth, can possibly neutral toward him, so great and so compelling is His life and message. We are either radically for him—willing to leave all that we have and follow him, or we are radically opposed to him—ready to fight to protect what we think is our own turf, even if it means killing others, or shedding their blood.

On the other hand, there is another race in humanity. The fruit of the Spirit is love, joy, peace, patience, kindness, goodness, faithfulness, gentleness, self-control. These are the attitudes of Joseph and Mary. They had those fruits in their lives, because the gospel lived in them. Its bounty and seed had been planted in their lives and was growing.

Those who have the fruit of the spirit in them react one way at Christmas, while those who do not react another way, with the fruit of the flesh.

Now, turn back to Mary.

C.   Mary = Attendant to God, as in 1:37-38.

What a magnificent attitude for us to emulate at Advent. Hers was not anything like Herod's. It was even different from Joseph's. Now it's time for the angel Gabriel to announce the glad tidings to Mary. In the 6th month (of Elizabeth's pregnancy), the angel heads to Galilee to speak to Mary. She is a descendant of David and a virgin. The angel greets her as the "highly favored one. The Lord is with you." (1:28). Mary was intensely disturbed. This had never happened to her before. But watch her attitude. After the angel calms her fears (v. 30), he informs her that she will give birth to s son, who will be named Jesus.

Pause for one moment, surely we can take time to observe the strong names used for Jesus in the passage:

II. Names of the Messiah, and what this should tell us (1:32,33, 35)

In these verses, the child born to Mary is described as:

- The Son of the Most High. In this ancient time, to call a person a "Son of" meant to identify them with the character of their ascribed father. Thus Jesus, the son of the Most High, was identified with the Most High, *El Elyon*, the God of awesome power in the OT. That was the Messiah in Mary's womb.
- Also, in v. 32, the heir of David's Throne. It had long been prophesied (e. g., in Ps. 2, 110) that David the great king of Israel would one day have a descendant who would be the Messiah. His throne would not remain eternally vacant. Messiah born to Mary was this ruler.
- Will reign over the house of Jacob forever. Jacob was also named Israel. Jesus would reign over the house of Israel forever.

- Accordingly, his kingdom will never end. Amazingly short when compared to world history are all the various administrations and kingdoms. But not so with this child born to Mary. His kingdom would have no end. It would not stop . . . and important for us to remember, it has not stopped today. Sure many rival claimants try to usurp the throne. But none do. Christ is the king whether we know it not.
- the holy one (35).
- the Son of God.

Now Mary asks a question in v. 34, which is similar to Zechariah's back in v. 18. Note: Zechariah asked: "How can I be sure of this"—with the emphasis on his certainty. Mary asked: "How will this be?"—not doubting, but raising the normal question, since a virgin had not normally conceived. Yet we see in Mary's attitude a willingness to learn from God, a quiet maturity that knew how to wait on the Lord; and accordingly as her request was a legitimate one, she received an answer.

The angel responded in v. 35, by telling her that the Holy Spirit would come upon her and the power of the MOST HIGH (*El Shaddai*) would overshadow her. She would give birth to a holy one, who would be called the Son of God. Why even old cousin Elizabeth was pregnant, and in her 6th month. Mary is surely amazed. Then the angel completes the announcement with these great words which were received by Mary: "For nothing is impossible with God."

Focus on two main aspects of her attitude.

a.   *Nothing is impossible.*

She knew God was able to do far more than many expected. Mary did not put a limit on what God could do. She knew him better than that. She knew him well enough to know that he is the God of the Impossible—and that God works over and above our expectations. He is the God who overturns a lot of things, and he is the God who is not prevented from doing a single thing, when it is his will to do such.

Mary understood that even though she was pregnant, God could still work in her. She had a great trust that he could deliver on all that his good word promised. Even the most unusual of circumstances were not barriers for him.

And in so doing, she joined a long line of those who'd learned the same thing. Abraham, nearly two millennia earlier had learned, "Is anything too hard for the Lord?" (Gen .18:14). Nothing is impossible with God. David had learned, "Our God is in heaven; he does whatever pleases him" (Ps. 115:3). Nothing is impossible with God. Jeremiah prayed, "Ah, Sovereign Lord, you have made the heavens and the earth by your great power and outstretched arm. Nothing is too hard for you" (Jer. 32:17).

Daniel learned that nothing is impossible with God, as he saw Nebuchadnezzar be broken and then confess, "All the peoples of the earth are regarded as nothing. He does as he pleases with the powers of heaven and the peoples of the earth. No one can hold back his hand or say to him, "What have you done.""(Dan. 4:35). Jesus himself taught, "With man this is impossible, but with God all things are possible" (Mt. 19:26). God has an "incomparably great power" (Eph. 1:19) and with him, nothing is impossible. He even does greater than we ask or imagine according to his power that is at work within us (Eph. 3:20).

According to the prophets, eye has not seen, nor have ears heard, all that God has in store for his people. Let us know our God at Advent, as Mary did: "for nothing is impossible with God." Of course apart from him, many things are impossible. What do you think to be impossible today? By that, I mean impossible to obey God. The Scripture certainly does not teach that we are to dream up the absurd, then ask God to jump through those hoops. It does, however, assure us that if it is God's will, but merely seems beyond the normal, that we're not to shy away from that. Take God's will back to him, and don't call anything impossible that God has commanded.

Also be sure to look in v. 38 at her attitude of servanthood.

b.   *Thy will be done.*

Mary responds with those words which are nearly magical to the ears of God: I am the Lord's servant." She confesses to being a handmaiden. Her answer shows the depths of her servanthood. She is the Lord's servant, and will act at his bidding. Whatever her God ordains is right; his holy will abideth.

He is master and we are servants. That is the attitude to have at Advent. She ends by saying, "May it be to me as you have said," or the equivalent of thy will be done. She'd learned to forget the world's commonest prayer: "Thy will be *changed*"; and to pray the world's greatest prayer: "Thy will be done." Can you say that to the Lord today? About those important decisions facing you? Can you rest as a servant, confident in your Master?

That's the attitude God wants us to have at Advent. Have you grown in Christ enough to follow him and take on the mantle of a servant?

Mary could, and her song, which maybe we can look at next week shows us how real her faith was. Where did she get this faith? This fruit? To further answer that question, look back to Romans 8:5-8. For there we're given once again the two great and divergent options in life: The mind that is opposed to God, and the mind that submits to God. That is what really explains these people's differing reactions.

Romans 8 tells us that our actions are based in our desires which are based in the state of our minds, whether we are believers or not. We are, you see, inter-related persons, and act rather integrally. It's just that often the root of our lives is not envisioned. According to Scripture, those who live according to the sinful nature have their minds set on fulfilling that sinful nature. On the other hand, those who live in accord with the Spirit live to fulfill it.

Then in v. 6, the mind of the sinful person leads to death, whereas the mind controlled by the Spirit leads to life and peace. Now remember carefully, v. 7, as it explains Herod's reaction: "The sinful mind is hostile to God. It does not submit to God's law, nor can it do so." You see, it will not, and furthermore, it is incapable.

This explains why some people react positively to Christ, while others find him to be inconvenient.

The Two Advents

Hebrews 9:27-28

We will spend our time on this final Lord's Day morning worship of this year on a verse that is sobering but encouraging. I pray that the Lord will permit us to think deeply and creatively about Hebrews 9:28. Having focused for several weeks on the Advent of Christ, on both the similarity between the two advents of Christ and the dissimilarity between them, we shall make some remarks concerning our personal interest in both advents as we conclude a fine year together.

I. The text asserts very plainly that as we are judged twice—once in a life of probation, and a second time in the day of judgment; so Christ shall be here twice—once in his life of suffering that began at his virgin birth, and then again in his hour of triumph. The two Comings of Christ have some degree of likeness.

First, let me list a few similarities between Christ's first and second advents.

1. Both happened in real histories; neither is mythical.
2. Both are personal comings of Christ.
3. Both had some measures of Glory.
4. Each had kings . . . and opponents.
5. Both are supernatural.

The Advent of Christ is described in royal language as a *Parousia*, the arrival of a king.

[Enjoy some notes from Spurgeon on this text.] First, they are like each other in the fact that they are both personal comings. Christ came the first time, not as a spirit, for a spirit has not flesh and bones as he had. He was one who could be pressed to a teenage virgin's bosom; one who could be borne in a father's arms. He was one who could afterwards walk in his own person to the temple; one who could bear our sins in his own body on the tree. We have done once for all with the foolish ideas of certain of the early heretics, that Christ's appearance upon earth was but a phantom. We know that he was really, personally, and physically here on earth. But it is not quite so clear to some persons that he is to come really, personally, and literally, the second time. I know there are some who labor to get rid of the fact of a personal reign, but as I take it, the coming and the reign are so connected together, that we must have a spiritual coming if we are to have a spiritual reign.

Now we believe and hold that Christ shall come a second time suddenly, to raise his saints at the first resurrection; this shall be the commencement of the grand judgment, and they shall reign with him afterwards. . . We believe that the Christ who shall sit on the throne of his father David, and whose feet shall stand upon Mount Olivet, is as much a personal Christ as the Christ who came to Bethlehem and wept in the manger. We do believe that the very Christ whose body did hang upon the tree shall sit upon the throne; that the very hand that felt the nail shall grasp the scepter; that the very foot that was fastened to the cross shall tread upon the necks of his foes. We look for the personal advent, the personal reign, the personal session and reign of Christ.

The Advents are also like each other in that they are both according to promise. The promise of the first coming of Christ was that which made glad the early believers. "Your father Abraham rejoiced to see my day, he saw it and was glad." The epitaph inscribed upon the slab which covers the sepulcher of the early saints has written upon it, "These all died in faith, not having received the promises, but having seen them afar off." And to-day we believe that Christ is to come according to promise. We think we have abundant evidence in the words that were uttered by the lips of inspired prophets and seers, and more especially from the enraptured pen of John in Patmos. Do they not testify that Christ shall surely come? We now, like Abraham of old, do see his day; our eye catches the coming splendor; our soul is overwhelmed with the approaching glory. Did the Jew look for Messiah, the Prince? So do we. Did he expect him to reign? So do we. In fact, the very Prince for whom Israel now looks in all her hardness of heart, is he whom we expect. They doubt Messiah's first advent and they look for him to come as the fairest among ten thousand, the Prince of the Kings of the earth. At his Second Advent the scales from the blind eyes of Israel's tribes will be removed, and the fullness of the Gentiles shall with Abraham's seed praise and magnify the Lamb once slain, who comes the second time as the Lion of the tribe of Judah. In both cases we think the advent of Christ fully promised.

In the next place, the second advent of Christ will be like the first in its being unexpected by the mass of people. When he came before, there were only a few looking for him. Simeon and Anna, and some humble souls of the sort knew that he was about to come. The others knew that the patriarchs and prophets of their nation had foretold his birth; but the vanity of their thoughts, and the conduct of their lives were at such entire variance with the creed to which they were trained, they cared nothing for him. The Magi might come from the distant East, and the shepherds from the adjacent plains, but how little sensation did they make in the streets of busy Jerusalem, in the halls of kings, or in the homes of business. The kingdom of God came not with observation. In such an hour as they thought not the Son of Man came. And now, though we have the words of Scripture to assure us that he will come quickly, and that his reward is with him and his work before him, yet how few expect him! The coming of some foreign Prince, the approach of some great event is looked for and anticipated from the hour that the purpose is promulgated among the people. But of Jesus' glorious advent—where are they that strain their eyes to catch the first beams of the sun rising? There are a few of thy followers who wait for his appearing. We meet with a few men who walk as those who know that time is short, and that the Master may come at morning, or at midnight, or at noon. We know a few beloved disciples who with longing hearts prepare songs to greet Immanuel!

Lord, increase the number of those who look for thee, and desire, and pray, and wait, and watch through the dreary hours of the night for the morning which thy coming shall usher in!

When Christ comes the next time, he will come to bless those who wait for him just as he did at the first. Blessed were the eyes that saw him; blessed were the hearts that loved him; blessed were the ears that heard him; blessed were the lips that kissed him; blessed were the hands that broke the tributary alabaster-box upon his glorious head. And blessed shall they be who are counted worthy of the resurrection and of the kingdom which he hath prepared. Blessed are they who, having been born of the Spirit can see the kingdom of God; but doubly blessed are they who, having been born of water as well as of the Spirit, shall enter into the kingdom of God.

There are some who see not yet the kingdom, and others who cannot enter because they will not obey the ordinance which makes them Christ's disciples. Thrice blessed shall they be who, in readiness and preparation, being obedient servants and having done his will, shall hear him say, "Come ye blessed, inherit the kingdom prepared for you from before the foundation of the world." He comes to bless his people.

Let me note one further likeness: he comes, not only to bless his people, but to be a stone of stumbling and a rock of offense to them that believe not upon him. When he came the first time he was like a refiner's fire and like fuller's soap. As the refiner's fire burns up the dross, so did he consume the Pharisees and Sadducees: and as the fuller's soap cleanses away the filth, so did he unto that generation when he condemned it, even as Jonah the prophet did unto the men of Nineveh and thereby condemned the men of Jerusalem because they repented not. Thus too, when he shall come the second time, while he shall bless his people, his fan will be in his hand and he will thoroughly purge his floor, and they who know him not and love him not, shall be driven away like the chaff into fire unquenchable. Long not for Christ's coming if you do not love him, for the day of the Lord will be unto thee darkness and not light. Ask not for the world's end; say not, "Come quickly, for his coming will be thy destruction; his advent will be the coming of your eternal horror. God grant us to love the Savior and put our trust in him; then, but not till then, we may say, "Come quickly, come quickly, Lord Jesus!" [Spurgeon then leads us:]

II. Now we shall turn to the second part of our subject, the difference between the two advents.

In the prophecy of his coming the first and the second time there was disparity as well as correspondence. It is true in both cases he will come attended by angels, and the song shall be, "Glory to God in the highest, on earth peace towards men he favors." It is true in both cases, shepherds who keep watch over their flocks even by night shall be among the first to hail him with their sleepless eyes-blessed shepherds who watch Christ's folds and therefore shall see the Great Shepherd when he comes. Still, how different his Second coming will be. At first he came an infant of a span long; now he shall come the glorious one.

Then he entered into a manger, now he shall ascend his throne. Then he sat upon a woman's knees, and clung to his mother's breast, now earth shall be at his feet and the whole universe shall hang upon his everlasting shoulders. Then he appeared the infant, now the infinite. Then he was born to trouble as the sparks fly upward, now he comes to glory as the lightning from one end of heaven to the other. A stable received him then; now the high arches of earth and heaven shall be too little for him. Horned oxen were then his companions, but now the chariots of God which are twenty thousand, even thousands of angels, shall be at his right hand. Then in poverty his parents were too glad to receive the offerings of gold and frankincense and myrrh; but now in splendor, King of kings, and Lord of lords, all nations shall bow before him, and kings and princes shall pay homage at his feet. Still he shall need nothing at their hands, for he will be able to say, "If I were hungry I would not tell ye, for the cattle are mine upon a thousand hills." "Thou hast put all things under his feet; all sheep and oxen, yea, and the beasts of the field." "The earth is the Lords, and the fullness thereof."

Marc Leverett of Bethel Baptist Church in Ft. Collins, CO, lists a nice summary, contrasting the first and second advents: (http://www.bethelcolorado.com/index.php?view=articleandcatid=34%3)

In the first Advent Jesus came in humility.
In the second advent Jesus will come in power.

In the first advent, Jesus came meek and lowly in heart.
In the second advent Jesus will come in authority.

In the first advent, Jesus rode on a donkey.
In the second advent Jesus will come on a white war horse!

In the first advent, Jesus was beaten with a wooden staff.
In the second advent Jesus will wield a rod of iron.

In the first advent, Jesus wore a mocking crown of thorns.
In the second advent Jesus will wear the royal crown of glory!

In the first advent, Jesus came as a Lamb to die for the sins of the world.

In the second advent Jesus will come as the Lion of the tribe of Judah!

In the first advent Jesus came to bring salvation to all [his people].
In the second advent Jesus will come to administer justice to all who
reject His mercy.

Not only will there merely be a difference in his coming; there
will be a most distinct and apparent difference in his person. He will
be the same, so that we shall be able to recognize him as the Man of
Nazareth, but O how changed! No more carpenter's smock! Royalty
will assume its purple. Where now the toil-worn feet that needed to be
washed after their long journeys of mercy? They are sandaled with
light, they "are like unto fine brass as if they burned in a furnace."
Where now the cry, "Foxes have holes and the birds of the air have
nests, but I, the Son of Man, have not where to lay my head?" Heaven
is his throne; earth is his foot-stool.

And to the Son of Man there is given "dominion, and glory, and a
kingdom, that all people, nations, and languages, should serve him."
Ah! who would think to recognize in the weary man and full of woes,
the King eternal, immortal, invisible. Who would think that the
humble man, despised and rejected, was the seed out of which there
should grow that full corn in the ear, Christ all-glorious, before whom
the angels veil their faces and cry, "Holy, holy, holy, Lord God of
Sabaoth!" He is the same, but yet how changed! Ye that despised him,
will ye despise him now? Imagine the judgment-day has come, and let
this vast audience represent the gathering of the last dreadful morning.

Will those who once despised his cross, come forward and insult
his throne! Will those who said he was a mere man, come near and
resist him, while he proves himself to be your Creator! Those who
said, "We will not have this man to reign over us," say it now if you
dare; repeat now if you dare your bold presumptuous defiance! What!
are ye silent? Do you turn your backs and flee? Verily, verily, so was
it said of you of old. They that hate him shall flee before him. His
enemies shall lick the dust. They shall cry to the rocks to cover them,
and to the hills to hide them from his face. How changed, I say, will
he be in the appearance of his person. But the difference will be more
apparent in the treatment which he will then receive.

The Lord's reception on earth the first time was not such as would
tempt thee here again. "All they that see me laugh me to scorn; they
thrust out-the lip; they say, He trusted in God that he would deliver

him, let him deliver him if he delighteth in him; I am become a reproach; the song of the drunkard, a by-word and a proverb." "When we shall see him, there is no beauty in him that we should desire him." This was the world's opinion of God's Anointed. So they did not salute Jehovah's Christ when he came the first time. Blind world, open your eyes while the thunder-claps of judgment make you start up in terror and amazement, and look about you. This is the man in whom you could see no beauty; dare you say the same of him now?

Listen to how Rev. 19 describes the appearance of the Lord of the Second Advent. His eyes are like flames of fire, and out of his mouth goes a two-edged sword; his head and his hair are white like wool, as white as snow, and his feet like much fine gold. How glorious now! How different now the world's opinion of him! Bad men weep and wail because of him. Good men clap their hands, and bow their heads, and leap for joy. Around him an innumerable company of angels wait; cherubim and seraphim with glowing wheels attend at his feet, and ever unto him they continually, continually, continually do cry, Holy, holy, holy, Lord God of hosts." He finally receives suitable praise and laud.

Let us suppose again that the judgment-day has come, and let us challenge the world to treat the Savior as it did before. Will it possibly be that:

- Crowds, come and drag him down, to hurl him from the hill headlong!
- Step forward, Pharisees, and tempt him, and try to entangle him in his words.
- Herodians, will you now ask him a difficult question to entrap him?
- What, Sadducees, have ye no riddles left?
- Laugh at the Scribes and at the wise men; see how the wise Man of Nazareth hath confounded them all. See how the sufferer hath put to nought the persecutors!
- Come Judas, arch-traitor, sell him for thirty pieces of silver! Come and give him another kiss and play the traitor o'er again!
- Pilate, come forward and wash your hands in innocency and say," I am clear of the blood of this just person!"

- See ye to it ye fathers of the Sanhedrim, wake from your long slumbers and say again, if ye dare, "This man blasphemeth."
- Smite him on the cheek ye soldiers; buffet him again ye praetorians. Set him once more in the chair and spit into his face. Weave your thorn-crown and put it on his head, and put the reed into his right hand. What! have ye ne'er an old cloak to cast about his shoulders again? What, have ye no songs, no ribald jests, and is there not a man among you that dareth now to pluck his hair? No, see them how they flee! Their loins are loosed; the shields of the mighty have been cast to the winds. Their courage has failed them.
- The brave Romans have turned cowards, and now come forward, if you dare, ribald crew, and mock him as ye did upon the cross. Point to his wounds; jeer at his nakedness; mock ye his thirst; revile his prayer; stand ye and thrust out your tongues, and insult his agonies if ye dare. Ye did it once! 'Tis the same person; do it over again.

But, no; they throw themselves upon their faces and there goes up from the assembled mass a wail such as earth never heard before, not even in the day when Mizraim's children felt the angel's sword, and, weeping worse than ever than was known in Bochim, hotter tears than Rachel shed when she would not be comforted for her children. Weep on, 'tis too late for your sorrow now. Oh! if there had been the tear of penitence before, there had not been the weeping of remorse now. Oh! if there had been the glancing of the eye of faith, there had not been the blasting and the scorching of your eyes with horrors that shall utterly consume you. Christ comes, I say, to be treated very differently from the treatment he received before.

The difference appears finally in this; he will come again for a very different purpose. He came the first time with, "I delight to do thy will, O God." He comes a second time to claim the reward and to divide the spoil with the strong. He came the first time with a sin-offering; that offering having been once made, there is no more sacrifice for sin. He comes the second time to administer righteousness. He was righteous at his first coming, but it was the righteousness of allegiance. He shall be righteous at his second coming with the righteousness of supremacy. He came to endure the penalty; he comes to procure the reward. He came to serve; he comes to rule. He came to open wide the door of grace; he comes to shut to the door. He comes not to redeem but to judge; not to save but to pronounce the sentence; not to weep while he invites, but to smile while he rewards; not to tremble in heart while he proclaims grace, but to make others tremble while he proclaims their doom. How great the difference between the first and the second Advent!

III. Let us conclude this last Sunday [of 2010] with a few questions.

What has this to do with us? It has something to do with every one of us, from the oldest to the youngest child who is listening with eyes of wonder to the thought that Christ shall come, and every eye shall see him. There are many spectacles which only a few among the children of men can see, but every eye shall see him. Some of us may be gone from this earth before the next great event or year passes, but every eye shall see him. There may be some grand sights which you feel no interest in; you would not see them if you might, but you shall see him. You would not go to a place of worship to hear him, but you shall see him, perhaps you went up to the House of God sometimes, and when there, vowed you would never go again. Ah! but you will be there then, without a question as to your choice. And you will have to remain till the close too, till he pronounces either the benediction or the malediction upon your heads. For every eye shall see him. There is not one of us that will be absent on the day of Christ's appearing; we have all then an interest in it. Will you be among that number that weeps? Do not look round upon your neighbor-will *you* be among that number? Alas for you! You will, if you never weep for sin on earth. If you do not weep for sin on earth you shall weep for it there; and, mark, if you do not fly to Christ and trust in him now, you shall be obliged to fly from him and be accursed of him then. "If any man love not the Lord Jesus Christ, let him be Anathema Maranatha;" accursed with a curse! Paul said that. In the name of the Church, by its most loving and tender apostle, the soul is cursed that loves not Christ. Heaven on that day shall solemnly ratify the curse with an "Amen;" and the day of judgment brings its thunders to roll in dreadful chorus the sound "Amen; let him be accursed if he loves not Christ. "But there will be some there who, when Christ shall come, shall greatly rejoice to see him. Will you be among that number? Will there be a crown for you? Will you share in that magnificent triumph? Will you make one of that royal court which shall delight to "see the King his beauty" in "the land that is very far off?"

Will you be among those who shall go forth to meet the King when he cometh with, "Hosanna, blessed is he that cometh in the name of the Lord?" "I hope so," saith one. I hope so, too, but are you sure? Well, I hope so." Do not be content with having a hope unless you know it is a good hope through grace. What say you today: have you been born again? Have you passed from death to life? Are you a new creature in Christ Jesus? Has the Spirit of God had dealings with you? Don't let this year end without attending to these matters.

Have you been led to see the fallacy of all human trust? Have you been led to see that no good works of yours can ever fit you to reign with Christ? If we have learned anything this year from that or from the last months preaching [from Romans], surely you will end this calendar year not trusting in self. Have you been led to discard your righteousness as filthy rags?

Humbly, feebly, but still earnestly, can you say, Christ is my all; he is all I desire on earth; he is all I need for heaven." If so, long for his appearing, for you shall see him, and shall be glorified in him. But if you cannot say that! We are almost to the end of this year. This is the last time I shall have the pleasure of addressing you this year. Oh that God may say in your heart, "Turn, turn until you have put your trust in Christ, and he is yours.

And may you be able to answer, "Yes, blessed be God, I am not afraid to come to judgment, for—Bold shall I stand in that great day; For who aught to my charge shall lay? While, through thy blood, absolved I am, From sin's tremendous curse and shame.

Remember, salvation is by Christ; not of works, nor of the will of man, nor of blood, nor birth; and this is the message which Christ bids us deliver, "Whosoever calleth on the name of the Lord shall be saved." Oh! may you be led to call on his name by prayer and humble faith, and you shall be saved. "Whosoever believeth on him is not condemned." Oh! may you believe on him today, or before this year ends, if you never have done so before. Touch the hem of his garment, and say, "Jesus, Son of David, have mercy on me," you with the blind eye; say, "Lord save me, or I perish," thou who art ready to sink; and the ready ears of Jesus, and the ready hands of the Savior shall now hear and bless if the heart be ready, and if the soul is asking mercy.

May you have the blessing of God living, and his blessing dying; his blessing in his advent, and his blessing at the judgment and Second Advent. The Lord bless you more and more; may he give you the happiest of new years, and to him shall be all the praise and the honor.[3]

---

[3] Much of the superb language in this sermon is Charles Spurgeon's. Occasionally, I find a few sermons to be so excellent and well-stated that I inform our congregation of the source and that the sermon is a light adaptation.

The Birth of Christ

Isaiah 7:13-14

Earlier this fall, Pastor Barry brought us 6 sermons from choice portions of the Book of Isaiah. Isaiah is one of the more Advent-oriented books in the OT. It prepares us for the coming of the Messiah. The words of Isaiah 40 are well known, and Ken Rolston also recently called us to review the comfort that God promises in the sending of the One who would prepare the way for the coming glory of the Lord. Isaiah predicted that the Sovereign God would arrive on a highway prepared, with valleys levelled and paths made straight. John the Baptizer would do that.

Also, the words of Isaiah 11 are well known . . . There the prophet predicted that a shoot would bloom from Jesse's line. This is the Davidic Messiah who would not judge by outward appearances but who would be full of righteousness, justice, wisdom, power, and the fear of the Lord. This Messiah would usher in an era in which peace would extend even to the animal kingdom with wolves and lambs resting at peace, while cobras and infants would be safe together. And the earth will be filled with the knowledge of the Lord as the waters cover the sea (11:9). Isaiah is fixated on the Advent of Messiah and its incredible benefits.

Further, the prophecies in Isaiah 9 are some of the most used for Christmas. There he foretold how an era shrouded with darkness would be illuminated with the dawning light of Messiah. A child would be born, a son given. And his 4-fold name would summarize his greatness: Wonderful Counselor, Mighty God, Everlasting Father, Prince of Peace. Messiah would reign on David's throne and he would extend this just kingdom of peace. *What a collection of focused prophecies*!

And the prediction of the virgin birth occurs in Isaiah 7:14. I want to focus intently on that passage this last Sunday of Advent. And be sure to notice how God interrupts human history, human powers, and pre-existing rules to bring about his Messiah. If he were giving this prophecy in our day, surely the characters would be Brexit, Saudi Arabia, China, yes those meddlesome Russians, and other rulers that nobody seems quite able to keep under control. Things like stock market volatility, massive institutional debt, crumbling social fabrics, and pressing moral issues might well provide the backdrop of similar modern prophecies. But in Isaiah's time, there were other players and dynamics. And among them was Israel's recurring disobedience and even callousness toward the things of God.

Isaiah put it in this context: Ahaz is trying to survive. The kingdom of Judah was in a condition of imminent peril. Two monarchs had allied themselves against her, two nations had risen up against the walls of Jerusalem with full intent to raze them to the ground and utterly destroy the monarchy of Judah. This is *SERIOUS*! Ahaz the king, in great trouble, exerted all his ingenuity to defend the city and, among the other contrivances which his wisdom taught him, he thought it fit to cut off the waters of the upper pool, so that the besiegers might be in distress for lack of water.

And God allowed him to request a sign—a thing very unusual in itself—and this initiative of God was spurned. Ahaz tried to be more spiritual than God and refused to ask for a sign, when invited. [10] Again the Lord spoke to Ahaz, [11] "Ask the Lord your God for a sign, whether in the deepest depths or in the highest heights." [12] But Ahaz said, "I will not ask; I will not put the Lord to the test." Ahaz may also have been asserting his self-sufficiency and lack of need for a sign. He may have boasted, although cloaked in spiritual terminology, that he had no need of a sign. This may have been an expression like we see in our own day of spiritual callousness. And God humbles him and us. Then God provided the most difficult of signs.

[13] Then Isaiah said, "Hear now, you house of David! Is it not enough to try the patience of humans? Will you try the patience of my God also? [God is obviously not pleased with Ahaz' reaction.] [14] Therefore the Lord himself will give you a sign: The virgin will conceive and give birth to a son, and will call him Immanuel." Is. 7:14, this rich advent prophecy, concerns itself primarily with 2 key things: the miraculous birth of Jesus and the majestic name of Jesus. You need to factor both of these into your lives at this time.

This text may be one of the most difficult in all the Word of God. Commentators are often divided on it, with one asserting one thing and another denying and interpreting differently. This verse is, to be sure, a high challenge.

This morning, then, [what if we focus on this] text as relating to our Lord Jesus Christ, and we have two things, here, that are abundantly clear about him.

First, the miraculous birth.

Secondly, the majestic name of Christ. So let us learn what we can about the Jesus of Advent by (1) the prophecy of his birth, (2) the prophecy of his name—all from Isaiah. Together, they inform us greatly.

I. Let us begin with the birth of Christ—'Behold a virgin shall conceive and bear a Son.'

And, first, we see here, in speaking of this birth of Christ, a miraculous conception. The text says expressly, "Behold, a virgin shall conceive and bear a Son." This expression is unparalleled even in Sacred Writ! Of no other woman could this be said. The only other possibly-close OT precursor is the birth of Isaac to 90-year old Sarah—miraculous to be sure, but nothing like this.

And from his birth down to his death he knew no sin, neither was guile found in his mouth. Oh, marvelous sight! Let us stand and look at it. A child of a virgin, what a mixture! There is the finite and the Infinite, there is the mortal and the Immortal, corruption and Incorruption, the manhood and the Godhead, time married to eternity! There is God linked with a creature, the Infinity of the august Maker come to tabernacle on this speck of earth—the vast unbounded One whom earth could not hold and the heavens cannot contain—lying in his mother's arms! He who fastened the pillars of the universe and riveted the nails of creation, hanging on a mortal breast, *the Creator depending on a creature for nourishment!*

Oh, marvelous birth! Oh, miraculous conception! We stand and gaze and admire. Verily, angels may wish to look into a subject too dark for us to speak of! There we leave it, a virgin has conceived and borne a Son. In this birth, moreover, having noticed the miraculous conception, we must notice, next, the humble parentage. It does not say, "A princess shall conceive and bear a Son," but a virgin.

Sinclair Ferguson explained, "If God was to speak the language and the mathematics and the physics that was necessary to express creation out of nothing and virginal conception, our minds would seek to expand to their limit—to take it in until we reach the point that we said, 'I'm sorry that I asked the question. I am just a man or a woman, a boy or a girl. This is too great for me!' And you see, that's the point that we come to recognize that here is the difference between the believer and the unbeliever. That's the point where the believer is content to say, 'You are God and I am not, and I'm content that it should be that way.' Whereas the unbeliever will say, with Friedrich Nietzsche, 'If there is a God who can do such things, how can I bear not to be that God; and so I will not believe.' Yes, it is an amazing, supernatural miracle; but like God's great works-creation, incarnation, crucifixion, resurrection-done safe from men's prying eyes. He brings light out of darkness. He brings his Son into the dark womb of a virgin."

C. S. Lewis answered objections to the Scriptural record of the Virgin's miraculous conception. In *Miracles: A Preliminary Study* (New York: HarperOne, 2001, 73-74), he wrote:

> You will hear people say, 'The early Christians believed that Christ was the son of a virgin, but we know that this is a scientific impossibility'. Such people seem to have an idea that belief in miracles arose at a period when men were so ignorant of the course of nature that they did not perceive a miracle to be contrary to it. A moment's thought shows this to be nonsense: and the story of the Virgin Birth is a particularly striking example. When Joseph discovered that his fiancée was going to have a baby, he not unnaturally decided to repudiate her. Why? Because he knew just as well as any modern gynecologist that in the ordinary course of nature women do not have babies unless they have lain with men. No doubt the modern gynecologist knows several things about birth and

begetting which Joseph did not know. But those things do not concern the main point--that a virgin birth is contrary to the course of nature. And Joseph obviously knew *that*. In any sense in which it is true to say now, 'The thing is scientifically impossible,' he would have said the same: the thing always was, and was always known to be, impossible *unless* the regular processes of nature were, in this particular case, being over-ruled or supplemented by something from beyond nature. When Joseph finally accepted the view that his fiancée's pregnancy was due not to unchastity but to a miracle, he accepted the miracle as something contrary to the known order of nature. All records of miracles teach the same thing.

Furthermore, He must be more than a man to die for the sins of the whole human race. He must be God in human flesh. Bishop Moule once said, "*A Savior not quite God is a bridge broken at the farther end.*" The miraculous birth of Jesus is at the very heart of him being fully God—a mystery, to be certain, but also a miracle.

In his classic book, *The Virgin Birth of Christ* (395), J. Gresham Machen wrote, "How, except by the virgin birth, could our Savior have lived a complete human life from the mother's womb, and yet have been from the very beginning no product of what had gone before, but a supernatural Person come into the world from the outside to redeem the sinful race? . . . A noble man in whom the divine life merely pulsated in greater power than in other men would have been born by ordinary generation from a human pair; the eternal Son of God, come by a voluntary act to redeem us from the guilt and power of sin, was conceived in the virgin's womb by the Holy Ghost." *All this, Isaiah predicted—hundreds of years in advance.*

And as the NT opens, we see:-Joseph responded in faith, and this virgin who would conceive also exhibited great faith. It's really kind of incredible if you'll think about it.

First, an angel approached Mary and told her that she would conceive and give birth to the Messiah of the world. She was young and had not yet had intimacy with a man. By the way, this is also a pretty far-fetched notion for a young virgin to think up. That's not usually what young women sit around thinking about, "Humm, how can I make a religious contribution to humanity by conception?"

Nonetheless, the angel tells her that she will give birth and she is shocked. She reels from the announcement. She has a moment to act, and she could have disobeyed the angel and God had she wished. She could have acted like it was not true or that God could not possibly speak that way.

Then, later, she obeys fully and travels with Joseph to report in for the census. All along, she trusts God—and does not waver.

At so many places in the journey, Mary could have disregarded what God had told her. She could have rejected his word and elevated her own thoughts or expectations above his own.

Then, she gives birth, and all kinds of visitors, from lowly shepherds to stunning royalty show up to worship baby Jesus, while mean Herod is breathing down their necks, determined like other arrogant dictators to rid the earth of Jesus and faith.

This birth of Christ deserves all our celebration, if ever anything did!

Christ owes no one anything because of a luxurious birth: To Princes, kings, Presidents, Chairmen, Christ owes nothing! Christ is no one's debtor! None of us swaddled him; he was not wrapped in purple, you had not prepared a golden cradle for Him to be rocked in! Queens, did not dandle him on your knees, he hung not at your breasts! And you mighty cities, which then were great and famous, your marble halls were not blessed with his little footsteps! He came out of a village, poor and despised,

Spurgeon continues to argue: If Jesus Christ was born in a manger in a rock, why should he not come and live in our rocky hearts? If he was born in a stable, why should not the stable of our souls be made into a house for him? If he was born in poverty, may not the poor in spirit expect that he will be their Friend? If he thus endured degradation at the first, will he count it any dishonor to come to the very poorest and humblest of his creatures and tabernacle in the souls of his children?

Then remember, concerning his birth, when did God ever hang a fresh lamp in the sky to announce the birth of any other king? Kings may come and they may die, but stars shall never prophesy their birth! When did angels ever stoop from Heaven and sing choral symphonies on the birth of a person or leader?

The representative men of the two bodies of mankind—the rich and the poor—knelt around the manger—and gold, and frankincense, and myrrh, and all manner of precious gifts were offered to the Child who was the Prince of the kings of the earth, who, in ancient times was ordained to sit upon the Throne of his father, David,

And Isaiah intended for his audience to know also that this miraculous birth would be of a real body that consumed normal food. He speaks of the One born to the Virgin as eating honey and butter and making moral choices (v. 15). He had a real digestive system and a real human brain—he was embodied God.

Some heretics taught, even shortly after the death of Christ, that His body was a mere shadow, that he was not an actual, real Man—but here we are told he ate butter and honey just as other men did—to teach us that it was actually a real Man who, afterwards, died on Calvary.

He knew the evil from the good. It is, usually, not until children leave off the food of their infancy that they can discern good from evil in the fullest sense. It requires years to ripen the faculties, to develop the judgment, to give full play to the man—in fact, to make him a man. But Christ, even while he was a Baby, even while he lived upon butter and honey, knew God's will perfectly.

He begins as a tiny piece of history, but it is real history. Jesus was in the fetal position in Mary's womb. It is a mystery beyond any experience. And amazing.

II. Now we come to the name of Christ—"And shall call his name Immanuel."

Names in the OT have meaning.
> Eve = mother of the living.
> Cain = I have gotten.
> Seth = appointed.
> Noah = rest.
> Abraham = father of many nations.
> Isaac = laughter.

Today, names still are filled with meaning. And God assigned a majestic name to the one who would be born to the Virgin: Immanuel = God (*el*) with us. Think of how ancient hymns develop this!

On several occasions when God institutes or renews his covenant, he chooses this concept to encourage believers. God tells Abraham that wherever he goes, he will be with him. In the covenant ceremonies in Genesis, God pledges to be "with his people and to be their God." To Moses, the name of God revealed as Yahweh means, I will be in whatever verb tense you are. I am what I am, or I will be what I will be. But in any case, I will be with you.

Elsewhere in the OT, God promises to be Immanuel, "God with us." And in John's first chapter, the word became flesh and dwelt "with us." God with us!

And in addition to this name, the Mighty God further defied all the wisdom of the world, in sending Jesus to be raised in the outback—not in the capital of power, commerce, entertainment, education, or finance. Jesus was born and reared in Nazareth.

Isaiah made several applications. Note v. 13: Don't try God's patience. Haven't some of you had numerous chances to please or obey him? Yet, we still serve self? If God stooped and made an offer to give you a sign, as he did to Ahaz, would you be too stubborn to accept it?

There are also applications in first century. These had waited a long time and were thrilled to see the dawning of the Messiah. God had not forgotten his promises! He keeps his covenant.

Of course, there are applications today: Do you know the Name and the Origin of Christ? How valued is it to you and your home?

On the name of Jesus, Philippians 2:1-11 gives us the point of view of Jesus and the Father; this is an open door into God's mind.

He comes into this world in such lowly conditions, so that—as the Book of Hebrews says—he knows all our darkness, depths, disappointments and desperation. There is nothing you may experience that he has not, *except sin!*

He is conceived in the womb of the virgin, so that he is the perfect savior. His name shows us that—he fulfills all previous predictions. He enters our history; he has a majestic name!

"God with you" meets all our needs. Will you trust him today?

How Some People Hate to Repent:
God and Man before Advent

Malachi 1:2-14

To begin this series in the final book before the First Advent, let me give three good reasons to Study of Malachi.

a. First, because it is often unstudied.

One of our Pastors taught an overview of the Minor Prophets this past summer in one Sunday School class. That was needed because this material is often unfamiliar but it is very helpful. The minor prophets are for many of us *terra incognita*, unknown territory, and I want us to overcome our sense that these prophets are inaccessible, inscrutable, or too far removed from the issues of your own lives. Many of us are not that acquainted with this material, which came from the best preachers of their day. (Rayburn)

b. Second, because fits modern spirituality.

In this short book, we find a rather progressive Christian community—maybe progressive in a bad sense. After centuries of plodding, Israel at the time of Malachi was fairly dulled. Sure, they'd had many opportunities and many callings, but over time, they'd grown not only callous to the things of the Lord but also they'd learned with too great precision how to justify themselves. Doesn't that fit closely with what we see all too often around us?

c. Third, because as final book of OT it is last word before Advent.

Since many of us don't know what's in this book, much less where it falls in biblical chronology, it may surprise you to note that:

(a) It was composed about 440 BC and is the final book of the OT.
(b) That also means that the Greek empire was developing, and this is roughly contemporaneous with the philosopher Plato's writing. Society was moving toward modern ideas. The world was becoming a fairly civilized place.
(c) As the final book of the OT, this is the last revealed word before Matthew. I frequently tell new bible students: to locate Malachi, open to NT book of Matthew and turn backwards 2 pages.

We tend to forget how late this book is and how it is much closer to the NT than any other inspired writing. Then, for whatever reasons, God halted his revelation for a while. Four and a half centuries of human history pass in relative silence, until John the Baptist comes on the scene. Speculation, of course, may be rife, but this is the Lord's last word in the OT; it is his final revelation until the Advent of the Messiah. Maybe this year, as we lead up to Advent, some chronological preparation is in order.

Watching people admit that they are or have been wrong is seldom pretty. Sometimes when you confront a child, he does not immediately own up to his mistakes. That avoidance syndrome only intensifies with age and ability. By the time we reach adulthood, with years of experience and highly developed verbal skills, most of us can plead innocent instinctively. We pack a ready laundry list of excuses. If someone confronts us with sin, either by omission or commission, we tend to say, "What? Me? Sin? How can you say such a thing?" And then when the Lord convicts us of our sins, we also find many rationalizations. Many of us find that when confronted with our own sins, often it takes many times for us to admit that we fall short of the glory of God. Are you quick to see and admit your own sin and guilt? Or will you argue and defend yourself for a long time before admitting guilt?

Last week, unfortunately, we saw an example of that in the latest inexcusable fall by another unaccountable, evangelical minister. Besides the sordid hypocrisy of this sin, it was also an example of how reticent most evangelicals are to admit sin. The leading Colorado pastor who denounced promiscuity, immorality, and homosexuality in particular was found to be a purchaser of illegal drugs and a frequent consumer of gay massages. Did he confess his sin on his own? No, only after the unbeliever painted him into a hypocritical corner.

Did he admit his sin, then? No; only after attempting several rationales, partial statements of truth, and series of denials. He claimed to be faithful to his wife and that he'd been in a Denver hotel writing a book. Pulling the truth out of him was worse than pulling your own tooth with a string tied to the door knob which was then slammed. Like the people in Malachi's day, he said, "How have I sinned?" And when God gave them a statement, still the sinners said, "but it's not me; surely something else is to blame. How have I sinned? Why can't I be excused like everyone else? What about my explanation or rationale?"

That presumptive, overly-human-centered attitude is symptomatic of how people treat God in our modern times. Well actually the times aren't so modern. This has gone on for centuries. Today as we begin a study of Malachi, let's see how people were treating God ca 400 BC, in the last book of the OT. And further, let's learn from Malachi, how we should have our attitudes in preparation for the Advent of Christ.

Background of Malachi

Malachi means "my messenger," and he lived around 450 BC. The situation Malachi faced was the same situation faced by Ezra, when he came to Jerusalem in 458 B.C., eighty years after the first return of exiles from Babylon, and by Nehemiah when he came to Jerusalem in 445 B.C.

This was a day that witnessed the rise of world empires from the West, an increase of international commerce, arts, trading, and society in general. Many of the modern trends and practices that we take for granted were developing in these centuries just before Christ's birth.

Israel had already been taken captive to Babylon (586) and returned. Nehemiah had rebuilt the Temple (516). But the city of Jerusalem remained a ruin, inhabited only here and there by squatters. Agriculture did not rebound quickly and many of the people remained poor. The taxes, tolls, and tributes that had to be paid to the Persian imperial treasury ensured that economic activity would remain sluggish. Already, things were deteriorating, after Nehemiah's time. Learn above all things *the spiritual law of entropy*: Spiritual life and love may diminish over time, if the fires of worship and dedication are not restoked. It would be a large mistake to think that this cannot still happen among us.

With little autobiographical material available about the author, it is clear that God wants us to concentrate on the message; and it takes a definite FORM, with a series of queries and answers. Some scholars of antiquity even believe that the book of Malachi follows the form of an ancient lawsuit. In each bloc of information, there is an:

- Indictment;
- A rebuttal by Israel, who pleads not guilty;
- A verdict by the Lord who sees all. All of this is because these people would not confess their sin in the first instance.

At a minimum, these sections record a disputation. Today let's look at the first two queries, or may I say, the 1st two excuses.

I. vss 2-5 How people mis-treat God.

"I have loved you," says the Lord. That is the opening statement; and it is an indictment. It will be argued about, but if God says he expresses his love, that should not be dismissed as minor.

However, the people reject that expression of love. They feel that God is not loving them as they wish, and they respond, "Oh Yeah? Just how is that." Note first the skepticism, the outright rejection of God's love, in that these people said, "Baloney, we don't believe you've even loved us." The reaction is like that of a jilted friend, whose expectations have not been met. The people of Israel turn and accuse God of not loving them. They allege: if you've loved us, we can't see it. They respond, "How. . . Just show us. We're from the 'Show me' state (Missouri). How have you loved us? Times are so bad, we can't see it."

Our kingdom has declined, our prestige is low again [why, our elections didn't go as we wished], we have little or no protections—being surrounded by warring Arab tribes—and you even let our Temple be sacked a century ago. Sounds like a child who is caught doing something bad, only to turn and accuse the parent or authority for not taking care of everything in life.

One of their underlying problems, was that they tried to squeeze God into a uniform way of treating everyone equal. These people imagined that God would treat everyone equally, identically the same. But his love is not that way.

God answers in v. 2 with that verse which sends anti-predestinarians into a frenzy. God says, "I have loved Jacob, but Esau Have I hated."

That's a hard verse. But just allow Scripture to speak for itself. The root or origin of this in Genesis 25. Abraham, after a long wait, finally had a son, Isaac. God had promised to work through that line of descent to bring great blessings. Isaac was old and about through with his course of life. God had provided twins, born within moments of one another, to Isaac; their names were Jacob and Esau. Esau was born split seconds ahead of Jacob. By birth order, he should have received most of the inheritance. He did, but on a whim, Esau sold his birthright to Jacob, who had a little assistance from a conniving Rebecca.

That led God to pronounce in the Book of Genesis . . . "the older will serve the younger." (25:23) And Malachi's phrase, "Jacob have I loved; and Esau I have hated," is repeated in Romans 9:13 to make the point that God has mercy on whomever he has mercy.

Some commentators have sought to soften the language of election by paraphrasing this as, "I have loved Jacob more than Esau, who seems hated in comparison." That might help some, but it still shows God treating different people differently, even if only relatively so. Also, that's cheating a little too much on Bible translation, because the Hebrew makes clear that the word chosen for Esau is 'hated.'

The Bible from Genesis to Revelation, despite all modern ideas to the contrary, teaches that God saves/chooses some and passes over others. That idea is well taught in the OT, and should be commonplace for those who read all of the Bible, instead of merely limiting their study to select portions of Scripture. May I say this as clearly and faithfully as possible: God teaches us in his own Word that he is an electing God. Those who know their true condition and the depth of his love realize that if he did not choose us, we would be hopeless and sunk. That's why that is good news for believers.

Do you fail to embrace what God's Word says here? Do you despise or not like something that our gracious, infinite, all-wise, powerful God has taught? Even worse, do you think you know better how God should work, and that he should choose all people? Or that you should raise objections ("How can this be?") to his plan? Will any of us be found to be arguing with the Lord? So much better to accept his word and adjust human theory, than to try to twist Scripture.

God states his general love in v. 2; then in answer to Israel, he states that he loved Jacob specifically and did not have the same love for Esau.

Continue on in v. 3. Not only that statement, but also it goes on to say, "and I have turned his mountains into a wasteland and left his inheritance to the desert jackals." That indeed is a pretty severe judgement. Esau's land has become a wasteland; and foraging animals sniff around his inheritance.

Mysteriously, but truly, God's love is like that. It is discriminating. To be faithful to Scripture and to avoid imposing a humanist agenda on God, we must accept and embrace that he does not choose every individual. Hell is real, and it will be populated with those who are not God's people. And every single one of them who are not chosen by God also reject him in their souls.

This teaching may not be accepted by Affirmative action and plans that strive for cookie-cutter equalism. But it is nonetheless thoroughly scriptural.

John Piper interprets: "In God's hatred of Esau, it means that God opposes their prosperity and brings their land under judgment. "I have laid waste his hill country and left his heritage to jackals of the desert." Also, it means that God will continue to oppose them when they resist his judgment. His judgment will not suffer resistance. Verse 4: "If Edom says, We are shattered but we will rebuild the ruins, the Lord of hosts says, They may build, but I will tear down." Third, God's hate for Esau means that they will by and large as a nation be given up to wickedness. Verse 4b: ". . . till they are called the wicked country. . ." This is the most devastating of the judgments and the one that makes all the others just.

Notice two ways that people mis-treat God in this area. These are two wrong reactions.

(1) Some reject that very biblical truth in principle. Some say, whether aloud or in their hearts of hearts, "I will not believe God, I will not follow him in this; surely modern, democratic folks know better." There are many different rationales, but some reject what God says in principle.

(2) Others reject that truth in *practice*. Vss. 4-5 described that.

In v. 4 we have recorded the inner thoughts of Edom after God has judged them. Do they accept his judgement? Hardly. Instead they vow to rebuild. In practice they reject the will of God. They attempt to defy it. They try to reject it. Do you know any people like that? Who try to go against God?

Even though God has worked and led in a particular way, some folks want to keep going in their own direction. To do that may not win a smile from the Lord.

But notice what God says at the end of v. 4 and into v. 5. The Lord says, regardless of man's plans, no matter what he builds, if it is not the Lord's will, it may be demolished. The particular people that God was dealing with were *Post-Mercies*. That's a new term I just coined. Israel had received:

> Chance after chance
> Opportunity after opportunity
> Mercy after mercy.

Still they insisted on doing things their own way—despite their heritage—and God said, "They will be called the Wicked Land, a people always under the wrath of the Lord." That is a challenge, isn't it, to thinking that ethnic Israel is still in God's favor. Here at the end of the OT, God promises, as the outworking of his covenant, that these will always be under wrath.

Not only does he promise to those who lived ca. 450 BC that they would see that in their own day, but he also promises that his mercy is larger than ethnic Israel five centuries before most of the NT was written. The Lord said that Israel was under his wrath and wicked, but his work did not stop. Long before Jesus' First Advent, God planned to show his great work "beyond the borders of Israel." It was never, you see, that God wished to work only inside the confines of Israel. No, his work is great beyond the borders of Israel. God, the Lord was working to draw people from many nations, tribes, etc. to himself.

God will be sovereign. "Great is the Lord—even beyond the borders of Israel." God is not confined in his working to Israel alone. He had a world-wide plan—even at this stage in the OT.

Yet people mistreat him by rejecting his plan. God will not stand for it. Sometime between now and Christmas, *will you come to God and admit that his plan is what you want for your life?*

II. The 2nd Query in vss. 6-14 contains the accusation:
    A. God is not honored, v. 6.

The Lord states a simple truism: A son honors his father. That is not extra-special, but normal. Similarly, a servant honors his master.

God states that he is a father in the middle of v. 6, but there is no honor coming from Israel. Nor is their respect given. Then things grow a little more specific.

    B. The religious leaders are the primary culprits (v. 6 = the priests), "It is you, O priests, who show contempt for my name." Not only did the religious leaders of Israel fail to give honor/respect to the Lord, but they also showed contempt for his name and all that it stood for.

That is God's indictment against these.

    C. Still the people profess innocence, as they ask, "How have we shown contempt for your name? They attempt to provide a rebuttal. They plead not guilty.

The Answer from God = "You've given shoddy sacrifices and offerings." Then, in v. 7 he adds that they had defiled food on my altar.

It was clear from the very first offering, Cain and Abel, that the Lord wanted to receive the best of offerings. It was an insult to give God what one would cast off anyway, such as:
    v. 8 blind animals for sacrifice
    v. 8 crippled animals
The OT was clear that defective animals were not appropriate.

"Try offering those to your civil leaders!" is God's reply. Verse 9 asks, "Is God stupid, Will God accept such?"

God is not fooled by second class offerings. Have any of you been skimping on this? Have you acted as if God is a poor huckster with a tent, trying to be negotiated with? Stop and think: how are your offerings to God? We don't give him animal sacrifices anymore, but are you giving any sacrifice? Too much comfort may go hand-in-hand with spiritual deafness.

In vss. 10-13, God states that he would rather have some sincere soul-searching on this matter, instead of extra temple services. In fact, he suggests something radical: *Close the church!!* Imagine!

That may take your breath away. The Lord said here, he'd just as soon have the temple doors closed so that people wouldn't come to church and go through the motions at the altar—if their hearts were not right. He is not pleased! God says, Close the church; there could be worse things. He will not accept offerings under certain conditions. Did you know that? All the offerings in the world from hearts that do not love God help very little. This may strike some of you as radical, but when the Lord speaks for himself, he clearly states that some acts of worship are not acceptable.

Instead, he desires (and re-states) that his name will be great AMONG THE NATIONS, from east to west. Wherever people truly love God, his name will be great.

But the people of Israel in Malachi's day were profaning the Lord's table, the place of sacrifice, by sniffing at it, acting above it, treating God's ways as beneath them. They showed contempt for God when they brought crippled or diseased offerings.

God's conclusion of the whole subject is given in v. 14. The Lord views us as "cheats" if we seek to give blemished sacrifices. Nonetheless, he repeats that he is a great king, a king to be feared, and that his name will be known among the nations.

This is how people were treating God immediately prior to the first advent.

Are any of us?   *Ways we may be doing so?*
- Do you dispute with God or change your ways to fit in with his?
- Do you think that you're immune from spiritual decline?
- Do you ever think about honoring God, about bringing glory to him? Why not make that a conscious target?
- Do you revere God? Or treat his presence as "ho hum"?

In sum what is required is REPENTANCE.

Many people use Lent as a period of repentance. This year I'm asking you as a congregation to use Advent for a season of repentance. Let Malachi challenge and lead us to such. Let every heart prepare him room.

There is a constant, regular need for spiritual renewal in the church of God. Malachi is all about preparing ourselves for God's blessing by presenting to him the kind of hearts and lives he delights to bless. It is a [seven-fold] wake-up call to renewed covenant fidelity. (Rayburn)

John Piper observes: "But the people had not learned their lesson from the exile. They had grown skeptical of God's love (1:2), careless in worship (1:7), indifferent to the truth (2:6-7), disobedient to the covenant (2:10), faithless in their marriages (2:15; 3:5), and stingy in their offerings (3:8)." The solution for each of these that may apply to you: come home, return back.

Why does God inspire Malachi to begin his message to these worldly Israelites, and to us, with such a revelation as this? "I have loved you, says the Lord. How have you loved us? Is not Esau Jacob's brother? Yet I have loved you and hated Esau? How have I loved you? I have loved you with free, sovereign, unconditional, electing love." "Why start a book or season with this?

- To humble you.
- To take away your presumption.
- To remove every ground of boasting in yourself.
- To cut the nerve of pride that boasts over Esau as though your salvation were owing to anything in you.
- To put to naught the cavalier sense of self-reliance that lets you dally in my presence as though you were an equal partner in this affair.
- To make you tremble with tears of joy that you belong to God.

But that is not all. God has another purpose in revealing the greatness of his electing love for Jacob and his judgment upon Esau. He tells us in verse 5: Your own eyes shall see this (you shall see the terrible judgments on Edom) and you shall say, 'Great is the Lord beyond the border of Israel!' That may help us meditate and prepare for Advent.

In other words, part of what it means to be loved by God is to know that God reigns—that he is great and mighty—even beyond the people called by his name.

The origin of careless Christian living is the failure to see the greatness of God. Piper again may be helpful: "In dealing with the problem of careless worship God unfolds the nature of his love not first as something warm, gentle, kind, and tender, but as something awesome and strange and fearful in its electing freedom. There is in God's love a great and awesome sovereignty. And that's what God draws attention to first" in this prophetic book.

To fail to see this may cause careless worship? Malachi warns: It makes a person bored with God and excited about the world. If you don't see the greatness of God then all the things that money can buy become very exciting. If you can't see the sun you will be impressed with a street light. If you've never felt thunder and lightning, you'll be impressed with fireworks. And if you turn your back on the greatness and majesty of God you'll fall in love with a world of shadows and short-lived pleasures.

I get this from verse 13: "What a weariness this is, you say, and you sniff at it, says the Lord of Hosts." They are bored with God. ["God loves us, Ho Hum."] Their basic attitude toward worship: "What a weariness this is!" And when you become so blind that the maker of galaxies and ruler of nations and knower of all mysteries and lover of our souls becomes boring, then only one thing is left— the love of the world. For the heart is always restless. It must have its treasure: if not in heaven, then on the earth.

Stephen Cole sums it up well: "They had drifted into routine religion instead of maintaining a vital personal relationship with a loving God. They followed God's program, but they had lost touch with His person. Their religious observance blinded them to their true condition, so that when God confronted them through Malachi, they responded, 'How has God loved us?'" This Advent, know the love of God; and don't take it for granted.

How (Unthankful) Hypocritical People
Treat the Lord Before Advent

Malachi 2:10-18

Advent in the Christian year follows upon the heels of Thanksgiving in America. That is probably a good thing. Today we bounce off a holiday that has most likely been excessive: I hope, at least, I'm not the only one who gluttonized. And we continue our season of Advent preparation. As you know, I am trying to lead up to Advent by having us study the final book of the OT. If ever there was a book to lead us to appreciate the birth of Christ, it is this one.

Today, however, I want us to explore what happens when unthankful or hypocritical people treat the Lord with contempt. It is a sobering but necessary message, and it should remind us to continue in thanksgiving, lest we become presumptive.

This morning, let's focus on a series of four tendencies in Malachi 2:10-18. God in this book is confronting the people with their need to turn from their sin. They say, they're not guilty, but they were. Not only did Malachi speak to a secularizing culture, but the church, just before the birth of Christ, was also an unfortunate example of a secularized church. These people were not so much "in open rebellion against God . . . but they are laboring under the delusion that because they have brought offerings they have been true to him all along." (G. Campbell Morgan in Boice) They had a form of godliness but contradicted its heart; and they were accommodating their culture too much. First, see:

A. Presumption of security based in paternity (10-12).

What happens if we believe we have a special "in" with God, and we do not?

The voice of the defendants is expressed in v. 10. God has charged them, and this is their answer. They plead, "have we not all one Father? Did not one God create us?" These two aspects claim common paternity. The people of Israel at this time, thought they had an automatic connection with God. They thought that an appeal to him as father permitted them to act wickedly without any punishment. It was a religious trump card.

If people think that, do you know what that does to their behavior? They expect the world and all around to serve them. They become selfish, arrogant, putrid—unthankful. These folks were speaking to one another and took quite a bit for granted. They thought that God was their Father and that they had a special privilege. Thus, they began to discount his claims on their lives.

Have you ever observed a child who misuses his father's influence? I once had a young man in a youth group that I led in a church; he thought he was a child of privilege and that the rules didn't apply to him. He would either say or infer: "you can't get on to me; don't you know who my daddy is? He's an elder." Obviously, this young man was not trying to please God by playing that card.

The Israelites with a few exceptions, 4.5 centuries before Christ were not either. They said, "we have our father on our side; all's well." Furthermore, they said, we're all made by the one Creator? At least they understood more about the origins of man than many moderns. But in both regards they believed that they needed to do nothing to have God's favor.

Two things recur when this privilege is asserted: profound unthankfulness and hypocrisy result when a person presumes God is his father but that person never acts like it. If we think God *owes* us things, if we take an entitlement mentality toward the Almighty with us, we have little need to be thankful. We also tend to look down on others and presume our superiority—this is exactly what Israel did. Will Advent find any of that attitude in you? Guard against it.

These people were breaking faith with one another. If they were all siblings, why were they so ruthless toward one another? Do you see how true faith works itself out in true brotherhood? The NT will later teach that you cannot truly love God and hate your brother (I

John). God took them to task and called them to repent for their personal relations.

God then answers in v. 11. He states that Judah had done a detestable thing. Something way bad had transpired. Judah had desecrated the sanctuary the Lord loves by marrying the daughter of a foreign god.

At the heart of the Lord's quarrel with Judah was that she had, in effect, married another god. She had given herself to false religion; and so defiled the sanctuary that God loves. This provides a lasting warning that one may correctly perform worship outwardly but be far from God inwardly.

God had expected that his sanctuary would be a place reserved for his people to meet with him. Instead, it had become a bazaar, a *commonplace* instead of a *sacred space*. Israel had brought into her worship all the world's trends, all the fashions of the day, she had married false religion, and joined herself to another spouse.

Not only did Israel believe herself better, but she was also way off the reservation, straying into adultery. If another human being did this, as v. 12 says, he should be cut off from the dwellings of the Lord. No matter, how much, in other words, a person wishes to cloak himself in outward righteousness, even if he brings offerings to the Lord Almighty, if he falsely worships God, outward acts will not matter.

This is also one of those verses that makes it clear that God never intends for a Christian to marry a non-Christian! No exceptions! You should no more pray about marrying a non-Christian than you should pray about whether it is God's will for you to commit adultery or murder your neighbor. God has made it abundantly plain that it is sin for his children to marry an unbeliever. It is never God's will for you!

From the contemporaneous books of Ezra (9, 10) and Nehemiah (13:23-29) we learn that one of the ways the priests had set a bad example and thus had led the people astray was in this sin of marrying foreign women who did not follow the Lord. In fact, they were even divorcing their Jewish wives to marry these foreign women (Mal. 2:13-16). Through the prophet, the Lord warns his people against the sins of marrying unbelievers and divorce. *For a believer to marry an unbeliever is to sin grievously against God.*

Do you observe how clearly God sees through our falsehood? Hypocrisy is condemned over and over again, in this book and

throughout the Bible. Don't think this morning that you can do a few
outward things or give extra money to cover over a heart that does not
love to worship God.

Just prior to the Reformation, the Roman Catholic church had—
much like Israel of old—created a system called "indulgences." Think
of these as back-taxes for spiritual matters. If you had committed
many sins, the Roman Catholic church thought, surely there should be
a make-up provision of some sort. And since they were in the middle
of a building program, why not let folks give a little "arrears offering"
and break even. The idea, not unique to any particular age, was: if you
do something public, you can cancel out private sins.

Think of the ways, evangelicals have developed similar customs:

- Some prayer requests, presented to be pious, really slander
  another person or bring attention to the requester.
- Agreeing to serve in church as a down payment for a sin you
  fully plan to commit.
- Some altar calls.

In fact, the next few verses amplify this theme. Another symptom
of heart-ingratitude is:

B. Attempt to pacify God with wrong-spirited offerings (13-14).

The people of Israel had to consider another accusation by the
Lord. In v. 13, God brings another indictment. He said, you flood the
altar with tears. You may weep and wail, surely outward emotion
does not prove the genuineness of one's heart, you may cry, you may
have great emotional affect, but that is not the same as resolutely
following the Lord.

These folks had learned to play a religious game, but God was not
fooled. Like some I've known, they'd say:

- "Great Sermon, Reverend," then not think anything of it. The
  verbal comment "You really touched me, today," with no
  action is like flooding the Lord's altar with tears.
- Closing one's eyes with rapture, but with no accompanying
  action, is like flooding the Lord's altar with tears.
- Coming to re-dedicate oneself again and again, with no action
  is like flooding the Lord's altar with tears.
- How do you flood the Lord's altar with tears?

God told Malachi to relay this message to the people: God no longer pays attention to your offerings or accepts them." (v. 13) He's not fooled! Others may be, but the Lord of all is not fooled. Think of Annanias and Sapphira in Acts 5.

The people of Israel were shocked. They'd never heard that God did not have to accept any and every offering. See how presumptuous they were. They pled not guilty, and they challenged the Lord, "Why? What's the deal? Why won't you just accept our offerings—that You instituted—and let us keep acting any way we want?"

Malachi answered (v. 14): God is acting as a witness because in your marital relationships, you have broken faith. The Lord believed that if these people were half as faithful as they said they were, then their marriages would be intact. But they were not. Divorce was becoming rampant, evidently, and church-goers/temple-goers thought they could break that relationship and just keep going—giving an offering would make the destruction of a home, spouse, and children all OK.

Does that ever happen today? Sure it does, folks will offer a devastating cancellation of all their words by an action of expedience if they're not careful. Profess to be a big Christian and have a wicked marriage, and watch what happens. Guess what, though: even if you fool some, God is not fooled.

Have any of you broken faith with the wife of your youth? She is your covenant partner. Either reconcile and have a nonscandalous marriage . . . or tone down the boasting/presumptiveness that you are such a great Christian.

I have no desire to heap guilt or condemnation on those who have already been traumatized by divorce. If you sinned in your marriage (inevitably both sides sin in divorce situations), I trust that you have confessed your sin to the Lord and sought the forgiveness of those you sinned against. We cannot undo the past. But we can learn from our mistakes and grow as we walk in daily repentance. So I don't want to add to anyone's pain. But I do want to call us back to God's standard of lifelong marriage. Even some well-known pastors and Christian leaders have gone through divorces. One survey showed that ministers ranked third among the professions in the number of divorces granted each year, behind medical doctors and police (*Leadership* [Fall, 1981], p. 119).

The Lord is not duped; he takes this area very seriously. So seriously, that he compares Christ's relationship to his church to marriage between man and wife. Each divorce is an assault on that!

And you cannot either give a make-up offering or cover over with additional good works, if certain basic relationships are disintegrating.

That's true on many levels.

- If I've just hollered at one of my children all Sunday morning . . . I'll not preach a great sermon.
- If I've treated an elder wrongly, and set myself up as a great pastor, I'm headed for embarrassment.
- If I say I'm a great Christian leader, real mature, and I cannot even speak to my spouse or say a few kind things to a fellow church member, God is a witness.
- If I am a leader of a ministry and I despise those that the Lord has provided as servants of the church, I'll probably not accomplish much until I repent and get things corrected.

There are many relationships that are crucial; and marriage is singled out here as ultra-important. The Lord here says that treating those right who are near us is more important than giving great gifts or showing emotion at the altar.

Here's an announcement that could get a pastor in hot water with the Treasurer, the Finance Committee Chairman, and the entire Session: "Don't give if your heart's not right." All the money you may contribute might only fool you, if you think that make-up contributions can pacify the Lord or make him happy. He could care less about all your money. The Lord wants something far more valuable: your heart, your mind, your moments, your soul, and your strength.

There is a temptation both by leadership and by members to confuse things on this score; and it can be deathly. You should not attempt to pacify God with wrong-spirited offerings. For that is a sign of spiritual presumption and superiority.

Go on to the next verses to see how seriously God takes the home as the proving ground of our faith.

C. Efforts to cover sin with "clothes" (15-16).

The Lord warns against the attempts to cover over some of these glaring sins, these relational ills. Verse 15 is a very important verse on marriage. It explains why God takes divorce so seriously. He believes that when people take a vow, they should keep them. That's in general. More to the point, in marriage, he also believes that when people are married, they create a one-flesh union, and that they should stay together unless there is an adulterous breach. God would rather have you *work through* your marriage than try to *work out* of it. He particularly finds it ugly when folks parade around as deeply spiritual and then cannot live minimally in their own homes.

Today, no one has to enter into marriage by coercion. No one is forced to marry another person that they cannot live with. Thus, be careful who you marry. We enter into this covenant til death do us part.

That requires work and preparation at times. Accordingly, v. 15b calls on you to "guard yourself in your spirit, and do not break faith with the wife of your youth."

The Lord says divorce is "breaking faith," it is belief, snapped in two by rebellion. And look at God's opinion of it: "I hate divorce!" No interpretation of these words can believe that this is a minor sin.

Why does the Lord express such a strong sentiment on this? For two reasons:

First, for all times, God planned for marriage to be a permanent bond that will also serve as an anchor for persons and society. The Lord meant for people to work through their problems in marriage, to learn how to give-and-take, and to abide through all the storms of life—not to run from problems or seek refuge in humanistic solutions or legal loopholes.

Even if well-meaning folks think of themselves as more loving with ever broadening divorce grounds, I cannot understand how one gets around this verse. It is so clear, so difficult to get around that one has to mangle several other doctrines just to accommodate that error. It is much like creation; when folks deny those verses, they are moved to deny other biblical teachings. Look how clear this is.

God, not man, is the author. He speaks for himself. He HATES divorce. He knows how much damage it produces, and the Lord calls for anyone who identifies with the name of Christ to hold the same view. The next time you hear a clever rationale for something God hates, remember that the God whose love exceeds all human loves *hates divorce*. The only way around this, as some contemporary arguments do, is to ignore this passage, and act as if humans are wiser or more compassionate than God. And the prophet here calls the people's hand on this, and the priests who were encouraging divorces 2500 years ago.

By the way, the rest of biblical teaching holds forth the same things. Our Lord Jesus taught that marriages were designed by God from the beginning to be lasting and that to put aside a believing spouse for a reason other than actual adultery was to cause that other person to become considered an adulterer as well. Jesus was quite emphatic about this, even going against the grain of his own culture's morality. In fact, his own disciples were shocked that he stressed marriage as having such a binding quality.

- In 1920, one divorce occurred for every 7 marriages.
- In 1940, one for every 6.
- In 1960, one for every 4.
- In 1972, one for every 3.
- By 1977, one for every two. The divorce rate in America doubled between 1967 and 1977.

Hasn't the church, sadly and this is our need to repent, contributed to this decline? At least, she has not slowed it down very much. And this verse calls on you, if you're a church leader, a pastor, or a teacher to repent from condoning something that God says he hates. Will you follow God's teaching on this with courage and consistency? Or will we contribute to the widespread ethical breakdown?

While our Savior and Scripture could have blessed the dissolution of marriages for any of the numerous grounds that society has blessed today, God's Word does not. So the first reason that God hates divorce is that it violates his own created pattern for marriage. Jesus knew that marriage was "so holy that of all social sins its violation invokes the most appalling consequences." "Instead of trying to find loopholes in God's commandment or trying to convince ourselves that our spouse is not a Christian or is at least not behaving as one and therefore divorceable, we ought to be shouting the holiness of marriage from the housetops. It is better to endure much personal unhappiness than to treat as expendable the solemn vows of the wedding service." (Boice, 588-9)

But the *second* reason for God's strong condemnation here—an even more convicting one—is that divorce was rampant among professing believers just before the First Advent; moreover, those who had identified themselves as public believers were showing their own hypocrisy by their inconsistent behavior in this area.

Let me put it this way: I'm not sure God expresses his anger to this degree to nonbelievers about their divorces. Certainly, that does not make it good for them; and their children and families are just as wrecked when divorce occurs. But it seems that God's white-hot hatred for divorce is for believers who talk about trusting God, wanting to follow God's plan, and lean on him and not their own understanding, who *then* resort to divorce without biblical grounds. Not only does that harm the person, the family, and society, but it compounds matters and *harms the witness and reputation of the Church.*

And that is compared to violence. Divorce for one who has professed faith is like putting on a clean suit to cover over a murderous, violent assassin. Remember the criminal who assaulted and murdered the 54-year old lady bicycling on the Silver Comet Trail back in July? Take him, scrub him, and put him in clean nice clothes and what do you have? A murderer in a suit. God is not fooled.

The same for those who cloak divorce and come up with a number of rationales and treat it as if a covenant can be annulled without consequence.

Today, our society is far more permissive towards divorce than it was 50 years ago, and this has flooded into the church. When Adlai Stevenson ran against Dwight Eisenhower for president in 1956, it was a big deal that Stevenson had been divorced. But when Ronald Reagan ran against Jimmy Carter in 1980, Reagan's divorce was hardly mentioned. It was Reagan who as governor of California signed the nation's first no-fault divorce law in 1969. Now all 50 states have such laws. It is now easier to get out of a marriage than it is to get out of a car-lease contract!

God is not mocked or fooled. So, guard yourself in your spirit and do not break faith. God hates divorce, especially among those who profess to be believers.

Do any of you need to repent of this? Or is your marriage not what it should be? God sees through the cloaks and he is not enamored with hypocrisy in this area.

D. Maintenance of moral reversitude.

Finally, these folks have about worn the Lord out. It is possible to "weary the Lord." That accusation is made in v. 17. God indicts the people and says, "you have wearied the Lord with your words." These folks before the Advent of Christ were *talking, talking, talking* about faith and obedience. But God knew it was all chatter. Are you ever a Christian who talks a lot about following the Lord but then when something's on the line, you don't practice what you preach? These people had wearied God with that tendency.

But when he confronts them, they do not accept his diagnosis of their illness. Instead, these folks plead innocence . . . "Not us; how have we wearied him."

God's answer is that these folks were maintaining a moral reversal. Just like their hypocrisy on the previous matter of divorce, they had extended their own Pharisaism—the practice of calling folks to hold to one standard while you practice sin in the same area—to many other areas of morality. They had destroyed the ethical foundation and redefining by saying, "all who do evil are good in the eyes of the Lord and he is pleased with them." (17) These folks had become unconcerned about keeping the law or doing what God wanted them to do. They'd also become insensitive to right and wrong. They thought that, the height of presumptiveness, God did not know what they were up to. Again, human beings think they might become so clever as to be able to fool God.

They asked in their hearts, if not aloud: "Where is the God of justice?"

This is the logical end for people who presume to have an in with God and who are not thankful. Instead, after taking thing after thing for granted, they grow callous to the Lord and walk away from him. After a while, they become more and more comfortable with false worship; and they also start to question God.

That is how things were headed just prior to the first Advent of Christ. This was the rise of Pharisaism; it was actually the continuation of an age-old pattern of hypocrisy, and God lets his people know that he hated it in every form.

Their need, and our need, at Advent, is not to have more clever rationales or find more loopholes to avoid what God says to do. We need to accept all that God loves and hates and conform our lives to those. No amount of covering will fool him.

Five times in these verses, we are called on not to break faith. Is there some area for you today where you have broken faith? Where you have chosen to disregard the calling of God? If so, our Advents will be much better if we repent.

In answer to "where is the God of justice," note God's remedy in 3:1-5.

Sometime at Christmas you may hear parts of Handel's great oratorio on "He shall purify." When you do, ask first, "What is being sung?" Then how can we possibly sing this at Advent?

The answer is because the Christian knows that judgement comes first before Advent of Christ. But also that Judgment is not all. It is like medicine—even if bitter. We must take it first, and then look for cure.

Malachi is dispensing such medicine to prepare us for the cure. Advent should take such balm.

The Final Word Before the First Advent

Malachi 3-4

God wants your ministry, your marriage, and your money. He also wants your love and your desire. All of these are more important to him than external religious acts. In our lead up to Advent this year, we have been following the topics of people just before the coming of Christ. In each one, we've seen how the Lord calls his people to repent and return. That age-old calling is for us, as well. I realize this may have been painful, as God shows us our own sin; but it will help us appreciate the coming of the Messiah all the more.

Malachi also shows how prone religious people can be to make excuses for themselves. Repeatedly in this book, God brought a charge against his people. A review of those indictments by God in the opening chapters of Malachi is both humbling (as we are quite similar) and useful. Each time they tried to defend themselves. But God, who does not change, is right in his charge.

As you know, after the close of the OT, there was a 400-year gap. The inspired scriptures are silent on those years. What happened we can, to some degree, construe from secular history. Things like:

. . . Alexander the Great and the rise of empires;

. . . the maturing of the arts, philosophy, and literature—in cultures that had stability;

. . . The beginning of Roman Empire;

. . . Maccabean revolts and the rise of the Sadducean and Pharisaic parties within Israel;

. . . many other secular events that are not recorded in Scripture.

But, as far as the inspired scriptures go, this is the final advent prophecy. If ever we wished to see the end of an era, which is on the verge of change . . . and if ever we wanted to observe the last prophecy before the time of and pointing to the birth of the Messiah, it is in the 3rd and 4th chapters of Malachi.

Now we are ready, with adequate background to see the final Advent Prophecy. The closing chapters of Malachi provide the last instance of a biblical prophecy before the actual coming of the Messiah.

Introduction: Waiting and Waiting and Wanting and Wanting.

You know what it is like to wait and wait and wait for a long time, don't you? And for that whole period to want something intensely. For decades, then centuries, God's people longed for the expected Messiah. Every sun-rise would cause some faithful saint to tilt his head and cup his ear to see if he heard the hoofprints of Messiah. People waited so long that by the time of Jesus' birth, the event (for Simeon and Anna) was called the "consolation of Israel." Some even gave up. But it was a long wait!

The people of God at the close of the OT, however, thought they wanted the Messiah to arrive; they presumed that they were just fine and that when he came, he would take their side against all comers. They said they wanted the Messiah to come, but their lives contradicted that in many ways. This prophet had to instruct them that for those who are at ease in Zion, the presence of the Messiah may bring as much judgment as it does blessing.

In answer to the question, "where is the God of justice," at the end of chapter 2, the opening verses of chapter 3 present God's remedy for that. He will send the Messiah who will be the Just-God in the flesh.

Sometime at Christmas you may hear . . . Handel's great oratorio, "He shall purify," which is taken from this passage of Scripture. It's a wonderfully stirring piece of music, rich with biblical content.

Taken from these verses, the Lord makes it clear that the people are not good in themselves, they are not ready by themselves, in fact, they need some serious cleaning up. They are definitely NOT Messiah-ready. Instead, they were way too presumptive and self-righteous.

The Christian knows that judgment comes first before the Advent of Christ, but also that Judgment is not all. It is like medicine—even if bitter. We must take it first, and then look for healing to follow.

Do any of you recall having to gulp down some bitter medicine or take a painful shot when you were little to get well. I can tell you remember if your face scrunches up. It's still a reminder when you have to give a baby a spoonful of something—for us it was castor oil—to get well, the little cherub tunes up, turns red, and soon bawls like it is being murdered.

The OT ended with such a dose of spiritual medicine, and God's people needed it. But the message of the Bible is not about the medicine, it is about the CURE. That's what Rev. Malachi was trying to tell us.

More than anything Advent is about Jesus Christ, even more than about gifts. The Lord's final prophecies present some clear things about Christ. Let's focus on them in our time today.

a. First, before Jesus arrived, there would be a messenger (3:1), who would prepare the way for the Lord.

This prophecy first occurred in Isaiah 40, which we've read. In that prophecy, Isaiah announces comfort, for Jerusalem's hard labor is about completed. Her sin is atoned for, and God will send a prophet from the desert. His voice will call out for roads to be straightened and for an expressway for the coming Messiah to be made, which will include leveling of rough ground and preparation for the revealing of the glory of the Lord.

Look just about anywhere in our neighborhood and one sees a construction illustration of this.

Just down the street from our building used to be cows grazing. Soon it'll be a subdivision. You may think that's progress or regress. It's amazing to see how quickly some construction happens. But what's the first thing that happens in building: dirt is moved. A road is built and leveling occurs, so that more workers and other builders can access the site. Some large equipment moves a lot of red clay, and all of that is preparation, prep for what is coming. But all of that preparatory work is not the finished product: homes themselves. So with this messenger: Before the arrival of the Messiah, God would send the prep crew. Roads would be leveled, and highways straightened. For 400 years after this prophecy concludes, God will be knocking crowns off of hills and building up valleys. The Messiah is so important that God would see to it that things were prepared, and access would be available.

Then in the opening of the gospel we're told who this messenger is: John the Baptist (Matt 3:3) who fulfilled Isaiah's prediction and picked right up on Malachi's theme, calling for folks to repent, for the kingdom is near.

b. Next, the coming of the Messiah would be sudden (3:2a); and that would catch some by surprise. Jesus later taught that the 2nd Advent would be sudden and surprising, too. If you think, you'll have a 30-day notice before the Advent of Christ, you'll probably be shocked. And after all, if we had Christ's calendar down, that would make us presumptive.

c. The Lord would come to his Temple. Is it too much to say that Jesus comes to his church first at Advent? Not so much the world? He comes with both comfort and judgment. Judgment begins at the house of the Lord, but there is also comfort for those who love the Messiah.

The work of God has a decidedly "inside-out" force. He begins with his own and calls them back to faithfulness. Then he radiates outward like the ripples in a calm lake disturbed by a rock.

d. Jesus, born at Advent, is fully God. He is described as "the Lord, whom you seek" . . . also "the messenger of the covenant." Christ is all these things; he is the announcer of God's covenant faithfulness, Jesus more than anyone would accurately relay the covenantal plans of God, and he is the Lord. John the Baptizer was the forerunner, but Jesus is the Messenger of the Covenant, the one that people seek if they truly love God.

Rob Rayburn notes that the parallelism in 3:1 indicates that "the Lord you are seeking" and "the messenger of the covenant whom you desire" are the same. But that figure is distinguished from "my messenger" at the beginning of the verse. We have two figures here, an interpretation confirmed in 4:5 and then in the New Testament where we learn that John the Baptist was the messenger the Lord sent ahead of "the messenger of the covenant."

However, the ministry of this "Lord who will suddenly come" who is "the messenger of the covenant" is clearly the ministry of a divine figure. He does the things that only the Lord has the power and the authority to do. What is more, in both 3:1 and 3:5 there seems to be an identification between the messenger of the covenant and the Lord Almighty. In 3:1 we have the messenger of the covenant "coming" and in 3:5 "I," that is, the Lord, "coming." He is both the sender and the sent. [Stuart, 1347] The messiah is a divine figure.

e. Then vss. 2-3 portray a startling bit of information. The Jews before Jesus' birth presumed that they had a corner on the spiritual market. They thought that whenever the Messiah came, he would surely pat them on the back, congratulate them for their longsuffering and faithfulness, and praise them to the highest heavens. Do you ever allow your satisfaction to lead you to believe that God is so pleased with you that he can hardly contain his praise for you?

Most Jews expected the Messiah's entrance to be a pat on the back for their past faithfulness as well as a future endorsement.

However, note what these verses teach. When Christ comes, he is a severe judge of sin. When he comes, it will be like a refiner's fire. Most of us have not been in a smelting furnace. But a fire is stoked to a very high temp., and the goal is to remove impurities from metals by that hot fire. The dross is burnt off and removed, but only by intense heat.

"Launderer's soap" was a form of lye used to soak the dirt out of clothes. Both fire and lye are agents by which what deserves to remain is separated from what does not.

That is a vignette of how Christ confronts and removes sin. Like a high-powered soap (launderer's), he washes away sin. But note this for future reference: when the Lord comes, he does not gloss over sin or treat it as normal. Jesus is not, and was not, easy on immorality or disobedience. No, sin is a blight, and Jesus wants to cleanse it and wash it away. And that "day of his coming" (v. 2) is not necessarily a pleasant one, at least for those who are going against him.

He will come like a refiner of silver. He wants to purify us. No, Jesus will not come to bless the people for already *having arrived* in all things spiritual. As much as we love his Advent, should not each one of us take stock of our own standing with him; and perhaps we need to admit that we need cleansing and purifying from sin? Even the leading religious leaders (Levites) needed purification; and sadly

I'm quite sure that ministers today need the Lord to start his purifying work in our own lives.

Christ's refining work, though, does not end there. Verse 4 tells us what results from that. After he cleanses us from sin, after he purifies his spiritual leaders, THEN the Lord will have men who will bring offerings in righteousness. Do you see how when the Lord works in us truly, one of the telltale signs is that we bring offerings in righteousness. We give our lives, our time, our best moments—all our offerings. The urge to give something back to the Lord is a token that he has worked in our lives and that we truly belong to him. If things are right between us and the Lord, our offerings reflect our heart's gratitude for Christ's deep cleansing work in our behalf. Israel was not doing this in Malachi's day; and God would change that.

A spiritual law is apparent: those whom Christ confronts and cleanses, he also changes/transforms and makes us into those who give offerings and do so trusting in the righteousness of Christ. Make sure that that is happening in your life this Advent.

When that happens, our offerings and those from other believers "of Judah and Jerusalem" (v. 4) will be acceptable to the Lord.

Rayburn is helpful as he preaches: "Again, like the refiner and the fuller he will separate from the Levites those who are covenant breakers and purify those who have kept the covenant. And the result will be a renewed and reformed worship. Worship is chosen as the object of reformation because it has already been mentioned as something in the life of God's people in that day that had become corrupt, because it is so much an indicator of the spiritual condition of God's people, and because it is the engine of everything holy and good in the life of God's people. Fix that and you fix much!"

But to ensure that we take this seriously enough, note how v. 5, then, reiterates that when the Messiah arrives, he will come bringing some measure of judgment. The Lord will oppose those who live in immorality. Does this modern Advent find you thinking that the Lord will either excuse or overlook immorality in your life, as if you have a pass? Those who are sorcerers (#2), adulterers (#7), perjurers (#9), defraud laborers (#8), oppresses the widows, fatherless, and aliens of justice, will not meet the approving smile of Jesus Christ. Instead, their lifestyles show that "they do not fear me." God is not fooled. Even if folks hang out in the temple, even if they present themselves as outwardly religious, when Jesus Christ comes, he sees through all our smokescreens, all our deceptions, all our rebellion. If the Lord came to our church or our home, this advent, would he find any: sorcerers (#2), adulterers (#7), perjurers (#9), defraud laborers (#8), oppresses the widows, fatherless, and aliens of justice?

Note how the ten commandments were still a superb measurement of morality; also note how God does not condone these things.

When people fear the Lord it shows in their living. Malachi was sure that the people of his time weren't living out that fear of the Lord. Might we not do well to think about the fear of the Lord a little?

Note how long ahead of time, over four centuries, that the Lord predicted how these things would come about.

The *very idea of prophecy* also teaches something very important about the God we worship at Christmas: He is the God who had a plan—for ages—and that plan is so certain that he can make future predictions. Prophecies, about the Messiah, or anything else, would make no sense, if God did not have a plan, or if he could not bring it about. Every time we sing an Advent prophecy, we affirm the sovereignty of God, as well as praise his ability to control the future. God is not waiting on our decisions to determine how to run the world as if in response to us. Do you love God for that this morning?

Quickly drop to 3:16 because we should see the reaction of those who fear the Lord. Following last weeks' section about tithing, v. 16 shows how true repentance works itself out. Those who feared the Lord conversed together. They did not want to fail to show the appropriate fear of the Lord. God listened to their prayers. And they did something interesting and symbolic: they made a scroll of remembrance. They wrote down their commitment. This was like making a vow. They promised the Lord, and promised together, to obey him. They were serious enough to write this down and place the scroll somewhere for posterity. What have you committed to the Lord with that much seriousness?

Make sure you also see, the promise and assurance in vss. 17-18. It's worth reading over again.

Now to the last section, the last word of the OT:

The Final Word Before Advent: Malachi 4:1-6

Again, the Lord needed to underscore for these folks that the day was coming when the Messiah would come. And when he did, it would not be a pleasant day. When that day arrived, it would be as described earlier, a holocaust, in which evil would be burnt.

Specifically, the evil would be those who were arrogant and who did evil. The Lord would reduce them to stubble and set them on fire. Do you sense how seriously opposed God is to sin, evil, and arrogance? In fact, the final aspect of 4:1 promises that God will not leave a shard of their evil around—so thoroughly will he clean them out. "Not a root or branch will be left to them." The wicked will be destroyed. Is that not what the Lord said in Psalm 2.

In contrast, however, those who are under God will be blessed. Verse 2 describes them as those who "revere God's name"; they treat God and what his name stands for with the utmost respect. Do you revere him? Or ever lapse into what John Piper calls "careless worship"? For those who revere God's name, there awaits a rich promise in v. 2. Righteousness will rise like the sun, with healing in its wings—health and immortal life will come—and they will leap and rejoice and kick up their heels like frolicking calves set free. Joy and health are promised for those who revere God; burnt stubble is the promise for those who oppose him.

Moreover, v. 3 assures another part of the life for believers: They will trample down the wicked: there will be victory. Many times in this life, it seems like such will never come. But here those who look to God see that he will finally vindicate his ways. Those who try to resist him will be burnt and serve only as ashes underfoot.

God is that powerful; and this verse seems to understand what it is like to wait a long time on this promise coming about. At long last, God will Triumph over all his foes—that's part of the message of Advent—and his enemies will be destroyed.

Verse 4 reminds these people, 1000 years after the origin, to remember the law of Moses that was given at Mt. Horeb. Of interest for all those who, today, think that they may be above the law or better than these old commandments, God said, "Remember the law of my servant Moses, the decrees and laws I gave him at Horeb for all Israel." The law has not gone out of date.

So at the root of wickedness or evil in God's sight is human self-reliance and self-centeredness. The person who thinks that he is good enough in himself to get into heaven is arrogant in God's sight. He does not understand how absolutely holy God is, nor how utterly corrupt his own heart is. He establishes himself as his own standard of righteousness and arrogantly thinks that his good deeds will commend him to God on the day of judgment. But God, who sees the heart, is not impressed! He describes them as chaff and that day as burning like a furnace. It will be so hot as to leave them neither root nor branch. In other words, no one will recover from this scorching heat. (S. Cole)

Finally, the OT concludes with vss. 5-6. The testament that began with creation, the volume that has so much, reaches its conclusion with these words:

- The Forerunner Prophet was an identifying sign; look for that. And when John the Baptizer came on the scene that was fulfilled.
- A fruit of the reviving work of the Spirit: fathers turning to children. Normally callous and busy men would take an interest again their children. They would prioritize their spiritual life.
- Or a curse.

We're primed and ready for good news; God has set the stage for the Messiah. And he bursts on the scene in Luke 2; For behold I bring you tidings of great joy!

But believers must wait at times. If you have "a biblical mind about the life of the church in the world, one thing you will know and expect is that there will be long stretches when little happens. Days of small things will be more the rule than the exception. We might well have thought that the return from the exile would herald a new golden age for Israel. But it did not. It ushered in another day of small things and that day was to last for five centuries or more. This is a very important recognition, because without it Christians are much more subject to the temptation to be dishonest about their faith and their spiritual situation." (Rayburn)

This fundamental requirement of waiting upon the Lord, related as it is to faith as the principle of the Christian life, is why spiritual writers see in this patient waiting of Christians for the fulfillment of God's promises a main difference between real Christians and unbelieving people. The unbeliever is all for the present; he wants his good now and is uninterested in the promise of it eventually. He doesn't believe enough in the Word of God to be comforted by such a promise. Whereas a Christian will wait and continue to wait in confident hope even though all appearances are contrary to what he is longing for. [Sibbes, *Works*, i, 251, as cited by Rayburn]

How will you be awaiting Advent this year? Eagerly, on your toes, looking and in a humble posture? Or rocked back, sitting in overconfidence? The Lord wants to draw us near to him. The Messenger of the Covenant calls and will come suddenly.

Maybe more than ever, with this study, we can see how *good* the Good News is. Against this backdrop of spiritual decline, hypocrisy, and sinfulness, God is still faithful, and he sends his Incarnate Son, the Lord whom you seek, suddenly came to his temple. Will our hearts make him room?

Even in the lowest of ebbs, according to Mal. 3:1 the people were expecting the Messenger of the Covenant in whom they desired. Do you desire him this morning? Does that work its way out in your life. When you rise for the rest of Advent, will you utter a prayer, "I desire you, O Lord, to live and reign in my life today? And do you desire him, if he comes suddenly . . . or slowly? He is and always will be the "desire of nations." Let that start in your heart and expand outward this Advent.

Baby Jesus, the I AM

The Gospel of John, selected verses

Grandfather's stuff: watch, glasses, phone, pen, keys, wallet, candy for you!! Things to see and things to think about.

This is a pretty exciting night, huh!

I watched a 4-year-old little guy go nuts this week when Miss Sherry, Sherry Secretary gave him a cool, remote-controlled jeep. Another godly lady gave this same lad some crisp dollars, and he was pumped. Some of you, I can tell, are the same.

God gave us a wonderful gift at Christmas, and it is a gift that lasts forever. Jesus is the only gift anyone ever got that lasts forever and ever. He lasts to infinity and beyond. Nothing else does.

Do you think Mary told Jesus about the night He was born? I think she probably told him that story many times. Maybe every year on his birthday.

And it is a really great time of year. We see love, special cousins, have gifts, and hear fantastic stories about baby Jesus and God's love.

And while some tales are tall, this one that gathers us now is absolutely true.

Tonight we celebrate the birth of Jesus. He had parents just like yours:

- Instead of riding in a car, . . . they rode on a donkey.
- Instead of being in a cozy, dry house/church . . . they were in a smelly, damp stable. There was lots of noise.

- Instead of receiving shiny gifts . . . Jesus' fam was fairly ignored.

He was born in an open barn. And instead of a nice bed, with soft, scented sheets, Jesus was born and placed in hay.

And do you know why Jesus came to earth as a baby? So that he could show us God. When grown, he later said: "If you've seen me, you've seen the Father."

And in many ways, Jesus points us to God. He compared himself to certain things that are symbolized tonight, and I want to share those with you, by using Seven 'I Am' statements of John Jesus told us who God was. He was God!

1. 8:12   I am the Light of the world.

Ever get up at night, when it is dark, and smack your toe on something hard? We need light, don't we? Jesus is the One who lightens up the whole world. That's why we put lights on trees and use candle lights at this particular service.

The shiniest, brightest star EVER shone in the sky when Jesus was born. Later on, when Jesus was teaching about who He was, He said, "I AM THE LIGHT OF THE WORLD!" What does a light do? Yes, it scatters the darkness. Jesus gets rid of the darkness in our hearts. He can get rid of the darkness that makes us sin. JESUS IS THE LIGHT OF THE WORLD.

2. 10:7   I am the door.

A door keeps bad things and harsh weather out; it protects what is inside. We have strong doors on this church building, don't we? Even though, Jesus was a baby, he was strong and he protects us. Your mommies and daddies lock the doors after they get you in bed. Jesus secures us.

3. 10:11   I am the good shepherd (also v. 14).

There were shepherds taking care of sheep when Jesus was born. An angel appeared to them.

They were pretty muddy and rough. But Jesus is a good shepherd. He takes care of us and gently guides us.

Candy Canes!! Remind us of these shepherds. We have a lot of pointers to what really went on.

4. 11:25   I am the resurrection and the life.

He who believes in me will never die. Jesus was born a baby, and
he was treated horribly by some people, but he came back from the
grave. He was first placed in a manger, perhaps in the side of a hill.
Later he was placed in a cave to be buried. But he came back. He is
life!

5. 14:6   I am the way, the truth, and the life.

How do you think Mary and Joseph found the town they were looking
for? They didn't have a GPS like most cars. They didn't have an
iPhone telling them where Bethlehem was. They probably used a
map; or asked. Later Jesus told us, "I AM THE WAY." He tells us
how to get to the best place of all. He tells us he is the way to heaven.

6. 15:1,5   I am the vine, you are the branches.

What comes from a vine? Grapes. And grapes make the wine the we
drink tonight.

7. 6:35, 48, 51   I am the bread of life.

How did Joseph and Mary have food for their long trip to
Bethlehem? Did they stop at *Chick Fil A*? No! There weren't
restaurants then. They probably brought food with them. Mary
probably baked bread and packed it. When Jesus was a grown man He
told us, "I AM THE BREAD OF LIFE!" That means that all of us
have things we need. We need things only God can give us. God gives
us all we need. We even say that when we pray the Lord's Prayer. .
."Give us today our daily bread." He always does.

We use bread in this service of communion to know that Jesus is
our bread. He fills us better than the best food you'll eat at Christmas.

Your father Abraham rejoiced to see my day," He said. Then,
when they questioned that assertion, He went on to insist that "Before
Abraham was, I am" (John 8:56, 58).

"Fear not, Abram: I am thy shield, and thy exceeding great
reward" (Genesis 15:1).

There are seven "I am"s in the Book of Genesis, the first being
Genesis 15:1, as already noted. The second is in Genesis 15:7, where
God, speaking to Abraham, said simply: "I am the Lord." The word,
"Lord," of course, is the Hebrew Yahweh (or Jehovah), and carries
essentially the same meaning as "I Am," or "The One Who Is."

Then, there are 21 (i. e., 3x7) "I am"s in the Book of Exodus, including the divine answer to Moses, already mentioned, "I AM THAT I AM" (Exodus 3:14).

In the Revelation, there are 6 "I am"s that stress His eternal existence, from eternity to eternity. Note the list below:

- "I am Alpha and Omega, the beginning and the ending" (Revelation 1:8).
- "I am Alpha and Omega, the first and the last" (Revelation 1:11).
- "Fear not; I am the first and the last" (Revelation 1:17).
- "I am Alpha and Omega, the beginning and the end" (Revelation 21:6).
- "I am Alpha and Omega, the beginning and the end, the first and the last" (Revelation 22:13).
- "I am the root and the offspring of David, and the bright and morning star"(Revelation 22:16).

Yes, God identifies himself. He wants you to know him. And to walk with him all year long and all your life. He is, as we've sung, "veiled in flesh, the Godhead . . . hail God born as a Baby!! Will you love him and ask him to be your Savior tonight?

Be sure to receive the gift of Jesus that God gives.

The Coming

Luke 2:13-14

Yep. I saw Adam and Eve when they sinned. They sure had it good before that. I even watched events unfold before they sinned. I saw Satan fall like lightening (Lk. 10:18). I was an eyewitness to his fall and his disloyal demons—who used to be angels (Jude 6). I saw that.

I watched as God punished Adam and Eve by casting them out of the Garden. He then erected the swirling, flaming cherubim to guard the entrance into Eden. I saw all that and was even asked to guard Eden and keep people from coming back in. That's why after all these years, no one has discovered Eden. One of my daily routines—to this day—is to guard Eden. It's not a bad job. I've seen the best and I've seen it all.

I even saw Noah (What a character!) and the flood. I watched Abraham leave his homeland and take Isaac to the place of sacrifice.

In fact I jumped in at the last minute to prevent the young lad's death. I was personally involved (as one of three messengers) in visiting Sodom and Gomorrah. You think you've seen wickedness! I've seen it all. I also was privileged to know Jacob, who I met one night in a dream. I've seen it all. And I've had quite a life of good experiences.

One of the other highlights of my life was in delivering the "Ten Commandments" to Mt. Sinai (Acts 7:30; Gal. 3:19). I knew Moses quite well and followed his whole life. I spoke with Joshua a few years later about some very important matters (Josh 5:14-15). I watched David defeat Goliath, Solomon build the Temple, and

Jeremiah (one of my favorites) tell it like it was. I saw all the ups and downs of thousands of years. I've seen it all . . . or at least thought I'd seen it all.

I was even right with Daniel as he conquered his enemies by faith. It was fantastic to be able to see and help out in all those triumphs. On two occasions, when Daniel the Dreamer had visions, I was allowed to see those and even sent to explain them to Daniel (Dan. 8:16, 9:21). It is quite an honor to be God's messenger and instruct some of these heroes of the faith. My name is . . . GABRIEL.

Now do you believe me when I say, "I've seen it all."? Well I have . . . or so I thought. All of this early history was really something and I thought I'd seen it all, but all of this was nothing like the . . . COMING.

Let me tell you about my highest privilege so far. It was to be involved in the COMING. Let me take you back to the beginning of that; for this is the greatest message in the world to tell, especially at Christmas time. It all started with an announcement to a quiet little couple in Jerusalem. He was a priest and she was unable to have babies. The couple, getting up there in years, were saddened at the possibility of having no children as they grew older. So God called me in one day and gave me this assignment. He always amazes me at how well He can take care of his people. He sent me to Zechariah, who was in the temple at the altar (Lk. 1:11). I was to speak this message to him,

> Do not be afraid, Zechariah (It always surprises people when a stranger calls them by name.); your prayer has been answered. Your wife Elizabeth will bear you a son, and you are to give him the name, John. He will be a joy and delight to you, and many will rejoice because of his birth, for he will be great in the sight of the Lord. He is never to take wine and . . . will be filled with the Holy Spirit even from birth. (1:13-17)

So I told Zechariah about the birth of John. Unfortunately, Zechariah like many of us had to be shown in order to believe. He asked for a sign, thinking that this was incredible. Zechariah asked me, "How can I be sure of this?" One of the pleasures of my job is in answering questions like this. So I answered Zechariah in this way: "I stand in the presence of God, and I have been sent to speak to you and to tell you this good news. And now you will be silent and not able to speak until the day this happens, because you did not believe my words, which will come true at their proper time." (Lk. 1:19-20) And as you know that was exactly what happened. Zechariah went out and could not speak, Elizabeth surprisingly became pregnant, and all the people were amazed. I thought I'd seen it all.

But then one day I was called to the Throne where God sat me down. We hardly ever have sit-down conferences. I remember thinking, "This must be important." And it was. What God would began to tell me was great and more earthshaking than all of the other experiences in my life put together. I only *thought* I'd seen it all when compared to the COMING.

About six months (Lk. 1:26) after I'd visited Zechariah, God sent me to a small, unimportant town in Galilee, called Nazareth. My assignment was to visit Elizabeth's cousin, a young unmarried virgin named Mary. She was planning to marry a carpenter named Joseph in a few months. But my message would nearly mess up this poor couple's plans. I couldn't believe that I'd been chosen for this assignment. I went to Mary and began with, "Greetings, you who are highly favored!" I truly felt honored to speak with one who was so favored by God.

Of course, May was terrified. I'm sorry that we are sometimes so frightening to people. We don't usually mean to be. Mary wondered what kind of message this could possibly be. So I said, "Don't be afraid, Mary, you have found favor with God. You will be with child and give birth to a son, whom you are to name, Jesus. He will be great and will be called . . . the Son of the Most High." (Lk. 1:30-32) I couldn't believe that I was so fortunate as to announce the name of the Messiah. His name was even linked to the nearly unspeakable name of the Most High God, which even angels are not permitted to ordinarily use. What a privilege was mine! I went on to inform Mary—that innocent young lass, that her child would be given "the throne of his father David, and he will reign over the house of Jacob forever, his kingdom will never end."

Mary was dumbfounded. She'd never expected something like this. I could tell. Knowing that she and Joseph were not yet married and had not tried to have a baby she sacked, "How can this be since I am a virgin?" So I answered this way, "The Holy Spirit will come upon you and the power of the Most High will overshadow you. So the Holy One to be born will be called the Son of God." I went on the tell her that "Even Elizabeth your relative is going to have a child in her old age . . ." (Lk. 1:35-36) You should have seen the look on Mary's face when I told her about Elizabeth. This was almost too much for Mary to Believe. So I added "For nothing is impossible with God."

I've always been impressed with her response. Mary meekly said "I am the Lord's servant. May it be as you have said." (Lk. 1:38) that was it. We should all be that way. Whatever God wanted, she wanted. She almost sounded like an angel. I had never seen a virgin bear a child. Like I said, I've seen an awful lot in my time, but never this. This was a new miracle not in the catalog. I'd be anxious to watch events unfold. Mary then broke into song and visited her cousin Elizabeth. I watched the whole visit, including the moment when young John the Baptist jumped in his mother's tummy as Mary said "Hello."

Meanwhile, Elizabeth had her baby. A cute little Baptist. I was asked to oversee the birth and make sure everything worked according to the plan. It did. And eight days later, the proud older parents some stared at them as if they were grandparents—and took Zechariah's son to be circumcised. The officiating priest asked what the child's name was, assuming that he would be named after his father. I had to prod Elizabeth to cause her to forcefully interrupt the ceremony. She shouted out "No! His name shall be JOHN." (Lk. 1:60) The priests were amazed. They went to Zachariah and sure enough he wrote on a tablet the name J-O-H-N. At the moment I restored his ability to speak. He was so thrilled and convinced of all this that he burst into song. (Lk. 1:67-79). And Zechariah didn't normally sing; nor should he in the future. I was pleased to watch one happy father and mother.

My name is GABRIEL. I was in charge of watching Mary as her pregnancy continued. You know a lot of things can happen, so God was careful to make sure that she was OK. As the time drew near, God who had been working behind the scenes to direct all of these events (did you ever stop and think about how hard it is to govern the whole universe, complete with all the various rulers?), led the ruler to take a census of his empire (Lk. 2:1). And Joseph had to go to his home town of Bethlehem to talk him out of divorcing Mary when people began to see she was having a baby. He was planning to divorce her secretly—to avoid disgrace. It's very wrong, you know to have babies before being married.

So I went to him and, in a dream said, "Joseph son of David, do not be afraid (I had to talk to every one about their fear.) to take Mary home as your wife, because what is conceived in her is from the Holy Spirit. She will give birth to a son, and you are to give him the name Jesus, because he will save his people from their sins." (Mt. 1:20-21) Again I was given the rare opportunity of revealing the name of the Son of God to one of his earthly parents. Joseph did the right thing and took Mary home to be his wife (Mt. 1:24). That took a lot of faith. I was beginning to realize how "Big" this COMING was.

So Joseph and Mary, at the very end of her nine-month pregnancy, had to take a journey to Bethlehem. I went with them through the Judean hill-country and saw to their safe travel each step of the way. There were some other characters involved in this drama, also. The wise men who came from the east followed the bright star. I was the one who was dispatched to guide it over the exact right spot. I nudged that brilliant star on its course and, exactly as planned, the wise men would arrive within hours. It's not easy to rearrange heavenly things, you know! I thought by now I had seen everything. But the COMING was just beginning.

It was also my job to rouse that ragged troupe of shepherds. Have you ever tried to get them to do anything? I had to resort to unusual measures and invoke the Supernatural Powers Act. I summoned some of the radiant glory to shine on the area above them. And once more, to a people scared out of their wits, I had to say, "Fear not for I bring you good news of great joy that will be for all the people. Today in the town of David, a Savior has been born to you; He is Christ the Lord." (Lk. 2:10-11) You should have seen them run for cover before I told them not to fear. They were amazed. They weren't even looking for a Savoir, for an angel, or for any good news. I described how they could find Him: "This will be a sign for you: You will find a baby wrapped in strips of cloth and lying in a manger." They took off on a furious search.

Now, after all my assignments were completed—all the characters were informed of the action —I checked over my list once more to make sure everything was completed. I could now return to Headquarters. JOB COMPLETED. But about half way back to HQ I was met by, what seemed like, a whole company of warring angels.

They were racing earthward at rapid speed. I wondered what could possibly be so urgent. I could only remember one other time when so many angels were feverishly dashing about at such a quick pace. I hoped nothing was the matter. Of course nothing could be the matter, knowing God's ability. I decided to join the group and see what was going on. I had a few hours before my next assignment was to begin. So along I flew.

Soon I noticed that we were headed to the exact spot from whence I had recently left. "Why," I wondered, "would all these angels be interested in a few wise men, some rough shepherds, and a couple having a baby. Certainly there were some pretty good miracles involved, but why all the fuss"? As we approached the manger where Joseph and May had settled, I began to realize that things were not as usual here. From our vantage point in the air, I saw all of the principal characters converging on one point. Zechariah and Elizabeth had pointed to Mary who was now about to give birth. The words I had spoken to them began to make sense. The wise men were approaching this one small stall in Bethlehem. The shepherds, also, only about two miles away, would soon meet at this point. It seemed to be the center of the world. Joseph was just now beginning to help May through a difficult labor. All these characters, summoned by God's Chief Angel were approaching the stable for a once-in-a-lifetime event. This was no accidental event. All of the sudden the names I had revealed to Mary echoed in my ears (And sometimes it's hard to hear among the sound of flapping wings.) "His name shall be called Jesus—He will save his people from their sins. He will be called the Son of the Most High—the Son of God." Was this really it?!?! Was this the long-awaited COMING?

Was this what we had waited for, for centuries? I recalled all those Old Testament prophecies which we'd given, I thought of the years of yearning. I thought I'd seen it all. Now I was about to see something that I wouldn't have believed if I hadn't seen it with my own eyes.

Now the event of the ages was unfolding before my very eyes. I, Gabriel, had been chosen to speak to Mary, Joseph, and the others. But far more important than me, was the One who would be born on earth. God was in the process of sending his own Son, and at the same time, God was taking on the outer shell of human flesh. THIS WAS IT! The Messiah was being born and we beheld his birth. The COMING.

Then at that moment Joseph delivered that crying little baby. It was majestic. Every birth is painted with the miraculous, but none like this one. This birth would change world history. It would change all things. We, in the angelic community had awaited this for so long that most of us had stopped really expecting it. But God was faithful to his promise. At the right time, he sent his son, born of a woman, to redeem his people (Gal. 4:4). There . . . in that cradle was the Promise of the Ages, the hope of Glory, the Way, the Truth and the Life, the King of Kings and the Lord of Lords. Born a child, yet a king. "Veiled in flesh, the godhead, see, Hail th'incarnate Deity; Pleased as man with man to dwell, Jesus our Emmanuel."

Now don't get me wrong. Even angels can be moved by certain things. This even was so magnificent, that even we were led to break out in joyous praise. And angels aren't prone to praise for no reason. All at once, the split second after Jesus' birth, we burst into a round of praise: "Glory to God in the Highest. God is truly glorious and great. For he has given people to his children on earth" who are blessed with his favor like Mary was. I thought I'd seen it all. But that was the greatest. It was so great that I found myself lost in wonder, love, and praise. If you're not careful, you may find yourself lost in that way, too.

The rest, you know is history. The shepherds did arrive and visit Jesus. They then went and told others. The wise men also arrived and brought gifts for the young King. And evil Herod tried to murder baby Jesus. I even had to appear to Joseph and warn him to flee the country (Mt. 2:13) because Herod was going to kill the children. And then when that threat was over I instructed Joseph to return to Nazareth. But no assignment can compare with the COMING.

That was my highest privilege so far. I say "So far" because, I still have an important job to do at the end of time. In fact you can read for yourself in *The Revelation* what Gabriel will do at the end of time. In the meantime, I'll keep on doing the two things I enjoy the most.

There are two things I most enjoy. One is watching young ones come to know and believe in Christ. Angels in heaven love to do that. In fact there is more rejoicing in heaven over a new one or a young one who repents (Lk. 15) than over 99 who are already in the kingdom. So it is my pleasure to watch chosen ones come to Christ. I'll plan to keep on doing that until the end. Would one of you be my Christmas present this year? I can't help but wonder if one of you little readers might not be among God's family. Do you want to come to Christ today? Is there a small child or an adult who wants to come to worship Christ, as did the wise men and the shepherds???

The other thing that I'll do is keep on reflecting and rejoicing about the first Christmas—the COMING. That was the greatest thing I've ever seen or hope to see. You humans do not understand what it's like to be an angel. We can't be redeemed like you are. Sure it's true that we don't sin like you do. We've not fallen into sin like you have. So in one sense we don't need to be redeemed. But on the other hand, we are not adopted into God's own family. You are highly favored, if you're adopted into his family.

I thought I'd seen it all. But I hadn't. Take it from me, Gabriel, the greatest thing I've ever seen was Christ born at Christmas. That sight was so great as to make grown angels weep. It made us sing. That birth changed our normal routines. It was more important than anything. It was the COMING. I, Gabriel, saw it. Now I've seen it all. Have you?[4]

---

[4] Readers may detect in this, or in a few other chapters, a presumed readership of children. Our churches have always had Christmas Eve services, pitched for the young and families. This particular one was even a free-standing booklet with classic artworks.

The Prince

Once, not too long ago, there was a king. He was a good king, a wise king, and most kind. However, he also must have been the most misunderstood king in all of history, for the neighboring people (not his own, of course) thought he was horrible, hideous, and filled with mean-ness. Although his own loyal subjects were grateful for his kind rule, whenever he tried to help others they ran off, as if he were the ugliest person in all of the Middle East.

Never content to give up easily, he wished to give a gift to the tribal group in Arabia, just across his borders. He knew he could help those people; for as it was, these crude tribes lived in tents, or caves, and were always on the move. They were never settled or peaceful. The children of the wandering tribes (Wanderers, they were called) had no shoes, never knew where their next meal would come from; and there was hardly ever any joy. But the good King wanted to give not one, but many, gifts to help them.

So he gathered supplies, food, colorful materials for clothing . . . and, of course lots of DVDs, PlayStations, Xboxes, and CD players. But guess what? As he loaded all these gifts and electronics on hundreds of camels, and headed toward his western border, the Wanderers fled as fast as anyone could remember. They took to the hills, left no tracks, and disappeared into their caves. They feared that the Good King—his name was Saleem—only wanted to conquer them and take away from them their moldy bread, the few ragged clothes they wore, and hurt them. That's what they had been told for years; and they believed it.

King Saleem, however, really wanted to help them. Perhaps he needed to make a peace treaty with them first. If only they would accept his gift or make a treaty, then they would have plenty of food, work, happiness, plus they would have King Saleem's protection against the evil ENEMY king, Serpentine.

So King Saleem thought things through this way—and he was very wise. He had two obstacles to overcome: (1) the people fled from any sign that the king or his helpful army was approaching. If a plane flew over, they hid. If he sent a caravan of care packages (as he attempted earlier), they hid. He'd even tried to send gifts on large ships, but to no avail. If he tried to sneak help in, they resisted all foreigners. The (2) second problem was that the King had to find an emissary to get through. For winter was coming, and these Wanderers would starve.

So, King Saleem thought and thought; and he asked all his royal advisors to come up with a plan. Finally one surfaced from an unexpected source, and the more King Saleem thought about it, the better it seemed. He needed to send a person that:

a)   He could absolutely trust; have his confidence.
b)   Would always represent the king and his goodness; not other ideas.
c)   At the same time, could fit in with the Wandering people.
d)   He might even have to assume deep, undercover for 20-30 years, but the errand was worth it. And here's the kicker, the best part of the idea:
e)   This helper would be from his own family—to make sure all of the above worked.

Of course, King Saleem couldn't send his wife—she was too well known and would be recognized. He had several daughters who would have been excellent, but the nomadic Wanderers would never listen to a princess. The only candidate left—and this plan was his idea to begin with—was the Prince, the only son of King Saleem.

But just before launching on this quest, King Saleem pondered, "What if something happens to my son, my only son? He's the only heir I have; and our own people are depending on him to succeed me?" Plus, he didn't know if a child of the palace could possibly pull off the great task.

Still, King Saleem was so loving that he was willing to try.

A program of Royal Prince training was begun. The prince had to learn:

- The wandering people's customs—some were very crude, and the prince could not be expected to approve of these behaviors.
- He had to learn their language, which was curious to begin with, but had grown even cruder over the years.
- The next challenge for the Prince was to learn to look like the Wanderers. He had to leave behind his beautiful clothes and learn to love rags. He also had to wear his hair like them— look like them in every way, in other words.
- He even had to learn to travel like them, sleep in dripping caves with bugs, and eat their stale food—the best dish was stale bread dipped in squash stew [Oh, what horrible food they ate!]
- Finally, he had to take all this and spend a long time making friends and building trust—this couldn't be done quickly—the Prince had to be one of them for so long that they never remembered he was not one of them. He couldn't be known as a "settled" person, who'd come over, but he had to be a full Wanderer, always roaming and never at home. And then, once he'd become like them, he would give the people the message from King Saleem: "Come, meet me at the border, and I'll bring everything you need, including protection from bad kings."

The Prince, then, could only come on foot, live in a cave, and work like Wanderers. He started on his journey, bravely so, although the goodbyes were very difficult.

There was only one major problem—for the Prince, the King, and the Plan were all supremely pure. The problem was the ENEMY, Serpentine. He had told the Wanderers for years that King Saleem was bad and mean. That's why they believed that lie, and loved darkness more than light. The ENEMY flashed a super-bright light from time to time that would blind the tribesmen. That drove them further into their caves. He also intercepted any letters from King Saleem. In fact, the GREAT ENEMY patrolled the border, long expecting a great plan involving the Prince.

So, when the ENEMY got word that the Prince had snuck into the country, he searched it and tried to kill all outsiders. Fortunately, the

Prince's preparations were so thorough that he passed for a Wanderer. But the evil ENEMY would not quit; he killed many of the pitiful Wanderers and their children in the process. He created more and more lies about King Saleem and did all he could to stop this rescue attempt by King Saleem.

Well, a lot of time went by and after surviving for a while, 20-30 years, the Prince knew what he had to do. He would have to get rid of the ENEMY and defeat him in a different way. Now that the Prince was fully grown, everyone thought he was just another Wanderer; they had no idea that he was royalty, and he didn't try to impress people. However, he had become a tribal chief, the first one who had never been married. The Prince was that respected.

Shortly after his 30th birthday, he activated the plan. He would do two things to finish his mission; then he could go home to his father. First, he would offer the message of peace and help from King Saleem. Those who had any sense would listen; only those who were permanently blind would not. Second, that would attract the ENEMY, and the Prince would destroy his power once and for all.

So, he convened a town council and all the chiefs gathered by torchlight in a huge cave. The Prince gave this short speech: "I am not merely a Wanderer. I am also a Prince, the only son of King Saleem, and I have brought you a peace treaty that will give you and your children life and light. Love the King and respect him, and he will take care of all of you and give you what you truly need. I have lived with you all these years to prove the truth of this message."

Several chiefs were skeptical, some downright unbelieving. But one, who the Prince knew from somewhere, was especially angry and insulting. He was enraged, said bad words about King Saleem, and made fun of the Prince. He said this was all silliness, and then he reached into his cloak and pulled out a super bright light, which he lit, to blind the elders. Then he pulled his knife, while everyone was dazed and blinded, and went straight for the Prince. At that moment, the prince remembered, "this is the face of the ENEMY; Serpentine has masqueraded as a chieftain."

The enemy headed right for the prince, and just as the blindness was subsiding among the chieftains, the Prince did something that was amazing; it was so brave that it would be talked about for centuries. He told the ENEMY: "come ahead, kill me, if you wish, for the people have heard and they will love my father. They have a seen a great light, which overshadows your blinding light." Enraged and still trying to silence the Prince, the ENEMY turned—before their very eyes—into a poisonous snake, slithered over to the Prince, bit him on the heel, and felled him. But before he collapsed, the prince did two things: (1) he stomped on the head of the snake, and (2) he told the Wandering chiefs: "Believe me, I'll live again, and you can trust my father."

Thus, the Prince defeated the ENEMY; his shriveled up snake-skin was all that was left, although some Wanderers who loved their old ways, spread stories that he was still alive and that the Old Serpent was better than the new Prince of Peace.

But many believed and guess what? The Prince did not die. At the last moment, outside the cave, the thunderous hoofbeats of a powerful army were arriving: it was the Prince's aged Father, and he had a healing potion that cured the snakebite. So the Prince lived again.

The people were freed from their blindness. And King Saleem got his message through by his only son, who had become like the Wanderers.

- The Love of the King.
- The Sacrifice and Success of the Prince.
- The offer of real peace . . . why that IS the message of Christmas.

I invite all of you to know Jesus, the Prince of Peace.

Messianic Prophecies: Hints in Genesis
of Jesus' Advent

This morning I shared with you how the Lord had been leading people to expect the First Coming of Christ. However, it is actually very early that God began to prepare his people for that, as early as the book of Genesis. Since we've been spending much time on that in our evening worship, I thought it might be helpful to review "Hints in Genesis of Jesus' Advent." If we review these, we'll see how long God had been planning this and how extensive his love is to plan so long.

1. First, Gen. 3:15.

Even surrounded by sin, God has a marvelous plan of redemption; and it involves a child born to a woman. After God cursed the serpent, he forecast that there would be a continuing hatred, enmity between the offspring of Satan and the offspring of the woman. That the offspring of Eve in mind is Christ can be seen since only he, in all of human history, was the one who crushed the head of Satan [on the cross] while he himself was bruised and pierced. But on the Cross, Jesus born of woman, defeated Satan. That was hinted at long ago, and it is part of the Christmas story when we see that Jesus was not born of a goddess or a spirit but of a woman, a virgin named Mary.

2. Next, if we think about Isaac's birth, we can see parallels and hints to Jesus' birth. [Excerpt below from A. W. Pink]

Isaac was the child of miracle. Sarah's womb was "dead" (Rom. 4:19) and before she could conceive a supernatural "strength" must be given her (Heb. 11:11). In this, of course, we discover a foreshadowing of the miraculous birth of the Lord Jesus—now, so generally denied. However, the vital importance of the virgin birth of our Savior cannot be overestimated. Sir Robert Anderson says, "The whole Christian system depends upon the truth of the last verse of Matthew one" ("The Coming Prince"). Returning to the miraculous birth of Isaac, do we not see in it, as also in the somewhat similar cases of Rachel, Hannah, the mother of Samson, and Elisabeth, not only a foreshadowing of the supernatural birth of Christ, but also the gracious way of God in preparing Israel to believe in it, facilitating faith in the Divine incarnation. If God quickened a dead womb and caused it to bear, why should it be thought a thing incredible if he made the virgin give birth to the Child!

The birth of Christ was markedly foreshadowed by that of Isaac and this in several ways at least.

- First, Isaac was the promised seed and son (Gen. 17:16); so also was Christ (Gen. 3:15; Isaiah 7:14).
- Second, a lengthy interval occurred between God's first promise to Abraham and its realization. When we are told, "And the Lord visited Sarah as he had said" (Gen. 21:1), the immediate reference is to Gen 17:16 and Gen 18:14, but the remote reference was to the original promise of Gen 12:7. So also was there a lengthy interval between God's promise to send Christ and the actual fulfillment of it.
- Third, when Isaac's birth was announced, his mother asked, "Shall I of a surety bear a child, which am old?" (Gen. 18:13), to which the answer was returned, "Is anything too hard for the Lord?" and the striking analogy is seen in the fact that when the angel of the Lord made known unto Mary that she was to be the mother of the Savior, she asked, "How shall this be, seeing I know not a man?" (Luke 1:34), to which query the answer was returned, "With God nothing shall be impossible" (Luke 1:37): so that in each case God's omnipotence was affirmed following the annunciation of the birth of the child.
- Fourth, Isaac's name was specified before he was born—"And thou shalt call his name Isaac" (Gen. 17:19); compare with this the words of the angel to Joseph before Christ was born—"And thou shalt call his name Jesus" (Mt 1:21)!

- Fifth, Isaac's birth occurred at God's appointed time (Gen. 21:2) "at the set time;" so also in connection with the Lord Jesus we read "But when the fullness of time was come, God sent forth his Son, born of a woman" (Gal. 4:4).
- Sixth, as we have seen above, Isaac's birth required a miracle to bring it about; so also was it with the incarnation of Immanuel.
- Seventh, the name Isaac (given unto him by Abraham and not Sarah, Genesis 21:3), which means laughter, declared him to be his father's delight; so also was the one born at Bethlehem—"this is My beloved Son in whom I am well pleased." Surely you can note the amazing consistency in Scripture and see how God is preparing us for Christ's miraculous birth—all in Genesis.

3. Another large hint about Jesus is contained in Genesis 22: Abraham's sacrifice of Isaac. In that famous passage, we see a father who is called on to sacrifice his son, his only son, his son of promise that he loves dearly. Abraham models the love of the Father; Isaac models the obedience and sacrifice of Christ. For several days, Abraham, his head servant, and Isaac hike to Mt. Moriah and prepare for the soul-agonizing struggle/sacrifice. "God himself with provide the lamb for the burnt offering."

Thankfully, at the end God saves Isaac and send a substitute animal. Surely, this is a picture of what Jesus did on the cross for us—when the father gave his utmost gift, and Jesus died in our place. The sacrificial scenes of Genesis 22 prepare the imagination for what would happen after Jesus' incarnation.

4. Also: Genesis 28: Stairway to heaven, with "Angels ascending and descending on ladder" = John 1.

5. Prophecies in Genesis 49 (Jacob blessing his sons): "The scepter will not depart from Judah, nor the ruler's staff from between his feet until he comes to whom it belongs and the obedience of the nations is his. He will tether his donkey to a vine, his colt to the choicest branch; he will wash his garments in wine, his robes in the blood of grapes."

The first book of the Bible is full of prophecies for the first Advent of Jesus. This year, unwrap as many as you can!

Ruler of the Nations

Luke 1:29-33

One of the Advent hymns we sang tonight, admittedly a bit Gregorian sounding, is "Let All mortal flesh keep silence." As you might know, that is taken from the Hebrew Prophecy that says, "The Lord is in his holy temple; let all the earth be silent before him."

And one of that hymn's stanzas that lends itself to communion at Advent says: "King of Kings yet born of Mary, as of old on earth he stood; Lord of Lords in human vesture in the body and the blood . . ." Now that phrasing is not limited to communion and may refer to Christ in any situation, but it surely draws the mind of the believer toward this sacrament.

Here's a question: Is the body and blood of Christ present at the communion table? How could it be? Which body?

Christ is as eternal as God the Father and the Spirit. He took on a body, uniquely I argue, at his incarnation. The timeless took on time; the infinite became finite; True justice stooped to injustice, and the immortal took on our mortality.

What was born was encased in soft, pink, infant flesh. Jesus probably did actually cry (contrary to "Away in a Manger"), unless crying always and only be coupled with sinful acts—but Jesus later wept (Jn. 10:35). All babies cry. All human ones, and Jesus was fully human. He had a body—a respiratory system, a heart, a brain, fingernails, eyelashes, a skeleton, just like ours.

Christ's body was wired in every way as ours, except he never acted, nourished, nor went along with a sin nature—which he did not have! And throughout his 33 years, his body carried him through this vale. And when he was tortured and hung on the cross, his human body reacted and behaved in all the ways of a normal human body— not as an appearance but in reality. That is part of the Christmas message; that is part of communion.

And when Jesus rose, he had a body—a confined corporeal existence. Jesus was not merely a spirit, but he rose, glorified— pointing us to what our bodies will be like when we, too, are glorified.

And, as I'm heading to communion, in contrast to some who teach that Jesus' body is incorporated in these elements, where was his body last seen? And what was it like?

Listen to how John 21 (on the shore, ate fish that the disciples caught) and Acts 1 describe this: Jesus arose and ascended to heaven. And his body was what went up. A body seems to remain attached to Jesus, after his Ascension—which would create a serious problem for Roman Catholics and others who think his body inhabits this bread.

So, as the Protestant Reformers (after, not, Luther) taught: Jesus' body is ascended to heaven and sits on the right hand of the Father. This also is the Lamb that John saw in Revelation 4-5.

So, of this table as of the tomb, we must say BODILY, "he is not here but he is risen." Yet, the Spirit of Jesus can transcend all things, and there is still blessing in this meal.

But it is blessing for those who know Jesus Christ as he wished to be known. This includes knowing his body, and tonight I wish to draw your attention to but one phase of that: his incarnation as announced to Mary.

I preached on Mary's great faith and great song a few weeks back. Tonight, to prepare us for communion, I wish merely to focus on a short segment of that Announcement. For when the Angel Gabriel reveals this miracle to Mary, he also tells us the kind of Savior/Messiah to expect. And *we should recognize no less in this meal. Same in Manger and at the Table!*

I want to highlight four phrases that are used to announce our Savior's birth, and see if you see these four things in your participation in communion tonight.

1. He will be your son, called Jesus (v. 31): he will save his people from sins.

Jesus is named for his mission. Taken from the Hebrew, *Jeshua,* Jesus (according to Mt. 1:21) will save his people from their sins. That means, tonight, that you have sinned, I have sinned, and we need a Savior—One who can save us while we cannot. Jesus rescues, delivers, saves, and forgives. Jesus' name means that he did not come to assist us in saving ourselves, nor that any could save himself. But to save helpless sinners, he was born in a human body and in this meal, we are pointed to how he loves and saves us.

Richard Sibbes famously wrote, "We have this for a foundation truth, that there is more mercy in Christ than sin in us." Grace exceeds all our sin!!

Tonight in this Christmas communion know that abounding grace and Jesus as the Savior, who has a people, who claims and redeems a people, who purchased a people, and who forgives us of our sins. He will be called Jesus, Mary's Son, who saves his people from sins. NEXT:

2. He will Be Great.

There is nothing average or mediocre about our Lord. In every category, he exceeds, he outperforms, he excels. Jesus will be great. He will not fade over history. Today, there are more people on earth who call him great than ever. Despite any societal decline in some places, people all over the world this year will cry out that Jesus Christ is our only Savior, and he is great, and his name is above every other name.

He has no rivals or close competitors. It is a slam dunk. The angel foretells to Mary that her son will be great. Will you know him, praise him, worship him as such tonight? "How can we be afraid of anything when there is no one and nothing greater than our Lord Jesus Christ?"

3. He will be the Son of the Most High.

He is also tied to God the Most High as a son. To be sure, the Trinity is still mysterious to us. Despite all his humanity, he is also Son of the Most High God, fully God and fully man.

The "Most High" God is rooted in the OT. Believers then saw him as incomparably above any other fictitious gods. He was above them all—the most high. Even demons (Luke 8:28) recognized Jesus as the Son of the Most High.

Geoff Thomas preached: "A son is everything his father is whether he is a genius or a handicapped child. The Son is everything the Father is. He has deity; he has godhead; whatever constitutes divinity the Son has it. Whatever the Father is then the Son is that too. He has every single perfection of the Father; every attribute and characteristic of the Father the Son has it also. As the Son of the Most High he is almighty, omnipresent, omnipotent, omniscient, omnicompetent. The Son of the Most High was the Maker of the heavens and the earth in the beginning. Without him was not anything made that was made.

4. He will reign (33).

Jesus will be the long-expected fulfiller of all OT political prophecies. He will reign on David's Throne; he will be not only a prophet, not only our merciful high priest, but he will be our king. And he will actively reign and bring together all events.

Interestingly, Jesus is not revealed as an Advisor or as a Facilitator. He's a powerful ruler. He does what is right; and he acts without and above our permission. He will reign.

Many Advent hymns proclaim Christ as Ruler in Advent Carols: Why are there no carols for pluralism? Uniformly, our carols proclaim Jesus as the Sole King.

> 195 "Joy to the World . . . let earth receive her *king* . . . Joy to the earth, the Savior *reigns* . . . He *rules* the world with truth and grace, and *makes the NATIONS* prove the glories of his righteousness."

> #196 "Born a child and yet a *king*; born to *reign* in us forever, now thy gracious *kingdom* bring."

> #197 ". . . bidding all men to repentance, since the *kingdom* now is here"

> #198 "Lift up your heads, you mighty gates. Behold the *King* of glory waits; the *King of kings* is drawing near, the Savior of the world is here."

#203 "Hark the herald angels sing, 'Glory to the newborn *king* ... joyful all ye *NATIONS* rise, join the triumph of the skies .. .

#207, "Earth and heav'n before him *bow*" (obeisance is fitting for a king)

The last line of "Christians, Awake, Salute the Happy Morn," (#209) is 'incessant shall sing eternal praise to heav'n's almighty *king*."

Silent Night sings "alleluias to our *king*."

"Come Adore on bended knee Christ the Lord, the newborn *king*." (#214)

"We Three Kings: "Born a *king* . . . *King forever*, ceasing never, over us all to reign."

And an early Christian carol sings: "*Ruler* of the Nation, Come." Moreover, the refrain from "Angels, From the Realms of Glory" calls us to "worship Christ, the newborn *King*." Christ is born to reign. It is for that reason that he came—not as one among equals but as the Sole Potentate and Perfect *Despotes*.

Mary's son will reign, will be the Son of the Unrivalled God, will be exceptionally great, and will be named Jesus and save his people from their sins! That is who was encased in Jesus' body; that is who we meet at this table tonight.

That returns us back to v. 30, which commands: "Do not fear. You have found favor." Elizabeth wondered why she'd found favor (1:43)

Can you believe how many times, freedom from fear is mentioned in these narratives?

- Luke 1:13 on first appearance to Zechariah, "Do not fear, your prayer has been heard ..."
- Luke 1:30: to Mary, "Do not fear, Mary, you have found favor..."

- God has enabled us to 'serve him without fear.' (1:74b)
- 2:10, first to the Shepherds, "Do not Fear."
- And Matthew 1:20 to Joseph: "Do not fear, take Mary home as your wife."

"His gentle encouragement 'Fear not!' not only soothes their present terror, but has a wider meaning. The dread of the unseen, which lies coiled like a sleeping snake in all hearts, is utterly taken away by the Incarnation."

At Communion. Our Lord reveals himself in the Manger and at the Table. And in both, he is Great, the Son of the Most High, The Savior of his people from their sins, and the ruling Son of David. God wants you to know that his favor rests on you—not that you're so special but because his grace is so powerful. Also that we need not fear him, so great his love.

Christmas is not hard . . . if you believe God.

John 1:14

There are a lot of takeaways, a lot of messages, you may derive from Christmas. You may associate this holiday with rest—as in a month-long college break after exams. Or you may think of it romantically, as a time when you fell in love. Or you may associate Christmas with lavish gifts . . . or even with an impoverished period that was rich beyond imagining. Or you may associate Christmas with great joy or deep sadness. Some even think of this as an impossible time of year because of the sheer miracles involved. But God wants us tonight to think of Christmas in a way that illumines who Christ is, what he did for us, and it's not hard . . . if you will just believe in God and what we're told in this one, short but incredible verse in John.

Tonight, I want you to hear and believe three things from this one verse.

1. *The divine Word became human.*

God expresses himself clearly at Christmas. He's above our understanding, sure; but God communicates in a word. He takes these amazingly high and deep thoughts, and communicates through words that humans can understand. And at Christmas, not only did God speak through words, his Word became human. Not only was there great truth, but the eternal God came into our world and was made like us. First, see the Word became human.

"Though he was rich, he thought it not robbery to be equal with God, but he's made himself of no reputation," and he's been born in a stable in Bethlehem, utterly dependent—utterly and completely dependent on Mary to feed him and nurse him, and change him. It's unimaginable. It's incomprehensible. He became man." Yet, that's the kind of God our Lord is. He is that great and so unthreatened as to be able to take on our flesh and still be perfectly God.

As Augustine so beautifully reminds us: "He was created of a mother whom he created. He was carried by hands that he formed. He cried in the manger in wordless infancy, he the Word, without whom all human eloquence is mute." [Sermons, 188.2]

At Jesus' birth, all the truths of God in words came in a person. Associate Christmas with that!

> 2. *Next: God in flesh tabernacled among us. He is not the DISTANT God.*

This Word became flesh. That is, he left heaven and the Spirit world and came to earth; and he wore our flesh—and all that came with that. God dressed himself in flesh. And he lived in a tent with us. That is a literal translation of this verse. It's a bit more colorful than he dwelt among us. This is the word used in the OT for living in a tabernacle or tent. God tabernacled among us. All of the glories of God, all of the traits of God—once seen in the tabernacle—became encased in the flesh of Jesus. Yes, God can do that. No, no one else can.

"Our God contracted to a span, Incomprehensibly made man."

A famous preacher (George Buttrick) once suggested, that God came down the back stairs at Bethlehem, lest he blind us by excessive light. God found a way to be known; and he was known as he lived with us.

The great God, the infinite God, who knows all things, who is everywhere present, who has all power and all authority; who merely has to speak, and it is done; who only has to say "Let there be light" and there was light . . . and he's lying there, in the manger as a little infant with a body, and arms and legs and eyes and nose and ears . . . and hair . . . a real baby. And all of you mothers and fathers, too, remember your first-born, and the sense of unbelief, disbelief that through all of this messy process, this little child would be born–

breathing, crying . . . making sounds, alive, warm. You can touch . . . and here's the great God of heaven and earth, and he's contracted to a span. He's become poor, for our sakes.

The Mind of God became expressed in a human; that human lived with us: and:

3.   *And we saw—have you? —that he is full of grace and truth.*

Christ carries about this infinitely beautiful combination of grace and truth. And we saw him, tabernacling among us—this limitless Word taking on the limitations of a human body, born to a regular woman in a stable. And those who lived in his day saw him. Have you? At this Christmas Eve, toward the close of a year, have you seen our Lord? So much hinges on this. Do you know his grace? And his truth?

There can be no salvation unless first there is Christmas as Luke and Matthew described it.

Christ is God, full of grace and truth—associate Christmas with that. If Christ were not God then, whatever he was, he is of no particular significance to you and me today. If he were a mere man, then the claims that Christians have made for him are genuinely preposterous. He would, if mere man, not be the way, the truth, and the life, the only way to the Father, as he once claimed. If there is a God we must discover some other way to find him because the long dead Jesus Christ can hardly help us now. If he was not the incarnate God—God come now also as a human being—the claims that he performed miracles, that he died for the sins of the world, that he rose from the dead as victor over sin and death, that he ascended to the right hand of his Father in heaven, that he is coming again to judge the living and the dead; I don't think any of us would believe any of it if we didn't first believe that he came into the world as the God-Man. are all rendered null and void. The incarnation is the foundation of everything else that we will learn about Jesus in the Gospels and the foundation of our faith in him as the Savior of the world and the King of Kings as we are taught in the rest of the NT. He must be both God and Man!

But it is true. We read these verses of Luke 2, but can we believe that angels announced his birth to shepherds, that magi came from the east following a star in order to worship him, that he would grow up to perform miracles, and after he was crucified rise from the dead? Is this true?

So God invites us, through John 1;14, to see this real baby, who is also the eternal Son of the Most High. He is two natures in one person, and he is looking around the place where he's been born. He sees from a baby's perspective these immense cows looking down at him. He is lying in their place, where they normally thrust in their noses and seize a mouthful of hay, and we can see the little Lord Jesus looking up at them. He is the one who made cows and donkeys. In other words, this is the Creator who in eternity said "Cow!" and "Cow" came into being; "Donkey!" and "Donkey" came into being.

This is the astonishment of the incarnation; he is lying there examining in close-up what he himself has made, thrilled and astonished by what he is discovering. These are the first glimpses of our life in a fallen world which the God-man has in his great voyage of discovery. The Lord of glory has begun a journey which is going to last over three decades, which will end on a cross. He will see for the first time from his creaturely perspective, from down below, the lowly human condition. At times he will be gasping with wonder, as we do when we see a champion bull as big as a little elephant; the Son of the Most High astonished at this new perspective that incarnation has brought to him, seeing through human eyes and close up what he the Son of the Most High has made. At other times he will weep.

Come to Christ! Come to Christ now! Just as you are come to him! From where you are to where he is . . . is the briefest of journeys. Think of it . . . a palace, the throne of Solomon, a scepter and a crown were all his by right, but from the beginning he shed all that regal paraphernalia; they might repel one inadequate little sinner. The manger of the Son of David can only invite. Its invitation comes out of tenderness, pity, and concern: its invitations come to our inquisitiveness: "Who is this? A King of kings born in a stable, and lying in a feeding trough? Do you know who this is? Who knows? Does anyone know? Let's go and see. Let's find out for ourselves . . . Let's all of us go now." The question was a living invitation to the ignorant and poor folks.

Jesus was born in a place that was freely accessible to all who were led to it, came to it, needed it and wanted it. Whosoever has the tiniest longing to come may indeed come to God's holy child Jesus. Here within his wide loving parameters full and free salvation is to be found. Sometimes men's embittered consciences tell them, "This gospel grace is not for you," but if God has not shut you out of the stable, don't shut yourself out. The door is open and yet there is room, and if you mean business with him you'll not quibble with a manger bed; better a manger with Christ than a palace without Him." *Don't make something hard that is not designed to be so! Associate this divine Word, Christ in the flesh, with all the God wants to tell us, and he is full of grace and truth. Why wouldn't you want that?*

As the manger is free, so Christ is free, and he is able also to save them to the uttermost that come to God by him. Venture on that and you'll find him free to all comers. God put this expectant mother and Joseph in a cave, and Mary laid the newborn child in a manger. Why? To show that Christ and his grace, salvation and redemption are free to those who humble themselves and come there to the one who says, "For I am meek and lowly of heart and ye shall find rest for your souls."

This, the Godhead, was veiled in flesh. See!

53850189R00231

Made in the
USA
Lexington, KY